PRICELESS MARKETS

PRICELESS MARKETS

The Political Economy of Credit in Paris, 1660–1870

PHILIP T. HOFFMAN, GILLES POSTEL-VINAY, AND
JEAN-LAURENT ROSENTHAL

The University of Chicago Press
Chicago and London

Philip T. Hoffman is professor of history and social science at Cal Tech. He is the author of *Growth in a Traditional Society: The French Countryside, 1450–1815*. Gilles Postel-Vinay is directeur d'etudes, Ecole des Hautes Etudes en Sciences Sociales, and directeur de recherches at the INRA. Jean-Laurent Rosenthal is professor of economics at UCLA and the author of *Fruits of Revolution: Property Rights, Litigation, and French Agriculture, 1700–1860*.

The University of Chicago Press, Chicago 60637
The University of Chicago Press, Ltd., London
© 2000 by The University of Chicago
All rights reserved. Published 2000
Printed in the United States of America
09 08 07 06 05 04 03 02 01 00   5 4 3 2 1

Library of Congress Cataloging-in-Publication Data

Hoffman, Philip T., 1947–
    Priceless markets : the political economy of credit in Paris, 1660–1870 / Philip T. Hoffman, Gilles Postel-Vinay, and Jean-Laurent Rosenthal
        p. cm.
    Includes bibliographical references and index.
    ISBN 0-226-34801-6 (cloth : alk. paper)
        1. Commercial credit—France—Paris—History.   2. Commercial loans—France—Paris—History.   3. France—Economic conditions.   4. Paris (France)—Economic conditions.   I. Postel-Vinay, Gilles.   II. Rosenthal, Jean-Laurent.   III. Title.
    HG3754.5.F8 H64   2000
    332.7'42'0944361—dc21

                                                                    00-008587

"A ... , pour la remercier de m'être si chère."

JULES SUPERVIELLE

Contents

Acknowledgments

LIKE ALL AUTHORS, we have a number of people and institutions to thank for their help, their expertise, and their financial support. Our research could not have been carried out without funds from a variety of sources: in France, the Archives Nationales and the Institut National de la Recherche Agronomique; in the United States, the California Institute of Technology and UCLA through the Dean of Social Sciences and the Academic Senate; the RBSL Bergman Foundation; the Albert and Elaine Borchard Foundation; Marcia Howard through the Adopt a Scholar Program; The National Endowment for the Humanities (grant number RZ-20044-97); the Young Investigator Program of the National Science Foundation (grant number SBR 9258498); and the Center for Advanced Study in the Behavioral Sciences (with support from NSF grant number SES 9022192).

For help with our research, we would like to thank Coralie Capdeboscq, who more than once saved us by getting critical data; Philippe Leroy at INRA; Claire Béchu, Perrine Canavaggio, Andrée Chauleur, Lucie Favier, and Pierre Portet of the Archives Nationales, who helped us get access to the enumerations from the Minutier Central; and Gildas Le Gonidec de Keralhic, who opened the doors of the archive of the Compagnie des Notaires de Paris. In the United States, we received able assistance from Erik Drabkin, Negar Ghashghai, Hajime Hadeishi, David Madero, Yovanna Pineda, Lacey Plache, Mark Potter, and Quan Vu. At Caltech, Rosy Meiron spared us many an error and continues to help us in multiple languages.

Our work has benefited from the reaction of audiences at Caltech, Cornell, Ecole des Hautes Etudes en Sciences Sociales, Harvard, Illinois, Indiana, Michigan, Northwestern, Rutgers, Observatoire Français des Conjonctures Economiques, Paderborn, Princeton, Stanford, Toronto, UC Berkeley, UC Davis, UC Irvine, UCLA, UC Riverside, Western Ontario, Vrije Universiteit Brussel, and Yale University; and at conferences sponsored by the All-UC Group in Economic History, the Cliometric

Society, CNRS Lyon, the Economic History Association, FUCAM Mons, the NBER, and the Society for French Historical Studies. We have also profited from comments, readings, and advice from Lance Davis, Marc Flandreau, George Grantham, Avner Greif, Steve Haber, Thomas Hubbard, Naomi Lamoreaux, Maurice Lévy-Leboyer, Tim Le Goff, Timothy Luckett, Thierry Magnac, Joel Mokyr, Larry Neal, Kathryn Norberg, John Nye, Howard Rosenthal, Paula Scott, Ken Sokoloff, Donald Sutherland, William Summerhill, François Velde, Michael Waldman, David Weir, Eugene White, and Mary Yeager. Finally, we want to thank the readers and staff of the University of Chicago Press, and especially the copy editor, Richard Allen.

Abbreviations

ACNP
Archives de la Chambre des Notaires de Paris

AD
Archives départementales de [name of department]

AN
Archives Nationales (Paris)

ANMC
Archives Nationales, Minutier Central

CFF
Credit Foncier de France

ODS
Outstanding Debt Series

SSOD
Steady State Outstanding Debt

Introduction

BENEATH THE VAST literature on the evolution of financial institutions, there lurks a beguiling story. It is a story told by historians and economists, and it goes something like this: Before the Industrial Revolution—and in developing countries, before modern economic growth—financial dealings were usually personal, and lending was consequently limited. The shortage of credit crippled the economy, for, with no way for entrepreneurs to borrow, investment stagnated, eliminating any chance for economic growth. In Europe, the impasse lasted until the late eighteenth and nineteenth centuries, when the continent passed through a drastic economic transition that transformed both finance and society as a whole. The transition created an impersonal and capitalist credit market, which fed entrepreneurial investment and made growth a reality.

One cannot unearth this story intact by digging in any single publication. But bits and pieces of it protrude through the surface of nearly every work on the history of European finance. It juts out of the books and articles of distinguished historians and economists. And it crops up in sociology and anthropology as well, where its roots reach back to the classic social thought of Karl Marx and Max Weber.[1]

Here we disagree. It is not that we believe credit markets to be unimportant or irrelevant for economic growth—quite the contrary. Credit is essential for economic growth, and that is one reason why it merits study. No, our disagreement with the traditional story lies elsewhere—in particular, with the assumption that impersonal lending was always limited before the Industrial Revolution. That premise we simply reject. We also dispute the sharp contrast that the traditional story draws between the capitalist and the pretransitional worlds. In our view, such a contrast simply obscures the workings of preindustrial economies by

---

1. For references, see Hoffman, Postel-Vinay, and Rosenthal 1999.

making economic behavior in the past (or in developing countries) seem stranger than it really was.

We base our argument on evidence gathered from the city of Paris, evidence that reveals how Parisians saved and went into debt and how borrowers and lenders met over the course of two centuries, from 1660 to 1870. Our evidence tells a very different tale about financial dealings in the past. Consider, for example, what the traditional story might suggest about Paris under the Old Regime, before the city possessed modern banks or other undeniable signs of a capitalist transition. Capital markets ought to have been feeble, with little lending and no impersonal credit. Yet our research demonstrates that financial intermediaries were arranging thousands of loans between borrowers and lenders who did not know one another. What rendered such impersonal lending possible (so economic theory suggests) was the financial information the intermediaries possessed, information about who had money to lend and who was a creditworthy borrower. The information invigorated the long-term capital market, allowing men and women alike to borrow, lend, and invest in ways that seem surprisingly familiar to modern eyes.

Although our evidence comes from a single city, it points to the same conclusions that are emerging from research on Asia, the Americas, and other parts of Europe. In all these places, scholars are rediscovering the importance of credit in preindustrial societies and casting doubt on the traditional dichotomy between the impersonal relationships under capitalism and the personal links and traditional financial structures in preindustrial societies.[2] But the havoc that development wreaks upon traditional channels of information may actually make personal relationships even more important for lending—and do so at the same time that other economic transactions become anonymous. Personal ties and other informal means of transmitting information about borrowers and lenders may substitute for the formal mechanisms of banks and stock exchanges, but they may also help the formal mechanisms out. It all depends on the historical circumstances. The lesson—for historians and economists alike—would seem to be that we should jettison older theoretical constructs and replace them with newer ideas drawn from historical studies of how information and capital flowed in the societies of interest. Such an approach could open up a fruitful dialogue between microeconomics and history, a dialogue that could yield new insights into the process of societal change.

Our research resulted in a number of findings that will interest histo-

2. Ibid.

rians, economists, and social scientists. Some of our findings address issues within history:

- The gray officials who drew up contracts and legal documents—the Parisian notaries—played a crucial financial role in the eighteenth century. They were in fact the very intermediaries who animated the Parisian credit market under the Old Regime. Institutional reforms after the French Revolution (in particular, the creation of a public lien registry) kept them from resuming the same role in the nineteenth century and thus condemned them to obscurity.
- The financial crisis in 1787–88 was intimately bound up in a political struggle that stretched far back into the eighteenth century and continued well into the 1800s, with heavy consequences for the economy. This crisis did not merely touch off the Revolution, as most historiography assumes; it did much more. The Revolution's financial drama was thus just as important as its political and cultural gyrations. We propose new models for the politics and economics of the ongoing battle over government finance, models that incorporate forgotten groups, such as women and the elderly.

Other findings concern economics and political economy:

- Prices did little to allocate capital or inform participants in the flourishing credit market of eighteenth-century Paris.
- The size of a capital market affects the development of financial institutions but not always in a favorable way.
- A financial market can prosper under a wide variety of institutions: it does not require secondary markets, representative political assemblies, or even governments that pay their debts. Institutions of this sort are neither necessary nor sufficient for a thriving capital market.
- Tampering with the currency, by contrast, can devastate a capital market. It did so in France in the early eighteenth century and again during the Revolution, with long-lasting consequences for capital mobilization.

Finally, all readers should gain a deeper appreciation of history. Here, by history, we mean not what historians write, but rather the past course of events, particularly the events that people remember and deem relevant. History in this sense matters for financial markets in at least three ways. First, indebtedness in any year—in 1660 as in 1870 — obviously reflects borrowing and repayment in the past. Second, many of the institutions that support lending are the result of events in the distant past; in other words, these institutions are a product of what economists call path dependence. Third, memory of past events shapes expectations about the future and has a profound effect on borrowers and lenders.

Why Paris?

Those are our conclusions, but before seeing how we reach them, most readers will want to know why we chose to study Paris. There were two reasons for doing so. In the first place, the city seemed to be an ideal laboratory for studying the evolution of financial institutions and the political economy of credit. As such a laboratory, it certainly has few equals. Buffeted by war, revolution, and political turmoil, it ran the gauntlet of all the social and economic transformations that sum up the seventeenth, eighteenth, and nineteenth centuries. Long the second largest city in Europe, it grew particularly rapidly between 1600 and 1750, and then again with industrialization in the nineteenth century. Meanwhile its architecture and neighborhoods were being developed— in a piecemeal fashion by kings, officials, and private investors in the years before the French Revolution, and then wholesale in the second half of the nineteenth century, when the government and Baron Hauss- mann transformed the entire city. Obviously, Paris was always a legal and political center, but in the eighteenth century it became—arguably— not just the intellectual and cultural capital of France but of Europe as a whole. In short, it experienced most of the changes that characterize both European history since the Middle Ages and the more recent course of events in the capitals of many developing countries.

Paris is particularly intriguing for scholars studying the evolution of financial markets. Although it did not rival Amsterdam as an interna- tional capital market in the seventeenth century, or London in the eighteenth and nineteenth centuries, it did dominate the financial life of France from the early seventeenth century on. It also endured spec- tacular financial shocks: an attempt to impose paper money and a cen- tral bank in 1719–20, hyperinflation during the French Revolution, and repeated financial scandals in the early nineteenth century. It also underwent significant institutional reforms. The political constitution of France was rewritten repeatedly during the Revolution and again in the nineteenth century. Even outside these periods of dramatic change, stat- utes and the court system evolved, making it possible to probe the rela- tionship between law, politics, and financial markets. All the while, new financial institutions arose. Modern banks emerged in the nineteenth century, as did a thriving stock market. But even in the eighteenth cen- tury, the city gave birth to the financial network of notaries, a network overlooked by historians even though it had an enormous impact on public and private finance.

One reason for the financial innovation was the wealth of Paris. The city was always far richer than the rest of France, always the home to numerous older, well-heeled investors. Some were nobles, office hold-ers, or civil servants. Others were merchants or industrialists. Still oth-ers—even under the Old Regime—were independent, unmarried women. All had savings to invest and powerful reasons to put their money to work. The unmarried women, for example, could not lean on children or pensions for support in their old age; for retirement, they had to count on investments. Could they (and other older savers too) find appropriate financial instruments for their investments? If so, where did their savings end up? Did they enter the state's coffers, thereby fund-ing the wars that were so common in the seventeenth and eighteenth centuries? Or did they find their way into private hands? Individuals had many reasons to borrow. Likely private borrowers included victims of bad fortune in an era before insurance. They also included the city's real estate developers and industrial entrepreneurs, either in Paris or out in the provinces. If the entrepreneurs lacked funds—as some economic historians maintain—then it would be easy to account for the halting pace of French industrialization. Finally, the private borrowers might simply be young couples who took on debt as they started families or careers. Financial markets would then be passing funds from the old to the young, facilitating life-cycle savings.

In all financial dealings, the key was how borrowers and lenders got information about one another. That was far from a simple task in a large and anonymous city like Paris, which counted more than half a million inhabitants in 1700 and well over a million by 1850. In a city that big, how did borrowers determine who had money to invest? How did they locate the lenders who offered the best terms? How, for their part, did lenders discover creditworthy borrowers? How did they tell whether borrowers were likely to default? What institutions, if any, fur-nished the necessary information and made financial transactions possi-ble? The answers, not surprisingly, depended on legal, social, and politi-cal forces. In Paris as elsewhere, there were many possible ways to gather the information needed to grease the wheels of financial transactions. The particular institutions that ended up doing the job were the off-spring of particular historical circumstances.

We chose to study the credit market in Paris between 1660 and 1870 in order to grapple with such questions. We also wanted to see how the Parisian credit market evolved. The questions we pose have parallels in modern developing countries, which share the same burden of political instability, rapid social change, and imperfect financial institutions. They too suffer coups, revolutions, and civil wars. They too possess burgeoning capitals, which dominate the economy and attract a disproportionate share of the wealth. They too endure financial institutions that may leave

capital idle. And even where their economies have boomed—in south-
east Asia, for example—their financial sectors can still crash, just as the
Parisian credit market did in 1720.

The second advantage to studying Paris is the extraordinary evidence
that lies at our disposal. Some of this evidence comes from diaries, letters, and untapped private archives, but the core of it is quantitative—
quantitative data that reveal, month by month for two centuries, how
much financial capital the credit market was mobilizing. The reason why
there is so much quantitative data can be traced back to the city's notaries. As in other countries influenced by Roman law, notaries in Paris
had to pass along the legal documents they drafted to their successors.
As a result, most of their legal documents have survived to this day, leaving us a detailed account of economic transactions in the past. For Paris
alone, the notaries' papers fill twenty-two kilometers of shelving, and
for many of their firms, the paper trail is nearly complete for three hundred years.

Understandably, the notarial archives have been a treasure trove for
historians, having yielded up rich nuggets of information about politics,
society, culture, and the economy, from the sixteenth to the nineteenth
century. Most historians who delve into the notarial records, though,
spade through the documents in an unsystematic way. Either they select
only a few notaries or they limit their research to brief periods or to a
restricted set of individuals. The reason, of course, is the effort involved.
With more than one hundred notaries in Paris alone, each recording
hundreds of acts a year, historians have to limit their archival excava-
tions. The result, unfortunately, is that certain topics remained buried
beneath the reams of paper. The study of credit has suffered particularly
hard, for although historians have long known that loan contracts
abound in the notarial archives, they have had no way to assess how
much lending was going on. Simply studying one or two notaries is no
indication, because there is no way to tell whether the one or two were
representative.

Our approach has been radically different. For reasons which will become apparent below, we focused on the amount of borrowing rather
than on its price. Thus, using statistical techniques, we estimate the total
volume of lending recorded in Parisian notarial archives over two centuries. We began by counting the number of new loans made by a random
sample of notaries, a technique pioneered by Jean-Paul Poisson (1985,
1990). We then multiplied the number of new loans made in any given
month by the average size of loans at the time, which we had estimated
by taking periodic samples of loans. That gave us the volume of new
loans, month by month, from 1660 to 1869. We also separated out differ-

ent types of loans and distinguish loans to private parties from government borrowing. Similar tactics let us construct the rate at which loans were being repaid, yielding a curve of total indebtedness for Paris as a whole.

Our figures, it is true, are estimates. We resorted to such estimates because it was simply impossible to count all credit activity given the mass of surviving documents. The accuracy of our procedure only falters for short intervals—months or quarters—but it stands up quite well for the longer intervals that are our central concern. To be sure, one would like to have series that are reliable at the monthly level or, even better, to be able to track the history of each particular loan. Yet such increased information would require years of additional research. Given how little is known about credit in Paris, the benefits of our approach far outweigh its drawbacks. Indeed, the financial activity series we have constructed allows us to answer important questions and to make comparisons that were previously impossible. We can decide, for example, how significant both private and public borrowing was under Louis XIV and then later during the Law affair (1716–20), when the Scottish banker John Law created a state bank and experimented with paper money. We can do the same on the eve of the French Revolution or during the financial scandals that serve as a backdrop for Balzac's novels. And we can determine how important institutions were for the development of capital markets—institutions ranging from central banks to decentralized networks of financial intermediaries.

The Boundaries of our Research

All studies have limits, and there are some things we have not done. First of all, we focus on medium- and long-term credit at the expense of short-term loans. In Paris, short-term credit typically involved loans from merchants or bankers to other merchants. These short-term loans were unnotarized private notes usually lasting for three months or less. Although such lending rose to particular prominence after the Revolution, it nonetheless left few tracks in the archives. It is thus impossible to trace the kind of curves for short-term credit that we have done for medium- and long-term lending. The lack of such curves, though, is not a serious problem for three reasons. First, individuals who were not merchants faced formidable legal obstacles if they tried to use private notes for other purposes than short-term credit. Second, there is little reason to believe that short-term loans were often renewed for long periods of time to create an alternative form of long-term credit. Finally, for legal reasons, long-term loans were nearly always notarized (see chapter 2). In all likelihood, then, our series give a reliable account of long-term credit in Paris.

A second limitation is that we cover the financial activity of notaries more fully than that of other intermediaries, such as merchants, bankers, stock brokers *(agents de change),* and government financial agents *(financiers).* Each of these intermediaries typically specialized in a particular type of transaction or client. The merchants and bankers, for example, might finance trade for private clients, while bankers and financiers offered the government short-term loans. Giving less coverage to bankers, financiers, and stockbrokers, though, may not be as great an omission as it seems. The stock market, for example, was just a secondary market. Although it added to the appeal of stocks and bonds (by making them easier to sell), it did not, by itself, mobilize capital, as the notaries did. Furthermore, when any of these intermediaries other than notaries participate in long-term credit, they creep into our data. We can therefore assess their contribution to the development of notarized debt, though we leave it to other scholars to investigate their role in other arenas.

We have decided then to concentrate on one of the most significant and yet least understood of all intermediaries—notaries—and to pursue them carefully across the two centuries. Their role as financial intermediaries has by and large been ignored in the historical literature, which emphasizes—all too anachronistically—banks and stock exchanges.[3] Yet the notaries dominated long-term credit into the nineteenth century, and they left the clearest trail in the archives—a trail that persists even after the notaries themselves receded in importance. We can therefore follow both their rise and their fall with a confidence that would be impossible for the other intermediaries. We realize, of course, that other intermediaries offered services that were sometimes substitutes for what the notaries could do. Consequently, we always try to keep in mind the actions of the other intermediaries as we follow the notaries through the years.

Finally, some readers may wonder why we pay so little attention to interest rates, the prices charged on loans. We did gather the interest rate for loan contracts that mentioned it, but we found that it did not vary. The absence of price variation, though, is not as severe a handicap as it might seem. Indeed, as we shall show, interest rates played a relatively minor role in allocating credit.

Even though interest was clearly charged on loans, it simply could not play the allocative role that economists expect of unconstrained,

3. Ibid.

publicly announced prices in perfect markets. Rather, debt transactions were based on shared knowledge about the availability of a lender's funds, for example, or about the soundness of a borrower's collateral. Allocation therefore depended on information flows between lenders and borrowers. There was a sound basis for the important role of information in credit flows. Indeed, each borrower presented different risks—risks that had to be discovered before any lender could decide whether or not to grant a loan and on what terms. Prices were thus second-order mechanisms in the equilibration of supply and demand. Such a limited role for prices may of course seem bizarre, but it has parallels in other situations where information is unevenly held. After all, even in modern credit markets, a simple willingness to pay a high interest rate is often not enough to get a loan.

A Preview of the Chapters

We begin by describing the institutions of Parisian credit markets and how we assembled our data (chapters 1 and 2). Chapter 3 then analyzes lending in the seventeenth century, while chapter 4 examines the debacle of the Law affair and its dramatic experiment with paper money. Readers will see the political risks and institutional failings that hobbled the credit market in the seventeenth century. They will gain a better understanding of the political economy behind the Law affair too: who lost, who gained, and why Law was allowed to experiment with public and private finance.

Chapters 5, 6, and 7 probe the growth of credit in the aftermath of Law: what was responsible for the rise of indebtedness, how financial intermediaries operated, and what groups—women, for instance—benefited as a result. A thriving economy and declining risk account for only a fraction of this growth. The bulk of it was the work of the notaries. Assuming a new role as financial intermediaries, they provided more information to borrowers and lenders and mobilized vast sums of capital as a result.

Chapter 8 takes up credit during the French Revolution, from the political economy of the public debt to the devastating private effects of the revolutionary hyperinflation. We hope to reawaken historians' interest in revolutionary finance—a burning issue to contemporaries—but we also argue against the models that economists have recently brought to bear upon the subject. Chapter 9 then considers the long-term impact of the Revolution. In Paris at least, mortgage lending stagnated for most of the nineteenth century, and credit in general remained very sensitive to political crises because individuals associated political instability with the risk of inflation. Other indicators of lending reveal that the financial stagnation was confined to Parisian mortgage credit. Outside of Paris, and for other debt instruments in the city, the declines associated with political instability were temporary and the long-term pattern was one of growth.

Finally chapters 10 and 11 consider the causes of the decline of notarial credit in Paris. We focus first on the notaries' inability to reconstruct their cooperative information network. The lack of cooperation led them to follow financial strategies that systematically increased risk taking. The result was a wave of scandals, which provoked the government to banish notaries from financial intermediation. In chapter 11, we look at the consequences of the rise of the Crédit Foncier de France on mortgage credit in the capital. We pay particular attention to the role of information technologies in moving credit from notaries to mortgage banks. In the Conclusion we return to the broad question of institutional change and financial development.

CHAPTER ONE

The Institutions of Credit Markets

FROM THE MID-SEVENTEENTH to the end of the nineteenth century, French credit markets evolved slowly and irregularly. Although financial institutions ultimately resembled those we have today, for most of the period the banks, stock markets, and quoted prices that we are familiar with played little role in allocating capital. Instead, credit was distributed by notaries on the basis of information on risk. The resulting institutions were thus so different from those prevailing in "modern" markets that many scholars have failed to recognize them as systematically organizing capital transactions and have omitted them from the genealogy of capitalist growth. Studying them here will not only help allay the reader's cultural shock but will also allow us to present a set of hypotheses about the impact these strange institutions had.

Credit markets occupy a hallowed place in economic history because scholars are keenly aware that the flow of loans is driven by precise institutions that reduce problems of asymmetric information.[1] In other words, lending depends on institutions that help borrowers and lenders know more about each other—about a borrower's creditworthiness, for example, or about the sort of loan terms that a lender may offer. But before discussing credit markets in particular, one might ask what a market is. We define a market to be any organized system of exchange, however centralized or decentralized, formal or informal. A market may allocate resources based on prices or information or a mixture of both. It may also be imperfect in the sense that the costs of transactions—the difference between what the buyer pays and the seller receives—may be significant. The list of these transaction costs is long; for credit, it includes not just fees for arranging loans or drawing up con-

---

1. Gerschenkron 1962; Postan 1935; Davis and Gallman 1978.

tracts but also taxes, effort expended in finding a suitable lender, losses from a borrower's default or from a lender's inopportune demand for repayment, etc.[2]

In analyzing the institutions that structure markets, we distinguish two types. Both consist of rules and an enforcement mechanism behind the rules. The first type, formal institutions, we define to be explicit rules enforceable by law. Formal institutions range from government regulation to private agreements, but they are all ultimately enforced by the state. In contrast, we define informal institutions to be rules that are either implicit, or, if explicit, not enforceable by law.[3] Examples of such informal institutions include both the French monarchy's practice of selective default in the seventeenth and eighteenth centuries and the reputational equilibria we detail in chapter 6. (For readers unfamiliar with game theory, an equilibrium is simply an expected pattern of behavior, once the actors in a strategic situation have made the best of their situations. In chapter 6, the actors are notaries and their clients, and the equilibria are reputational because the clients' actions depend on what the notaries have done in the past—in short, on their reputations.)

Formal and informal institutions may be substitutes for one another. They may also be complements, in the economist's sense that formal and informal institutions help one another out. Here it is impossible to generalize, except to say that in France in the eighteenth and nineteenth centuries, the formal and informal institutions developed interdependently. Chapter 10 details the coevolution of two systems for keeping records of mortgage loans, one a formal institution, the other informal. In some areas, these two institutions were complementary while in others they were substitutes. Complexity of this sort means that we have to evaluate the contribution of both types of institutions to the development of notarial credit and to further institutional innovation.

The present chapter describes the key institutions that affected lending in Paris. It begins by examining the difficulties that Parisians had in getting the information needed to borrow or lend. Financial intermediaries could help solve the problem, and after we introduce the intermediaries active in France, we describe the laws that governed their behavior. We pay particular attention to notaries, the least known of all these intermediaries. We explain what notaries did in France and focus on the special privileges they had in Paris.

2. Kreps 1990a.
3. Davis and North 1978; North 1981.

Intermediation and Information

In the 1650s Paris was already a large city with some 450,000 inhabitants.[4] If we leave out children and women by assuming that they did not borrow or lend (an assumption that was certainly false for many women), there were still on the order of 100,000 potential borrowers and lenders by the beginning of our period. Even if we restrict our attention to wealthy groups such as the nobility, the clergy, or the commercial classes, thousands of participants in credit markets would remain who could have conceivably undertaken tens of thousands of transactions. Such a large population could hardly organize its asset transactions without some form of financial intermediation.

Precisely how financial markets are organized varies over time and across space. The causes behind financial innovation are equally diverse. In Renaissance Europe, private banking houses intermediated credit at seasonal fairs.[5] In London financial innovation was driven by the government's founding of the Bank of England in 1694, although the capital market remained privately organized.[6] In early nineteenth-century New England, the banking system rested more on family reputations than on any regulatory structure.[7] In nineteenth-century New York, the stock exchange was privately organized but with formal rules.[8] In the late nineteenth century, German farmers could rely on credit cooperatives that had few professional administrators.[9] Their counterparts in the Midwest of the United States at the same time borrowed from the Eastern seaboard and Europe via loans that were arranged by bankers like J. P. Morgan and local mortgage agents.[10]

In the case of Paris, the formal institutions of credit changed infrequently; yet five distinct groups—merchants, financiers, notaries, private bankers, and corporate banks—all offered financial intermediation. One set of intermediaries dominated in most periods, but no group was ever able to shut out all the others because none of them were ever able to control both short- and long-term credit. A particular group of intermediaries increased its share of business whenever it offered better service than its rivals. As we shall see, the key to high-quality service (given the regulatory structure) was the ability to resolve informational asymmetries.

---

4. De Vries 1984; Lepetit 1988; Benedict 1990.
5. Boyer-Xambeu et al. 1986; Ehrenberg 1922.
6. Neal 1990; North and Weingast 1989; Dickson 1967.
7. Lamoureaux 1994.
8. Davis and Cull 1994.
9. Guinnane 1994, 1997.
10. Snowden 1995.

The Regulation of Credit

In preindustrial Europe, credit markets were subject to a number of laws and court decisions. Much of this legislation reflected the condemnation of lending money at interest in the Bible, the church fathers, and canon law. Although the inspiration for these strictures was religious, the laws themselves were drawn up by royal officials, and enforcement (at least in France) was completely in the hands of royal courts.[11] Curiously, little of this changed with the French Revolution. Although it transformed French society in many respects, much of the legislation relevant to credit remained intact throughout the nineteenth century.

Until 1789, lenders who charged interest could face prosecution in royal courts for two distinct reasons. First of all, only certain debt instruments could stipulate interest charges. Those charging interest in other cases were breaking the law. Second, even when charging interest was allowed, lenders had to keep the interest rate below a legal ceiling. Exceeding this limit could cause the lender to lose the money he had loaned. The first rule had its roots in the argument that jointly specifying term and interest in a debt contract was usury.[12] Profits could only be earned from money when the lender surrendered control of the capital or assumed some of the risk of the investment. If he permanently surrendered control over the capital, the debt was considered as the sale of a perpetual annuity rather than as a loan. Similarly, when investors took on risks, they were entitled to a portion of the profits, which was not considered interest.

Had these rules been interpreted literally, they would have stymied the development of long-term credit. However, there were obvious ways to circumvent the regulations, including the tactic employed for bills of exchange *(lettres de change)* and notes *(billets)*—discounting. (With discounting, a borrower promised to repay a lender a larger sum than he had received, a larger sum that included interest and repayment of principal.) Discounting was common for short-term loans among merchants, but it posed grave problems for long-term credit because after a few years the accumulated interest grew and came to dwarf the principal. To solve the problem, early modern financiers, lawyers, and theologians devised three different types of contracts, which eventually allowed the flows of long-term credit to swell.

11. Dumas 1935–65. For the theology, which was far from rigid, see Noonan 1957; Clavero 1991, 1996.

12. De Vourric 1687. As always there were exceptions here. Merchants, for example, could often lend to one another at authorized fairs at rates above any interest ceiling.

The first, the *obligation,* specified the date of repayment. The second, the *rente perpétuelle,* specified an annual interest payment but let the borrower decide when to repay the capital. The third, the *rente viagère,* stipulated annual payments, but they came to an end when a person named in the contract died. Although these contracts resemble certain modern financial instruments, the modern analogies can be misleading. Let us therefore consider each of the three debt instruments in detail.

Obligations were promissory notes, whose structure changed dramatically over time. In the seventeenth century, these contracts, often for relatively small sums, usually lasted only a few months or perhaps a year or two. At this point, they were a close substitute for other forms of short-term credit. When the sum involved was trivial and the loan of particularly short duration, the borrower and lender would economize by not having the notary keep a copy of the contract after he had drawn it up. In this case, obligations were known as *obligations en brevet,* and they were even more closely related to short-term commercial credit or to the privately drawn up IOUs that came to be prevalent in England. Over the course of the eighteenth century, they grew larger and more common, and by the nineteenth century, they came to dominate the credit market.

Under the Old Regime, obligations could not openly specify the payment of interest, but evidence shows that it was paid on the side.[13] Suppose, for example, that Monsieur Martin lent 1,000 livres to Baron du Pont for a year at 10 percent interest.[14] The contract might stipulate that du Pont had to repay 1,100 livres in a year's time. Alternatively, it might require him to repay 1,000 in four months, but he and Martin could agree privately that the loan would be extended for another four months provided he pay fifty livres. If the loan were extended twice and the principal repaid at the end the year, du Pont would have paid the same amount—1,100 livres—over the course of the year. The practice of extending obligations in this fashion explains why many of them ultimately lasted longer than was stipulated in the original contract.

There are, to be sure, many other ways to arrange for interest payments on the side in obligations. In the late eighteenth century, notaries in fact developed payment schedules that joined interest payments and capital repayment in obligations. The payment schedules were an important improvement in many respects, and they had the particular advantage of circumventing the usury legislation. Suppose, for example,

13. Courdurier 1974:67–74. Probate inventories, estate division records, and court records also reveal that high rates of interest were paid on obligations.

14. This and the following examples are purely hypothetical.

that Martin lent du Pont 1,000 livres to be repaid in five equal annual installments at an interest rate of 10 percent. The notary might draw up a contract stating that du Pont had borrowed 1,320 livres, which he would repay at the rate of 264 livres a year. After the Revolution, the usury legislation changed, and obligations could mention interest rates. Increasingly, they rested on the surety of real estate, and they played the role of modern mortgage loans. (When we use the word mortgages to refer to loans, we mean any loan backed by real estate as collateral. The word mortgage can of course refer to the legal claim on the collateral; the context will make clear which sense we have in mind.)

In contrast to obligations, *rentes perpétuelles* (perpetual annuities in English—we will use the terms synonymously) could stipulate interest, so long as it did not exceed a legal maximum.[15] Usually, the rate on perpetual annuities lay below what was actually paid on obligations.[16] The other key difference between rentes perpétuelles and obligations involved repayment of the principal. With a rente perpétuelle, a lender surrendered his principal in return for an annuity that was to be a stream of fixed annual interest payments from the borrower and his heirs. The lender had no right to demand repayment of the principal. The annual payments included no amortization and they could continue indefinitely, as the loan was transmitted from generation to generation.[17] Only when the borrower repaid the principal would the payments stop. If the borrower did want to return the capital of a rente, the lender had to accept it and do so quickly.

To illustrate how the rentes perpétuelles functioned, let us imagine that Martin lent du Pont 1,000 livres at 5 percent interest. The loan contract would require du Pont to pay Martin fifty livres of interest a year. The interest payments would continue until du Pont returned the 1,000 livres of principal to Martin. If du Pont died, his heirs would be held to the same contract; if Martin died, his heirs would take his place.

Why would du Pont or Martin enter into such an agreement? There are many reasons, but one might be that du Pont needed money to establish himself in a trade or profession. He could pay the interest out of the income that his business generated, and could rest assured that he would not have to pay the principal until he retired or inherited

---

15. Using the blanket term *rente perpétuelle* masks a certain shift in legal terminology toward what was called a *rente rachetable;* see Schnapper 1957.

16. Hoffman, Postel-Vinay, and Rosenthal 1992; Courdurier 1974:132.

17. While most rentes were repaid within a generation, some lasted an extraordinarily long time.

money. As for Martin, he might simply want to give his family and his heirs a stable annual income.[18]

With the third type of loan contract—the rente viagère or life annuity in English—the structure of payments was different. Here, in return for the lender's principal, the borrower agreed to pay an annual amount until one or more individuals (the "lives") specified in the loan contract died. At that point payment stopped. The annual payments were therefore expected to include not just interest, as with the rente perpétuelle, but principal as well. The only way for the borrower to pay off the life annuity was to return the entire capital to the lender—something few borrowers did. Obviously, the contract involved risks, because the number of payments depended on the life span of particular individuals. Most often the life specified in a life annuity contract was the lender's, making the life annuity a retirement contract.

To imagine how a rente viagère worked, suppose that Martin had 1,000 livres, which he wanted to use to provide for his own retirement. Du Pont might be willing to borrow the 1,000 livres and, based on Martin's age and health, promise to pay him 100 livres a year until he died. The notary would then draft a life annuity in which Martin's would be the "life" in the contract. Du Pont's heirs would have to continue the payments should he die before Martin.

Alternatively, Martin might want to use the 1,000 livres to provide his two young and healthy daughters with income for the rest of their lives. In that case, du Pont would reduce the payments to take into account their life expectancy, and the rente viagère would mention their lives.[19] He could do so freely because the state imposed no limit to the size of the annual payments.

Although the three loan contracts had different purposes, they were all typically backed by collateral. The collateral might be a specific piece

18. One might ask whether borrowers and lenders manipulated the principal and interest payments stated in rentes perpétuelles so as to achieve interest rates above the usury ceiling, as they did in obligations. We have found no evidence that such things happened, and accounting evidence suggests that the terms of the perpetual annuity contracts were respected. That evidence is particularly good for interest payments, though there may have been some manipulation of principal. But if such manipulation were widespread, then rente perpétuelle contracts would not have been sensitive to changes in the usury ceiling, as they in fact were. In short, while borrowers and lenders may have occasionally connived to fiddle with the principal in perpetual annuities, the practice must have been limited.

19. Before the 1720s, when little had been published about life expectancy, life annuities were relatively rare. Thereafter, information about life expectancy increased, and life annuities grew more common—especially after the publication of Antoine Deparcieux's *Essai sur les probabilités de la durée de la vie humaine* in 1746. See Weir 1989:112; Rohrbasser 1997.

of real estate or it might be all of the debtor's assets. (In that case, the loan contract would mention as collateral "all the borrower's property both now and in the future, whether personal or real.") If the borrower defaulted, the lenders would have a claim on the collateral, but they could not simply take possession of it.[20] Instead, it had to be sold at auction—a slow and expensive judicial process, particularly when real estate was involved.[21]

Real estate was the most common form of collateral, as might be expected in an era before extensive industrialization. What is somewhat surprising, though, is that real estate meant more than just land and buildings, at least under the laws of the Old Regime. Until the French Revolution, government offices were legally considered real estate, and they could serve as collateral to secure loans. The same was true of perpetual annuities. If, having lent du Pont 1,000 livres via a 5 percent rente perpétuelle, our Monsieur Martin himself wanted to borrow, he could mortgage the rente perpétuelle to secure his own loan. As real estate, the perpetual annuities offered certain other legal advantages as well. Indeed, under Old-Regime inheritance law, they were the ideal instrument for converting cash into an asset that profligate heirs could not dissipate.[22]

All three types of contracts (obligations, perpetual annuities, and life annuities) survived the Revolution, but, once the strictures on usury were removed in 1789, perpetual annuities became a rare and exotic form of credit. Life annuities also diminished in importance—a puzzling turn of events. The demand for life-contingent income could hardly have declined since life expectancy was rising and since the rich still wanted to provide for their old age. Perhaps they turned to the burgeoning insurance industry and replaced life annuities with tontine insurance. In any case, the credit instrument of choice in the nineteenth century was not the life annuity but the obligation. It dominated lending just as perpetual annuities had in the seventeenth century. Only in the eighteenth century did all three types of contracts coexist.

In some credit markets, lenders can offset the relative danger of default across debtors by charging them different interest rates. In early modern Europe, however, their ability to vary interest rates was constrained by public authorities. Individuals who did not avail themselves of notaries had greater freedom in setting interest rates—in part because

20. Guyot 1784, s.v. "hypothèque" and "saisie réelle"; Schnapper 1957.
21. When a borrower defaulted on short-term commercial credit, the lenders usually recovered their losses much more quickly than with notarized debt. That was true under the Old Regime, and it was even more likely to be so in the nineteenth century.
22. Schnapper 1957; Giesey 1977.

non-notarized loans were most often short term and thus interest was part of the sum to be repaid.[23] For notarial credit, the legislation was more restrictive. Until 1789, the interest rate cap affected perpetual annuities exclusively, falling from 10 percent in the fifteenth century to 5 percent in 1665.[24] The 5 percent rate would serve as the golden rule for most of our period, and it would remain in force until World War I, except for three brief intervals. First, during the Regency (1715–23) the legal interest rate dipped below 5 percent from 1719 until 1725.[25] Second, in 1766 Louis XV attempted to reduce the interest rate cap to 4 percent, but the traditional interest cap was reimposed in 1770.[26] Finally, although the Revolution abolished a part of the usury regulation in October 1789 by legalizing interest-bearing notes, it did not remove the 5 percent cap. It was not until July 1796 that interest rates were freed, but the freedom was brief, for Napoleon reintroduced the 5 percent cap for mortgages in 1807. This 5 percent ceiling endured into the twentieth century.[27]

Why did the 5 percent interest rate cap persist for so long and across so much political change? And what were the consequences of the rigid prices? It is worth digressing here to consider both questions, if only because economists might otherwise conclude that credit in Paris was severely rationed. Although inflexible prices may have initially restricted lending, the constraint disappeared as a result of financial innovation. In the long run, the credit market created enough new debt instruments to offset the negative consequences of interest rate regulation, and the interest rate cap affected more who had access to what kind of loan than the availability of credit overall. The reason perhaps is that 5 percent may well have been the long-run price equilibrium in the mortgage market, where evidence from the ratio of the rental to sale price of land suggests implicit interest rates at or below 5 percent.[28] In such a market,

23. The law of 3 September 1807 fixed the legal interest rate at 6 percent for commercial paper and at 5 percent for private parties. See Bigo 1947:48.

24. Guyot 1784, s.v. "taux légal"; Schnapper 1957; Isambert 1822, 18:69–71. An edict of September 1679 did raise the limit back to 5.56 percent, but it is not clear that it took effect (Isambert 1822, 19:217).

25. Isambert 1822, 20:293–94.

26. Felix 1999.

27. Decree of 3–12 October 1789; laws of 5 thermidor, an IV (23 July 1796) and 3 September 1807. See *Archives parlementaires* 1862: première série, 9:337–38.

28. In the second half of the eighteenth century, the rental/land price ratio was about 3.5 percent in England and usually between 3 to 4.5 percent in various French provinces. The ratio does almost equal 5 percent in Beauce, southwest of Paris, during the last decades of the Old Regime. See Clay 1974; Allen 1988; Clark 1988, 1996; Frêche 1974: 568–73; Poitrineau 1965:513–14; Deyon 1970: 310–19; Saint-Jacob 1960:292; Béaur 1984:316–17; Velde and Weir 1992:19.

the task of financial intermediaries was to use their information to allocate borrowers and lenders to different types of contracts. The effects
of the interest rate ceiling were therefore felt at the margin rather than
in the aggregate. Some borrowers were denied access to rente loans and
forced to rely on shorter term obligations, while others were shut out of
notarial credit altogether. But loans overall, as we shall see, were broadly
available.

Another important rationale for the 5 percent cap was the effect it
had on lenders. With a 5 percent interest cap, lenders reserved their
loans for the safest of borrowers—those who could provide secure collateral. As a result, the 5 percent cap boosted the demand for information
about collateral: whether a particular piece of land was already burdened
with liens, for example. There are two ways for lenders to gain access to
such information: it might be collected by the state or by private intermediaries.

For its part, the state recognized the value of gathering information
about collateral at an early date, but it made only slow progress towards
this goal. Prior to 1771, public information about liens was only available for liens on government offices and government loans.[29] In the late
eighteenth century, mortgage *(hypothèque)* registers were put in place,
but their use remained limited through the 1790s. The popularity of
the hypothèques increased after a set of reforms under the Convention.[30]
By the early nineteenth century most Parisian debt contracts with land
as collateral were registered with the hypothèques. As we discuss in chapter 11, the diffusion of the hypothèque system to the rest of the country
was hampered by transaction costs. With the hypothèques, a creditor
could learn from his notary what debts a given borrower had registered
and what loans used a particular piece of land as collateral.

The alternative to public mortgage registers was the private provision
of information. In our case, that was the task of notaries, a task that they
accomplished efficiently, as chapters 5 and 6 will show. Their effectiveness offers a partial explanation for why a hypothèque system failed to
catch on under the Old Regime. The informal institution effectively

29. Isambert 1822, 22:530–37; Boucher d'Argis 1786.
30. The hypothèques reform occurred in three stages, the Code hypothécaire of messidor, an III, the Law of brumaire, an VII, and the Code Civil. On the Code hypothécaire,
see *Procès verbaux de la Convention Nationale* (An III, 64:146–232) and *Bulletin des Lois de
la République Française*, law of 9 messidor, an III (code hypothécaire), law of 9 messidor,
an III (déclarations foncières), and laws of 2 brumaire, 26 frimaire, and 21 nivose, an IV.
The key law of 11 brumaire, an VII is also in the *Bulletin des Lois de la République Française*.
For an analysis of the issue, see Flour de Saint-Genis 1889. See also Archives du Ministère
des Finances, B 31141, 38916–19, 38921, 38923.

blocked the formal institutional change. Notaries could provide a substitute for mortgage registers because they accumulated information about individual debtors and creditors in the course of drawing up contracts. They simply had all the relevant information about assets and liabilities, and they could provide it more cheaply than any mortgage registry. One might argue that the decline of notaries reflected the creation of more efficient informational institutions, which released financial brokerage from informational services. Such an argument, though, ignores another factor that continued to affect financial markets throughout the nineteenth century: the memory of the financial cataclysm during the French Revolution. As we shall see, this same cataclysm scattered the notaries' private store of information like a pile of straw.

There was one other rationale for the 5 percent cap on interest rates that deserves mention—namely, politics. Prior to the Revolution, the state was a huge borrower, and it feared having to compete with the private market because of its history of default. Limiting private interest rates was a way to reduce competition, even if the limits were advertised as private credit relief. Only in the nineteenth century did such competition turn in the government's favor as public debt became a safe investment.

Government debt was exempt from all credit regulation. Under the Old Regime, the crown created long-term interest-bearing debt with preannounced redemption schedules, while its short-term debt either bore interest or was discounted. Under Louis XIV, for instance, perpetual annuities were issued by the state at rates up to 8 percent a year. In the eighteenth century, discounting of initial issues allowed government investors to earn far more than the 5 percent limit in the private market. And after the Revolution, government investors could do the same, at least until 1824.

Under the Old Regime, the monarchy marketed a large amount of debt of varying types, from short-term notes sold by financial officials (financiers) to a number of different long-term loans, most of which were peddled by notaries. The long-term debt includes term loans, and life and perpetual annuities. For each type of contract, different nominal interest rates were proposed, and issues were tied to different funds for service.[31] The crown showed the greatest ingenuity with life annuities. It sold ones that depended on the lives of one, two, or even three persons. In some instances, the annuity payments depended on the age of the person whose life determined the length of the contract; in others, they did not. Sometimes, in loans known as tontines, lenders were

31. Marion 1927, vol. 1.

grouped together with others of similar ages, and the government divided a constant payment among the living members of each group until the last one died.[32] The government could sell so many life annuities because, in an era before old-age pensions, demand was high. In addition, the government had an advantage when it came to borrowing via life annuities. It sold so many of them that the risks it faced were relatively small.

With all of its debt, the monarchy could unilaterally rewrite the terms of the contracts. Term debts might be transformed into perpetuals, interest payment cuts, and tontines turned into life annuities.[33] After the Revolution, such capricious practices came to a halt and government borrowing was reformed. The debt was consolidated. All new issues became perpetual bonds underwritten by bankers rather than notaries. And after the default of 1797, the state honored its debts.

One could thus characterize the state's history as a borrower by dividing it into two distinct periods. The first period lasted until 1797 and was one of repeated defaults. The second, from 1797 on, featured a commitment to debt payments despite the absence of any real constraints on the central government. The history of government debt raises several questions we aim to answer. First of all, what was the impact of the Old Regime's policies on financial markets? On the one hand, repeated defaults ought to have retarded the development of the credit market. On the other hand, the inventiveness of government officials in finding new ways of attracting savings made it a positive force in financial innovation. Similarly, in the nineteenth century, the state's record of paying its debts and maintaining monetary stability should have encouraged financial growth. At the same time, though, the state was excluding notaries from government borrowing, which damaged their role in financial markets.

Beyond regulating the credit market, the French state also controlled the monetary system. Under the Old Regime, money included a theoretical unit of account (the *livre*) and coins either of gold or of silver. It was up to the crown to define the relationship between specie and the unit of account. The state's ability to manipulate the value of the unit of account threatened the credit market, and for a simple reason: until the Revolution at least, individuals had to specify all long-term debt contracts in units of account. The threat was particularly serious during three periods: the bout of currency manipulation that eroded the gold or silver value of the livre between 1688 and 1726, the paper money

32. Velde and Weir 1991. There was at least one private tontine as well.
33. Marion 1927, vol. 1; Velde and Weir 1992.

experiment under Law in 1717–20, and the issue of paper notes known as *assignats* during the Revolution.[34] In each of these three episodes, creditors suffered significant real losses from devaluations. The Revolution brought the monetary manipulations to a halt, though, for after 1797 the gold and silver value of the franc (the currency that replaced the livre) remained unchanged until the First World War.

Each of the devaluations struck when the state faced major budgetary problems. Like inflation, the devaluations were in fact disguised defaults because they cut the value of the crown's debt payments. At the same time, as we shall see, they redistributed enormous amounts of wealth in the private credit market. Indeed, private claims plummeted just as much as public debts.

As scholars have shown, shifts in the value of the currency offered the opportunity for substantial gains to those who correctly anticipated changes.[35] Such profits, though, were usually out of reach in the long-term credit market, because the transaction costs of using long-term loans for speculative purposes were too high. That left lenders vulnerable to devaluation, and they were well aware of the danger. To protect themselves, lenders could demand repayment in coin (most loan contracts contained clauses to this effect), but such demands provided little protection. In the first place, when the state issued paper money (in the Revolution, for example, or during the Law affair), it simply invalidated these specie clauses. And in the seventeenth and eighteenth centuries, rentes and obligations—the only available loan contracts for long-term credit—had to be stipulated in money of account. Because the state cut the silver and gold value of the money of account in a devaluation, a lender reimbursed after the devaluation received less bullion than he had loaned.[36] The specie clauses thus could not protect against changes in real value of the unit of account, leaving the credit market with the equivalent of exchange rate uncertainty. The hyperinflation accompa-

---

34. Between 1688 and 1726 the livre lost nearly half of its value in silver. During the Law experiment the Billets de Banque lost more than half their value. The assignats lost more than 99 percent of their value. See Nathalis de Wailly 1857; Caron 1909; Lüthy 1959; Goubert 1960; Faure 1977.

35. Neal 1994; Murphy 1986.

36. Bullion clauses, specifying that a loan should be repaid in units of silver or gold, were illegal. It was also illegal to require in-kind payment. See Isambert 1822, 15:275–6 (Edit sur les monnaies, 1602) and Schnapper 1957:175–200. After the Revolution, it became legal to specify debt either in silver or gold or in bags of wheat with no monetary equivalent; see AD Vaucluse, Actes Civils Publics, L'Isle-sur-Sorgues, 1807 or AD Aube, 4Q3794, no. 195, année 1822. See also AN, MC, XXXI, January 7, 1831 for an obligation for 8.749 kgs of fine gold.

nying the Revolution (which we explore in chapter 8) offers a striking
example of just how vulnerable lenders could be to continued changes
in the value of the livre. And while the problem disappeared after the
Revolution, Parisian creditors still feared inflation's return well into the
1850s.

Before indexation became legal in the nineteenth century, the only
solution was for lenders to structure debt contracts in a way that would
allow them to recover their funds quickly. (Here indexation means writing a loan contract that compensates lenders for inflation by tying the
payments they receive to a price index or the value of a commodity like
gold.) Fears of devaluation thus pushed creditors to move resources
from long-term to short-term loans. Yet there were limits to how far such
a shift could go. If a lender was funding a long-term project, he and the
borrower would have to renegotiate the loan repeatedly. If renegotiation
was costly, long-term contracts might well have been preferable despite
the risk of monetary manipulation.

In addition to institutions governing financial markets, we must consider those affecting property rights in general. When debts went sour,
creditors had to go to court and seek redress in the same way as any
other civil litigants. Litigation was costly, particularly under the Old Regime. The judicial problem remained largely intact through the Revolution. The end of the Old Regime may have diminished the costs of litigation, but it did not reduce the complexity or time required to recover
resources.[37] In the first place, goods and real estate pledged as collateral
could not simply be repossessed by a lender, for a borrower only surrendered his property up to the value of the debt. To determine what the
pledged assets were worth, it was necessary to auction them off. The
debtor was entitled to whatever remained from the public sale of assets,
after the debt itself and the cost of repossession had been paid off. In
the case of real estate, the legal process to arrive at the auction of an
uncooperative debtor's property could be particularly expensive, if the
courts had to force the sale. The only way to avoid the expense was for all
the creditors to contract together and reach a settlement with the debtor.
Such a settlement could take many forms, from *atermoiement* to *abandon.*
In the case of an atermoiement, the creditors simply rescheduled a large
fraction of the debts. In the case of an abandon, the debtor handed over
all his present possessions in return for a discharge of his debts.[38] But any
such agreement required the consent of the debtor and of all the creditors.
If they could not agree, the courts had to settle the matter.

37. Woloch 1994.
38. Luckett 1992.

These judicial arrangements indicate that the institutions of credit in France generally favored debtors in cases of default. Such a bias undercut the efficiency of credit markets, because in the long run the efficiency of markets depends on protecting the property rights of investors and lenders. In societies where such protection is lacking, savers will try to keep as little of their wealth in financial assets as possible. Strengthening the property rights of lenders can therefore boost both savings rates and the extent of financial contracting. The latter is especially important, for in the short and medium term, financial market growth is often driven by increases in the proportion of assets that are financial instruments. That is particularly true for preindustrial societies where the savings rate appears to have changed only slowly. Thus the evolution of financial markets permits us to test the real effects of changes in judicial procedure. If the judicial system of the Old Regime was significantly worse than the meritocratic system of the nineteenth century, then it should have limited credit growth. However, if creditors and debtors were usually able to resolve their differences without recourse to formal institutions, then the impact of judicial reforms might be small.

Notaries

Notaries take the center stage in our story. In fiction, these scriveners could not hope for a leading role. Indeed, in nineteenth-century novels, they were often ridiculed for their supposed sloth, corpulence, and greed.[39] Yet in our financial drama, these men were the stars. To understand their role, we must understand the legislation that governed them, first in France as a whole and then just in Paris.

Notaries are a legacy of the Roman law that influenced the legal systems of France and other continental European countries. With its emphasis on written rather than oral contracts, Roman law proved difficult to administer in societies where few individuals knew how to read or write. To ease the problem, medieval courts appointed notetakers to record what were really oral contracts. The medieval notary provided two services. He drew up written contracts and thus helped the parties involved avoid disputes that would inevitably arise with purely oral agreements. As an agent of the court, he was not a party to the contract and

39. In *Cousin Pons,* Balzac (1962:253) describes an honest notary in these terms: "C'est un homme lourd et pédant. . . . C'est patriarche; ça n'est pas drôle et amusant." Roguin in Balzac's *César Birotteau* (1898a) is the very epitome of the greedy and dishonest notary. See also Flaubert 1926, 52:294.

thus had no incentive to mislead illiterate people about the contract's terms.[40] Further, as a judicial official, the notary helped to guarantee the legality of the contract. Indeed, a notarized contract had the burden of proof in its favor. It was presumed to be valid unless the plaintiff could bring dramatic evidence to the contrary.

By the early modern period the notary drew up two types of contracts. For one kind, contracts *en brevet,* he provided only the scribal service and kept no detailed record of the agreement. For the other kind, contracts *en minute,* he drew up at least two copies. One, called the *grosse,* was handed to the creditors or more generally to the buyers of the assets; another copy, the *minute,* remained in perpetuity in the archives of the notary and his successors. Here the notary performed both the role of a scribe and a record keeper. If a grosse was ever lost, the lender could always return to the notary for a second copy, as could his heirs.

The notarial positions themselves were bought and sold in the early modern period. A would-be notary had to buy his position from an existing notary and also be approved by the local notarial corporation and by public authorities.[41] By the eighteenth century, there were tens of thousands of notaries and they blanketed France. Individuals either came to notarial offices (known as *études*) or notaries went to private homes to draw up marriage contracts, wills, probates, land sales, rental contracts, loans, and any other private agreements. In Paris, the typical notary had an office with a safe, books, and archives. There was only one notary in each étude, but he usually employed domestics and several skilled clerks.

The sale of their businesses gave notaries an incentive to accumulate information, because the information could be sold along with their notarial offices. Because the information varied greatly in value depending upon the location, the disparity in the value of notarial offices was great. By the eighteenth century, offices in Paris, for example, were worth fifty times that in small towns, and rural notaries purchased their positions for less than a hundredth of the price in Paris.[42] The Revolution abolished the sale of notarial businesses, but it was quietly reintroduced in the early 1800s and fully acknowledged by 1808.[43]

40. One might wonder whether the wealthy bribed notaries to take advantage of the illiterate parties in contracts, but that was apparently not a problem, probably because the contracts would still have to be introduced in court and because the penalty for a notary who defrauded a client was high.

41. Faure-Jarrosson 1988:4–11; Woloch 1994.

42. For Paris, see below. For notarial offices in Burgundy see AD Côte-d'Or C 9875 July 1777, and 9671 September 1740.

43. AN BB[10] 100; *Archives parlementaires* 1862, deuxième série, 15:527, 542.

In many respects, notaries' credit activities were unregulated. However, they were only permitted to draw up contracts that were legal. They were therefore liable to prosecution, for example, if a loan they drafted did not respect the interest cap. The state also refused to let them engage in certain financial practices, which became the specialty of bankers: lending out money on deposit, for example, or dealing in negotiable short-term credit, such as bills of exchange. Although their role in arranging transactions was either tolerated or encouraged, their attempts to compete directly with bankers worried the government greatly. The state therefore tried several times to stop the notaries from acting like bankers. It was not until the 1840s in Paris (and the 1880s and 1890s in the provinces), though, that the notaries truly relinquished control of credit activity. In our period, they were by and large free to shape the credit market with their own unique form of financial intermediation.

Parisian Notaries

The notaries of Paris were by far the busiest in the country. Like notaries in the provinces, they were organized into a company, which settled disputes, approved newcomers to the notarial profession, and lobbied on behalf of the notaries as a group. Although the business of the Parisian notaries resembled that of their provincial counterparts, they did enjoy a number of special privileges. These privileges made Parisian notaries more stable and more visible than their provincial counterparts, at least until the Revolution, when their special status was abolished.

To begin with, the number of Parisian notaries remained extraordinarily stable. From 1639 to 1790, there were exactly 113 notaries in Paris. Only in 1790 did the number rise to 114 when the city annexed the neighborhood of the Roule (behind the present Champs Elysées), incorporating its notary. Under the Second Empire, Paris annexed outlying municipalities, and again the number of notaries was increased to 122. The number of notaries thus grew less than 10 percent, while the city's population jumped by over 300 percent—a sharp contrast with the rest of France, where the government freely changed the number of notaries to reflect changes in legal business.

Prior to the Revolution, notaries drew up contracts for state borrowing. The Parisian notaries benefited from this role since they had a near monopoly on drafting the state's credit contracts. They also competed intensely for and garnered a disproportionate share of the business of issuing the debt floated by provincial institutions. These privileges lasted until the Revolution, when the state consolidated all its

borrowing into a single standard contract, dispensed with the notaries'
services, and turned instead to bankers to underwrite government debt.

One final privilege enjoyed by the Parisian notaries was the right
they had to draw up contracts anywhere in France. A provincial notary
could only operate within the jurisdiction of the court to which he was
attached. Parisian notaries could do business anywhere, even though
they were attached to the Châtelet, the local royal court for Paris.[44] Although Parisian notaries rarely ventured beyond the confines of the
Paris Basin, they did draw up lucrative contracts in an area of about one-
hundred kilometers around Paris.

Notaries charged fees for their services that varied by type of contract,
length of the document required, and the value of the transaction. Each
local notarial corporation negotiated, for different types of contract, a
tariff of fees, which did not change frequently. In Paris, for instance, the
tariff negotiated in the late seventeenth century remained the reference
for more than a century.[45] Yet despite this official tariff, the total fees
that a notary charged were at his discretion. In the first place, he controlled the actual number of contracts necessary to realize a transaction
as well as the length of each contract. Furthermore, he could add on a
charge for finding a suitable partner for a contract—finding a lender
for a borrower, for instance. Unlike the fees for services as a scribe, the
surcharges for arranging transactions were unregulated.

The king and the notarial corporation itself taxed notarial contracts.
In Paris, though, notaries actually escaped the major tax on notarial contracts, the royal government's *Contrôle des actes*. The capital's notaries
had paid a lump sum to the crown shortly after the tax was instituted
in 1693 so that the contracts they drew up would be exempt from it. As a
result Parisian notaries had an additional advantage over their provincial
rivals, an advantage that grew when the *Contrôle des actes* was increased
in 1722.[46] In the eighteenth century, Parisian notaries periodically paid
lump sums to the monarchy plus a stamp tax levied on all legal documents. It was only after the Revolution that they paid the same taxes as
their provincial counterparts. Parisian notaries then owed the tax *(enregistrement)* on all notarial acts. For credit agreements this was almost
always 1 percent for debt initiations and 0.5 percent on debt repay-

44. Limon 1992:42.

45. For an example outside Paris, see Gaston 1991:329–42. For Paris, see Limon 1992:
46, 61; El Annabi 1994:189–90; "Tarif des salaires et vacations des notaires, commissaires
et substituts du procureur du Roy, procureurs et sergents, précédant le règlement de 1690"
(AN Y 17609); and *Statuts et règlements des notaires parisiens* (1766).

46. Limon 1992:102; Marion 1927, 1:32–33.

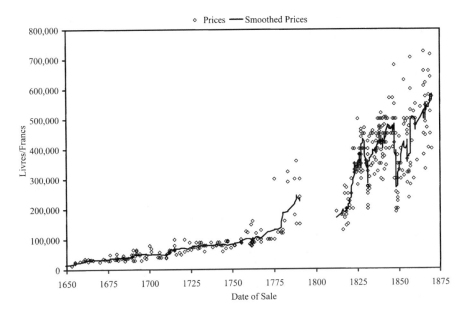

FIGURE 1.1   The Price of Notarial Offices in Paris, 1650–1870. Source: ANMC; AN BB[10]; ACNP; Limon 1992; and *Archives parlementaires* 1862, 1st ser., 31:201.

ments.[47] They also had to pay a fee for registering their clients' liens with the mortgage administration *(hypothèques)*. These fees had a fixed component and a part that varied with the amount of the transaction.

Since notaries' offices were sold, the sales prices give us an index of how their business changed over time because the prices should reflect the discounted value of expected future profits net of taxes. The sales prices can be found in sales contracts, a task that Limon (1992) has largely accomplished for the late seventeenth century and that we have continued up to 1789. Thereafter, the ministry of justice and the corporation of notaries both kept records of office transmissions, giving us information on sales from 1815 onward (figure 1.1). With the exception of the nineteenth century, when credit transactions actually declined as a portion of the notaries' total business, the value of notarial offices is consistent with the development of notarial credit that we will chart in the rest of the book. After about six decades of slow growth, the price of notarial offices began to rise in the 1760s. The growth in prices accelerated up to the 1780s, in parallel with credit activity. The Revolution

47. Since Parisian notaries did not pay the contrôle des actes under the Old Regime, borrowers and lenders outside Paris had an incentive to have their loans arranged in Paris.

then cut the value of notarial positions in Paris by at least 40 percent.
Yet by 1825 the value had rebounded; a notary's business was worth
about as much as it had been in the eighteenth century. By 1869 the
typical business had doubled in value.

———————

This brief description of the formal institutions affecting credit in Paris
highlights their remarkable stability over time. Unlike contemporary developing countries, which undergo frequent major reforms, France
evolved slowly. The pace of legal change gave informal institutions ample
time to adapt. Take, for example, the interest rate cap. What were the
costs of a regulation prohibiting charges above 5 percent for certain
types of contracts for two hundred years? In the absence of informal
institutional evolution, the costs would have been great because, as chapter 3 will show, when risk increased the market stagnated. Over time,
however, notaries and their financial allies developed the obligation until it became in effect identical with interest-bearing term debt. By the
1770s notaries were drawing up obligations that circumvented the 5 percent cap and that required borrowers to reimburse the lender in installments containing both capital and interest. As a result, the interest rate
legislation was of little practical importance except in allocating borrowers among types of contracts. Yet the process of innovation began only
in the 1740s, and the obligation did not become a real competitor to
rentes until the 1770s, even though the 5 percent cap had been put in
place in 1666. The delay between the change in interest ceiling in the
1660s and the rise of obligations nearly one hundred years later drama-
tizes historical contingencies, whose effects can be felt decades later as
people learn and adapt. Although economic theory may predict that
informal innovations will occur when formal rules are changed, it says
little about the timing of the specific response.

CHAPTER TWO

From Notarial Archives
to Credit

BECAUSE THE NOTARIAL ARCHIVES contain mountains of data, it is
simply impossible to study lending in Paris without sampling. All the
figures we present in this volume are thus estimates from samples rather
than exact totals. This chapter details the steps we took in constructing
our estimates: first the counts of the number of different notarial acts
concerning credit, next the value of new loans taken out, and finally
total outstanding debts. The rest of the chapter then describes the general patterns in the data and the other evidence we used. Readers who
are willing to accept our figures—at least for the moment—may want
to glance at the concluding section of this chapter and then jump ahead
to chapter 3. They can return later if they have questions about the evidence or want to know how it was assembled.

Before they jump ahead, though, many readers may want to pose one
question: namely, is it possible that many long-term loans were never
notarized and hence left no trace in the notarial archives? If the answer
is yes, then estimates like ours, derived as they are from notarial records,
will inevitably undercount the amount of lending.

Fortunately, for long-term credit, such unnotarized loans were probably rare. Indeed, probate inventories show that few long-term debts
were unnotarized.[1] The reason was simple. As explained in chapter 1,
there were powerful legal reasons to notarize any long-term contract,
particularly a long-term loan.[2] In the case of a default, a lender with
an unnotarized loan lost seniority for his rights, and worse yet, he
had little or no claim against the borrower's real estate, the most important form of collateral in the long-term credit market. Even in
the nineteenth century, most long-term credit was backed by real es-

1. Furet and Daumard 1961; Daumard 1973.
2. Guyot 1784, s.v. "hypothèques."

tate, and the registration of the real estate liens required the intervention of a notary. The same was true for corporate banks, including
the Crédit Foncier, the most successful mortgage bank in the late nineteenth century. Since the law created an incentive to use notaries, we
are confident that our data and our estimates cover nearly all long-term
credit.[3]

Our Sampling Strategy

Studying notarial credit requires dealing directly with the problem of
data collection. To begin with, no sources provide aggregate statistics,
and each individual notary did an enormous amount of business. Every
year, on average, a notary in Paris witnessed about 520 acts in the mid-
eighteenth century and slightly more by the mid-nineteenth century.[4]
Of these, at least 160 concerned private credit. To recover the entire
set of notarial loan contracts for a single year in the middle of the eighteenth century would require wading through some 60,000 contracts to
collect information on between 20,000 and 25,000 public and private
loans. While that is not beyond the capacities of a small team of researchers, it would preclude collecting more than one or two years' worth of
data. The two centuries we considered would mean wading through
more than twelve million contracts to collect information on the five
million acts related to credit. With such a torrent of data, one has to
sample, and we chose a sampling strategy that relied on the notaries'
efforts to manage their own records.

Notaries were required to keep copies of most contracts they recorded. When they retired, they sold their archives to their successor
or to another colleague. Upon buying an office, a notary therefore acquired several hundred yards of shelf space filled with copies of the
contracts that his predecessors had witnessed—the minutes, which were
preserved because they helped establish property ownership. Periodically, the notary would have to locate particular acts at the request of
his clients. To find his way through the mounds of contracts, he kept
both alphabetical and chronological indexes. Most of the alphabetical indexes are unavailable or have disappeared, while the chronological ones survive and have been microfilmed.[5] These indexes are terse,

3. We also leave out long-term loans that were incorporated into other transactions,
such as land sales. As a result, there was surely more lending than what we have found.

4. Poisson 1985:298–99.

5. It appears that the archives received the chronological indexes when they accepted
the minutes, but they seem to have been less successful in collecting the alphabetical in-

TABLE 2.1   THE SAMPLE COUNTS AND THE
POPULATION

Type of Acts	Our Sample	114 Notaries
New private credit	98,440	1,122,216
New public credit	83,186	948,320
Total new credit	179,473	2,045,992
Other acts	255,606	2,913,908
Total acts considered	437,232	4,984,445

Source: Our series; for details see text and Archival Sources.

but at the very least they record the type of act and the names of the parties.

The indexes make it possible to count the number of credit contracts drawn up by notaries. All that is required is to total the number of each type of loan month by month, notarial index by notarial index. To make the counts, we chose ten notarial businesses (études) and followed all the notaries who worked in them, from 1660 to 1870. That proved more economical than randomly sampling new études every year, and it also had the advantage of allowing us to track the evolution of business practices without worrying about differences among notaries.[6] For these ten études, we collected monthly totals for fourteen different types of contracts.[7] While differentiating among these different contracts gives us a good deal of detail, it still squeezes all the different types of government debt into only two categories.[8] Table 2.1 displays the broad categories of contracts that we counted. It also shows our estimate for the total number of contracts for Paris as a whole, which we derived by extrapolating from our sample. The same process of extrapolation was applied to the monthly totals, yielding time series of lending and indebtedness for

dexes. Nonetheless, a few of the alphabetical indexes have found their way into the archives. See, e.g., ANMC études XXIII, VII, X, XV.

6. The ten études were IX, XXI, XXVII, XLIII, LXII, LXX, LXXVIII, XCI, CXV, CXVII.

7. New private credit broken down into perpetual annuities, obligations, obligations in brevet, and life annuities; new government credit broken down into perpetual and life annuities; repayments, broken down into private and government; secondary sales, lien releases, apprenticeships, and prorogations. In the nineteenth century we also counted credit lines and the loans of the Crédit Foncier.

8. The government perpetual category includes all long-term bonds that are not life contingent. These include the direct borrowing of the crown, and loans secured through corporations, the clergy, or provincial estates. Some of these contracts were term bonds while others had no defined duration. The government life annuity category includes all life-contingent assets, be they tontines, single life annuities, or multiple life annuities.

all of Paris. This process, which we describe below, is delicate and some-what involved. Throughout, however, we tried to keep the method as simple as possible and to reduce the number of assumptions needed to construct our series.

The first step was adjusting for brief gaps in the indexes of some of our études. The problem was particularly severe for the seventeenth cen-tury, for which a number of indexes have been lost. There were in fact so many gaps in the indexes before 1690 that we had to collect data from two additional études.[9] To fill in the gaps, we had to adjust our counts for years when one or more of the notaries' indexes were missing. To do so, we took each notary with a gap in his index and calculated the number of credit acts he drafted for the five years before the gap and the five years after. We performed the same calculation for the other nine notaries in our sample, and the ratio of the two numbers gave us two weights for the relative importance of the notary with the gap in his index, one weight before the gap and the other after. Linear interpola-tion of the two weights then let us adjust the counts from the nine other notaries for the gap in the one notary's index. We checked this adjust-ment procedure against other, simpler procedures, but they all led to similar results.

Having filled in the gaps, we turned to the problem of extrapolating our counts for ten études to the whole of Paris. Since we wanted to esti-mate lending for Paris as a whole, we had to find ways to insure that our sample was representative over time. We did so by comparing the counts for our ten études with similar counts done periodically for some thirty other études.[10] The comparison gave us periodic measures for the rela-tive importance of our ten études, and we used linear interpolation to extend these measures of relative importance to every year from 1660 to 1870. Admittedly, the thirty additional notaries are still not all of Paris, but they do represent 26 percent of the city's notaries. We feel thus quite confident that investigating additional études would not change the re-sults of our extrapolation greatly. We can actually check this assumption thanks to special indexes of all notarial acts that the Archives Nationales compiled for two years, 1751 and 1761. In those two years, the thirty additional notaries (and the ten études in our sample) in fact turn out to be representative of the whole universe of Parisian notaries, at least as far as credit is concerned.

9. Etudes IL and LXXII.
10. The other notaries included études I through VIII, X through XX, XXII through XXVI, XXVIII through XXXIII, and XCIII. The counts were undertaken in 1670, 1700, 1725, 1751, 1761, 1780, and then every ten years starting in 1800.

TABLE 2.2   THE DETAILED SAMPLES

Minutes of Études	Date	Number of Observations
IX, XXI, XLIII, LXII, LXX, LXXVIII, CXV	1662	367
IX, XXI, LXII, LXX, LXXVIII	1690	305
IX, XXI, XLIII, LXII, LXX, LXXVIII, CXV	1700	2314
IX, XXVII, XLIII, LXII, LXX, LXXVII, CXI, CXV	1718–20	666
IX, XXI, XLIII, LXII, LXX, LXXVIII, CXV	1740	681
LXX, CXV	1750–59	1574
IX, XXI, LXX, LXXVIII, CXV	1760–66	1000
IX, XXI, LXX, LXXVIII, CXV	1770	274
IX, XXI, XLIII, LXII, LXX, LXXVIII, CXV	1780	1330
IX, XXI, XXVII, XLIII, LXII, LXVIII, LXX, LXXVIII, CXI, CXV, CXVII	1790–96	1843
IX, XXI, XLIII, LXII, LXX, LXXVIII, CXV	1807–10	266
IX, XXI, XLIII, LXII, LXX, LXXVIII, CXV	1840	230

Note: To these samples we added information for government loans from the P series for 1682 (P6115, $n = 923$), 1711 (P6120, $n = 213$), 1747 (P5934, $n = 1,675$), 1751 (P5936, $n = 101$; P6055, $n = 150$; P6056, $n = 97$; P6057, $n = 157$), 1754 (P5937, $n = 1,808$), 1757 (P5939, $n = 127$), 1758 (P5947, $n = 100$), 1778 (P5970, $n = 22$), 1779 (P5973, $n = 25$), 1781 (P5975, $n = 66$). For additional information about the detailed samples, see Archival Sources.

Constructing the Long-term Series

The next step was to take the monthly counts of new loans and multiply them by average size of each type of loan in order to get the volume of the new debt that was issued. To get the average size of each type of loan, we began with evidence from the samples of notarial records described in table 2.2. We added several additional samples so that we ended up with observations on average loan size nearly every ten years from 1662 to 1826.[11] We then interpolated linearly to get an estimated average loan size for all the intervening years. After 1826 we took down the size of loans directly from the notarial indexes. The evolution of average loan size by type of contract is displayed in figure 2.1.

One problem with this whole procedure was the large variance in the size of loans. In estimating loan sizes, we therefore limited ourselves to samples with at least one hundred loan contracts, in order to reduce the errors to manageable proportions.[12] A second problem we faced was

11. The additional samples were from the years 1665, 1666, 1670, 1682, 1690, 1715, 1725, and 1788; for these years—in contrast to the samples described in table 2.2—we did not gather detailed information on borrowers and lenders. Finally, we collected information on the size of government loans from the issue registers in the AN series P, as described in table 2.2.

12. For each type of debt contract, the mean loan size was approximately equal to the standard deviation of the loan size. With samples of one hundred or more contracts, the

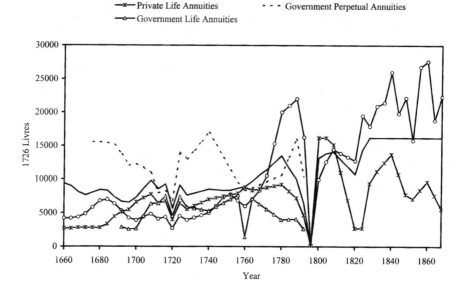

FIGURE 2.1   Size of Notarial Loans by Type of Contract, 1660–1870

the possibility that errors might have been introduced by the process of interpolating loan sizes. Fortunately, because we can observe loan sizes directly after 1826–they are listed in the indexes after that date—we can see whether interpolation actually distorts our series of loan volumes. It turns out that the series based on actual loan sizes do deviate from those constructed using interpolation. Over the short run, the deviations can be quite large: indeed, for a few isolated trimesters one series can be twice the size of the other. But such differences disappear in the long run and seem completely unimportant for the medium- or long-term evolution of the credit market. Indeed, in every decade after 1826, both the interpolated and the exact series show the same pattern of either growth or decline. Furthermore, if we rank decades by growth rates, both series have the same ranking. Admittedly, interpolation does reduce the variation in the series of loan volumes, because the series are no longer jolted by the chance appearance of very large loans. Because such gigantic loans occur irregularly, they create variance in the time series, which our statistical approach cannot capture. Still, these enormous acts are

estimated standard error of the loan size is thus about 10 percent or less of the mean loan size. A 95 percent confidence interval for loan size is thus within 20 percent of the mean. As figure 2.1 shows, long-term changes in average loan size were large and thus unlikely to be statistical flukes. Our estimates of loan durations are equally accurate.

more curiosities than typical of notarial credit, and thus for most lending our method appears reliable.

To make lending volumes comparable across time despite the changing value of the French livre, we converted all monetary amounts to a livre of constant silver weight. Unless stated otherwise, the livres and francs in all our series are therefore corrected to both be worth 4.45 grams of silver, the value of the livre from 1726 to 1789.[13] For 1718, 1719, and 1720, dates for which the silver value of the livre is suspect, we checked with French-British and French-Dutch exchange rates.[14] Since neither the British pound nor the Dutch guilder suffered devaluations, most of the variation in the exchange rate in this period reflected the declining value of Law's paper money, the *billet de banque*. For the period of the Revolution, when paper assignats were legal tender, we relied on the published depreciation tables for Paris.[15]

With series for the volume of new loans in place, the next task was estimating the level of outstanding debt. Essentially, we wanted to include debts when they were first contracted and then remove them when they were repaid.[16] In theory, we would have recovered the expected and realized duration of every loan that we examined from the minutes. We could have then attempted for debt something akin to the family reconstitution of demographers. Such precision, though, proved impossible. Repayments, unlike loans, were sometimes unnotarized, and even when they were notarized, the repayment might not take place before the notary who had drafted the original loan. It would therefore be difficult to find many of the repayment contracts, and even if they could be located, they would have to be matched to the original loans, an ordeal that would demand years of research in the notarial minutes.

Instead, we used yet another approximation that was inspired by demography and has the advantage of simplicity. Faced with a similar problem, Lee, Wrigley, and Schofield devised the method of back projection to estimate the population of England.[17] For our part, we resorted to an

13. Nathalis de Wailly 1857.

14. McCusker 1978.

15. Caron 1909; Crouzet 1994. The exact value of the franc after 1797 was 4.5 grs. silver (5 grs. silver 9/10 fine).

16. As with all stock series, we needed a starting value. For each type of contract, we simply took the average volume for the first five years of our data and multiplied it by the average duration of that contract. Since the market was remarkably steady in the 1660s, variations in the starting value do not affect our series.

17. Wrigley and Schofield 1981; Lee 1974. The use of a forward or backward method depends on having either a good end point or a good start point for the total of outstanding debts. Since we had neither and because we faced the near total extinction of debts during the Revolution, we decided to use a forward projection.

analogous technique—forward projection—to recreate private indebtedness in Paris. After all, debts, like people, are born and die. The population of debts therefore can be tracked with a two-step procedure that
involves adding new credit acts (births) and removing repaid debts
(deaths). Adding the new debts is straightforward since we have such
information on a monthly basis. To deal with the repayment of loans
we used information on duration and on debt repayments to remove a
fraction of all outstanding debts in each period.[18]

If the demography of debt was simple, repayments could be derived
directly from duration evidence: the inverse of the duration $(1/d)$
would serve as an estimate of what was repaid in each year. But debts,
like human lives, face periodic epidemics that cut short their duration.
To account for periodic crises, we relied on variations in the rate of
quittances, or repayment contracts, in our notarial series. Admittedly, the
quittances are not a perfect indicator of credit repayment. Many quittances did not involve credit but rather sales, inheritances, or past business associations. Furthermore, not all repayments gave rise to a quittance, for a lender could simply return the original credit contract to
the borrower after having signed it as repaid. Still, we assume that variation in quittance rates do reflect variation in credit repayment rates, and
we let the repayment rate be a function of both the duration d and the
ratio of the current quittance count (Q^t) to a moving average of quittance
(Q^{*t}). While there is little to justify the last assumption, it seems reasonable to assume that the relationship between quittances and total repayments was stable, outside of periods of crises. Fortunately, the variability
in quittance rate has little effect on our long-term series, although it
can matter in the short run. We therefore set the repayment rate equal
to (Q^t/dQ^{*t}) during the years 1660–1717 and 1721–1789. Between
1718 and 1720 and after 1789, we used alternative procedures described
below.

We estimated indebtedness separately for each type of contract. For
the obligations, we gathered information on their duration from the
same samples that provided data on loan sizes. Before 1800, the duration
of obligations rarely extended far beyond the time agreed upon in the
initial loan contract, a fact that can be verified from repayment contracts.
As a result, we have confidence in our duration figures for obligations,

---

18. We did not attempt to adjust our series for bad debts. In effect, we are assuming
that the duration of bad debts equals that of debts that are properly serviced and then
paid off. This assumption may seem surprising, because a debt becomes bad when the
debtor defaults on a scheduled payment—either of interest alone, in the case of a perpetual or life annuity, or of interest and principal, in the case of an obligation. In either case,
the default must occur before the end of the life of the loan.

and, with the durations and the quittance rates, we constructed estimates for the stock of obligation debt before the Revolution that seem quite robust.

Quantifying the stock of rentes perpétuelles was more problematic. First, we had only three solid estimates of the duration of perpetual annuities: 1662–66, 1717, and 1789. But we could glean additional information about the age distribution of rentes from two periods of crisis (1718–20 and 1790–95), when many rentes perpétuelles were repaid. Both periods suggest that eighteenth-century perpetual annuities lasted a long time—on average, about fifteen years.

That still leaves the seventeenth century in the dark, when the data about the durations of rentes perpétuelles are difficult to interpret. The evidence from 1662–66 contained two types of information about perpetual annuities' duration. The first type comprised 68 durations recovered because the notary annotated the margin of the original loans with the date of repayment. The second type was made up of 31 durations gathered from quittance contracts. Although the marginal annotations were easier to collect, we decided not to use them, because they were inherently biased.[19] Obviously, notaries only entered such marginal annotations infrequently—about a third of the time in seventeenth–century perpetual annuities. As table 2.3 shows for both 1665–66 and 1718–20, the marginal annotations were particularly prevalent on loans that lasted only a short time. The duration in the margins was in fact so much shorter than the duration in the repayment contracts that it was as if we were drawing samples from populations with wildly different mean durations. In the end, the durations garnered from the quittances seem more reliable, even though the quittance contracts are scarcer. As a result, we ignored the marginal annotations altogether and adopted 7.8 years as the initial duration for rentes perpétuelles, which was their average duration in quittance contacts in 1662, weighted by loan size. We then let the duration rise linearly to 12.7 years in 1718, when we had our next reliable measure of duration, and thereafter let it rise linearly to 15 years in 1789. Further research may uncover more variation in the duration and repayment of perpetual annuities, but unless it is extreme it will not influence the aggregate evolution of financial markets in Paris.

For private life annuities, we assumed that during the whole period they lasted on average 15 years and that they were never repaid before the death of the person named in the contract (the so called "life").

---

19. The marginal annotations create bias in two ways. Notaries were very unlikely to make such annotations for acts that had been outstanding more than a decade, and they could not annotate acts where the quittance was drawn up in front of another notary.

TABLE 2.3   REPAYMENTS OF RENTES IN SELECTED YEARS

Duration in Years	1662–66 Margins	1662–66 Repayments	1718–20 Margins	1718–20 Repayments	1790–97 Repayments
		Number of Contracts			
1	30	1	39	28	10
2	11	2	47	16	16
3–4	15	7	29	37	26
5–6	5	4	1	25	37
7–8	3	3	2	14	25
9–10	4	9	2	6	23
11–15	6	3	3	29	85
16–30	2	2	3	51	124
>30	1	0	0	38	115
N Observed	77	31	125	243	461
N Total	221	31	259	266	480
Cumulative Distribution		Percentages			
1	38.2	3.2	31.2	11.5	2.2
2	53.2	9.7	68.8	18.1	5.6
3–4	72.7	32.3	92.0	33.3	11.3
5–6	79.2	45.2	92.8	43.6	19.3
7–8	83.1	54.8	94.4	49.3	24.7
9–10	88.3	83.9	96.0	51.8	29.7
11–15	96.1	93.6	98.4	63.8	48.2
16–30	98.7	100	100	84.8	75.0
>30	100	100	100	100	100
		Average Duration in Years			
Unweighted	4.6	8	2.82	15.6	23
S.E.	0.89	0.99	0.32	1.38	1.03
Weighted	1.7	7.8	1.43	12.7	15.1

Source: The detailed samples described in table 2.2 for the years 1662, 1718–20, and 1790–96; plus samples of loans sizes and durations in ANMC IX, XXI, LXII, and LXXVIII for the years 1665–66. Note: We added data from 1665–66 because in 1665 the interest rate ceiling dropped from 5.56 percent to 5 percent.

This duration was estimated from the life expectancy of persons whose "lives" figured in private life annuities during the second half of the eighteenth century (the only time when such contracts were quantitatively important). We ruled out early repayment because a borrower who paid a life annuity back early had to give back all of the capital—an unattractive option. It is true that some early repayments of life annuities occurred during the French Revolution, but there were too few of them to study systematically. On the whole, the only bias this procedure is likely to have created is an excess number of life annuities outstanding in the early nineteenth century. But since the overall number of life annuities at that time was small, the bias is unimportant.

In the crisis years of 1718 to 1720 and 1790 to 1796, our standard procedures did not work. As a result, we had to estimate repayment rates year by year in these two periods, using methods detailed in chapters 4 and 8 and in appendix 3. Estimating the debt stock correctly in these two periods is crucial, for in one case it was cut in half and in the other it dropped 90 percent.

Finally, from 1797 to 1869, we relied on information from the indexes to improve the precision of our estimates of the evolution of the stock of obligations. We were faced with two problems. After the Revolution, loan durations were unstable and sensitive to political crises, and many obligations were renewed instead of being repaid on their due date. (Formal loan renewal began in the eighteenth century but was relatively rare; for details, see chapters 1 and 8.) To account for such renegotiation of loans, we relied upon a different procedure that is explained in appendix 4 and that uses the extra data available for the nineteenth century.

We ended up computing two different outstanding debt series (ODS): a nominal ODS, which ignored the effects of variations in the value of the livre, and a silver ODS, in which the outstanding stock of debt is constantly revalued at the current value of the livre. Nominal ODS is the financial equivalent of a capital stock measured without regard for price variation, as one might compute from pure quantity indicators. The silver ODS is akin to a capital stock series in which the capital is evaluated at market value in every period. It provides the current cost of repayment for debtors.

Interest Rates and Other Data

Studying Parisian credit markets is made easier by the existence of published time series for economic, demographic, and financial activity. In particular, prior research has made available building indexes, wage rates, numbers of bankruptcies, grain prices, rental rates, population totals, and decennial marriage rates. Beyond these series, we relied on alternative sources (for instance, numbers of apprenticeships) and on cross-sectional analyses of the financial business to test our explanation of the evolution of notarial lending. To understand changes in the clienteles of notaries, we gathered detailed information from samples of loans in order to establish the identities of borrowers and lenders. (For the sources used, see table 2.2.) We also scoured probates and secondary sources on the wealth holdings of Parisians, and we examined the archives of the corporation of notaries (the Chambre des Notaires) and those of the Ministry of Justice to glean information on notarial practices. Similarly, we perused diaries, literary sources, and the correspondence of contemporaries to understand how the role of notaries changed over time. Finally, to the greatest extent possible we tried to recover evidence from records of litigation involving notaries.

On the financial side, we have interest rate data from the mid-eighteenth century onward, and good information on government debt and the activities of some Parisian financial institutions after 1805. Given that prices play a subordinate role in our analysis, the published data bear some review. For the Old Regime, there are two interest rate series, one for government bonds and the other for short-term debts.[20] Since they both begin after 1740, they reveal nothing about interest rates during the period of monetary instability under Louis XIV. For the period after the Revolution, there are a government bond series and a short-term series. Because the Banque de France maintained a 4 percent discount rate, the short-term rate (which is inferred from letters of exchange drawn in London on Paris) tended to hover around 4 percent in the nineteenth century. The long-term series suggest that interest rates remained close to 5 percent, at least in the periods of stable money before the Revolution and from 1820 to the middle of the century. Most of the shifts away from 5 percent involved movements upward during political crises, because the long-term rates were sensitive to any threat that the government might not repay its debts in full. In any case, with both the long- and short-term rates, it is remarkable how little a connection there was between interest rates and the state of the economy.

At least in part, the long-run stability of the published interest rates reflected government policy. The Old-Regime monarchy, in particular, did not encourage the trading of a single publicly traded government bond. It issued many kinds of debt, and the few that were listed on the Paris stock exchange had less risk and hence less variation in interest rates. The riskiest government long-term debt was not traded on a public exchange because the monarchy did not encourage the creation of a homogenous asset like the British consol.[21] Similarly, the available short-term rates refer to the very best commercial paper traded between London and Paris. Marginal letters of exchange, no doubt, paid higher inter-

20. Our source on government bond yields under the Old Regime and after the Revolution was a tape generously provided by David Weir. For short-term rates, see Luckett 1992; Boyer-Xambeu, Deleplace, and Gillard 1995.

21. In the seventeenth and early eighteenth centuries, British public debt involved a wide of variety of bonds. But during the 1720s a process began whereby it was consolidated into perpetual annuities—hence the name consols. See Dickson 1967.

TABLE 2.4   SHARE OF LOANS AT OR ABOVE THE USURY CEILING IN ENGLAND AND
PARIS

	Above or at Usury Ceiling		Strictly Above		Number of Observations	
	England (percent)	Paris (percent)	England (percent)	Paris (percent)	England	Paris
1660	31.0	72.1	7.1	0.0	42	202
1670	33.8	92.2	9.2	0.0	65	155
1680	18.2	84.5	9.1	1.7	33	118
1690	8.3	100.0	0.0	3.1	36	64
1700	0.0	88.8	0.0	1.0	46	98
1710	—	100.0	—	46.2	—	13
1720	37.0	—	0.0	—	27	—
1730	22.2	97.8	5.6	0.0	36	—
1740	31.8	79.7	9.1	0.0	22	48
1750	25.0	89.2	4.2	1.2	24	416
1760	40.0	93.3	0.0	1.3	10	150
1770	28.6	100.0	0.0	12.5	14	40
1780	31.3	99.3	12.5	0.7	16	145

Source: England data generously communicated by Gregory Clark; see Clark (1988) for details. Paris, our periodic sample.

Note: The sources are not strictly comparable. Clark's data come from Charity commission reports and thus involve a very select group of lenders dispersed all over England. Charities were exempt from the usury-ceiling legislation. The data for Paris comes from samples of the population that capture a very wide group of lenders, all of whom were subject to the interest rate caps. Further, in France at least, interest payments were taxable and lenders and borrowers were free to decide who would pay the tax. Since the tax was 10 percent of the interest payment, contracts at 5 percent paid either 5 percent or 4.5 percent to the lender depending on who paid the tax.

est rates, but these rates were not published. Finally, for the nineteenth century, public bond rates reflected the government's reputation as the safest possible borrower. Following the variations of either the long- or short-term interest rate series is thus unlikely to tell us much about the scarcity of credit except when that scarcity was driven by politics.

In any case, it was information not prices that allocated capital in private transactions, as we shall show below. In the nineteenth century, the 5 percent rule was almost universally adhered to in Paris at least for mortgage credit. In the eighteenth century, there were a few instances of private contracts at either 4 or 4.5 percent, in particular from 1740 to 1770. Leaving aside the period of the Law affair, one has to go back to the 1670s or earlier to find any substantial variation in interest rates. Further, as table 2.4 shows, what evidence is available from England suggests that there were significant differences in the organization of the French rente market and that of British rents. In Britain the usury ceiling does not appear to have been as binding as in France. That finding has a simple explanation, at least in the years between 1664 and 1714, for then the British cap was 6 percent, while in France it was a more restrictive 5 percent. The period after 1720 is more complicated. After that date, both countries limited mortgage charges to 5 percent. In England less than two-fifths of rents stipulated an interest charge of 5 percent or more, while in Paris that number was never less than four-fifths. The question remains somewhat clouded by the fact the British data are restricted to loans made by charities and thus may not be as representative as the Parisian data.[22] Until further research yields more systematic evidence of mortgage interest charges in England, we cannot hope to explain this divergence.

As chapter 3 will show, in Paris interest charges ranged from 4 to 5.5 percent during the early 1660s. An even broader range of interest rates prevailed in the early seventeenth century and before. Because the spread of interest rates in any cross section is rather limited during our period, we have not tried to explain the evolution of the system from this earlier equilibrium to the one that was in force in the eighteenth century.[23] Yet it seems that the riskless interest rate was below 5 percent. Indeed, we know that there were defaults and that resolution of arrears could take years and be extremely costly.[24] Lenders could thus not expect to earn 5 percent, but rather somewhat less. And given the limited variations in interest rates (table 2.4), it was not prices that matched the demand and supply of credit. The question we must answer is whether credit was rationed or whether it was allocated by shifting debtors and creditors across contract types.

The Aggregate Series over the Long Run

Although the next nine chapters analyze the evolution of notarial credit in detail, the long-run changes in the series bear some comment. Indeed, if we examine loans over the two centuries from the 1660s to the 1860s, key features of the credit market become clear, features that explain why we divided our book into chapters focusing on particular periods.

Figure 2.2 divides the total number of notarial credit contracts into three categories. The upper line in the figure traces government credit

---

22. For French evidence that charities may have had a steeper risk return tradeoff than other lenders, see Potter and Rosenthal 1997a.

23. Schnapper 1957.

24. Given the risks involved in lending, some readers may wonder why anyone with capital would want to lend money. Why not simply buy a farm? The trouble is that farms and other productive assets also involved risks and entailed certain costs—for example, the risk that a tenant might not pay the rent or not maintain the property's value.

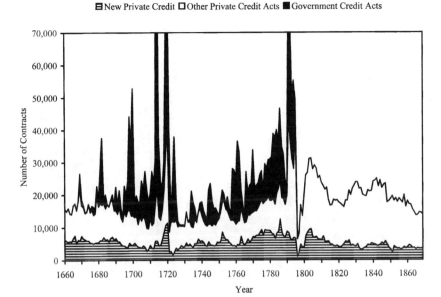

☐ New Private Credit ☐ Other Private Credit Acts ■ Government Credit Acts

FIGURE 2.2 Annual Number of Credit Contracts by Type, 1660–1870

contracts, primarily borrowing or debt consolidation—hence the sharp spikes, usually after wars. The middle line displays private credit contracts other than loans (repayments, transfers, and lien releases). Just below it lie new private credit loans, a remarkably stable series, which never rises to much more than seven thousand loans each year. Despite the stability, one can clearly make out the Regency (1715–23), with its two sharp spikes, and the Revolution with its dramatic decline after 1789. Two long-term developments are also worthy of note. From 1770 to 1789, the number of new loans grew rapidly, while after the Revolution, it slowly fell.

The volumes of new loans are the next step in our estimation. Figure 2.3 displays the volume of new private loans. Now the chronology is clearer, with five key periods standing out in the data: decline during the personal reign of Louis XIV (1661–1715); crisis during the Regency, followed by growth in the eighteenth century; collapse during the Revolution; and finally an unstable recovery.

The volume of new private debt, however, is a potentially misleading measure of private lending, for different types of loans were made for different lengths of time, and hence the different credit contracts imply different levels of indebtedness. We can overcome the problem by examining private indebtedness. Figure 2.4 provides information for two se-

⊞ Private Perpetual Annuities   ☐ Obligations   ■ Private Life Annuities   ⊞ Banks

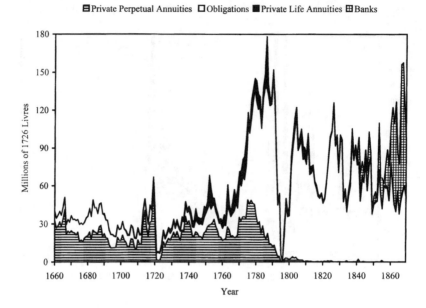

FIGURE 2.3   Annual Volume of New Private Loans in Paris, 1660–1870. The graph
includes notarized loans only.

—— Nominal   —— 1726 Livres

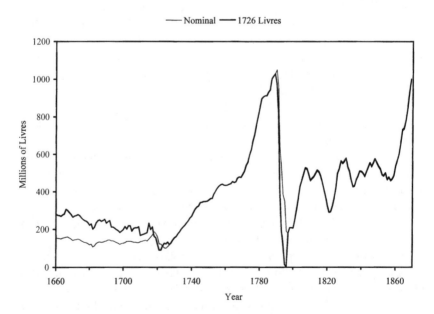

FIGURE 2.4   Private Outstanding Notarial Debt in Paris, 1660–1870

⊟ Private Perpetual Annuities ☐ Obligations ■ Private Life Annuities ⊞ Banks

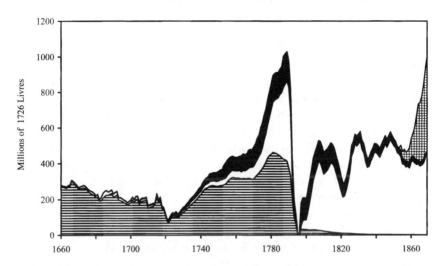

FIGURE 2.5 Real Private Outstanding Debt in Paris by Type of Contract, 1660–1870. The graph includes notarized loans only.

ries we compiled: nominal and real private indebtedness. Except for the reign of Louis XIV and the two periods of crises, the nominal and real series are indistinguishable, and once again the same five periods stand out in the data.

If we break up the real indebtedness series by type of loan, it becomes clear that much of the eighteenth-century boom in private credit was accounted for by the rise of the obligation (figure 2.5). The obligations, which amounted to less than 5 percent of all outstanding debts as late as 1742, constituted half the stock by the time of the Revolution. Another striking pattern in figures 2.4 and 2.5 is the devastating effect of paper money during the Law affair and the Revolution. During the Law affair, private indebtedness fell some 50 percent; it also took nearly two decades to recover. The Revolution knocked private credit even lower. Nominal indebtedness plummeted by nearly 90 percent (real indebtedness plunged even deeper), and it did not regain its 1789 level until the 1860s.

So far we have looked at indebtedness and the volume of new loans in the private market. What about lending to the government? Unfortunately, it is difficult to estimate government indebtedness, forcing us to rely on the volume of new government loans. The chief problem in estimating government indebtedness is the difficulty of sampling, for government debt was quite complex. The government sold its bonds in distinct issues, with notaries competing to place most of them. Many notaries were usually involved, but the number of bonds that each notary sold varied greatly, because certain notaries served as the equivalent of underwriters and drew up a disproportionate number of contracts. A reliable estimate would therefore require reading the indexes of many more notaries.[25] Another complication stems from the growing role of bankers, who placed government debt abroad. These bankers relied on notaries who are not in our sample (études XLVIII or L, for example), cutting the accuracy of our government series, particularly after 1770. Finally, if we examine the size distribution of government loans, it has an even fatter tail than the equivalent distribution for private loans.[26] The problem is particularly serious for life annuities. There bankers pooled large sums of foreign capital to invest in life annuities, with each pooled sum far larger than the average loan to the government.[27] We know that such innovations were taking place, but in our series their impact is muffled.

Still, we believe that our estimates of the volume of new government debt reveal the long development of the public bond market (figure 2.6). As the graph demonstrates, the volume of new government loans traced out a pattern dramatically different from that of private credit. The path of government borrowing is highly irregular, with large spikes punctuating the seventeenth and early eighteenth centuries, followed by more regular activity until 1790, when the notaries lost control of government debt. The graph also shows the growing importance of life annuities after 1730, and it reveals the pattern of short-term borrowing followed by consolidations that characterized the reign of Louis XIV. That pattern blessed the notaries with an immense amount of business.

The graphs presented here form the core of our evidence. They also suggest the questions we will pose, allowing us to define the key periods and the key transitions in the history of Parisian lending. The aggregate evidence offers three possible explanations for the rise and fall of notarial credit. One explanation focuses on the link between lending in Paris and the state of the French economy. Here the assumption is that lending would move in parallel with economic growth. The lending might fund investment (and thus be a cause of the growth), or it might simply be a consequence. The second explanation focuses on financial innovation, such as the rise of the obligation under the Old Regime, the grow-

---

25. The problem is compounded when considering corporations, which often used a single notary. See Potter and Rosenthal 1997b.

26. In laymen's terms, very large contracts amounted to a greater share of all the funds lent to the state than to private individuals.

27. For details on foreign investment in French government debt, see Lüthy 1959.

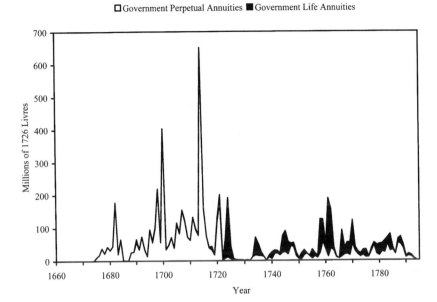

FIGURE 2.6 Annual Volume of New Government Loans in Paris, 1660–1795. The graph includes notarized loans only.

ing role of notaries as financial intermediaries, or the dramatic growth of the Crédit Foncier in the nineteenth century. The final explanation invokes political factors: warfare, monetary manipulation, or revolutions and political instability. The rest of the book investigates each of these themes beginning with the seventeenth century.

CHAPTER THREE

Stagnation and Decline,
1660–1715

WHAT THEN DOES OUR examination of the notarial archives reveal about credit in Paris? For the seventeenth and early eighteenth centuries, the answer seems clear: private lending declined, no matter which data series we examine. If we consider the level of outstanding private debt, it peaked in 1666 and then fell inexorably until after the Law affair of 1716–20. It did not regain its former heights until the 1740s (figure 2.4). The slump during these decades did not merely reflect the erosion of old loans by successive devaluations, for the volume of new loans slipped as well. It in fact subsided without interruption throughout the 1660s and 1670s. And once the abortive revival of the early 1680s had passed, the volume continued to sink until Law (figure 2.3).

This decline in lending may, of course, come as no surprise, since most historians paint the economic history of seventeenth-century France in grim hues: indeed, they keep bright colors off their palettes until the last half of the eighteenth century. Yet stagnation and decay still require explanation, even during the seventeenth century. After all, the Old Regime's economic history has been revised drastically in recent years: it is no longer the monotonous story of a *société immobile,* where economic growth was impossible. Growth, we have learned, could erupt even in agriculture, which is usually considered the most backward sector of the preindustrial economy. And economic fluctuations were far more common than historians once supposed.[1] Furthermore, dwindling credit in seventeenth-century Paris is particularly surprising. The city grew rapidly in the seventeenth century, at least until the 1680s, and its expanding population would seem to be evidence of a boisterous local economy, one that thrived upon the burgeoning tax receipts feeding into the city. Why then did the credit market not keep pace?

1. For agriculture, see Chevet 1983; Hoffman 1996; Moriceau and Postel-Vinay 1992; Moriceau 1994; Grantham 1995, 1997.

In part, the answer does lie with the health of the French economy. Yet it also lies with the uncertainties that frightened both borrowers and lenders. The uncertainties included the temporal shocks that hammered the credit market repeatedly in the seventeenth and early eighteenth centuries, from monetary manipulations to wild variations in real returns from loans. Legal and political institutions eliminated most defenses against these shocks, leaving many borrowers and lenders with no option but to shun the credit market. Those who ventured into it faced yet another daunting task: the seemingly insurmountable difficulty of finding who had money to invest or who would be likely to repay a loan. Such problems—problems of what economists call asymmetric information— forced borrowers and lenders to rely on personal ties with one another because there were as yet no financial intermediaries who could put borrowers and lenders together. That in turn severely restricted the scope of the market.

The Credit Market and the Evolution of the Economy

That the health of the economy influenced lending is no surprise. If Paris's population increased and incomes rose, lending, presumably, should have jumped too. The argument could be investigated directly using our series if the supply and demand for loans could be disentangled. Doing so, however, is far from easy. We do not know the savings rate, which presumably influenced the supply of credit, and we lack time series of interest rates, which might allow us to tease out the supply and demand for loans via a clever use of econometrics. All that we do have is the net level of indebtedness and the volume of new loans, plus periodic observations of the interest rates on rentes (figures 2.3, 2.4; table 3.1).

Yet we can still explain much of what drove borrowing and lending. As we shall see, eighteenth-century evidence demonstrates that much of the lending in Paris was driven by the life cycle. It revolved around older lenders granting loans to younger borrowers, who in turn built houses, established businesses, or purchased government offices. There is no reason to believe that seventeenth-century lending was any different in this regard.[2] And since nearly all of the borrowers came from Paris itself, we might reasonably suppose that the demand for credit would rise with the number of young people in Paris and with the return on the sort of assets that young people would eventually inherit and use to pay off their loans. We can fashion a crude measure of the number of young people

2. See chapter 7 and Hoffman, Postel-Vinay, and Rosenthal 1992.

TABLE 3.1   PERPETUAL ANNUITY CONTRACTS: FUNDS LENT AND LOAN SIZES BY
                       INTEREST RATE

Interest Rate (percent)	1662	1670	1682	1700	1718–20
Percentage of Rente Contracts					
0–2	0	0	0	0	11.9
2–4.9	1.5	7.8	16	11.2	50
4.9–5.1	26.4	92.2	82.8	87.8	37.4
>5.1	72.1	0	1.2	1	0.7
Percentage of Funds Lent					
0–2	0	0	0	0	17.1
2–4.9	3.4	18.5	38.4	26	66.2
4.9–5.1	56.5	81.5	61.6	73.9	16.6
>5.1	40.1	0	0.1	0.1	0.0006
Average Loan Sizes (Livres)					
0–2	0	0	0	0	19,329
2–4.9	11,766	8,971	12,200	10,952	17,733
4.9–5.1	11,061	3,594	3,800	3,981	5,960
>5.1	2,871	0	600	500	1,050
Sample Averages					
Average loan size	5,163	4,017	4,228	4,728	13,395
Average interest rate (unweighted)	5.56	4.93	4.93	4.96	4.04
Average interest rate (weighted by loan size)	5.16	4.92	4.82	4.85	3.34
Sample size	202	155	118	98	254

Source: Reprinted, by permission, from Hoffman, Postel-Vinay, and Rosenthal 1995, table 1.

from the number of marriages in the city and use estimates of the city's population when marriage statistics are lacking. We can do the same for the return on assets using late eighteenth-century estimates of Parisian incomes and information about revenues from the government and local real estate.

If marriages, asset income, and the city's population were all moving up or down, then we might argue that the demand for loans was doing the same. That would be the case, for example, after 1750, when all three curves were on the upswing (figure 3.1). But for the period at issue here—the late seventeenth and early eighteenth centuries—the curves do not always move together. On the one hand, one could argue that the evidence is consistent with demand for loans that is stagnant or gradually declining. But particularly in the period between the 1650s and 1680s, when asset income is falling slowly and the population is still rising, it might seem that demand ought to be increasing. How then do

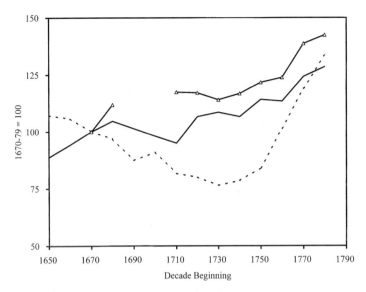

FIGURE 3.1 Parisian Marriages, Population, and Asset Income: Decennial Indexes. Marriages and asset incomes are decennial averages of the annual number of marriages and of income per year. Population is a decennial estimate. All three series are indexes with 1670–79 = 100. Source: The marriage index was compiled from Charlot and Dupâquier 1967, with adjustments explained in Hoffman, Postel-Vinay, and Rosenthal 1995, 261–62. The population estimates were derived from figures for baptisms, using the sources listed in Hoffman 1996, 236–37. For the asset incomes, we began with the late eighteenth-century estimates for after-tax income in Paris of Lavoisier (1864–93) and projected them back using information about revenues from the government and local real estate. The procedure and sources utilized are described in Hoffman, Postel-Vinay, and Rosenthal 1995, 261–62.

we explain the inexorable drop in real indebtedness, which continues unabated from the start of our series until the 1740s? In all likelihood, something beyond anemic demand was sapping the credit market.

Was it a shrinking supply of credit? Probably not. If the supply of credit had contracted relative to demand, lending would decline. In that case, we would also expect to see pressure on interest rates—pressure that would boost average interest rates and eliminate rentes below the usury ceiling of 5 percent. Yet nothing of the sort occurred. Average interest rates actually dipped slightly between 1662 and 1700, and the fraction of funds lent at 4.9 percent or below remained large (table 3.1). Interest rates dropped particularly low in 1718–20, during the Law affair, when (as we shall see in the next chapter) the government was

trying to push interest rates down. In any event, diminished supply is
not the secret that explains declining indebtedness.

Alternatively, private indebtedness could conceivably have been
driven down by the government's own borrowing. When the government
arranged loans, so the argument would go, its operations may have en-
ticed away lenders, thereby crowding out private borrowers. Now in early
modern Europe, governments did borrow considerable sums, chiefly to
pay for war; the French government was no exception to this rule. In
the period at issue here—the late seventeenth and early eighteenth centuries—it borrowed from a number of financial intermediaries. Bankers
did bring funds, but tax farmers (individuals who paid a lump sum to the
crown for the right to collect taxes) and other financial officials (whom
contemporaries called financiers) were even more important.[3] It also
borrowed long term by selling government offices and rentes. Most of
the rentes were actually sold after the wars were over, when the government consolidated the short-term debts run up during warfare, often
in what were in effect government defaults (figure 3.2).

It is impossible to tell exactly how much the government raised in
the short-term market in the late seventeenth century.[4] Nor is it possible
to determine precisely how much of the long-term debt was simply the
consolidation of earlier short-term loans. But if we make the reasonable
assumption that most of the short-term debts were contracted during
wars, then it is hard to see how government borrowing could have depressed private indebtedness. Although the decline in private lending
did begin just as Louis XIV was preparing for the War of Devolution
(1667–68), it nonetheless persisted through the years of peace between
1678 to 1688, when the government was borrowing relatively little (figure 3.2). If the government stopped crowding out private borrowers,
why did private lending not recover?

A simple regression suggests that government borrowing did not
crowd out private loans. If government borrowing depressed private
lending, its effect ought to be apparent in a regression of the volume
of new private loans on long-term government borrowing and a dummy
variable for warfare. The dummy variable for warfare would serve as a
proxy for short-term government borrowing, and both it and long-term
government borrowing should have regression coefficients that are negative, statistically significant, and large in absolute value. But when the
regression is run, it reveals little or no evidence of crowding out. (See

3. Dessert 1984; Lüthy 1959, vol. 1.

4. The short-term market, whether public or private, is simply beyond our ken, for
reasons discussed in the Introduction.

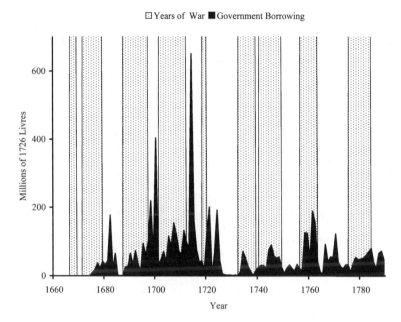

□ Years of War ■ Government Borrowing

FIGURE 3.2 Warfare and Long-Term Government Borrowing, 1660–1789. The graph shows the annual volume of new long-term government loans raised in Paris alongside the years of war. As explained in the text, much of the long-term government borrowing was actually the consolidation of older debt, and it did not therefore represent an actual increase of indebtedness.

the regression for the years 1660–1725 in table 3.2.) In the regression, government borrowing is included with leads and lags of two years, for borrowers could have withdrawn from the private market in anticipation of a government loan or, alternatively, abandoned private lending after a government issue was sold. Only one of the regression coefficients turns out to be significantly different from zero, and that one happens to be positive. As for the other coefficients, the two that are negative are both small in absolute value: even when added together, they imply that a thousand livres of government debt would only cut private borrowing by less than eighteen livres. Meanwhile, the cumulative effect of the led and lagged values of government borrowing is actually positive, as is the effect of war. Such positive coefficients are actually sensible, for they no doubt reflect private borrowing by the financiers who lent to the government. To advance funds to the government, they raised money privately, which appears in our series of new private loans. The ease with which financiers did so suggests that crowding out is hardly the explanation for the decline in private lending. One could perhaps argue that

TABLE 3.2   CROWDING-OUT REGRESSIONS

Dependent Variable	Private Borrowing in Year t		
Years Covered in Regression	1660–1725	1726–89	1660–1789
Independent variables:			
Dummy variable: 1 if t is a year with a war, 0 otherwise	28,519 (1.00)	−70,992 (−1.61)	−28,178 (−1.15)
Government borrowing in year $t + 2$	0.0075 (0.70)	−0.046 (−1.12)	−0.0013 (−0.11)
Government borrowing in year $t + 1$	0.026 (1.95)	−0.031 (−0.68)	0.011 (0.80)
Government borrowing in year t	0.012 (0.86)	−0.029 (−0.63)	0.000031 (0.002)
Government borrowing in year $t − 1$	−0.00071 (−0.05)	0.008 (0.21)	−0.0046 (−0.33)
Government borrowing in year $t − 2$	−0.017 (−1.55)	0.025 (0.72)	−0.013 (−1.07)
Observations	61	62	123
R-squared	0.13	0.09	0.02
Standard error	88,102	112,645	103,436
Durbin-Watson statistic	1.97	2.13	2.18

Source: Estimated annual volumes of new government and private loans in Paris; see chapter 2 for details.
Note: Because all variables are measured as first differences and there is no time trend, the regressions lack a constant term. Government borrowing equals the annual volume of all new government rentes (both perpetuelles and viagères) estimated from the notarial registers; private borrowing equals the annual volume of all new private rentes and obligations. If private borrowing is measured in a given year t (say 1700), then government borrowing in year $t + 2$ is what the government borrowed in 1702, etc. Both private and government borrowing have been converted to 1726 livres. It is reasonable to assume that the government borrowed without keeping an eye on interest rates for all three regressions. A simple OLS regression is thus reasonable; for further discussion and instrumental variable estimates, see chapter 5. On the other hand, government borrowing is measured with error, which will bias our coefficient estimates. *T*-statistics are in parentheses.

their private borrowing boosts our private loan volumes artificially, causing us to miss the crowding out. But in that case, the volume of private loans ought eventually to suffer, and the lagged values of government borrowing should be negative, sizeable, and statistically significant. Yet as we know, they are not.

Unavoidable Uncertainties

The government did cast a pall over the medium- and long-term credit market, and its actions help explain the collapse of private credit.[5] The

5. The collapse was not the result of flight by wealthy Protestants after the revocation of the Edict of Nantes in 1685. The decline began well before the Protestants fled, and

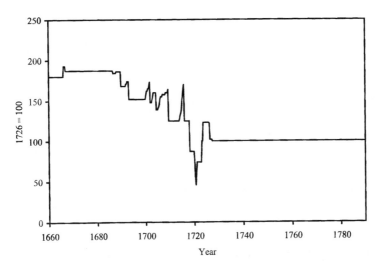

FIGURE 3.3 Index of the Value of the Livre in Silver, 1660–1789. The index is calculated relative to livre's value in 1726, which is given the index 100. Source: de Wailly 1857.

worst actions, at least for private markets, were the monarchy's currency manipulations. The state repeatedly tampered with the value of coinage, by fixing a new bullion equivalent for the legal money of account and by requiring coins to be reminted. It did so both to profit from mint fees and (since the usual course of action was devaluation) to repay its own debts in depreciated money of account.[6] The long-run effect on private credit markets was severe, particularly in the late seventeenth and early eighteenth centuries (figure 3.3). As we know, it was illegal for a rente contract to require in-kind payments of interest (for example, a loan for 200 bushels of wheat in return for 10 bushels annually). Nor could notarized debts specify payments of a fixed amount of specie (for instance, a loan of 200 grams of gold in return for 10 grams of gold annually), at least in the years of interest here.[7] As a result, parties to long-term private credit contracts had no way to escape the effects of currency manipulation. And because devaluation was the

---

even the dip in indebtedness in the 1680s, which was caused by the repayment of perpetual annuities, seems unrelated to their departure. The Protestant exodus did, however, affect the short-term market; for details, see Lüthy 1959, 1:28–31.

6. Lüthy 1959, 1:98–104. Devaluation sometimes addressed problems of chronic undervaluation of coinage: Glassman and Redish 1988. But for the late seventeenth and early eighteenth century it was the fiscal motive that was paramount, at least in France.

7. Isambert 1822, 15:270–76 (Edit sur les monnaies, Monceau, 1602); Schnapper 1957:175–200.

most likely course of action, it was lenders who shouldered the greatest
risk.

The government threatened the private credit market in other ways
as well. The wars it fought disrupted the economy, pushing borrowers
into default and depleting savings that could be lent. Worse yet, the
government defaults that followed the wars could spill over into the private market. The reason, again, was that the financiers were borrowing
privately and then relending to the state, and they were often compro-
mised during the government's recurrent financial debacles.[8] A financier might, for instance, be brought up short by one of the government's
frequent defaults. An even grimmer prospect was that he might become
the target of a *chambre de justice,* a judicial investigation that could single out financiers and tax them to the point of ruin. That was the fate,
for example, of the tax farmer François Bossuet; in the early 1660s, a
chambre de justice seized all of his assets. In cases like Bossuet's (or
in instances when the state defaulted), the financier's private creditors
watched their loans turn sour, and they had to contend with the state's
own claims to the financier's assets.[9] How widespread such predicaments
were we can only guess, for many of the private loans to financiers were
short-term affairs that have left no trace in the archives. Daniel Dessert
has argued that private loans to financiers were quite common in the
seventeenth century, and it is perhaps symptomatic that in the years
1665–73 the crown moderated its claims on financiers' assets in order
to protect the financiers' own private credit. In any event, it would be
difficult to predict whether a particular financier was likely to run into
trouble. The state's defaults were selective, often depending not just on
the costs of war but on personal politics. And a chambre de justice could
punish a seemingly prosperous financier for government business he
had carried out years earlier.[10]

The government was not the only source of risk. Both borrowers and
lenders faced sudden fluctuations in the real value of loan payments
because of the gyrating price of grain, the most prominent commodity
in early modern budgets. Grain prices varied far more before 1726 than
they would thereafter: in Paris the coefficient of variation of the price
of wheat rose to 0.42 in the years 1660–1725, versus only 0.28 in 1726–

8. Dessert 1984:128–29.

9. Dessert 1984:124, 143, 205–206, 743, 771.

10. Dessert 1984:60, 203–10, 239–41, 266–70, 341–68, 743, 750, 771; Bosher 1973;
Hoffman 1994. In addition to the chambres de justice themselves, there were legal proceedings against individual financiers, and the threat of a chambre de justice could be
used to extort money from financiers, as in the period 1656–61.

88.[11] Part of the variation in grain prices stemmed from the government's currency manipulations; the rest was driven by inelastic demand, meager storage, and the vagaries of the harvest. Since loan contracts were nominal, there was of course no way of indexing the contract to hold the real value of loan payments constant. Nor could interest rates be raised enough to compensate for the risk, because of the 5 percent cap on rentes, the dominant credit instrument in the private market. Again, lenders bore a disproportionate share of the risk, for they had no way of demanding repayment of a rente when, say, high grain prices suddenly cut their real income.

It would hardly be surprising then if the high variability of grain prices depressed the Parisian credit market, by frightening away lenders and perhaps borrowers as well. There is in fact some evidence for such an effect, though it is not unassailable. It comes from a regression of the logarithm of the volume of new private loans on the coefficient of variation of grain prices over the preceding nine years (table 3.3). The explanatory variables in the regression also include a measure of the state of the local economy—the logarithm of the number of apprenticeship contracts signed before notaries in our sample—and a dummy variable for periods of war, when private borrowing might be artificially inflated by the dealings of financiers. As expected, a thriving economy clearly boosts lending—the coefficient of apprenticeships is large, positive, and significant—and there are also some signs (albeit weaker ones) of the effect of price variability. The regression coefficient associated with the variability of grain prices is negative and sizeable: the difference in the coefficient of variation of grain prices from between the two periods (1660–1725 and 1726–88) would translate into a 7 percent decrease in the volume of new loans.[12] The associated T-statistic is anemic, though, particularly after we correct for the statistical problem of serial correlation. In laymen's terms, the effect of price variability may in the end just be a statistical fluke.

In an ideal world, the risk of sudden price changes (and others as well) could perhaps be dealt with by varying the terms of a loan. A borrower might have to repay if the lender fell on hard times, but the borrower might be able to suspend payments himself when he encountered

11. The wheat prices are from Baulant 1968, with corrections explained in Hoffman 1996:337–38.

12. Strictly speaking, the variable in table 3.3 is not really the coefficient of variation of wheat prices. Rather, it is the percentage variation of prices about a moving average, as the note to the table explains. It dropped by nearly the same amount as the coefficient of variation, though, going from 0.39 in 1660–1725 to 0.26 in 1726–88—enough to cut the volume of new loans by 6 percent.

TABLE 3.3   REGRESSION OF THE LOGARITHM OF THE ANNUAL VOLUME OF PRIVATE
                   LOANS ON ECONOMIC INDICATORS, 1660–1770

Independent Variables	Coefficients	*T*-Statistics
Constant	15.36	13.60
Logarithm of estimated annual apprenticeships	0.28	3.01
Coefficient of variation of wheat prices	−0.51	−1.14
Dummy variable for war (1 in years with war, 0 otherwise)	−0.027	−0.41
Number of observations	111	
R-squared	0.59	
Standard error	0.25	
Durban-Watson	—	
Rho (for autocorrelation correction)	0.61	
Mean of dependent variable	17.31	

Source: Estimates of annual loan volumes and annual number of apprenticeships are from notarial samples described in chapter 2. Annual Paris wheat prices are from Baulant 1968, with corrections explained in Hoffman 1996:337–38.

Note: The dependent variable is the logarithm of the annual volume of private loans, measured in 1726 livres. The estimated annual number of apprenticeships serves as a proxy for the state of the local economy. Because of legal changes, it could not be used after 1770, and for that reason the regression was restricted to the years 1660–1770. The regressions were run on the whole period because the coefficients of interest were unaffected when we split the sample. The coefficient of variation of wheat prices is a proxy for price and currency uncertainty. To calculate it, we first created a moving average of nominal wheat prices over the current year and the nine previous years. We then averaged the squared deviations of nominal wheat prices from this moving average over the same period, took the square root, and then divided by the moving average price of wheat. First stage autocorrelation was corrected for via a two-step estimation procedure, but higher order autocorrelation may remain. A simple OLS regression led to similar results. The estimation assumes that price variability and apprenticeships cause changes in the volume of loans and are uncorrelated with the error term. Although we cannot check that price variability is orthogonal to the error term, it is unlikely that borrowing affected price variability (because most of the variability in this period was the result of weather and of monetary manipulations) or apprenticeships (because long-term loans were not used to finance human capital).

difficulties. Economists have a name for this type of loan: they call it state-contingent debt.

The problem, obviously, is that state-contingent debt contracts often pose too many problems of moral hazard to exist in the real world. Here moral hazard is the label economists apply to undesired behavior that is difficult to detect or control, such as a borrower's falsely invoking hard times to suspend repayment of a loan even though he himself is in fact doing quite well. State-contingent debt contracts were in any case certainly not part of the institutional arsenal available in Old-Regime credit markets. A more practical alternative would have been shorter term loans, which lenders could prolong if they desired. A lender could then refuse to renew a loan if his budget was pinched or if he feared some impending disaster, such as devaluation. Obligations eventually played such a role, but in the seventeenth and early eighteenth centuries they probably frightened away borrowers, who feared being summoned to repay and having no other lender ready to grant a new loan. In a large and anonymous city such as Paris—its population in 1660 was already some half a million—it would not be easy to find a new lender. Only with a smoothly functioning network of financial intermediaries would the task be simple, but the requisite network did not yet exist.

What the credit market needed here—so one might argue—were universal banks. They would have pooled lenders' funds as demand deposits, which could be withdrawn at the lenders' whim. They would then lend the funds out, either short term or long term for borrowers who wanted the security of a long-term loan. They would successfully balance a borrower's preference for a long-term loan against a lender's desire for a short-term investment. Yet that sort of financial intermediation was simply unfeasible until the late nineteenth century. It was too difficult to manage both short-term demand deposits and a portfolio of long-term loans, and it was all the harder without a lender of last resort, who could step in to bail out the intermediaries during crises and financial panics. For that, credit markets had to wait until well into the nineteenth century.[13]

Without universal banks, without even a network of brokers who could arrange new short-term loans, it was difficult for borrowers to accept obligations. That is perhaps one reason why obligations constituted such a feeble part of private credit in the seventeenth and early eighteenth centuries (figure 2.5). With private lending by and large limited to rentes, many lenders had reason to spurn the market. They faced grave risks, yet legally they were unable to draw up contracts that would protect their investment from devaluation or rising prices. And they could not demand repayment if they were suddenly short of cash. It is thus hardly surprising that private lending was confined to a wealthy elite. In 1662, for example, some 69 percent of the funds lent (and 43 percent of the lenders) came from the nobility or Paris's officer class (table 3.4).

The elite alone had the resources (essentially cash and a wide variety of assets) that made it possible to ride out currency manipulations and financial disasters without feeling pinched for funds. Much the same was true of those who lent to the state, at least in 1682 and 1700 (table 3.5). True, government debt was perhaps easier to sell than private rentes, but it was still quite risky and it too demanded lenders whose wealth and other assets cushioned the risk. Having spurned the market, investors with moderate income would have to hoard their cash or invest in real assets such as land, which had the advantage of protecting against price

13. Schwartz 1986; M. Collins 1992.

TABLE 3.4   PERCENTAGE OF CONTRACTS AND FUNDS LENT BY PROFESSION:
PRIVATE BORROWERS AND LENDERS, 1662

	Private Lenders		Private Borrowers	
	Contracts	Funds Lent	Contracts	Funds Lent
Nobles and officers	43.1	68.8	44.5	74.3
Clergy	5.2	8.5	3.3	2.5
Merchants and bourgeois	27.8	15.2	21.9	11.7
Artisans and masters	11.4	4.6	9	4.1
Professions and services	7.1	1.2	8.7	4
Rural	1.4	0.3	10.9	1.2
Unknown and institutions	4.1	1.3	1.6	2.2

Source: Detailed samples of notarial minutes described in table 2.2.
Note: Nobles include military officers. Merchants and bourgeois tended to be richer than artisans and masters. They were also wealthier than individuals in the professions and services, who included lawyers, doctors, innkeepers, teamsters, and domestics. In 1662, the domestics were generally well-paid servants in noble households. Because of rounding, columns do not sum to 100. There were 367 credit contracts in all.

TABLE 3.5   PERCENTAGE OF CONTRACTS AND FUNDS LENT BY PROFESSION:
GOVERNMENT LENDERS, 1682–1711

	1682		1700		1711	
	Contracts	Funds Lent	Contracts	Funds Lent	Contracts	Funds Lent
Nobles and officers	44.5	61.2	47.2	57.9	37.6	35.8
Clergy	5.7	4.6	9.2	8.8	3.3	2.9
Merchants and bourgeois	24.8	18.1	22.3	16.8	33.3	26.6
Artisans and masters	3.5	2	5.4	3.6	8	11.6
Professions and services	3.8	2.8	4.1	2.7	6.1	11.1
Rural	0.2	0.1	0.2	0.1	0	0
Unknown and institutions	17.5	11.1	11.6	10	11.8	12.1

Source: For 1700, we used the government loans in the detailed samples described in table 2.2. For 1682 and 1711, we relied on AN P6115 and P6120.
Note: The occupational categories are as in table 3.4. Columns may not sum to 100 because of rounding. There were 924 contracts for 1682, 2,138 for 1700, and 213 for 1711.

fluctuations and currency devaluations but which carried its own costs and risks. The elite would of course appreciate the same advantages, which is one reason why they too kept the bulk of their assets in land.

Asymmetric Information

The lack of intermediaries in Paris caused other problems besides the trouble borrowers had in finding lenders. Lenders themselves faced the daunting task of determining whether a borrower could provide secure collateral. As we know, long-term loans depended on sound collateral. That was especially true of perpetual annuities, which constituted the bulk of long-term private debt in the seventeenth century. A borrower might offer specific assets or a general claim on all of his property, but what lenders preferred was extensive real property—land, buildings, but also government offices and even other rentes. It is no surprise then that most loans went to wealthy nobles or officers (table 3.4). They had the real property that would best guarantee a loan.

The difficulty—as always in credit markets—was that a lender could not easily observe dealings by a borrower that undermined the value of the collateral and the security of the loan. The collateral might already be mortgaged, and in the case of a bankruptcy, the lender might receive only a pittance after lenders with senior claims had been paid. Furthermore, there was no easy way to determine whether property had already been mortgaged, for the earlier mortgage remained a secret between the borrower and the earlier lender. A lender who wished to make a second loan might thus remain unaware of the first mortgage unless he knew the first lender well. Contemporaries were fully aware of the dilemma, and to resolve matters, a 1673 edict sought to create a system of public registration for mortgages. The stated purpose was to render it "possible to make loans with assurance. . . . Creditors will be certain about a debtor's wealth. They will neither fear for his fate nor anxiously watch over his assets."[14] The edict, though, was revoked only a year later. Perhaps registration was too difficult to establish. Or perhaps the edict fell victim to the contemporary argument that a registry, by revealing the vagaries of private fortunes, would actually destroy the existing system of access to private credit, which was based on a lender's personal knowledge and "opinion" of a borrower and the borrower's "reputation."[15]

A mortgage registry was in fact created for government offices pledged as collateral, but for most private property there was no practicable way of knowing whether it had previously been mortgaged.[16] Nor was there any way of preventing a borrower or his heirs from selling part of the mortgaged collateral without the lender's knowledge—an obvious risk with perpetual annuities. An aggrieved lender could certainly sue

14. Clément 1861, 2:332–33; Isambert 1822, 19:73–86. Another reason for the legislation was to facilitate sales, and a fiscal motive may have been lurking in the background as well.

15. D'Aguesseau 1759, 13:620–23.

16. Bien 1988; Vilar-Berrogain 1958. It was also possible to keep track of mortgages on certain government rentes; see Isambert 1822, 19:83–86. One could have a court post public notices asking mortgage holders to come forward, but the process was long and costly.

and even pursue the purchaser of the mortgaged collateral for a portion
of the interest due. But he would have to bring his case before courts
where justice was expensive and excruciatingly slow. The various troubles
he faced were far from theoretical. In the late sixteenth century, the
Wars of Religion had devastated so many borrowers and crushed so
much collateral under multiple mortgages that the noted jurist Charles
Loyseau judged rentes to be little more than a "will o' wisp right, at
bottom just a fragment of parchment." Loyseau was grasping for rhetorical effect, but there is no denying the reality of the problem.[17]

What the lender needed was a network of financial intermediaries. If
universal banks were impossible, one could at least imagine intermediaries who would know borrowers. They could then find borrowers and
match the lender up with those whose collateral was secure. They could
pinpoint other risks as well—whether borrowers were involved in risky
business, such as government finance. They would of course help borrowers with their problem of finding lenders, and they might even be
able to facilitate other financial transactions, such as the sale of assets.
They would, in short, help resolve the problems of asymmetric information that bedevil all credit markets.

Such musing might seem far removed from the Old Regime, but it
was not. In the sixteenth century, for example, the writer Montaigne
reported that his father wanted cities to have a place where buyers and
sellers would come together to exchange not only goods but assets and
information. Like his father, Montaigne had high hopes for the idea,
writing in *Les Essais:* "This method of mutual information would bring
no slight convenience into public commerce, for at all times there are
conditions which seek one another and from not being able to come to
an understanding, leave men in dire need." Although Montaigne did
not specifically address borrowers and lenders, his idea was put into practice in Paris by Théophraste Renaudot, a physician and protegé of Riche-
lieu, who did have credit in mind. The *Bureau d'Adresse* that he founded
in 1630 created a place where, among other things, buyers could meet
sellers, and goods and services could be advertised for purchase or sale
via a newsheet full of announcements. Renaudot believed that borrowers
and lenders would find his service useful, as would sellers of financial
assets. Advertisements by creditors desiring loans actually appeared in
his newsheet, but Renaudot's Bureau never seemed to realize its potential as a financial exchange.[18]

17. Loyseau 1606; Schnapper 1957:119–29, 261–80; Dewald 1980:232–33; Guyot
1784, s.v. "hypothèque" and "rente."

18. Montaigne 1946: Book I, Essay 35; Renaudot 1654:28; Hatin 1866:18; Bellanger
1969, 1:84–85.

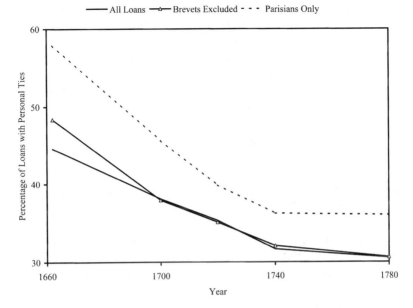

—— All Loans ——◇—— Brevets Excluded - - - Parisians Only

FIGURE 3.4 Personal Ties in Private Credit: Family, Profession, or Neighborhood. The graph shows the fraction of borrowers and lenders who were bound by personal ties in the sense that came from the same family, or profession, or neighborhood. Same family means that the borrower and lender are related by marriage or by blood. Same neighborhood means the same parish within Paris and the same department outside Paris. In the absence of a direct measure of personal ties, we take kinship, shared profession, or same neighborhood to indicate a higher likelihood that borrowers and lenders knew one another than if they had none of these characteristics in common. The fraction is shown for all loans, for loans involving Parisians only, and with brevet loans excluded. For the significance of the brevet loans and loans involving Parisians, see the text. The source for the graph are the samples in table 2.2 for 1662, 1700, 1718–20, 1740, and 1780. Loans from 1718–20 have been lumped together here. For details about the samples and a discussion of the definition of family, profession, and neighborhood, see Hoffman, Postel-Vinay, and Rosenthal 1999.

For the moment, however, the only practical alternative was for borrowers and lenders to rely on their own information—on knowledge they developed through their own personal contacts. That by and large was all that most borrowers and lenders could do, before the middle of the eighteenth century. Lenders therefore tended to restrict their loans to borrowers they knew well: borrowers from their own family, their profession, or their neighborhood, borrowers whom they could trust and whose collateral was in their view. In 1662, 45 percent of the loans that our notaries recorded involved borrowers and lenders drawn from the same family, the same neighborhood, or the same profession (figure 3.4).

Such personal ties were more common still if we leave out the short-term obligations that notaries rarely preserved—the brevets. Even these almost always brought together parties who were no doubt well acquainted, such as an artisan and one of his clients. And if we consider only loans involving Parisians, the frequency of the personal links rises higher still.

Defining a personal tie is, to be sure, a bit arbitrary. But whatever the precise definition, lenders who relied on personal knowledge of borrowers were more numerous in 1662 than in the late eighteenth century, and the difference is too large to be explained by chance. Even where no personal bond was evident, lenders were likely to have links to a borrower. They might have been involved in other dealings that established a relationship of trust.[19] Or they may have lent him money in the past. All were means of observing a borrower's actions and of verifying his collateral.

Such personal bonds were also the way borrowers gained information about lenders. When seeking loans, borrowers too sought out their relatives, neighbors, professional associates, and other close acquaintances. Or they turned to individuals whose repeated lending made it clear that they had funds to loan. In our 1662 sample, for example, only 16 percent of the lenders made more than one loan, but these repeat lenders were involved in 31 percent of the loan contracts and provided 41 percent of the credit. The result was to restrict credit, at least relative to the eighteenth century, when lending gradually escaped the bonds of personal relations (figure 3.4). Credit was limited to the channels of personal relations, or to borrowers and lenders who were well known via past dealings. It was restricted to borrowers who possessed secure collateral and to lenders who could survive currency devaluations and other financial disasters without any means of demanding repayment of their loans. As we know, lenders therefore came disproportionately from the elite, and the same was true of borrowers (tables 3.4 and 3.5).

Who then was excluded from the market? Those with less wealth obviously, but also some of the wealthy themselves, who kept much of their savings in assets such as land rather than lending it out in a risky and illiquid market. The most striking of the excluded investors were affluent women. There were no doubt many such women—in particular, older women who possessed funds that they would like to invest to support their retirement. In 1662, though, women made less than 12 percent of all the private loans (table 3.6). The problem was that women had less of a chance of meeting reliable borrowers. They were not directly

19. The tax farmer François Bossuet borrowed, for example, from the *tuteur* of a relative's children: ANMC, Etude CXV, 159 (23 October 1662).

involved in government finance, like many of the officers; nor were they in business, like wealthy merchants. They could of course rely on family and friends for information about investment opportunities, but as widowhood and old age approached, such channels of information might dry up. Clearly, they would have profited from the sort of financial intermediaries who slowly developed over the course of the eighteenth century to match borrowers and lenders and provide investment advice. But until those intermediaries were in place, women were rare as lenders (tables 3.6 and 3.7).

Perhaps the long-term private capital market would have flourished

TABLE 3.6   FEMALE LENDERS AND THE FUNDS THEY PROVIDE: PRIVATE LOANS, 1662–1780 (WITH AND WITHOUT OBLIGATIONS)

	All Private Loans		Private Loans without Obligations	
Year	Percentage Lenders Female	Percentage Funds from Females	Percentage Lenders Female	Percentage Funds from Females
1662	11.8	16.1	14.4	18.4
1700	18.9	12.7	24.5	14.1
1720	20.8	15.4	24.5	17.5
1740	27.6	23.5	35	28.5
1780	20	14.7	31.6	28.3

Source: Detailed sample of notarial minutes described in table 2.2.

TABLE 3.7   LENDING BY WOMEN TO THE STATE, 1682–1789

Years	Percentage of Lenders	Percentage of Funds Lent
1682	13.9	12.3
1690–99	30.2	12.3
1700–09	25.8	23.3
1740–49	29.4	18.6
1750–59	29.3	19.0
1760–69	27.4	15.4
1770–79	21.2	11.8
1780–89	21.1	27.6

Source: For 1682, the source is AN P6115; for the other periods, the data come from detailed samples of notarial minutes for the notaries described in table 2.2.
Note: There were 924 government loan contracts for 1682, 192 for 1690–99, 2,087 for 1700–09, 272 for 1740–49, 75 for 1750–59, 702 for 1760–69, 132 for 1770–79, and 829 for 1780–89. Note that the number of loan contracts and the periods involved are slightly different from table 3.5.

earlier had there been an institution that conveyed information between borrowers and lenders: specialized loan brokers, public registration of mortgages, or banks that would pool lenders' funds. It might have flourished too had the state not compounded the risks of lending by manipulating the currency and bullying its own creditors. But as we shall see, the appropriate institution did not yet exist, and the state's vicious behavior was inherent in the politics of Louis XIV's bellicose reign. A thriving credit market in Paris would await the rise of a new informal financial institution and a shift in the practices of public finance.

CHAPTER FOUR

The Crisis of Public Finance and the Law Affair, 1712–26

AFTER TWELVE YEARS OF BATTLE, the War of the Spanish Succession finally ground to a halt in 1712. Treaties then resolved the international crisis that had been bedeviling Europe for over a generation. No treaty, however, could fix what was wrong with the kingdom of France. The treasury was empty, and the economy had been bled dry by years of fighting. Measured in real terms, the public debt had reached per capita levels that were unprecedented—levels that would not be attained again until the end of the Old Regime. The monarchy obviously had to grapple with public finances, but the three ministers who succeeded one another between 1713 and 1718 failed to solve the problem. The solution came only after John Law's dramatic experiment with paper money and inflation, and the harshest default that France would witness until 1797.

Borrowers and lenders in the private credit market could not simply stand by and escape the consequences of what was happening to public finance. Indeed, as the repercussions of the inflation and the government default echoed through the economy, private indebtedness plummeted, falling by some 50 percent. How borrowers and lenders contended with the crisis is not at all clear, for historians have ignored this side of the Law affair. We therefore do not know how borrowers and lenders reacted, and sometimes their behavior seems unfathomable: why, for example, did lenders make a host of new loans just before the private market collapsed in 1720? Nor do we know who ultimately bore the cost of the government's default and the disintegration of private lending.

In this chapter, we analyze what happened in both the private and the public credit markets. We begin with a brief account of the public debt and the various measures that were taken to deal with it between 1712 and 1726. In order to understand the consequences of inflation and government default, we construct a model of how borrowers and lenders reacted. The model takes into account both inflation and changes in the value or type of currency—changes from paper money to coins and money of account, for example. We then use the model to analyze four distinct phases of the crisis and then calculate what the losses were and who bore them.

The losses were large; they were born by lenders. Those who lent to the government lost half of their initial investment to default and more still to currency depreciation. In the private market, they forfeited a third of what they had lent out. The magnitude of the losses, though, are not the only reason this crisis deserves attention. The whole affair foreshadowed what would later happen during the Revolution, with borrowers rushing to repay loans in worthless paper currency and manifesting striking differences of opinion about how the crisis would end. Even the politics of the crisis resembled what happened on the eve of the Revolution.

There is one other reason why this crisis deserves our attention. Traditionally, the Law affair is held to have stifled financial innovation in France. In particular, it supposedly kept France from developing the sort of banking system that seemed so essential to England's economic growth. Yet as we shall see, the Law affair did not usher in a period of financial stagnation in Paris. It may have frightened lenders, but it did not drive them away from the credit market forever. And it allowed the notaries to take on an important role as loan brokers—a role that they would exploit by mobilizing enormous sums of capital later in the eighteenth century.

The Problem of Public Debt

Because the origins of the crisis lay with the government debt, it is worth reviewing the steps taken by the monarchy to resolve its horrendous financial problems at the end of Louis XIV's reign. Such a review seems all the more necessary since the remedies the government adopted were as confusing as they were ineffectual. We will run through the essentials of the story, so that all readers will be able to follow our analysis. (For this complicated period, readers may wish to refer to the list of key events in table 4.1.)

At the outset one thing was clear: the public debt was simply unsustainable at the end of Louis XIV's reign. Government borrowing, which had mounted to about 3.5 billion livres, now absorbed 70 to 80 percent of fiscal revenues. In real terms, the debt that the Sun King bequeathed

TABLE 4.1   KEY EVENTS OF THE LAW AFFAIR

1715	Death of Louis XIV
1716	John Law forms Banque Générale, which later becomes Banque Royale
1717	Law founds Compagnie d'Occident, the future Compagnie des Indes
December 1718	Bank notes become legal tender
1719	War with Spain; Compagnie takes over tax farms
January 1720	Law appointed finance minister
February 1720	Bank and Compagnie united
May 1720	Law loses confidence of Regent
October 1720	Bank notes demonetized
1726	French livre stabilized

to his five-year-old great grandson in 1715 was of the same order of magnitude as that which touched off the Revolution in 1789, but it was spread over a smaller population and economy.[1] Of the 3.5 billion livres, about one billion was short-term debt. Roughly twice that amount was in long-term bonds, mostly perpetual annuities. Finally, the crown owed more than half a billion livres to royal officials for the capital invested in their offices—in other words, money that had been raised by selling government posts. The officials received salaries, and the salaries represented the return on the money paid to purchase the offices.

Virtually all the debt had piled up because of warfare, either from the cost of fighting itself or from paying the military expenses of allies. Taxes certainly had increased during the repeated wars under Louis XIV (1667–68, 1672–78, 1688–97, and 1701–13), but tax revenue could not keep pace with military expenses, which jumped every time armies took the field.[2] Debt in the form of offices increased. Current office holders were slapped with *augmentations de gages,* which required them to advance additional capital to the crown in return for higher salaries. At the same time, new offices—often of no social value—were offered to the highest bidder. The long-term debt grew both because of direct placement with investors and because short-term debts were consolidated by fiat into perpetual annuities yielding between 5 and 7 percent. The short-term debt had grown most of all because the crown sought advances both from its own financial officials—the so-called financiers—and from bankers.[3]

1. Marion 1927, 1:63–64; Lüthy 1959, 1:279–80, 422; Sargent and Velde 1995:478, fig. 1.

2. Hoffman 1994, esp. table 1.

3. Lüthy 1959, vol. 1.

Between 1713 and 1726 the crown did little new borrowing. Its intrusions into the credit market were confined to mopping up Louis XIV's financial mess, which by and large meant consolidation and default. What appears as an enormous debt issue in 1713–14 in figure 2.6, for example, really turns out to be a consolidation undertaken by Nicolas Desmarets, Louis XIV's last finance minister. In the consolidation, Desmarets attempted to turn all government debt (much of it contracted at relatively high interest rates) into 4 percent perpetual annuities. Two years later, though, Desmarets had still not succeeded in curing France's financial woes, and when Philippe of Orléans became regent upon Louis XIV's death in 1715, he promptly dismissed Desmarets, whose policies were too harsh for the politically feeble Regency.

In Desmarets's place, Orléans appointed the Duke of Noailles, who undertook a tentative compromise. On one hand, Noailles chose to target politically unpopular financiers by ordering a *visa*—the authentification of all short-term loans and their consolidation into long-term debt. To squeeze even more relief out of the financiers, he also ordered a chambre de justice—a judicial audit of their activities. Both measures amounted to a partial default on what the financiers were owed, and at the same time Noailles tried to gain the support of the elite by abandoning extraordinary taxes they disliked. Although such policies were politically popular, it was clear that they could not staunch the flow of red ink. The chambre de justice, for example, imposed some stiff fines, but relative to similar audits in the past, it actually treated the financiers leniently, netting less than 100 million livres, a pittance relative to the state's enormous debts. In the end, neither it nor the other steps Noailles took seemed feasible ways to resolve the monarchy's financial problems. Politically, it was simply impossible to push the remedies such as a chambre de justice or a visa far enough to eliminate the deficit. And for the same reasons, it was impossible to cut the deficit by taxing the wealthy.[4]

With Noailles's policies failing, the regent was willing to consider the more radical treatment proposed by the Scottish banker John Law.[5]

4. Marion 1927, 1:63–89; Faure 1977:93–95; Dessert 1984:238–76; Lüthy 1959, 1: 282–87; Touzery 1994:2–54; and Lavisse 1911, vol. 8, pt. 1:190–99; pt. 2:7–14. The difficulties involved in taxing the elite emerge quite clearly if one examines how the privileged eventually subverted or escaped the new taxes imposed at the end of Louis XIV's reign, the capitation and the dixième.

5. The literature on Law is vast. We based our summary on Dutot [1738] 1935; Faure 1977; Hamilton 1938; Harsin 1933; Du Hautchamp 1739; Marion 1927; Lüthy 1959, 1: 275–428; and Murphy 1997. Poisson (1985) began an investigation similar to ours, but since he counted the activity of just two notaries, he could only sketch the impact of Law on private credit.

Law wanted to create a bank that would provide funds to the crown. He was allowed to form the bank—the Banque Générale—in 1716, and it issued large quantities of notes—some 150 million livres worth in 1717 and 1718. The notes went into circulation rapidly, funding short-term loans—in particular, short-term loans to the government. After April 1717, they also became legal tender for taxes.

Law was then allowed to accelerate the pace of financial innovation, as the threat of hostilities with Spain (the two countries were at war throughout most of 1719) increased the government's thirst for money. Law purchased the rights to commercial development of Louisiana from Antoine Crozat, a financier, and founded the Compagnie d'Occident to exploit it in August 1717. To fund the company, he issued shares tradable on the Paris stock exchange. In December 1718, the bank was renamed Banque Royale, and its privileges were increased. Banknotes became legal tender and were issued in large quantities.[6] In August 1719, the company took over the general tax farms, which collected the most important indirect taxes, and it was authorized to convert the national debt into its shares. By October, the company (now renamed the Compagnie des Indes) was granted the rights to collect all taxes. Not long thereafter, Law became Controller General (minister of finance), and the Banque Royale—which was using short-term loans to fuel speculation in company shares—was merged with the Compagnie des Indes. Meanwhile, bank notes became the only permissible legal tender for payments above 100 livres.

From there, the end came quickly. In May 1720, Law lost the confidence of the regent, and his system began to collapse. In October 1720 the bank notes were demonetized (meaning that they could no longer be used as currency for payments), and in 1721 the state consolidated its debts at 2 percent interest with substantial cuts in the nominal capital of short-term debts.

The denouement of the crisis came in 1721–26, as state finances were slowly reorganized. The interest rate cap on private loans, which had gyrated wildly since 1713, was returned to the conventional 5 percent in 1726. The currency was stabilized at 4.45 grams of silver per livre— a 40 percent drop from its mid-seventeenth-century value but an increase of 50 percent relative to the terminal value of the paper currency.[7]

---

6. Although the total number of billets in circulation is unknown, Du Hautchamp (1739, 6:200) suggested that nearly two billion livres were printed.

7. The extent of the devaluation suffered by the Billet de Banque is difficult to determine. Nathalis de Wailly's (1857) compilations of monetary values suggest 50 percent, as do Hamilton's (1938) commodity price data. If we use exchange rate data, however, the figure is between 67 percent and 75 percent (McCusker 1978).

And in 1721, government debt was consolidated once again. As in the earlier consolidation of 1713–14, the Parisian notaries were deeply involved, for they had to draw up the new government debt that replaced older loans. The operations of public finance, though, were not their only concern. As we shall see, they were busy in the private credit market as well, for it too was buffeted by the currency revaluation and the inflation of the Law affair.

A Model of How the Crisis Affected Private Credit

What effect did the crisis have on the private credit market? At first glance, one might assume that the consequences would be easy to predict. One would simply have to consider the effect of the bank notes on the price level and the limits that the interest rate cap imposed on lending. The bank notes would naturally provoke significant inflation, and that in fact was just what occurred in 1719 and 1720, with the currency plummeting nearly 50 percent in value. (Here noneconomists should keep in mind that inflation translates into a loss of a currency's value in silver. Hence inflation and currency depreciation go hand in hand.) Since the nominal interest rate could not vary with the primary instrument of private credit—the rente—the result of the inflation would be straightforward: private lending would shrink, as prices rose and the real return on private loans fell.

Yet that is not at all what happened. In nominal terms, private lending in 1719 and 1720 actually loomed three times larger than it had on average in previous decades. Adjusting for the decline in the livre's value reduces the extent of private lending somewhat, but the flow of new debt in real terms was still twice as large in 1719 and 1720 than it had been for nearly thirty years. How do we comprehend this paradox?

The answer requires that we return to the rules governing private credit and use them to understand the behavior of the lenders and borrowers in the private credit market. Of all the rules in effect in the early eighteenth century, two prove to be crucial in understanding what the lenders and borrowers did. The first is the rule that all notarized debt contracts had to be specified in livres (the unit of account); the second, that interest payments were fixed in the rentes which nearly all borrowers and lenders used.[8] Under such constraints, any change in the inflation rate or the value of the livre was of great importance, for inflation and devaluation of the livre redistributed income from lenders to bor-

---

8. Some 90 percent of outstanding private debts in 1717 had been negotiated as rentes.

rowers, while deflation and appreciation of the livre did the reverse. Given the wild variations in the inflation rate and the livre's value during the Law affair, contemporaries were of course fully aware of the problem.[9]

How then did borrowers and lenders react to the monetary uncertainty? To grasp their behavior, we have formulated an economic model, which the more mathematically inclined reader may consult.[10] It highlights the differences between expectations about inflation and expectations about what we call monetary stabilization. Here stabilization is taken to mean that the government revalues the livre upward and requires borrowers to repay even old debts in livres which are suddenly worth more. Stabilization of this sort is actually what the government decided upon at the end of the Law affair. Of course, such expectations could vary from individual to individual.

How would expectations about inflation and stabilization affect borrowers' and lenders' behavior? If lenders expect inflation, they will try to call in their loans. Borrowers with such beliefs will put off repaying loans because inflation will further reduce the real value of what they owe. As for stabilization, if lenders believe it to be near at hand, they will try to delay any repayments in order to receive livres of higher value. Debtors with the same beliefs will hurriedly reimburse their creditors.

The intuition for these opposed effects is simple: inflation reduces the real cost of repaying nominal debt contracts, while stabilization increases it. Because borrowers want to minimize this cost, they will refrain from repaying so as long as inflation continues to erode the value of their loans. Once they see stabilization as imminent, though, they will rush to pay off their loans.

That stabilization can increase the real cost of repayment may of course appear odd and certainly different from what twentieth-century governments do. They typically choose a new unit of account equal to the old one with a few zeroes shaved off. A single conversion rate from old to new currency then applies to all outstanding contracts from the past—including loan contracts. But that need not be the case. The government could just as well apply an inflation index, with the real cost of repaying an outstanding contract equal to the nominal value of the contract divided by the inflation index's value at the time the contract was originally signed. That was, in fact, the policy adopted in France during the Revolution. The third, and most ominous, possibility for debtors is for the government to return to the preinflation unit of account—

9. See, among others, Véron de Forbonnais 1758a; Melon 1734; Dutot [1738] 1935.
10. See appendix 1.

to effect a revaluation of the currency. It can do so by setting the unit of account's metal value to what it was worth before inflation began. The British government in effect did so when convertibility of the pound was resumed after the Napoleonic wars; similarly, a number of governments attempted to resume convertibility at prewar parities after World War I.

When Law's system collapsed in 1720, the Regency government actually chose the third course of action. Rather than indexing any of the debts contracted in billets de banque, the government returned to a unit of account of relatively high silver content.[11] The Law affair offered borrowers a wonderful opportunity to reduce their debts, but the opportunity depended on seizing the right moment. For debtors, repaying in 1718 was not nearly as advantageous as doing so in early 1720, but either one was better than carrying debts through to 1721.

In 1718, though, the problem was that no one knew how the Law affair would end. No one knew for certain how long the inflation would last or when stabilization would occur. The uncertainties made it possible for individuals in similar situations to come to different conclusions about the future of the monetary system: they simply held different opinions about when a monetary transition would take place and what it would entail. Our task is therefore to determine how divergent such opinions were. Fortunately, we can use loan repayment contracts, for they allow us to infer what individual borrowers thought likely to happen. After all, it was the borrower's decisions that mattered here, and not the lender's. The reason, quite simply, was that nearly all private notarial debt took the form of rentes. With rentes, as we know, repayment was left to the discretion of the borrower, because the lender had no way to force repayment or to avoid inflation. It follows that the rate of repayments yields an index of borrowers' expectations—their expectations that stabilization was imminent and that it would favor lenders. As those expectations rose, the repayment rate ought to have risen too. It should have declined if they expected continued inflation.

Borrowers had another option besides outright repayment: they could refinance their loans. If nominal interest rates were low (as they were in 1720, for example) and if stabilization seemed unlikely, then borrowers might actually want to borrow money to pay off more expensive older debts. Such a strategy would allow them to lock-in the gains from lower interest rates and past inflation, but it would involve the no-

---

11. We say relatively because the livre in 1726 was still worth somewhat less than it had been back in 1717. It is worth noting here that the billets themselves were consolidated into long-term bonds (Marion 1927, 1:109).

tarial fees that borrowing and lending always entailed. Because of these fixed fees, a borrower would be more likely to renegotiate larger loan contracts, for the losses to fees would be swamped by the potential profits from the lower interest payments on a big loan.[12]

Lenders faced a simpler problem, for by law they were required to accept repayment in whatever currency was legal tender. From 27 December 1718 to 31 October 1720, billets de banque were legal for nearly all notarial debts, and when lenders were repaid in billets they had to decide what to do with the rapidly depreciating currency.[13] They could either consume the resources or buy long-term assets. Among the assets they purchased was additional long-term debt, and while that may seem surprising or even perverse, simple economics can explain their decision. What seems most likely is that the lenders who acquired the debt expected the imminent collapse of Law's system and a rapid monetary stabilization favoring lenders. With such expectations, they quite reasonably lent money out in the hope that the loans would not be repaid before stabilization took hold. Our model in fact confirms this intuition, because it suggests that individuals who believe in impending stabilization will be more likely to lend in periods of inflation. It follows that the volume of new loans will gauge (at least roughly) lenders' expectations that an approaching stabilization will be favorable to them. In a perfect market, expectations about stabilization and future inflation too would have converged, and the divergent beliefs would have disappeared. In this case, repayment and renegotiation would have occurred all at once just before the monetary transition. Yet the Parisian credit market offered no such perfection in 1719. True, it was limited to a small number of people, but even with a small number of participants, there was no mechanism to aggregate information. There was a rudimentary stock exchange, but it remained unorganized until after the Law affair and limited in its scope.[14] Neither it nor decentralized private trading could aggregate the information and help expectations converge.

If we apply our model to the notarial records, it becomes clear that few individuals perceived Law's system as stable. Beliefs about the likelihood of stabilization, though, were heterogeneous. Not that rational ex-

12. Aggregate indebtedness did not enter into the decision. What mattered was the size of each loan because transaction costs were assessed contract by contract.

13. The edict of 27 December 1718 required payment of all sums above 600 livres in billets (Faure 1977:64–66). On 21 December 1719, the ceiling dropped to 430 livres (Du Hautchamp 1739, 5:191), and on 27 February 1720, it fell to 100 livres (Du Hautchamp, 1739, 6:46). Our sample of debt contracts suggests that the initial ceiling of 600 livres was often ignored; see table 4.6.

14. Ehrenberg 1922, 2:300–301, 309–11; Lüthy 1959, 1:110–11.

pectations failed. On the contrary, Parisians made every effort to anticipate the gyrations of the Regency's monetary policies. The problem was
that they had no previous experience on which to base their decisions.[15]
Meanwhile, the crisis was so brief that erroneous beliefs could not be
corrected. Divergent beliefs of the same sort would also divide Parisians
during the turbulent assignat phase of the French Revolution. Because
Parisians looked back to the Law affair as a reference point, it is no
surprise that they behaved in the same way that their ancestors had in
1712–26.

The Evolution of the Long-Term Private Credit Market

Having sketched our model, we can now use it to analyze what happened
in the long-term private credit market between the end of 1712 and
1726. During these years, the private credit market passed through four
phases. In the first, from 1712 until 1715, it remained active despite
ongoing deflation. In the second, from 1715 to 1717, the volume of
private credit subsided, even though the currency was relatively stable
after an initial 25 percent devaluation in 1715. Wild variations in the
currency did not really strike the credit market until the third phase,
from 1718 to 1720, when the livre lost nearly two-thirds of its value.
Even so, the volume of new private loans attained levels as high as anything seen in nearly thirty years. Private credit then sank into a deep
depression in the final phase, from 1721 through 1726—all this in spite
of an eventual return of monetary stability.

In the first phase (1712–15), it was no doubt clear that the government would have to reorganize public finances, and that reorganization
would obviously affect private incomes in a city dependent on government business. Everyone knew that the wars had opened up an enormous deficit, and the monarchy was already late in paying office holders
and owners of government rentes. Still, it was not yet clear precisely what
measures the government might take, nor how drastic they would be. A
state bankruptcy was in the offing, but the financial minister, Desmarets,
nonetheless succeeded in maintaining confidence in some of the key
short-term government notes that were likely candidates for default. His
upward reevaluation of the livre, which caused deflation, may in fact
have been an attempt to soften the effects of any default, and it perhaps

---

15. There had been a number of proposals to create a bank of issue prior to Law, but
none had been enacted. See Harsin 1933.

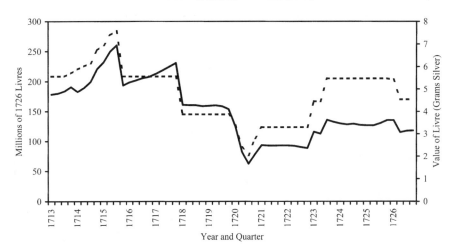

FIGURE 4.1 Real Private Indebtedness and the Value of the Livre in Silver, 1713–26

reassured the government's creditors.[16] The first period was thus one of heightened uncertainty, but new private lending nonetheless increased. The volume of new private loans in 1713 and 1714 was in fact nearly double what it had been during the last years of the War of the Spanish Succession. The only reason the outstanding debt series did not rise rapidly was that loan repayments were climbing at an even faster rate (figures 4.1 and 4.2).

Although firm evidence is lacking, we can at least speculate about the reason why both repayments and new lending jumped. On the one hand, many Parisian investors were probably waiting for the payments due from offices, government rentes, and short-term government credit. Others awaited money from financiers and bankers, to whom they had advanced funds to finance state loans. In either case, with the state late in repaying, these investors might themselves have been obliged to borrow in the private credit market, and if they had had short-term debts fall due, they might have tried to convert them into longer term obligations. Such a story does of course remain speculative, but it does fit accounts of what happened to certain bankers and financiers, who found themselves short of cash. There were, of course, some exceptions in the realm of banking and finance—lucky or influential individuals who had

16. Lüthy 1959, 1:102–103, 226–62, 277–82; Marion 1927, 1:45–47, 64–69; Faure 1977; and Lavisse 1911, 8, pt. 1:164–99.

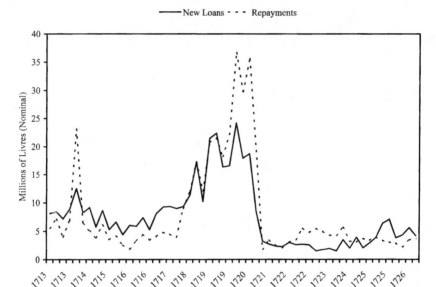

FIGURE 4.2 New Loans and Loan Repayments, 1713–26

safely liquidated their holdings of government debt or who had succeeded in pulling strings to get paid. They could well be the source of
the rise in repayments, for they might naturally have feared that the
government would eventually come after them and seek to reclaim their
cash. For them, one plausible strategy might thus have been to reduce
their cash holdings by repaying debts. That way, they would at least have
preserved their reputations and could have eventually resumed their financial dealings, once the government investigation had passed. They
could of course have purchased physical assets as well, but physical assets
could be confiscated too. Drawing down their cash balances by repaying
old debts might well have been the superior strategy.[17]

The second phase (1715–17) opened with the death of Louis XIV
in September 1715, which ushered in a period of even greater unpre-
dictability. By his testament, Louis XIV left the government in the hands
of a regency council until his young successor, Louis XV, reached the
age of majority. Although the Duc d'Orléans was named regent, he exer-
cised no power over the regency council, and he therefore sought to
have the testament overturned by the country's highest law court, the
Parlement of Paris. Allying itself with him, the Parlement gave the regent

17. For evidence about bankers that fits our story, see Lüthy 1959, 1:226–62.

what he wanted. In return, the Parlement regained the right to remonstrate (that is, to request amendments and delays before implementing
royal legislation and decrees), a right that had been suppressed under
Louis XIV. What is important in all this—at least for our purposes—is
that the Parlement could now question financial edicts. It regained a
voice in the game of public finance and could thus protest against tax
increases and government default. The Parlement began to use its voice
against the government, and although it was not yet as effective as it
would later be, it did put obstacles in the government's path.[18] A rapid
end to the state's deficit was thus unlikely, because the remedies that
were politically feasible—the visa or the chambre de justice—could simply not eliminate enough debt.

With Paris so dependent on a solution to the government's financial
problems, it is not surprising that new private loans declined swiftly. By
the end of 1715, the volume of new private loans had fallen 66 percent
from its peak in the previous year, and it remained depressed until 1717.
Repayments fell even more, though, so that outstanding debt actually
rose (figures 4.1 and 4.2). In all likelihood, both trends reflected public
anticipation of an upcoming devaluation. Serious adjustments to the
public debt in the past had usually included devaluations, and the state's
financial situation probably suggested that one was in the offing. If so,
lenders had reason to stop lending until the devaluation was in place.
Given the interest rate ceiling on the rentes that dominated private
credit, lenders could simply not make new loans at interest rates high
enough to compensate for the losses from devaluation. Their sole recourse was to stop making new loans in order to avoid even greater losses
to devaluation. As for borrowers, they would want to hold off repaying
outstanding loans and to keep their cash until the devaluation was past,
for then they too could repay their loans in cheapened currency—hence
the decline in repayments.

As Law's bank swung into action, the long-term private credit market
revived. The private market's third phase (1718–20) had begun, a phase
in which paper money would play an ever more important role. New
long-term private loans increased steadily from 1717 to a peak in 1720,
and interest rates began to fall significantly (table 4.2). This surge of
private lending, occurring more than five years after the battle of De-
nain, was clearly not the result of financiers' borrowing to fund the war
in Spain. One might argue that the new private loans simply tapped
the growing supply of paper money issued by Law's bank, but on closer
inspection that argument falters. The problem with it is that through

---

18. Lavisse 1911, 8, pt. 2:15–17; Flammermont 1888, 1:i–xii, 1–123.

TABLE 4.2   INTEREST RATES DURING THE REGENCY

Year	Quarter	Average Interest Rate		N
		Unweighted	Weighted	
1718	1	4.80	4.81	28
	2	4.53	4.50	29
	3	4.45	4.75	11
	4	4.60	4.81	14
1719	1	4.35	4.32	32
	2	4.66	4.74	12
	3	4.14	4.15	19
	4	4.58	4.02	17
1720	1	3.15	3.06	39
	2	3.22	2.31	32
	3	1.99	1.99	16
	4	1.96	1.99	10

Source: Interest rates were culled from new rentes contracts found in a 20 percent sample from the minutes of notaries IX, XXI, XLIII, LXII, LXX, LXXVIII, CXV.
Note: The legal interest rate was reduced from 5 percent to 3.33 percent in August 1719 and to 2 percent in March 1720.

the end of 1718 most long-term loans in Paris were still transacted in coins rather than the sort of bank notes one would expect if Law's money were driving the new lending. In fact, notes from Law's bank hardly appeared in any notarial transactions before February 1719, and it was not until March of that year that they became the dominant currency for repaying debts.

A more likely explanation for the rise in new private lending between 1717 and 1720 lies with lenders' beliefs. At least some lenders apparently thought that the threat of inflation and devaluation was over, even though the livre declined in value early in 1718. In their view, there was little further risk that the government would disrupt private credit transactions as it grappled with its financial problems. Perhaps these lenders were reassured by the Paris Parlement's regaining the right to remonstrate, for even though the Parlement seemed momentarily meek, it had traditionally defended creditors. Or perhaps they were financiers who found themselves pushed into the arena of private credit as Law's bank took over more and more of the state's financial dealings. In any case, their sanguine view of the future was shared by at least some of those who had borrowed in the past. Convinced that further inflation and devaluation were unlikely, these borrowers hurried to repay their debts. The amount repaid was not negligible: it came to over half the volume of new private loans in the years 1715–18. It is thus clear that both many borrowers and many lenders had concluded—wrongly to be sure—that devaluation and inflation were over.

Not all individuals shared this rosy view of the future. Other borrowers and lenders in fact anticipated not monetary stability but more inflation and devaluation. Lenders with such beliefs spurned the private credit market. As for borrowers who expected inflation and devaluation, they were the ones who amassed new debts. Presumably they were investing the loan proceeds in assets that would be unaffected by monetary manipulation.

In December 1718, Law began to turn his bank and the Compagnie des Indes into the French equivalent of the Bank of England. To do so, he not only made the bank's notes legal tender for all payments above 600 livres but he also encouraged speculation in Compagnie des Indes shares. His goal was to carry out a debt for equity swap of the government debt. In return for their fixed-interest-rate government bonds, the monarchy's creditors would receive shares in the Compagnie des Indes, which were liquid and also appreciating in value. For the operation to be profitable to Law and the state, though, it had to be carried out on favorable terms. In Law's view, that meant roughly doubling the price of the company's stock (so that it would reach 10,000 livres a share) and paying shareholders a guaranteed dividend of 2 percent. To get the stock to double in value, Law's bank began to lend on the security of the company's shares with low margin requirements.

Others have described the resulting speculative frenzy that gripped Paris in 1719 and early 1720; what matters to us is that Law's billets had multiple uses. By January 1719 Law's bank was lending the billets to private individuals at 3 percent interest, and then at 2 percent. Borrowers could use them to reimburse older private debts or to speculate on the value of Indies shares. They could also borrow at 3 or 4 percent from private individuals for similar purposes. From the evidence in notarial acts it does not seem people actually used the private loans to purchase Indies shares.[19] The reason, no doubt, was that bullish investors found it easier to finance their shares with a low margin loan from Law's bank than with privately contracted rentes, which required sounder collateral. But paying off outstanding debts was another matter. In fact, a number of private borrowers used loans contracted in the years 1718–20 to repay older, more expensive debt. One sterling example was the chevalier Joseph Jean-Baptiste Fleuriau, who in January 1720 borrowed nearly 400,000 livres in coins and billets from his son to repay thirteen old debts, some of which dated back as far as 1706. Fleuriau used the money to extinguish old rentes, cancel a debt due the Jesuits, and settle an

19. Speculation in shares was also fed by the international capital that flowed into Paris via the short-term market in bills of exchange. See Neal 1990:62–76.

inheritance due his daughter. Once he had wiped out his old debts, he borrowed 75,000 livres in billets from a Parisian bourgeois and then used the inflation cheapened paper to pay back part of what he owed his son.[20] Not even family ties could keep debtors like Fleuriau from taking advantage of Law's system.

Many of these borrowers made their repayments while Law was still gaining power. They presumably believed that the easy credit would soon come to an end, even though Law's most fantastic plan—his debt for equity swap of March 1720—was still in the future. They accelerated their repayments in 1719, lifting them up past the volume of new loans and driving outstanding debt levels down (figures 4.1 and 4.2). Even the nominal level of outstanding debt, which was unaffected by inflation, began to drop in 1719, while Law was still firmly in control (figure 2.4).[21] Apparently, many Parisians thought that Law's regime was unstable.

After Law's dismissal in April 1720, the regent initiated an extraordinarily messy transition from paper money to specie currency. In May 1720, the government decided to put off debt consolidation. At the same time, it announced that it would retire the paper money in the fall and fold it into the state's other obligations. What exactly would become of the billets was not yet clear, but the government did reveal that a new visa or verification of short-term government debt was in the offing. In the meantime, the paper money remained legal tender until November 1. Under these circumstances it is no surprise that borrowers continued to use billets to repay private debts right through the end of October, pushing the outstanding debt level even lower (figures 4.1 and 4.2). It reached a nadir in the fall of 1720, when in real terms outstanding indebtedness was only a third of the level attained in 1713. Thereafter, although it revived slightly, the private market remained depressed well past 1726. In this fourth phase of our story (1721–26), some repayments continued, but few lenders dared make new loans.

What mattered, throughout all four phases of the crisis, were expectations about the steps the government would take to restore the monarchy's finances. In the second phase (1715–17), for example, the public anticipated a currency devaluation. Lenders therefore stopped making new loans, because they could not raise the interest rate to compensate for the expected losses that devaluation would entail. Expecta-

20. ANMC, CXV, 386 (27 January 1720).
21. While the real series provides a more reliable measure of the value of the debt, the nominal series tracks the extent to which each livre of repayment is matched by a livre of investment in each period.

tions, though, could differ radically from person to person. In the third phase of the crisis (1718–20), some lenders believed the risk of devaluation was over, but they made loans to borrowers who had exactly the opposite opinion. Believing devaluation was imminent, these borrowers wanted to amass paper debts which could be paid back in cheap currency.

The Broader Effects of the Crisis

At the end of the third phase of the Law affair, real outstanding debt plunged. The collapse obviously raises the issue of redistribution—of who lost and who gained, both in the private credit market and in the public market. Other questions naturally arise as well. Why did the monarchy tolerate such a financial disaster? And what impact did the crisis ultimately have on the credit market? Did it stifle financial innovation, as accounts of the Law affair have long maintained?

As far as the public credit market is concerned, it is clear that the financial schemes of the Regency had cost the state's creditors enormous sums. In nominal terms, they lost about half their claims on the state.[22] In real terms they lost even more because the currency had depreciated.

Private lenders were hurt too, but no one has ever tried to estimate how much money drained from their hands into those of private borrowers. Thanks to our series, we can guess at their losses in Paris and from that extrapolate to the rest of France, albeit with a greater margin of error. Among the various ways to compute the redistribution from private lenders to private borrowers, we have selected a method that gives a reasonable order of magnitude, although it probably underestimates lenders' losses.[23] What we do is to break the private lenders' losses into two parts: those due to devaluation of the livre between 1718 and 1727, and those due to repayments made by borrowers who took advantage of the depreciated paper currency during the Law affair.

22. The losses came to about 34 million livres in annual interest charges from a 1715 total of 86 million a year (Marion 1927, 1:65, 112).

23. There are several reasons why we underestimate private lenders' losses. First, we ignore losses due to the depreciation of the livre before 1718. Second, we overlook redistribution that is difficult to quantify. Some lenders, for example, accepted interest cuts to avoid being repaid in paper money. Such interest rate cuts entailed a loss for the lender, but we could not quantify the magnitude of the loss. There are similar problems estimating the losses suffered by lenders who were repaid in billets but who did not bring the billets in for redemption (cf. Marion 1927, 1:109). The final reason we underestimate the losses is that we overlook repayments made in the countryside.

TABLE 4.3   REDISTRIBUTION AND THE DECLINE IN OUTSTANDING DEBT, 1718–27

	Paris			France	
	Nominal Livres	1726 Livres[a]	1726 Livres[b]	Nominal Livres	1726 Livres[a]
Debt stock in January 1718	185	231	231	740	938
Loss to devaluation, 1718–27	0	−46	−46	0	−184
Loss to repayments during Law Affair	0	−43	−48	0	−174
Market flight, 1718–27	−66	−23	−18	−264	−90
Debt stock in January 1727	119	119	119	476	476
Percent change, 1718–27	36	48	48	36	49
Government default					−1,500
Private redistribution (loss to repayments during Law plus loss to devaluation)					−358
Loss to repayments during Law relative to government default					11.6%
Private redistribution relative to government default					23.8%

Source: The government debt estimates come from Marion 1927, 1:67, 112, and Lüthy 1959, 1:279–80, 442. For the source of the other figures, see the text and Archival Sources.
Note: All amounts are in millions of livres. The silver value of the livre is taken from Nathalis de Wailly 1857, and, because there are doubts about his data for the Law Affair, we also calculated the silver value of the livre relative to British and Dutch currency, using exchange rate data in McCusker 1978. Because of rounding, the sums may not total. The data on private outstanding debts comes from our estimates of private credit. We assume that Paris represented twenty-five percent of all private credit for France as a whole. That is somewhat less than what we found for the 1780s (see chapter 10), but it seems reasonable to believe that Paris's share of financial activity rose in the eighteenth century. We define devaluation as the loss due to the declining value of the livre in silver between January 1718 and the end of 1726. The losses are expressed in terms of 1726 livres and are calculated using two methods. We define losses from repayments during the Law Affair as the difference in 1726 livres between what the repayments cost at the time they were made and what they would have cost once the livre was restabilized in 1726. They represent what borrowers gained by making repayments in depreciated paper currency. Finally, market flight is the remaining decline in private indebtedness. It is the drop in private indebtedness that cannot be attributed to devaluation and premature repayments, and it represents lenders' abandoning the private credit market.
[a] Silver value of the livre from Nathalis de Wailly 1857.
[b] Value of the livre calculated from exchange rate data in McCusker 1978.

The first part of the private lenders' losses covers what it would have cost them if there had been a serious devaluation alone, without the Law affair. It simply involves computing how much the outstanding debt series declines as the livre went from its value in January 1718 (5.56 grams of silver) to its value at the end of 1726 (4.45 grams of silver), when it was stabilized until 1789. The devaluation cost private creditors in Paris some 46 million livres, or 20 percent of the value of outstanding private debt in January 1718 (table 4.3). Parisian lenders would have lost that much even if borrowers had been unable to repay their loans with depreciated paper currency during the Law affair.

To calculate the additional losses from repayments in paper—the second part of the redistribution from lenders to borrowers—we estimated in a simple way how much borrowers gained. For each quarter when borrowers were repaying lenders in paper (1719 and 1720), we calculated the difference in silver between what the repayments cost at the time they were made and what they would have cost once the livre was restabilized in 1726. That is what the borrowers gained by taking advantage of the depreciated paper currency. The resulting damage suffered by Parisian lenders lies between 43 and 48 million livres, depending on the way one calculates the silver value of the currency in 1719 and 1720.

Whatever the precise figure, the total loss to private lenders fell well below what the monarchy's default cost the government's creditors. In real terms, the monarchy's default came to 1.5 billion livres. The total loss to private lenders from both devaluation and repayments was less than a quarter of that, even if we consider the entire kingdom of France (table 4.3). Overall, the Law affair cost private lenders about one third of their initial investments, whether we look at Paris or France as a whole.

That was certainly enough to anguish private investors, but as we shall see, it pales beside the havoc wrought by the French Revolution. There are two reasons why the damage remained limited during the Law affair. First, paper money was legal tender for less than two years; during the Revolution, paper money—the assignat—would circulate for a full six years. Furthermore, Law's paper money did not depreciate as much as the assignat would.

Still, during the three brief years that constitute the height of the Law affair, borrowers repaid 125 million of the 166 million livres of rentes that had been outstanding at the beginning of 1718. The implication is that Parisian borrowers rushed to take advantage of Law's billets by repaying their creditors in depreciated paper. One might argue that it was easier to do so in 1718–20 than in the past, because somewhat fewer borrowers were linked to their lenders by personal ties of family, neighborhood, or profession. Yet even when borrowers and lenders shared such personal ties, they did not hesitate to pay in paper. Indeed, loans between individuals with personal links were just as likely to be repaid as were credit contracts in which the parties had no social, professional, geographical, or family ties.[24] As the economist Mirabeau observed several decades later, during the Law affair, "the brother reimbursed his sister, and the son, his mother."[25]

In the end, the losses during the Law affair frightened away lenders. They hesitated to make new loans and did not reinvest the sums they received in repayment of older debts. We can estimate how much money left the market by assuming it equals that part of the decline in indebtedness which cannot be attributed to devaluation or losses from repayment

24. Hoffman, Postel-Vinay, and Rosenthal 1995:278.
25. Marion 1927, 1:102.

TABLE 4.4   THE SOCIAL DISTRIBUTION OF BORROWERS AND LENDERS IN PARIS BY PERCENTAGE
OF FUNDS LENT, 1718–20

Year	Nobles and Officers	Clergy	Merchants and Bourgeois	Artisans and Masters	Professions and Services	Rural	Unknown and Institutions
	Lender's Occupation in New Debt Contracts						
1718	62.6	5.5	18.7	1.2	5.1	2.1	4.8
1719	78.0	5.0	7.2	3.8	1.9	0.1	3.9
1720	80.1	1.9	12.4	0.8	2.2	0.1	2.5
	Borrower's Occupation in New Debt Contracts						
1718	68.5	2.2	12.9	1.2	11.8	1.2	2.1
1719	73.4	12.7	7.5	2.7	2.4	0.5	0.8
1720	80.4	3.6	4.6	0.9	4.6	0.7	5.2
	Lender's Occupation in Repayment Contracts						
1718	75.3	3.9	14.2	0.4	1.6	0.1	4.6
1719	64.0	3.1	16.8	0.0	11.8	0.0	4.3
1720	50.1	4.1	33.9	2.0	6.2	0.1	3.6
	Borrower's Occupation in Repayment Contracts						
1718	65.9	0.0	15.2	4.3	9.9	0.3	4.3
1719	71.1	2.7	11.0	2.2	10.8	0.5	1.8
1720	86.6	2.1	4.9	0.5	3.8	0.8	1.2

Source: Samples of loan and repayment contracts from notaries IX, XXI, XLIII, LXII, LXX, LXXVIII, CXV. For
details, see Archival Sources.
Note: The occupational categories are as in table 3.4.

in depreciated paper. For Paris, it comes to somewhere between 18 and
23 million livres, or 8 to 10 percent of the outstanding debts in January
1718. It is true that some of the funds withdrawn from the long-term
private market might have fed speculation in shares of the Compagnie
des Indes in 1718–20, but the sums involved were probably not high.
It is more likely that lenders simply hoarded specie while they waited for
the livre to stabilize. Apparently, they wanted clear signs that monetary
manipulations were over, for they shunned long-term private credit until
after 1727.

Who then were the lenders who lost so much money in the private
credit market? By and large, they came from the elite. One reason was
that notarial credit was still an affair of the rich—in Paris, essentially
the nobility, royal officers, and the commercial classes. Lenders came
overwhelmingly from the elites, both before the Law affair (as we know
from chapter 3) and during it (tables 4.4 and 4.5). Obviously, they had
the money to lend.

But during the Law affair there was yet another barrier that kept more

TABLE 4.5   THE SOCIAL DISTRIBUTION OF BORROWERS AND LENDERS IN PARIS BY PERCENTAGE
OF ALL LOAN CONTRACTS, 1718–20

Year	Nobles and Officers	Clergy	Merchants and Bourgeois	Artisans and Masters	Professions and Services	Rural	Unknown and Institutions
			Lender's Occupation in New Debt Contracts				
1718	32.1	5.4	33.0	5.4	10.7	2.7	10.7
1719	44.6	6.2	22.3	8.9	5.4	0.9	11.6
1720	57.2	3.8	17.6	6.9	8.4	1.5	4.6
			Borrower's Occupation in New Debt Contracts				
1718	49.1	2.7	22.3	7.1	11.6	4.5	2.7
1719	46.4	5.4	21.4	11.6	9.8	4.5	0.9
1720	46.6	3.8	11.5	9.1	9.9	16.0	3.1
			Lender's Occupation in Repayment Contracts				
1718	48.7	5.1	17.9	2.6	2.6	5.1	17.9
1719	55.6	1.8	22.2	0.0	13.0	0.0	7.4
1720	45.7	3.3	28.6	6.7	8.1	0.5	7.1
			Borrower's Occupation in Repayment Contracts				
1718	51.3	0.0	12.8	10.3	12.8	10.3	2.6
1719	55.6	3.7	18.5	3.7	9.3	5.6	3.7
1720	61.9	1.4	10.5	3.3	10.0	8.1	4.7

Source: As in table 4.4.

Note: The occupational categories are as in table 3.4.

modest lenders from being repaid in worthless paper: the size of Law's
billets. At least initially, the billets came in extraordinarily large denominations of 1,000 and 10,000 livres. Since a skilled worker earned roughly
a livre a day, a 10,000 livre note could only be used to repay a very large
loan. These 10,000 livres notes actually constituted 40 percent of the
total billet issue, while 1,000 livre billets—also out of bounds for most
of the population—formed yet another 40 percent.[26] Still another obstacle to redistribution in modest social circles was the lower limit to the
size of contracts in which billets were legal tender. Some borrowers ignored the limit, but most loans that were repaid involved sums well over
the legal limit (table 4.6).

Many of the lenders whose private loans were repaid had also advanced funds to the government (table 3.5). And many of them were
nobles, officers, and privileged bourgeois, who were exempt from taxation. That they lent money to the government and yet paid no taxes
suggests a possible explanation for Law's system—an explanation pro-

26. Du Hautchamp 1739, 6:200.

TABLE 4.6   SIZE OF CONTRACTS AND THE TIMING OF REIMBURSEMENT OF PRIVATE LOANS, 1718–1720

| | | By Size Class in Livres | | | | | | Whole Sample | |
| | | Numbers of Contracts (percent) | | | Share of Funds (percent) | | | Number of Contracts | Value in 1000 Livres |
Legal Status of Billets	Period	≤100	>100 and ≤600	>600	≤100	>100 and ≤600	>600		
Not legal tender	1718	5.5	19.4	75	0.01	1.3	98.6	36	177
Legal tender above 600 livres	1719	6.1	10.2	83.6	0.01	0.6	99.3	49	289
Legal tender above 300 livres	Jan–Feb 1720	0	6.4	93.5	0	0.2	99.8	78	847
Legal tender above 100 livres	Mar–Dec 1720	1.5	23.7	74.8	0.01	1.0	99.0	131	1079
Total		2.4	16.3	81.3	0.02	0.7	99.3	294	2393

Source: As in table 4.2.

Note: Columns may not sum due to rounding.

posed in other contexts by Alesina and Drazen and by White.[27] The idea is that the monarchy's financial problems could be solved either by a tax increase or by a reduction in spending, which in our case would come from a default on government debt. But a default and a tax increase would have vastly different distributional consequences. A default would impose costs on the sort of nobles, officers, and privileged bourgeois who held government debt. They presumably would oppose default and favor a tax increase instead. A tax increase, by contrast, would leave them unscathed because of their tax exemptions and would push the burden of fiscal adjustment onto the less prosperous groups who actually paid taxes.

These taxpayers would of course resist added taxation and push for default. Both they and their opponents, the privileged lenders, would then fight for the financial solution they preferred—default for the taxpayers and a tax increase for the lenders. Each group might well believe that its opponent was ready to cave in and absorb a disproportionate share of the costs. Each group would therefore want to hold out until its opponent conceded, and the result would be a long war of attrition, during which the government deficit would grow, compounding the problem.

At first glance, such a story appears to fit the Regency. The Regency, one could argue, was politically weak and took a very long time to solve the problems of public finance left by Louis XIV's reign. The regent, the argument might go, was beholden to the government's creditors once he appealed to the Parlement to break Louis XIV's will. He could not openly default as kings had in the past. Yet he could not raise taxes either, after so many years of warfare and high taxes. In the end, it was the privileged lenders who paid, via the default and inflation of the Law affair. They were the ones who ultimately lost the war of attrition and footed the bill.

Such a story might seem convincing, but it would actually be a grave error to apply it to the Regency—or indeed to any episode of financial history under the Old Regime. In the first place, the elite itself was divided in many ways: it was not composed of lenders alone. Women and the elderly might well lend, but young males in the elite often borrowed heavily. They might not lose at all from the Law affair. With the elite divided, a simple story that pits them against taxpayers assumes a unity that was really not there.

More important, this simple version of the war of attrition leaves out the monarchy itself, which had its own interests, distinct from those of

27. Alesina and Drazen 1991; White 1995.

any coalition of lenders or taxpayers. Even under the Regency, the crown was concerned with preserving autonomy for its policies, and the regent wanted to leave the young king with all the powers Louis XIV had enjoyed.[28] For that reason, a tax increase after Louis XIV's death was unthinkable, for it would have required political concessions that would undercut the monarchy's autonomy in war and foreign policy, the affairs of state that mattered most. The problem for the French kings was that they could really only raise taxes during periods of warfare, and once the fighting was over, the tax increases usually had to be rolled back. The only way to get a permanent tax increase after a war—a tax increase that could fund all the debt run up during the battles—was to summon the Estates General or get the assent of the Parlements. Calling the Estates always posed grave dangers to royal authority, and kings after Louis XIV had difficulty getting the Parlements to agree to peacetime tax increases. The Parlements had regained their ability to remonstrate, and when presented with tax increases, they might well balk and demand a role for themselves in the government's financial affairs. The Regency was no exception in this regard: as early as 1717 the Parlement of Paris was objecting to tax increases and poking its nose into royal finances.[29]

The crown could still default on its debts, but even defaulting was made difficult by enormous political obstacles. To begin with, the Parlement of Paris had traditionally defended the government's creditors. It was particularly vociferous in its support of creditors who (like the magistrates of Parlement themselves) did not happen to be financiers. Although the Parlement would have gone along with a selective default that struck unpopular financiers, such a measure could not by itself have solved the monarchy's fiscal problems. In effect, the chambre de justice of 1716 was just such an operation, yet, as we know, it netted less than 100 million livres of government debt, or less than 3 percent of what the monarchy owed.[30] A larger default would hence be necessary, but it would hit the magistrates themselves as government creditors. The Parlement was particularly vigilant when its own interests were at stake.[31]

28. Shennan 1979.

29. Lavisse 1911, 8: pt. 2:15; Flammermont 1888, 1:vii–viii, 50–65.

30. Marion 1927, 1:76–77 and his appendix 1; Dessert 1984:262. Although members of the Parlement of Paris did serve on the chambre de justice, its operations eventually provoked the opposition of several provincial parlements and of the Paris Chambre des Comptes. Strictly speaking, the chambre was supposed to tax the excess profits that the financiers had amassed, but the financiers paid nearly all the taxes due by surrendering government debt.

31. Flammermont 1888–98, 1:vii–viii, 50–65.

Faced with such a debacle, the regent no doubt saw two clear advantages in letting John Law move into public finance. Even if his system failed, he would provide the regent with an obvious scapegoat, and in the meantime the Scotsman was providing all the cash necessary to see France through its war with Spain in 1719. True, the Paris Parlement did oppose Law, but the regent gave him enough support to overcome the Parlement's opposition in August 1718. And the regent continued keeping the Parlement at bay as Law pursued his projects.[32]

One might of course imagine the Law affair's having a different ending. Among the many possible outcomes, it is even conceivable that it might have given France a financial system like the one that sprang up in eighteenth-century England. There, the state did not raise taxes temporarily during wars and then default on its debts afterwards, as in France. Instead, England raised taxes after every war in order to pay for the borrowing that the fighting entailed, and most of the bonds it issued were traded on a public exchange.[33] It is true that the Law affair did spell the end of one of the French monarchy's worst financial practices: the crown stopped manipulating the currency to raise revenue or lower the value of its debts. Yet the rest of its financial habits persisted. The monarchy still peddled illiquid debt, still hid its financial situation, and still tended to fund wars by selective defaults rather than permanent tax increases. These habits survived not out of blind custom but because they preserved the king's autonomy in foreign policy. Doing otherwise— in particular, getting permanent tax increases to fight wars—would have necessitated constitutional change.[34]

Because the crown left most of its traditional borrowing mechanisms intact, bankers would lurk in the shadows of Parisian notaries until at least the 1770s, while notaries would remain the chief brokers of government debt. Yet curiously, notaries had come close to losing this role during the Law affair. Had Law actually consolidated the monarchy's debt into shares of the Compagnie des Indes, the shares would have been sold on the stock exchange, as in England. The sales would be the responsibility of the company and regulated by the commercial code. Notaries would not have been involved in any way, not even in the drawing up of documents. Naturally, Parisian notaries were quite alarmed by Law's proposals and demanded an interview with him. But Law re-

32. Flammermont 1888–98, 1:viii–xii, 66–140.

33. Sargent and Velde 1995; North and Weingast 1989; Jones 1981; Neal 1990.

34. For a formal model and a discussion of evidence from various parts of early modern Europe, see Hoffman and Rosenthal 1997.

buffed them, feigning ignorance of their role as brokers of debt and arguing that the government would no longer need their assistance.[35] It is no wonder then that notaries were alarmed. Had Law succeeded, they would have been forced out of marketing public debt in the 1720s, rather than during the French Revolution. And they would never have gone on to their extraordinary success as brokers of private credit in the late eighteenth century.

But because Law failed, Parisian notaries retained their lucrative role as the chief intermediaries for the government's long-term debt. They also profited greatly from the government's default and consolidation of 1720–21. As the eighteenth century wore on, they became the crucial source of new funds for the crown, and the monarchy issued more and more of its debt in the form of rentes and other long-term loans sold directly to the public by the Parisian notaries. The government did permit trading in the shares of the Compagnie des Indes to continue on the Paris stock exchange. A secondary market would also eventually develop in certain rentes.[36] But the original placement of most of these rentes was assured not by bankers but by notaries.

The Parisian notaries had the good fortune to emerge from the Regency rich and untainted by the monetary speculation that had cost French investors so dearly. Their riches came from the countless acts of credit and repayment they had drafted between 1713 to 1721. For each one, they collected their fees. And they were unscathed because they had not been the central financial figures of Louis XIV's regime. Furthermore, because they opposed Law's projects, they managed to retain the public's trust after the Law affair. When the credit market rebounded, the public turned to them as the intermediaries of choice for long-term investments.

In the crisis surrounding the Law affair, lenders lost perhaps a third of their investment in the private credit market. They lost it not just to currency devaluation but to borrowers who were ready to pay off even relatives and friends in worthless paper currency. Those who advanced money to the government watched even a larger fraction of their investments go up in smoke.

35. ACNP, Deliberations 1703–19 (10 September 1719); Deliberations 1719–34 (17 September 1719). Law's ignorance was clearly feigned, because he had his own notary. See Poisson 1985.

36. Velde and Weir 1992; Le Goff 1996.

The lenders were of course frightened, much like the investors ruined by the inflation and the paper money of the French Revolution. Yet fear was not the only similarity between the Law affair and the Revolution: the behavior of borrowers and lenders and their widely differing expectations about how and when the Law affair would end—these all had parallels after 1789.

But there were also some striking differences between the two crises. The losses during the Law affair were large, but they pale by comparison with the reverses of the Revolution. Having suffered less damage, lenders were not so timid about returning to the credit market in the aftermath of the Law affair, and when they did, the market revived and flourished until the end of the eighteenth century. Traditionally, of course, the Law affair is held to have blocked financial growth in France, by ruling out the sort of banking system that existed in England. But it actually ushered in a long period of expansion and financial innovation in the Parisian credit market. One reason was that it allowed the notaries to take on the role as loan brokers—a role that they would exploit with great success later in the eighteenth century.

CHAPTER FIVE

An Explosion of Private Borrowing, 1726–89

FROM THE ABYSS of the Law affair, private indebtedness began an unparalleled ascent. Although private credit did not reach its former level for over a decade, it rose inexorably, climbing without interruption until 1789 (figures 2.4 and 2.5). Such unchecked growth was unknown in the past, and it cannot simply be dismissed as the result of inflation or of population growth. To begin with, the private indebtedness sketched in figures 2.4 and 2.5 is already calculated in livres of constant silver value. Converting it to bushels of wheat traces out the same incline, and so does per capita indebtedness, whether in wheat or livres of constant silver value (figure 5.1).

By the eve of the French Revolution, lenders were thus making more private loans than they had ever done in the past. Their achievement is all the more striking when we take into account the relative size of Paris and the embryonic state of the French economy. After all, the level of private indebtedness attained in 1789 was not surpassed for eighty years, and by that time the economy was much bigger, and Paris had nearly twice the population. That so much capital was mobilized in 1789 was hardly what one would expect of the Old-Regime economy.

These loans, it should be stressed, represented nearly all the medium- and long-term private credit in Paris: it was not as if the surge of lending in the notarial registers simply replaced unnotarized credit—from bankers and merchants, for example, or informal advances by family members. True, banks and merchants did make loans to private parties, usually without recourse to a notary. Until the last half of the nineteenth century, though, such credit was only extended for short durations—typically, the several months needed to finance trade. Friends and relations also advanced money, but if large sums were involved, they too (like all lenders) had compelling legal reasons to draw up the sort of notarized loan contracts that our curve takes into account. In all likelihood, then, figures 2.4 and 2.5 really do capture the bulk of long-term private lending.

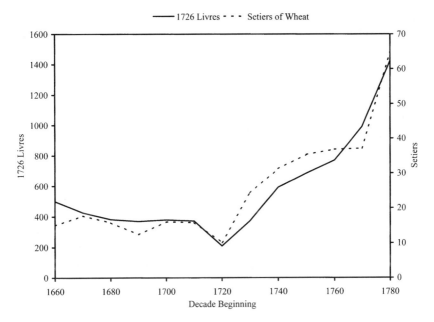

FIGURE 5.1 Private Per Capita Indebtedness in Paris by Decade in 1726 Livres and Setiers of Wheat. For the calculations, the indebtedness figures are averaged by decade. The wheat prices come from Baulant 1968, with corrections explained in Hoffman 1996:337–38. One setier equals 1.56 hectoliters of wheat, which weighed roughly 240 pounds.

How can we explain the thriving Parisian credit market? Was it a decline in government borrowing after Louis XIV's disastrous wars that freed savings for private loans? Was it the expansion of the economy in the eighteenth century? Or was it the stability of the French currency after 1726, which preserved lenders from the sort of devaluation that had wreaked such havoc in the Law era and before? Each of these three hypotheses seems promising, but as we show below, they cannot explain the rise of private lending in the eighteenth century. Obviously, another cause must have been at work. In part, it was new credit instruments. Yet it was also new financial intermediaries—the notaries themselves, who began to arrange loans on a large scale.

The Supply of Funds and the Effect of Government Borrowing on the Private Market

To understand why credit flourished in eighteenth-century Paris, let us return to the two indicators of private loan demand invoked in chapter

3: the number of marriages in Paris, and the return on assets like farm land, government offices, and Paris real estate. Both indicators rise after the 1730s, suggesting that the demand for loans was climbing (figure 3.1). The available evidence points to a burgeoning supply of credit as well. If the supply had not grown, interest rates would presumably have mounted, and lenders would have shunned private rentes with their interest rate cap. Ultimately, rentes would have disappeared as lenders shifted to obligations, where there was no interest rate cap. Now it is true that from the 1760s on Paris did witness a jump in the volume of obligations. But the volume of new rentes expanded as well, at least until 1780 (figure 2.3). Furthermore, many lenders continued to agree to rentes at rates below the interest rate cap, something they would not have done had interest rates been on the rise. That was true in every decade from the 1740s through the 1770s, except one—the 1760s, when, as we shall see, the government frightened lenders by temporarily reducing the interest rate cap from 5 to 4 percent. Once that disquieting episode was over, lenders set a post-Law record for the volume of new rentes, many of them agreed upon at rates below 5 percent (table 5.1). Only in the 1780s did new rentes—and particularly ones below 5 percent—subside.

Other interest rates were also stable in the late eighteenth century, yet another sign that the supply of credit was expanding. Short-term rates have been collected by Thomas Luckett from newspaper accounts of the market for bills of exchange. Although his series vary a great deal, they show no upward trend between 1740 and the 1780s.[1] Furthermore, all of these interest rate data—both from the rentes and Luckett's short-term loans—are nominal. Real interest rates were actually falling because of price inflation in the late eighteenth century.[2] With real interest rates dropping and loan demand on the rise, the supply of credit must have been growing.

Where did the supply of new funds come from? One possible explanation is a decline in government borrowing, which at least theoretically could have released funds for private borrowing. One bit of evidence supporting such an argument is the drop in the real value of total government debt between 1715 and 1789. Measured in livres of constant silver value, the state's total debt fell some 10 percent between 1715 and 1789 (table 5.2). Also in favor of the argument is the diminishing volume of

---

1. Luckett 1992. A graph of Luckett's interest rate suggests that the interest rate was only oscillating about 5 percent throughout the period; regressions of his interest rate figures on a time trend lead to similar results.

2. Labrousse 1933; Baulant 1968; and Riley 1986:7–13.

TABLE 5.1   INTEREST RATE ON PRIVATE RENTES PERPÉTUELLES, 1730–89

Years	Number of Loans	Mean Interest Rate	Percentage of the Number of Loans and Total Loan Volumes at Interest Rates of					
			4.9 Percent or Less		Between 4.9 and 5.1		5.1 Percent or More	
			Number	Volume	Number	Volume	Number	Volume
1730–39	48	4.98	2	3.2	98	96.8	0	0
1740–49	267	4.84	20	45	80	55	0	0
1750–59	310	4.92	10	27	89	72.9	1	0.1
1760–69	80	4.98	2.5	4.4	96	94.5	2.5	1.1
1770–79	40	4.74	25	38.3	75	61.7	0	0
1780–89	134	4.98	2.2	3.4	97	96.6	0	0

Source: Reprinted by permission, from Hoffman, Postel-Vinay, and Rosenthal 1992, table 4, which is derived from detailed samples of private rente contracts.
Note: The mean interest rate is an unweighted average. The data suffer from one deficiency: for the 1760s our sample does not include loans negotiated after 1765, so the reported interest rates do not show the effect of the 1766 reduction in the legal ceiling to four percent. Similarly, because our sample for the 1770s was drawn from 1770–71, it does not reflect properly the return of the legal ceiling to five percent in early 1771.

TABLE 5.2   TOTAL GOVERNMENT DEBT, 1715 AND 1789

Type of Debt	1715 (nominal)	1789 (nominal)	1789/1715 (both in 1726 livres)
Short term (millions of livres)	919	322.3	0.23
Long term (millions of livres)	2,000	3,775.5	1.23
Rentes viagères as a percentage of long-term debt	1	31	
Percentage of long-term debt for which Bourse price quoted in newspapers	0	18	
Offices (millions of livres)	542	735.9	0.88
Total debt (millions of livres)	3,641	4,833.7	0.91
Long term as a percentage of total debt	58	78	

Source: Lüthy 1959–61, 1:279–80, 422; Marion 1927–31, 1:63–64; Véron de Forbonnais 1758b, 5: 235, 258; Doyle 1996: 51; Sargent and Velde 1995, especially table 1; and Velde and Weir 1991. Note: All the amounts above are approximate. The numbers from 1715 are taken from Lüthy, who gives the same numbers as Marion except for the long-term debt, which Marion estimates at 1.2 billion. Both Marion and Lüthy acknowledge the uncertainties involved, but evidence from Forbonnais suggests that Lüthy's estimate is probably closer to reality. One reason for the difference in long-term debt is the problem of double counting the *augmentations de gages*, which should appear under offices but sometimes end up under long-term debt. Doyle supports the 1715 figure for offices given here and suggests that additional augmentations are in fact included in the category of long-term debt in 1715. The same problem reoccurs with the amounts for 1789, which come from Sargent and Velde. They actually publish a slightly different estimate of total debt reported in November 1789, whereas most of their figures for types of debt date from May. The most uncertain number in the entire table is that given in 1789 for the fraction of the long-term debt for which prices were quoted in newspaper accounts of trading on the Paris Bourse. That the fraction is zero in 1715 is clear, but the percentage for 1789 is only a rough estimate based on information in Velde and Weir.

new government rentes that Parisian notaries recorded. In livres of constant silver value, annual sales of new state rentes slipped from an average of 67 million a year in 1660–1725 to 43 million a year in 1726–89. Was it the 24-million-a-year difference that invigorated private borrowing?

The answer is no. In the first place, the government's retreat from long-term borrowing hardly coincided with the revival of the private market (figure 5.2). The same conclusion emerges even more strongly from the crowding-out regression in chapter 3. There we regressed the volume of new private loans on warfare and new government loans in order to determine whether government borrowing crowded out private credit in the seventeenth century (table 3.2, regression for 1660–1725). We deduced that crowding out was minimal: even Louis XIV's gargantuan appetite for loans did not depress the private credit market. But if his borrowing did not weaken private credit in the seventeenth century, then reduced borrowing by his successors was unlikely to have revived it a century later.

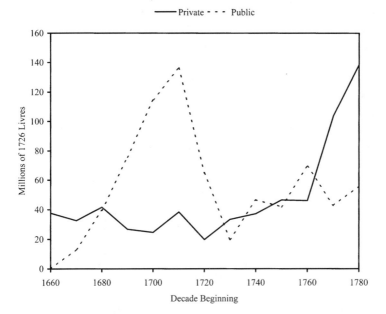

FIGURE 5.2 Decennial Averages of the Annual Volume of New Public and Private Loans

The regression discussed in chapter 3 covered the years 1660–1725, but we can repeat it for 1726–89 and for the entire period from 1660 to the end of the Old Regime (table 3.2). Whatever years are chosen, crowding out is too small to explain the rise of private indebtedness after the Law affair. In the table, all the regressions take into consideration the government's borrowing over a range of years, because investors may have withdrawn from the private market in anticipation of a government loan or, alternatively, abandoned private lending after a government issue had been sold. The coefficients of government borrowing then measure the impact that government loans have on private credit—in other words, how much each livre advanced to the government drew away from the private credit market. For crowding out to be sizable, the coefficients of government borrowing must be negative and large in absolute value. They must also be statistically significant, for otherwise they could just be chance results. Moreover, the same must hold for their sum, which gauges the total cumulative effect of government borrowing. It too must be negative, large in absolute value, and statistically significant.

The coefficients never turn out that way. In all three regressions, the coefficients of government borrowing are frequently positive. They never fulfill all three criteria of being negative, statistically significant, and large in absolute value. Of all three regressions, the one that yields the largest crowding out is the one for the years 1726–89 (table 3.2). Even in that regression, the cumulative effect of government borrowing is minuscule. The sum of the coefficients is −0.07, suggesting that every one hundred livres of government debt cut private lending by a total of only seven livres. At that rate, the decline in government borrowing could explain less than 6 percent of the increase in annual private loan volumes after 1726. In the other regressions, crowding out is even weaker, and in none of them can we rule out the hypothesis that it is actually zero.[3]

There are several reasons why crowding out was so small. To begin with, the supply of savings in Paris must have always been plentiful, even in the seventeenth century.[4] The government itself, though it borrowed a lot, could simply not absorb it all, even in the short run. Savers were always there with money to invest, and some of them might conceivably possess enough cash to add both public and private loans to their portfolios at the same time. After all, both the public and the private loans might be attractive: both, for instance, might be perpetual rentes, and holding both might help investors diversify their portfolios. If such behavior were common, it would be a second explanation for the low crowding out.

The final reason for the minimal crowding out comes from the very nature of government borrowing in the late seventeenth and early eigh-

3. Deciding whether crowding out is zero amounts to testing the hypothesis that the coefficients of government borrowing sum to zero. In none of the regressions in table 3.2 can we come close to rejecting this hypothesis, even at the 25 percent level. One could of course raise questions about the regressions. One worry might be autocorrelation, but tests on the residuals suggested that it was not a problem. A second concern might be the possible endogeneity of the government's decision to borrow: in making its decision, the government was perhaps influenced by the very economic variables that determined private lending. But early modern governments usually decided to float loans more for reasons of foreign policy than because conditions in the credit market were favorable. Treating government borrowing as exogenous therefore seems reasonable. Furthermore, we can reestimate the regression with British military expenditure as an instrument for French government borrowing. Once again, we cannot reject the hypothesis that crowding out is zero. Finally, the regressions might underestimate actual crowding out, because some of the government loans were made by lenders from provinces and abroad. They would probably not have switched to making private loans in Paris if the government stopped borrowing, and their government loans should therefore not be counted as part of the explanatory variable in the regressions. A reasonable estimate suggests, however, that the amount of the underestimate is very small.

4. In the very short run the available investment funds were cash, but even in the short run individuals could forego consumption to make investments. That was true in particular for the rich, who where numerous in Paris.

teenth centuries. Many of the government's loans in those years actually represented the consolidation or liquidation of older debt, particularly short-term loans. When writing down such debts, the monarchy gave its creditors new rentes in exchange for their claims. With little or no cash changing hands, creditors were not advancing new funds to the government, and because older debts were retired, the state's net indebtedness did not rise. Indeed, it often fell because the new rentes usually represented only a portion of the older debt that was cancelled. Such a process brought the Law affair to a close, and the Law affair was hardly unique in this regard.[5] It is no surprise then that the notarial registers could burst with new government rentes, even though the private market remained by and large unaffected. Many of the new rentes simply transformed one kind of government debt into another and did not siphon money away from private credit.

Although this practice persisted after the Law affair, government borrowing did begin to change in a way that deserves a digression, for it makes the revival of private credit in the eighteenth century even more remarkable. The government did continue to use rentes to consolidate short-term debt—particularly after wars, when short-term debt mounted—but increasingly the rentes also served as an independent source of funds that could be tapped to fund warfare directly, once the fighting began and not just after the war was over (figure 3.2). The visual evidence that the government was beginning to issue long-term loans during wars (and not just afterwards) is confirmed by a regression of the volume of long-term government borrowing on dummy variables for warfare (table 5.3). Warfare enters the regressions both for the years the loans are floated and for the preceding year, and the coefficients measure the increase in long-term government borrowing in years of war. If the government was raising money via long-term loans during war (rather than simply using them to consolidate short-term war debt after the fighting was over), then the regression coefficients for warfare should be positive and significant and should sum to a number greater than zero.

When we run the regression for the years 1660–1725, the war coefficients actually sum to a negative number. None of them is in fact significant, and given the weakness of the relationship, we cannot reject the hypothesis that the sum is in fact zero.[6] In short, before 1725, there is no clear evidence that long-term government loans were being floated while wars were actually being fought.

5. Marion 1927, 1:107–12; Dutot 1935, 2:198–99; Véron de Forbonnais 1758a; Shakespeare 1986.

6. A test of the hypothesis that the sum of the war coefficients is zero yields a T-statistic of 0.94 with 62 degrees of freedom.

TABLE 5.3　　WARFARE AND THE ANNUAL VOLUME OF GOVERNMENT LOANS:
REGRESSIONS FOR 1600–1725 AND 1726–89

Independent Variables	1660–1725	1726–89
Constant	79.96	26.78
	(3.91)	(3.02)
Dummy variable: 1 if there is a war in the year in question, 0 otherwise	−33.51	8.22
	(−0.96)	(0.68)
Dummy variable: 1 if there is a war in the preceding year, 0 otherwise	6.12	29.70
	(0.18)	(2.47)
Number of observations	65	64
R-squared	.05	0.34
Standard error	100.99	31.59
Rho (for autocorrelation correction)	0.16	0.44
Mean of dependent variable	68.09	43.47

Source: As in table 3.2.
Note: The regressions were estimated using a two-stage GLS procedure to correct for first-order autocorrelation of the errors. Estimation via OLS led to similar results, and analysis of the residuals suggested that more complicated autocorrelation was not a problem. The dependent variable is the annual volume of new government loans in millions of 1726 livres.

After 1725, the results are different. Both coefficients are now positive, and at least for war in the preceding year, the coefficient is estimated with enough accuracy so that the positive sign is not likely to be a chance result (table 5.3). What the coefficients suggest is that the onset of war raised the monarchy's long-term borrowing one year later by 69 percent over the usual levels in Paris. From the same regression, the cumulative effect of war over two years was an 87 percent increase in the crown's long-term borrowing in Paris, and that figure too is not likely to be due to chance.[7]

The government, then, had begun to use long-term loans not just to sop up the short-term debt that it continued to run up during wars but to raise money directly for fighting. It did so within a year or so after the soldiers marched off to battle—probably to supplement the ordinary sources of short-term loans once they came under strain. For the government, the advantages of the long-term market were clear. It offered an additional supply of funds from savers who might not be willing to lend short term, and it came at a time when need for the money was most

7. The cumulative effect of warfare is calculated by summing the two coefficients of war in the regression. A test of the hypothesis that this sum is zero yields a T-statistic of 2.81 with 61 degrees of freedom. We experimented with different lags and with other variables (a dummy variable for the end of war, for example), but the only variable that really mattered was warfare with a one year lag.

pressing—while the fighting was under way. In addition, the debt management might be less burdensome, for at the very least the loan could be spread out over a number of years. It is no surprise then that long-term debt gained in importance in the government's borrowing after 1725, particularly after the repeated military conflicts in eighteenth-century Europe. We can see as much by comparing the composition of government debt in 1715 and 1789. Although total government debt as a whole declined nearly 10 percent in real terms between 1715 and 1789, long-term debt actually rose at the expense of borrowing via short-term loans and the sale of offices (table 5.2).

Long-term government borrowing thus grew in importance as a direct source of funds; less and less of it simply went to consolidate short-term loans. But that only makes the expansion of private notarial credit all the more astonishing, for at the same time that private indebtedness was skyrocketing, long-term public debt was rising too. Its ascent was not as dizzying, but it was climbing nonetheless. Somehow, the Parisian credit market not only managed to fund millions of livres a year in private long-term loans, but millions a year in public loans as well. And in contrast to the past, these public loans no longer simply reshuffled other forms of public debt.

Prosperity and Currency Stability

If crowding out cannot explain the explosion of private credit, perhaps the thriving eighteenth-century economy can. Prosperity might have pushed more individuals to borrow, while rising incomes provided more savings to loan. At the same time, the halt to monetary manipulations after 1726 might have convinced lenders that they would not see their profits eroded or fall victim to another Law affair. Reassured by the stability of the currency, they would resume making loans. They would even return to rentes, which offered no protection against devaluation.

We already have strong evidence that prosperity buoyed up the credit market, and somewhat weaker evidence that monetary manipulations and price variations drove it down. The evidence comes from the regression of the volume of private loans discussed in chapter 3 (table 3.3). This regression does not run to the end of the eighteenth century, but it does at least go as far as 1770. Included among its explanatory variables are the annual number of Parisian apprenticeships (to gauge the state of the local economy) and the coefficient of variation of nominal wheat prices (to measure risks to lenders from currency manipulation and fluctuating prices). The number of annual apprenticeships did rise after

1726, a sign of economic recovery. At the same time, variations in wheat prices subsided. Those changes are enough to explain slightly over half of the rise in private credit volumes between 1660–1725 and 1726–70, according to table 3.3.[8]

That leaves nearly half the increase through 1770 unexplained. To account for this unexplained residual, one might try making the most out of the small amount of crowding out that we uncovered. If crowding out were not zero but seven livres for every one hundred the government borrowed—the maximal rate in all of our crowding-out regressions— then the unexplained growth of lending would almost be accounted for, at least up until 1770.[9]

The trouble, of course, is that all the other regressions in the two tables point to less crowding out. And as we have already shown, we can not reject the hypothesis that crowding out was in fact zero, even with the regression that yields the figure of seven livres for every one hundred the government borrowed. Finally, even if we were to make the implausible assumption that crowding out were that high, it could only explain the residual up to 1770. After that date, it would utterly fail to do so. Public borrowing, after all, remained relatively stable after 1770 (figures 2.6 and 5.2). It simply did not fall enough to explain the sudden jump in private credit after 1770 (figures 2.3 and 5.2), even if crowding out were seven livres for every one hundred the government borrowed.[10]

It is equally unlikely that the post-1770 boom in private lending derived from further economic growth and the continued stability of the French currency. Unfortunately, legal changes cut short our apprenticeship series in the 1770s, so we lose our measure of the state of the economy. That is why the regression in table 3.3 stops in 1770. That is also why we did not push beyond the period 1726–70 when we calculated

8. Average private loan volume climbed 24 percent between 1660–1725 and 1726– 1770, while the mean logarithm of private loan volumes—the dependent variable in table 3.3—rises by 0.25 between the same two periods. As for the change in the explanatory variables in the table over the same two periods, the logarithm of apprenticeships increases 0.31, war moves up by 0.005, and the coefficient of variation of wheat declines by 0.10. Together, these changes would add 0.14 to the logarithm of private loan volumes, which is just over half the 0.25 increase between 1660–1725 and 1726–70.

9. If we use the regression with the highest crowding out—the 1726–89 regression in table 3.2—then the change in public borrowing between 1660–1725 and 1726–70 predicts that private loan volumes will rise 1.8 million livres a year, or about 25 percent of their actual increase between 1660–1725 and 1726–70.

10. If we look past 1770 and consider the growth in private loan volumes between 1660–1725 and 1726–89, then crowding out cannot even account for 6 percent of the increase in private lending, even at the maximal rate of seven livres of crowding per every one hundred the government borrowed.

the effect of economic growth and currency stability. But we can at least try to carry the calculations beyond the year 1770. We have a reasonable substitute for the missing apprenticeships—namely, the asset incomes in figure 3.1. Apprenticeships and incomes were correlated before 1770.[11] If we use the income numbers to extend the apprenticeships into the 1770s and 1780s, we then can estimate how much lending was due to a thriving economy and a stable currency over the longer period 1726–89, and not simply bring our calculations to a halt in 1770. If we do so, then prosperity and a stable currency turn out to explain only about a third of the growth in private lending between 1660–1725 and 1726–89. They thus account for even less of the increase than was the case with the shorter period 1726–70. Furthermore, even if we were to add crowding out at the maximal rate of seven livres per one hundred borrowed, over half the total rise in private credit over the years 1726–89 would still remain a mystery.[12]

One might have qualms about extending the calculations past 1770, but the conclusions are supported by other evidence. In the late eighteenth century, private indebtedness rose dramatically relative to figures we have for the city's income, all of which would be hard to explain if economic prosperity and higher incomes alone were driving up increased indebtedness.[13] Per capita debt service also climbed sharply rela-

11. The asset incomes (in 1726 livres) are decennial averages. The correlation between their logarithm and the logarithm of the decennial average of annual apprenticeships is 0.54 ($n = 12$). The correlation between the absolute numbers is the same. Both the incomes and the apprenticeships trace out a similar path over time, and correlation between them is stronger than that between apprenticeships and variables like marriages.

12. The logarithm of private credit volumes jumps by 0.59 between 1660–1725 and 1726–89. If we apply the coefficients in table 3.3 to the actual changes in warfare and the variability of wheat prices and the estimated change in the logarithm of apprenticeships over the same two periods, we can explain an increase in the logarithm of private lending of only 0.20. Crowding out at seven livres per one hundred borrowed would add perhaps another 0.06, leaving over half the increase unaccounted for. We estimated the change in the logarithm of apprenticeships by taking decennial averages for the annual number of apprenticeships and then regressing the logarithm of this decennial average on the logarithm of annual income per decade. We then multiplied the regression coefficient times the change in the logarithm of incomes between 1726–70 and 1726–89 and assumed that the result would tell us how much the logarithm of apprenticeships increased between 1726–70 and 1726–89.

13. The asset income shown in figure 3.1 actually projects back Lavoisier's estimates (1864, 6:403–513) for Paris income. If we take the portion of total private indebtedness furnished by Parisian lenders (say between 66 and 91 percent according to table 7.6) and divide it by Lavoisier's income estimates, we get a ratio that is about one for most of the seventeenth and early eighteenth century. It drops below one in the 1720s and then rises, reaching an unparalleled three by the 1780s. Changing interest rates cannot explain the increase.

tive to wages, from perhaps under 30 percent of the annual unskilled wage in the years 1660–1720 to nearly 100 percent of unskilled earnings in the 1780s. Such results may seem surprising, but it was of course not unskilled laborers who were borrowing in Old-Regime Paris. Rather it was the city's numerous merchants, officers, and nobles, who earned far more than laborers.[14] They were the ones borrowing, typically from wealthy, older members of the same social classes.

In the end, all these calculations may actually underestimate how much of the growth in private lending remains unexplained. The reason is that the regression in table 3.3 probably exaggerates the role that a stable currency played in stimulating the private credit market. The regressions suggest that currency stability alone was responsible for perhaps a tenth of the increase in private credit between 1660–1725 and 1726–89. It is true that the French livre was stabilized in 1726 and that its silver value remained constant up until the Revolution. It is not clear, though, whether people at the time realized that currency manipulations were over. French monarchs had fiddled with the coinage repeatedly ever since the Middle Ages. Although they relented periodically, the respites never survived the monarchy's repeated fiscal crises. As far as lenders in the eighteenth century knew, devaluations might soon be raining down on their heads again. True, lenders might assume that the government remembered the devastation wrought by monetary instability during the Law affair. They might also expect the government to be influenced by perceptive denunciations of currency manipulation that were published during the eighteenth century. But currency manipulation had been decried by writers and by the populace ever since the Middle Ages, and the outcry had never stopped kings throughout Europe from resorting to it. In France, devaluation still had its advocates— from memorialists like the Marquis d'Argenson to philosophes like Montesquieu and Voltaire—and rumors of impending devaluations were still circulating as late as 1751.[15]

Even the edict that set the value of the livre in 1726 announced addi-

14. The calculations assume that 25 percent of the Parisian population worked two hundred days a year, earning the unskilled wage. They also suppose debt service at 5 percent on 89 percent of total indebtedness. Here 89 percent is the fraction of private debt in our samples that was taken out by Parisian borrowers in the years 1770–89; the percentage for other periods was similar. For further details, see table 7.6.

15. Marion 1927, 1:140–41; Picard 1912:343–67; Bloch 1953:145–58, 433–56. For rumors of revaluation in 1738 and 1751 and d'Argenson's opinions in favor of devaluation, see Barbier 1885, 5:8; and Voyer de Paulmy, Marquis d'Argenson 1859, 1:341–46; 3:434–35. For Parlementary attacks on the currency manipulation in 1718, see H. Carré 1911:10-17; and Flammermont 1888-98, 1:68–107.

tional changes in its value six months later. The additional manipulations were put off repeatedly for only six months at a time until 1738,
when the value of the livre was finally fixed for good. Yet who knew
whether the monarchy would not resume tampering with the coinage?
Both Louis XIV and the regent had broken promises not to manipulate
the value of the livre. Other monarchs could do the same. To suppose
then, as the regressions in effect do, that momentarily stable prices
would mean no devaluations in the future is to assume that the actors
in the eighteenth century could foresee what we know only now: the
monetary history of the rest of the Old Regime. How could a lender in,
say, 1751 know the currency would remain stable? How could he be
confident that the value of his investments would not be affected by price
volatility in the future? To avoid such anachronism, it might be better
to remove price variability from the regressions altogether. But in that
case, we can explain even less of the rise in private lending in eighteenth-
century Paris.

New Instruments and Intermediaries

What then was responsible for the half or more of the increase in private
lending that remains unaccounted for? In part it was a new credit instrument, the obligation, which allowed lenders to cut short loans menaced
by currency devaluation or price inflation. As we know, obligations were
initially short-term loans. If the lender felt threatened by prices and currency manipulations, he could simply refuse to renew the obligation,
and he would get his capital back. He could also evade the legal ceiling
on interest rates with an obligation. None of that was possible with a
rente.

Obligations had of course existed for centuries; there was no legal
change that suddenly put them at the disposal of lenders and borrowers.
But they became much more common after 1766, when the government
briefly cut the interest rate ceiling to 4 percent on private loans. The
lower ceiling was part of an attempt to cope with the grave fiscal problems engendered by the Seven Years War, which had driven the crown
to tax the interest paid on government rentes. The tax naturally drove
lenders into the private market, and to lure them back the government
tried to make its own debt more appealing by limiting the interest rate
that could be charged on private loans. Although the supply of private
rentes fell, lenders were no more willing to lend to the state, and by
1770 the government was forced to return to the 5 percent limit. In the
interim, however, many lenders switched to obligations, which circum-

vented the ceiling.[16] Lenders came to appreciate the flexibility that obligations offered and grew accustomed to them, even though the loans required more follow-up and monitoring than rentes. Obligations lasted a much shorter time than perpetual or life annuities. Using an obligation to fund a loan of the same duration as an annuity would therefore require a series of renewals, all of which would involve follow-up. In particular, the lender would want to reevaluate the borrower's creditworthiness at each renewal, and that is monitoring. By the 1780s, notaries had reduced the cost of monitoring, and lenders were forsaking rentes for obligations, which became the contract of choice for new loans (figure 2.3).

The rise of the obligation was paralleled in the public market by the ascent of the rente viagère, the fastest growing type of government debt in the eighteenth century (table 5.2). Viagères (life annuities) too had a long history in both private and public borrowing, but they became the monarchy's loan of choice in the late eighteenth century (figure 2.6).[17] Demand was strong, particularly among investors without children. Rather than making bequests to heirs, they preferred the secure retirement that a life annuity afforded. But who sold them the new viagères? One can ask the same question of the obligations, for like the viagères, the obligation was a legal instrument that had long existed and yet did not gain favor until the late eighteenth century. Who convinced lenders to switch to obligations? Who helped them to monitor the loans? And who reconciled borrowers to obligations, which, unlike rentes, might be cancelled, leaving a borrower squeezed for cash?

The answer, in large part, was the Parisian notaries, the very people who drew up the loan contracts. As the next chapter will show, the notaries were not just scribes and record keepers but important brokers of loans. Of course, we should take care not to exaggerate their role, at least in the public market, for there they did have considerable help. To begin with, bankers sold many of the government's viagère loans, particularly to foreigners. The Swiss bankers who marketed Necker's viagère loans in Geneva are perhaps the best-known example.[18]

16. Marion 1927, 1:239–40; Le Goff, 1997:178–85; idem 1996; Guyot 1784, s.v. "intérêts"; Hoffman, Postel-Vinay, and Rosenthal 1992.

17. Velde and Weir 1991, 1992; Lüthy 1959, vol. 2; Roche 1981; Riley 1986; White 1989.

18. The Swiss bankers did employ Parisian notaries to draw up the necessary contracts, but in such transactions the notaries were limited to being scribes and record keepers. The key innovation of the bankers was to pool viagères contingent on the lives of thirty healthy young Genevan women; they would then sell shares in the pooled asset, which offered high returns and low risk. See Lüthy (1959, 2:464–591) for details, particularly about the Genevan bankers, but also about bankers in London and Amsterdam; see also Velde and Weir 1992; White 1989; and Riley 1986.

The sale of government loans was also facilitated by legal changes that, from the late 1740s on, made it easier to trade certain types of state debt on the Paris stock exchange. The initial sale of such a government loan might pass through a notary, but thereafter the loan could be traded by individuals or on a secondary market without having the notary draw up an expensive transfer contract. The effect was to make the debt easier to sell and thus more attractive to investors (table 5.2). And at the same time, the government even began to sell some of its debt directly, without using notarial contracts even for the initial sale.[19]

Yet for all the legal changes and accomplishments of the bankers, the Parisian notaries still had an enormous part to play in marketing the monarchy's debt. Even for the viagère loans in which banks were deeply involved, half or more of the funds lent probably still passed through the notaries' hands. And for the government's long-term debt as a whole, Parisian notaries still must have made the initial sales of at least half or two-thirds of the funds raised.[20]

Contemporaries certainly recognized how important Parisian notaries were to marketing the state's long-term debt. In 1742, for example, an official of the Estates of Burgundy was seeking to raise money in Paris for an important kind of long-term government loan—the debt issued by provinces. In his view, Parisian notaries were essential to any such undertaking. They were, he said, the "holders of the purse strings," and the "information gatherers for lenders," who determined where investors placed their money.[21] The same held for the long-term private mar-

19. Initially, most of the loans that could be traded without a notarized *transport* were term loans or lotteries, but eventually certain other loans became transferable too. For the importance of this change, Le Goff (1996:16–18) is essential. See also Martin 1789; Velde and Weir 1992; and Vührer 1886, 1:207–209.

20. For one viagère for which detailed documentation survives (December 1783), Lüthy (1959, 2:532–38) finds that 44 percent of the loan was placed via bankers who were engaged in the telltale practice of pooling viagères contingent on young women. In our detailed samples of government loans from 1770–89—a period when viagères were popular—only 18 percent of the loan funds came from foreigners; another 19 percent came from outside Paris (table 7.6). Notaries did have a hand in some of the sales of government debt outside Paris and some foreign sales as well, but let us nonetheless assume that all loans by foreigners were arranged by bankers and that all of the money from outside Paris was put together by someone other than the Parisian notaries. If so, and if the same percentages apply to all of the government's long-term loans in the late eighteenth century, then 63 percent of the money raised was still likely to enter via Parisian notaries.

21. AD Côte d'Or C4565 (15 September 1742). For provincial debt, see Potter and Rosenthal 1997b. One can find similar observations from the 1730s to the 1780s. In 1734, the writer and financial official Jean François Melon noted that "les notaires négocient les contrats sur la Ville (de Paris) et sur les tailles, les agents de change les actions et les

ket. As early as the Regency a well-informed author like Forbonnais could take the Parisian notaries' domination of long-term credit for granted. By the 1780s, the popular writer Louis-Sébastien Mercier could exclaim that the notaries had become "speculators, movers of money" who sought out nothing less than "every possible way to borrow here and to lend there. They are involved in all loans of any size."[22]

What the Parisian notaries were doing was to facilitate the task facing borrowers and lenders. Bit by bit, they were releasing credit from the personal ties to which lending had been condemned by fears about collateral. From their work drafting probate records and other contracts, the Parisian notaries knew who had money to lend and who had secure collateral. They had the information needed to put borrowers and lenders together. Precisely when they began their matchmaking we cannot say, but by providing an impersonal solution to the problem of collateral, they lifted the credit market higher than it ever would have climbed on its own. They helped create a secure atmosphere for lending and they furnished new credit instruments, from obligations to viagères.

At other times and in other places, different intermediaries played a similar role, but in France it was the notaries. They had begun matching borrowers and lenders before Law, as we can see from the decline in personal connections from 1660 to 1700 (figure 3.4). But the Law affair gave them an added impetus to arrange contracts and pushed them to become the dominant brokers in long-term credit. They had survived Law and even profited by drafting thousands of acts during the frenzy of borrowing and repayment. They thus acquired further information about potential clients, and the information was all the more valuable because the Law affair had wiped out private fortunes and made it difficult to distinguish the solvent from the insolvent. As one contemporary remarked,

> The reimbursements in paper money [during the Law affair] had destroyed all financial confidence one could have in individuals, and all their credit as well. The mistrust was all the greater because no one knew anyone else's financial situation. One knew that most people were ruined, but it

billets" (quoted in Ehrenberg 1922, 2:310). Over fifty years later the author of a pamphlet on financial affairs could remark, when speaking of Parisian bankers: "C'est encore par leur entremise et celle des notaires, que s'effectuent les emprunts du gouvernement" (Martin 1789:90).

22. Véron de Forbonnais 1758a, 2:530; Mercier 1783, 2:31–35.

was impossible to tell who had had the good fortune to escape the general disaster.[23]

Notaries, though, could still tell who had money to lend and who possessed secure collateral, because they had recorded the transactions during the Law affair. They now knew more than other intermediaries—more even than the borrowers and lenders themselves, who had to rely on outmoded information. Given the notaries' advantage, it is no surprise that they matched more and more borrowers and lenders, and, as they did so, personal ties between debtors and creditors continued to decline in importance. Meanwhile, as resurgent credit came to dominate the notaries' activity, the value of their own businesses rose (figure 1.1).

The change was not instantaneous: intermediation by notaries began before Law. It also took time for the economy to recover after the ravages of warfare in the late seventeenth and early eighteenth centuries. It took time as well for private lenders to shed their fears of currency manipulation and other attacks by the crown. And it took time for notaries to hone their skills in the private credit market and learn how to peddle the new obligations. But as they did, the credit market took off. Perhaps as much as half the subsequent growth in private lending stemmed from the economic recovery and the reduced threat of currency manipulation. The rest resulted not from less crowding out but from the spread of the obligations and, above all else, the deals arranged by Parisian notaries.

23. Quoted in Marion 1927, 1:103. Marion does not give a precise citation here, but the author was apparently someone who had written in response to Dutot's *Réflexions politiques*—perhaps Paris-Duverney. Cf. Dutot 1935.

CHAPTER SIX

Overcoming Asymmetric Information in Financial Markets

IN THE SEVENTEENTH CENTURY, borrowers and lenders used personal connections to cope with the problems that bedevil credit markets. Borrowers sought out parties with funds to lend in their neighborhoods, in their families, or in their professions. Lenders found creditworthy borrowers in much the same way, by exploiting information gleaned from social or occupational contacts. Gathering such information anywhere else was a daunting task. The difficulty—what economists usually call the problem of asymmetric information—is in fact inevitable in credit markets and in any market where buyers cannot easily ascertain what they are purchasing. Personal connections provide one means of surmounting the problem, but in modern financial markets, there are usually brokers or intermediaries such as bankers and venture capitalists who help arrange transactions for borrowers and lenders and furnish them with accurate information about investment opportunities. Some of these particular intermediaries may be relatively new, but the phenomenon itself is ancient. Indeed, many European cities have long been able to boast of intermediaries who matched borrowers and lenders and put together financial transactions.

In eighteenth-century Paris, it was notaries who took on this role. As they did—and it was a gradual process—personal ties between borrowers and lenders declined in importance. The notaries served as brokers, not investment bankers: they did not pool lenders' funds or manage a portfolio of loans. Nonetheless, we know that they mobilized a huge amount of capital. Precisely how they operated is the subject of this chapter.

The trouble for a notary (or for any broker) was that his duties gave him ample opportunity to mistreat his clients for his own personal gain. In going about his business he naturally acquired much confidential information about his clients' dealings in the credit market and other asset markets. He knew, for example, whether they had cash to lend, whether they had recently sold property, or whether they were teetering on the edge of bankruptcy. Other notaries, however, would not know their rival's clients so well and so would be reluctant to take them into their business. But their reluctance would then make it difficult for the clients to leave their original notary if he failed to serve them well. And because the original notary would no doubt realize his clients' dilemma, he could easily take advantage of them by failing to exert himself on their behalf. He could take advantage of lenders, for example, by holding their money and waiting for borrowers from his own étude even though he knew that other notaries probably had ready reliable borrowers available—thereby costing lenders foregone interest. Similarly, the notary could take advantage of borrowers—for instance, by waiting for lenders from his own étude to materialize and thereby delaying investment projects. What the notary gained in each case was that he did not have to exert himself to find suitable matches outside of his étude. More generally, the notary had better information than his clients, and that gave him an opportunity to profit at the expense of his clients by keeping his knowledge to himself.

If the notary took advantage of his clients, why could they not simply change études? For borrowers, the problem was that other notaries knew nothing of their affairs, collateral, and credit histories. Other notaries were therefore unlikely to deem them creditworthy. For lenders, the problem was that they would have to convey to the other notary all the information relevant to making an investment. It was not simply enough to show up with 10,000 livres; the notary had to know what sort of loan would fit the lenders' investment goals—something they themselves might not know. In general, clients who deserted their notary would pay high costs to convey information to another notary. For that reason, they risked being "locked in"—tied to their notaries in the jargon of economics.

One might doubt whether such conspiratorial reasoning could apply to the world of early modern Paris, but decent service from a notary involved far more than just drafting legal contracts. It depended, as one notary put it, on "the effort and care" with which he sought out appropriate matches for his clients—finding a creditworthy borrower for a lender, or matching up an entrepreneur with an investor. Dishonest notaries could—and did—take advantage of their clients.[1] The notaries would only succeed as intermediaries if the lock-in problem were resolved.

1. AN Y 18581, bankruptcy of notary Hurtrelle, 17 June 1756.

Here we shall explain how the notaries overcame this obstacle in eighteenth-century Paris. We argue that the solution lay in providing clients with a second notary to whom they could turn for help. The presence of this second notary would induce most notaries to serve their clients well. It would amount to what economists call "second sourcing of informational services," and it would ensure that notaries competed with one another.

This solution was in fact extremely important for the history of financial markets in Paris, and it illustrates how institutional innovations can improve the performance of markets. How formal and informal institutions reduce the costs of transactions is, of course, a question that has long intrigued not just economic historians but economists in general.[2]

Understanding the solution does require a new methodological tool: game theory. We must analyze how the notaries interacted with one another and their clients, and here game theory is the key to grasping the significance of their actions. Some historians may find the game theory forbidding. If so, they should glance at the next section and then jump ahead to the final part of this chapter ("Implications of our Model"), where we lay out the importance of our game theoretical model of the notaries' behavior and do so in terms that anyone can understand.

As for economists, when they inspect our model, they may wonder why we do not entertain some alternative explanations of the notaries' behavior—for example, that the notaries formed a cartel. In fact, we have considered several alternatives of this sort, but we have rejected all of them. In particular, as we have shown elsewhere,[3] we can rule out the following three hypotheses about the notaries' actions:

1. The notaries formed a cartel.
2. They specialized in certain types of contracts or clienteles.
3. They were grouped into small coalitions held together by reciprocity.

None of these hypotheses corresponds to what the notaries were doing. By contrast, our game theoretical model does fit their behavior and fits it quite well.

Like other economic historians, we use game theory here in order to see how institutions resolve market imperfections.[4] Yet we seek to push this methodology one step further by pairing the theoretical analysis of

2. North 1990; Davis and North 1971; Williamson 1975, 1985.
3. Hoffman, Postel-Vinay, and Rosenthal 1998.
4. For excellent examples of the use of game theory in economic history, see Greif 1989, 1993, 1994; and Levenstein 1991.

institutions with quantitative evidence. Doing so requires a different type of data, for the samples used so far will no longer suffice. Limiting ourselves to a sample of notaries would blind us to how they interacted with clients and referred business to one another. To view these interactions, we must follow each notary's dealings over a lengthy period so that we can see not only isolated contracts but repeated interactions with clients. Fortunately, we have an extraordinary data set at our disposal—an enumeration of nearly all the contracts drawn up by Parisian notaries in the year 1751. Thanks to this data set, we can follow all the Parisian notaries for an entire year at a time when their role as financial intermediaries was already assured.[5] With it, we first explore possible solutions to the problem of asymmetric information in the thriving long-term private credit market in mid-eighteenth-century Paris. We then formulate the game theoretic model of the notaries' and clients' actions. As is often the case in game theory, the model has multiple equilibria. (In plain English, that simply means that the game has a variety of likely outcomes, once the notaries and their clients have played the game against one another as well as they possibly can.) Fortunately, the data allow us to pick the equilibrium (in other words, the likely outcome) that characterizes the notaries' role.

This equilibrium is one that illuminates the notaries' behavior not just in the eighteenth century but in the nineteenth century as well. It was the institutional innovation that made possible the notaries' success. It involved notaries' referring clients to one another and thereby sharing precious financial information. Thanks to the referrals, clients always had another notary to whom they could turn besides the one who usually did their business, and it was therefore difficult to mistreat them, for they could easily switch to this second notary. The clients did most of their business before their usual notary, but the referrals brought a threat of competition that insured he would serve them well.

Notaries and Information

As we have seen, the notaries took on greater and greater financial duties during the course of the eighteenth century. The transformation of their

5. The data set is an enumeration, drawn up by the French Archives Nationales, of nearly all the notarial documents surviving from the year 1751: some 59,000 documents involving roughly 137,000 individuals. The year 1751 was chosen at random for the enumeration by Archives Nationales and was a normal year economically. For further description of the enumeration, see Hoffman, Postel-Vinay, and Rosenthal 1999.

role was gradual, as the letters of contemporaries demonstrate. The correspondence of Voltaire provides a perfect example of the changes. Back in the 1730s, Voltaire was still dealing with a wide variety of financial intermediaries—bankers, stewards, merchants, factors, and at least seven notaries. Angered by one of the notaries, he could even turn to a Jansenist clergyman as a business agent and ask him to "take charge of the money of someone who is not a church goer. . . . My dear Abbé, I like your safe a thousand times more than a notary's."[6] But by the middle of the century, Voltaire had a favorite notary, and he turned to him for the bulk of his financial dealings.

Many Parisians did the same. The capital's notaries had come to dominate the long-term credit market, handling a wide variety of transactions. And with no public registry of mortgages or other public source of information about borrowers or lenders, they held all the essential information about long-term lending and most other asset transactions as well. The information put them at the apex of the largest and safest financial network in the eighteenth century, leading clients to use them for a wide variety of financial transactions. The notaries not only drew up contracts and arranged the sales of assets; they also screened prospective borrowers, matched them up with prospective lenders, chose the appropriate credit instruments, and, in the case of the obligations, undoubtedly gave advice about loan renewals.

Given the different tasks involved, one might assume that the notaries (and other intermediaries as well) would have divided up the various asset markets. Yet such specialization did not develop, and, as we shall see, the notaries dealt in all long-term credit instruments and most other assets too. The reason was that they held the information needed to arrange all kinds of financial contracts. It was natural that they ended up at the center of the financial system.

One might of course argue that the notaries were in fact superfluous. There was really no need for them to match borrowers and lenders, the argument might go, for borrowers and lenders could do this themselves. We can reject this hypothesis for a number of reasons. The size and anonymity of Paris made it difficult to find trustworthy partners.[7] Moreover, many of a notary's clients were wealthy but not fully engaged in economic activities—among them were clerics, unmarried women, and many widows. These clients lacked information about appropriate investments and would be unlikely to find suitable borrowers on their own.

6. Voltaire 1953–77, 8 and 21 March 1736, letters 994 and 1,005.
7. For remarks on the anonymity of Paris, see Mercier 1783–88, 1:61–64.

Other clients might have information about borrowers but would be too busy to manage their affairs themselves. They would seek a notary's help in managing their portfolios.

Here, our data—the enumeration of all the notarial records drawn up in Paris in 1751—effectively rebut the argument that notaries did little besides drawing up documents, leaving borrowers and lenders to solve the problems of asymmetric information on their own. The logic is as follows: if notaries provided no informational services, then individuals would presumably deal repeatedly with the same partners in loans and other financial contracts in order to reduce information costs. In this scenario, a given individual would presumably interact only with the small number of partners whom he knew well, and he would keep them honest by denying them his business if they ever misbehaved.

The evidence seems to argue against a story of this sort, at least in 1751. Such repeated business with the same partners was extremely rare, particularly for loans. In fact, the probability that borrowers and lenders dealt with one another more than once was trivial. Each time that a borrower or lender engaged in a new loan, he in effect matched himself with a new partner. We can see as much by regressing the number of different lenders that borrowers used on the number of loans they took out (table 6.1). The coefficient is nearly one, a sign that each new loan meant a different lender. The addition of a quadratic term shows that the coefficient does not drop noticeably for frequent borrowers, and a regression for the number of borrowers lenders used leads to similar results.

Instead of coming back to the same lender, borrowers in Paris in 1751 returned to the same notary. Some 80 percent of all loans were drawn up before a borrower's or lender's favorite notary (table 6.2).[8] Parties in other contracts were less faithful, suggesting that when information became more important—as in credit dealings—loyalty increased. In the credit contracts, a regression shows that the number of different notaries used by borrowers rose only slightly with the number of loans they took out. The borrowers thus kept most of their business with the same notary, and a regression for lenders leads to the same conclusion (table 6.1). There was not even a tendency for large-scale borrowers and lenders to use many notaries, as they presumably would if they could convey information independently of their notaries. Furthermore, the typical client was not faithful to his notary simply because he lay close

8. We define a person's favorite notary to be the notary that he used most frequently during the year 1751.

TABLE 6.1   REGRESSION OF THE NUMBER OF ETUDES USED AND NUMBER OF PARTNERS IN
                 LOAN CONTRACTS

Dependent Variable	Number of Different Lenders (Borrowers)	Number of Different Borrowers (Lenders)	Number of Notaries Used (Borrowers)	Number of Notaries Used (Lenders)
Independent Variables:				
Constant	0.083	0.263	1.125	0.981
	(1.88)	(2.40)	(16.36)	(7.91)
Number of loans per (borrowers or lenders)	0.935	0.779	0.175	0.202
	(52.55)	(13.73)	(6.21)	(3.15)
Number of loans squared	−0.004	0.010	−0.0006	−0.002
	(−4.33)	(1.94)	(−0.41)	(−0.38)
Dummy variable for individuals appearing in more than 20 notarial contracts	—	—	−0.079	0.116
			(0.53)	(0.61)
R-squared	0.933	0.796	0.168	0.12
Number of cases	920	564	925	592

Source: See text.

Note: The regressions were run only for borrowers or lenders who appeared in two or more loans. The quadratic term (loans squared) was included to see if the number of études or partners would change for large-scale borrowers and lenders. The dummy variable for people appearing more than twenty times was added to the number of études regressions to see if individuals who appeared frequently could convey information independently of their notaries. If so, they should have used more notaries than other people, and the dummy variable's coefficient would presumably be large, positive, and statistically significant. Since it is not large and significant in either regression, the implication is that individuals did not convey information independently of their notary. *T*-statistics appear in parentheses.

One might object that the number of loans is endogenous and hence that restricting the regression to individuals who appear in more than one loan might lead to inconsistent coefficient estimates. Restricting the regression is probably more plausible, but running it for all borrowers and lenders does not change the coefficients enough to disturb our argument. The same holds if we use information on occupation and family status to estimate the regressions via instrumental variables, with one exception: the regression of the number of notaries used per lender. Even with that regression, though, the changed coefficient estimates are not statistically significant.

at hand. Indeed, there is no indication that notaries and their clients were neighbors, at least in the eighteenth century.[9] Most Parisian notaries were in fact clustered in the center of the city, within a stone's throw of one another but quite far from most of their rich clients. All of this evidence suggests—as do contemporary descriptions of notaries' activities—that notaries did serve as financial intermediaries.[10]

9. For one example, see El Hannabi 1994:292–94, 348. The clients of the notary Henri Boutet were scattered in the various parishes of the city, and "the parishes closest to Boutet's étude are not the ones that harbor most of his clientele." For a contrasting view, see Limon 1992:197; and Jurgens 1980:39.

10. See, for example, Véron de Forbonnais 1758a, 2:535; Mercier 1783–88, 2:31–32; AN Y 9529 (11 April 1777); AD Côte d'Or C4565 (15 September 1742).

TABLE 6.2　　　LOYALTY RATE BY TYPE OF CONTRACT

Number of Total Contracts per Individual	All Contracts	Credit Contracts: Private Borrowers	Credit Contracts: Private Lenders	Credit Contracts: Private and Government Lenders
2–3	0.73	0.77	0.81	0.81
4–9	0.66	0.77	0.80	0.84
10–19	0.67	0.80	0.83	0.74
20 or more	0.70	*	—	—
All	0.71	0.77	0.81	0.82

Source: See text.
Note: Loyalty for all contracts equals the fraction of each individual's contracts drafted by an individual's favorite notary—the one who records most of the individual's contracts. For credit contracts, the definition is analogous, except that for borrowers we restrict the calculation to contracts in which the individual appears as a borrower and for lenders we restrict it to contracts in which the individual is a lender.
*Only three individuals borrowed more than 20 times; their loyalty indices were 0.29, 0.59, and 0.70.

If so, then the notaries had to persuade their clients that they could resolve the problems inherent in matching borrowers and lenders. They also had to overcome a problem of moral hazard when they decided how much effort to put in. One might of course maintain that a notary's good behavior would be guaranteed by the value of his office—in effect a bond for performance. Or it might be insured by the courts and by the notaries' own corporate organization. Here, though, one must distinguish between the actions of a notary that are observable and those that are not. Convicting a notary in court or removing him from his office would require proof—proof that could only concern observable actions. Yet there were a host of unobservable decisions that each notary made. He reached decisions, for instance, on the basis of private information in his archives, to which he alone had access. It would be difficult to know how the notary used that information. It would be even more difficult to demonstrate that he had misbehaved.

It could still be argued that the typical notary had an incentive to build a reputation for good service because a large fraction of his work came from repeat business.[11] The notary himself would want to maintain the value of his office, and thus he would have to serve his clients well, for poor service would drive them away.[12] One can imagine a variety of

11. Kreps 1990b.

12. Initially, it would be difficult to discover whether a notary's service was poor. Once the transaction was completed, however, clients did know how long it took to arrange and how happy they were with their match. While information of this sort was not exactly the same as quality of service, it could be compared with what acquaintances had experienced with other notaries.

such reputational models. In the simplest, clients would remain loyal to the same notary so long as their interactions with him were satisfactory. If mistreated, clients would jump to a competitor, and the threat of leaving would keep the notaries from offering bad service. The result would be near perfect loyalty. Alternatively, one might imagine that clients would move from notary to notary, seeking one who treated them well. Or the notary might send his own clients to a colleague whenever it was efficient, in order to protect his reputation. Or perhaps clients might monitor notaries' behavior imperfectly, as in models of oligopolistic collusion.[13] Given such imperfect monitoring, clients would punish their notary periodically, either by mistake or to sanction misbehavior: the punishment would consist of taking their business elsewhere. Yet each notary would still cultivate a reputation for high-quality service.

There are in fact so many reputational models of this sort (and so many equilibria in the related repeated games) that one can tell a reputational story about nearly any pattern of client defections from their favorite notary. That is one problem with reputational models, but there are others as well. At bottom, the reputational models depend on two assumptions that remain quite dubious insofar as the notaries of the Old Regime are concerned. The first assumption is that clients could switch notaries at low cost, independently of their notary's behavior. If clients could not do so, then they could not quit (or even threaten to leave) a notary who mistreated them, and they thus had no credible way of inducing him to provide high-quality service. Yet the fact is that switching costs were clearly high for nearly all Parisian clients. Apart from a few extremely wealthy individuals, most clients were tied to their notary because of his private information about them—the "lock-in" problem. Shifting to another notary would be costly unless something besides reputation was at work.

Beyond the difficulties of conveying information about themselves, clients might well find it hard to punish a notary who had mistreated them or even to tarnish his reputation by spreading tales of his misdeeds. Indeed, the possibility that clients themselves were lying would undermine the credibility of a report about the notary's misconduct, and the size of the city would limit the report's impact. A notary could thus abuse many of his clients—though probably not all—at low cost. Some clients would leave, but the rest would remain unaware or unconvinced. The problem would be particularly severe for the many individuals who carried out asset transactions only rarely, such as women, clerics, and poorer notarial clients. Abusing these episodic clients would be especially tempting for a notary

13. Green and Porter 1984; Abreu, Pearce, and Staccheti 1986.

because their future business was limited. Moreover, these clients would have to exert themselves to report any wrongdoing, and their efforts would in all likelihood be unwarranted given the limited use they made of notarial services. To be sure, a notary would be easy to police if his clients could threaten to leave as a block, as soon as any one of them was mistreated. But we find no trace of such coalitions in our data.[14]

Broad reputation mechanisms thus seem to offer at best an incomplete account of the behavior of notaries and their clients in eighteenth-century Paris. We can gain further insight into their dealings with one another by focusing on how information passed among them. The pattern of their interaction has implications for how information flowed. And since information was crucial to policing notaries, the information flows can suggest what kept the notaries honest. In short, focusing on the structure of interactions can allow us to recover the precise reputational mechanism that underlay asset transactions in Old-Regime Paris.

The pattern that emerges from the notarial transactions is one of loyalty punctuated by defections. Clients did do most of their business before their favorite notary, but they also took it to other notaries. Such defections were not permanent—the clients would soon return to their favorite—and we would argue that the defections were not a sign of disloyalty. Indeed, the clients may well have been encouraged to go elsewhere by their favorite notary himself. The reason is simple. The defections were the very mechanism that allowed the notary to guarantee his clients quality service.

The evidence from 1751 supports the argument that clients who appeared unfaithful to their usual notary were in fact relying on him for referrals in order to carry out business with the clients of other notaries. (Henceforth we call such deals involving clients from two different notaries cross-étude transactions.) If notaries did not consent to such cross-étude dealing, it would not have accounted for 30 percent of all notarial contracts; nor would loyalty have been constant across all social groups. Women, for instance, were nearly as likely as men to contract outside their favorite étude, and while slightly more women than men were perfectly loyal to their principal notaries, the proportion is hardly staggering (28 instead of 25 percent). Women are a particularly interesting case, for in the mid-eighteenth century few women were as immersed in commerce as men. Presumably women would have depended more heavily on their favorite notary for information.[15] Yet it is impossible

14. Hoffman, Postel-Vinay, and Rosenthal 1998.

15. True, some men were utterly incapable of managing their affairs—profligate aristocrats, for example. But on average more men were involved in commerce and credit than women.

TABLE 6.3   TOBIT ANALYSIS OF THE LOYALTY RATE FOR
                     NOTARIAL CLIENTS

Independent Variables	
Constant	0.87
	(10.32)
Dummy variable: for merchants and artisans	−0.026
	(−3.94)
Dummy variable: women	0.011
	(1.56)
Number of contracts	−0.022
	(−18.7)
Number of contracts squared	0.00015
	(12.3)
s^2	0.149
Log likelihood	−12,659
n	20,253

Source: See text.

Note: The dependent variable in the regression is the loyalty rate for all contracts, as defined in table 6.2. Since the loyalty rate is one or less and frequently takes on the value one, we estimated a tobit equation $y = bx + u$ if $bx + u < 1$ and $y = 1$ otherwise. Here y is the vector of loyalty rates, x is the matrix of observations of the independent variables, b is the matrix of their coefficients, and u is the error term, which is normally distributed with standard deviation s. The observations here concern individuals who appear in more than one contract. T-statistics are in parentheses.

Since the loyalty rate y is also non-negative, one could argue that we should have estimated a two-limit tobit, but in fact y never gets close to zero, its lowest value being 0.125. One might also object that the number of contracts (call it n) is endogenous and that the tobit should therefore not be restricted to individuals appearing in more than one contract because $y = f/n$, where f is the number of contracts drawn up by the favorite notary. If we multiply y by n, we get an equation for f which can be estimated as a Poisson regression, and n will no longer be the denominator of the dependent variable. Doing that leads to similar results, although we have to eliminate the two observations with the largest n to get the Poisson estimation procedure to converge. (Dropping these two observations changes the tobit estimates by only a slight amount.) That still leaves the problem of the endogeneity of n, but we can tackle that via a two-stage use of instrumental variables. If we do so, the coefficients do not change enough to challenge our argument.

to find any statistical difference in loyalty by sex (table 6.3). Similarly, social status does not appear to matter, except for merchants and artisans who were only marginally less loyal to their usual notary than other groups. Their behavior is not altogether surprising, since they were the most involved in economic activity and thereby the most likely to have channels of information other than notaries. Their business may have also made it imperative that asset transactions be finalized quickly—thereby requiring more frequent shifts from one notary to another. In any event, if the evidence from 1751 is any indication, cross-étude agreements were an essential part of the relationship between a notary and his clients.

Yet there remained problems in carrying out cross-étude agreements, because a notary had privileged information about his clients. A notary could use this information to bilk a client, as Simon Hurtrelle did with his clients, the Sisters of the Holy Cross, who in 1750 rushed him 15,000 livres from their convent in Saint-Quentin only to have him spend months without finding them a suitable investment. Hurtrelle knew from the sisters' letters that they had few alternative investments or sources of information near their convent, 150 kilometers from Paris. He delayed buying them a government bond for months even though there were many on the market. A notary could, however, use information about clients to serve them well. That meant rapidity and proper matching, whether it was of borrowers or lenders or parties in any other contract. Voltaire's Parisian notary, Jean-Baptiste Dutertre, apparently provided such service: he answered Voltaire's request about his portfolio the same day he received it and sped his reply back to Voltaire at his home near Geneva. The whole exchange between the two men took less than ten days—as fast as a rapid public coach.[16]

When seeking a match for a financial transaction, a notary could look within his own clientele, but that might force the client to wait. More rapid service would then depend on referring clients to another notary, and that required cooperation among notaries, since they could communicate information about clients more reliably than the clients could themselves. A notary of course had incentives to keep his clients to himself, because referring clients created competition among notaries. Indeed, for a referral to work, a notary had to share information about his client. The notary to whom he referred the client would then be in a position to attract the client if the original notary failed to provide satisfactory services. In order not to lose his clients, the original notary would therefore find himself under pressure to find appropriate matches outside his own clientele, all of which would demand greater exertion. The resulting scheme would assure decent service in a way that was flexible and did not impose a heavy burden, since referrals also improved efficiency.[17]

16. For Hurtrelle, see AN Y 18581, and for Voltaire and Dutertre, see Voltaire's letters of 18 and 28 February 1777 in Voltaire 1953–77. For travel duration see Arbellot 1973.

17. In contrast to the other hypotheses we examined, the important relationship here is the one between the notary and his clients. Notaries communicated information honestly to each other because they could easily publicize to the rest of the notarial corporation the ill-doings of a dishonest colleague. While such publicity might not have led to any explicit sanction, it would cost a misbehaving notary the ability to arrange cross-étude

A wide variety of evidence—from contemporary letters to the 1751 enumeration of Parisian contracts—thus suggests that the notaries had risen to the apex of a vast financial network in the eighteenth century. The typical client consulted them to arrange loans and other financial transactions; he did not find financial partners on his own. Most of the time, he went to the same notary: that was the case, for example, for 80 percent of borrowers and lenders. But periodically his usual notary would refer him to a colleague, and it was these referrals (and not the courts or the value of the notarial office) that kept the notaries honest.

A Game-Theoretical Model

The ideas here can be formalized by constructing a game theoretical model of the interaction between notaries and clients.[18] Once a client requests a transaction, a notary has two distinct decisions to make. First of all, he must decide whether to seek out potential outside matches for his client by sharing information. He may or may not find a better match outside of his clientele than what he has available internally. But if he seeks an external match it will be costly because it will require him to expend effort beyond what is needed for deals within his clientele. Given the available matches, he must choose among them or tell his client to wait for a better partner. The client cannot observe how much effort the notary expends in doing all this, for all he sees is the speed at which the notary fulfills his request and whether or not his partner is from a different clientele. But here cross-étude deals are important to the client precisely because they can only occur if information is shared between notaries. Thus we simplify the game to a pair of decisions on the part of the notary: whether or not to provide a high-quality match and whether or not to share information.[19] The extensive form game is displayed in figure 6.1.

---

transactions. He would lose clients and ruin the value of his office. One other virtue of the scheme is also worth noting: because notaries communicated only a part of the information they had, the one who knew the client best was likely to do most of the clients' business—just what we observe in 1751.

18. The model here is inspired by the industrial relations literature on hold-up problems and second sourcing. For references, see Hoffman, Postel-Vinay, and Rosenthal 1998.

19. In arranging transactions, notaries can potentially face a conflict of interest, because on some dimensions the parties' preferences are opposed. In the case of loans, for example, conflict could occur over the amount of security or over the interest rate. On a number of dimensions, however, their preferences would coincide—speed of service, for instance, or duration and size of the loan. The dimensions over which the parties were

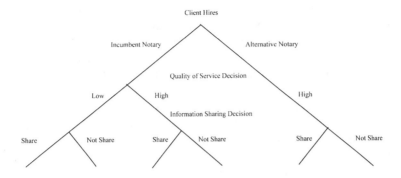

Note: Pay offs depend on how much information is available to each player.

FIGURE 6.1 The Stage Game for Notary-Client Relationships

Referrals can entail the client being sent to a second notary to do business with someone from that notary's clientele or they can entail the second notary's sending someone to do business with the client before the client's own notary. By symmetry one can assume that each sort of referral is equally likely: in other words, a fraction α of the client's transactions will involve referrals to another notary, and the same fraction α will involve referrals to the client's own notary.[20] Both sorts of referrals will necessitate information sharing between the client's notary and one of his colleagues, and the client will always know the identity of this other notary.[21] For 2α of the transactions, therefore, the client knows the identity of a notary who has recently received information about him. If he decides that his own notary is behaving unsuitably, he can switch at low cost to this second notary, who has recent information about him.

Each time a client wants to carry out a transaction, he must hire a notary. He has an incumbent notary—the one he most recently hired—as well as an alternative. The two notaries are either informed or uniformed about the client's current financial situation, and the client can

opposed could be negotiated. To the extent that a notary's conflict of interest was a problem, the parties had an incentive to bargain these out themselves. But to get to that point the notary had to make a proper match, and that is where quality of service really matters.

20. For simplicity, we assume symmetry of referrals period by period. Although that is not required for our results, it is what we observe in the data. Furthermore, the life cycle of wealth would tend to produce symmetry over time.

21. To the extent that α is large relative to what one would expect under full information (because of the need to ensure information transmission to allow clients to switch), there is some social cost to this mechanism. Yet if a notary's clientele is small relative to the overall population, the cost may be very small because it is efficient for most deals to occur across clienteles.

either rehire the first notary or switch to the second. For simplicity we assume that if the incumbent notary is uninformed about the client then so is the alternative notary. If the incumbent notary is informed, we assume that the alternative notary can either be uninformed or informed, provided that there have been recent exchanges of information. The client faces fees that are either low or high depending on whether the notary he chooses is informed or uninformed about him. If he transfers his business from the first to the second notary, he also faces a switching cost. Only the hired notary is active. In each period the client moves first by choosing a notary, and then the notary decides on sharing information and quality of service. More formally, the assumptions of the model are as follows:[22]

1. The fees of uninformed notaries are F, while those of an informed notary are f and the cost of switching to another notary is s. Here $F > f$ because an uninformed notary must bear the cost of learning about the client.[23]
2. High-quality service yields the client R^h before fees, while low-quality service gets him R^l with $R^h > R^l$.
3. The profits of an idle notary are 0. The notary's profits are π^h if he provides high-quality service and π^l if he does not with $\pi^l > \pi^h > 0$.
4. The gains to a notary for providing low-quality service are small relative to his client's losses; in other words, $\pi^l - \pi^h < R^h - R^l$. Hence, it is socially efficient for notaries to provide high-quality services.
5. The cost of sharing information is denoted e (the effort required to contact other notaries).
6. Lock-in can occur if the incumbent notary is informed but the other is not: $F - f > (R^h - R^l - s)(1 + 1/r)$ where s is the switching cost and r is the common rate of interest.
7. A notary who receives no information for n periods is uninformed. Here n is the time that it takes information about clients to decay and lose its value.

It is easy to show that the social optimum cannot be attained in a one-shot version of the above game. The one-shot game has two possible equilibria, depending on switching cost s and information cost F. Either the client hires the alternative notary ($R^h - R^l \geq s$) and receives high-quality service, or the client stays with his incumbent notary and receives low-quality service. We thus focus on an infinitely repeated game, for although the three players will not live forever, their families and successors will, making the infinitely repeated game a reasonable model. If a

22. See appendix 2 for proofs and a more rigorous treatment.

23. For simplicity, we take fees to be fixed. Variable fees, though, will not solve the problems clients and notaries faced: for a discussion, see Hoffman, Postel-Vinay, and Rosenthal 1998.

client is old, his notary will still be concerned about retaining his family's business. Indeed, families most often remained loyal to the same notarial étude for generations. Similarly, if a notary is about to retire, he will wish to preserve the value of his business, because he will sell it or bequeath it to his heirs.

Several remaining questions about our model require a detailed knowledge of how Parisian notaries operated. To begin with, were there any notaries who were informed about a given client at the beginning of play? Could they commit to high-quality service for one period? In eighteenth-century Paris, the beginning of play was the moment the client first entered into a relationship with a notary. It might be the beginning of adulthood, when the client married or secured an economic position, such as a government office, trade mastership, or commercial license. Both marriage and professional independence began with a visit to the notary. Clearly, at least one notary would henceforth be informed about the client. But this sort of contract was in fact likely to involve several notaries. Marriage contracts typically involved the bride's notary and the groom's as well. Purchase of a government office or a commercial license brought in the buyer's notary and the seller's. All the notaries present would come to know the client's social and economic position, and the client would enter active life with both a primary notary and an obvious fallback. As a result our assumption that clients have alternative notaries seems warranted.

What then about a notary's ability to commit to high-quality service? Would a client who contemplated leaving his notary for a competitor be confident that he would receive high-quality service? The competing notary knew that he could only attract the client if he promised to deliver high-quality service. Now such a promise might not be credible if the client switched before determining the quality of the competing notary's service. But in reality a client who considered leaving his notary could simply take his list of desired transactions to the competitor in order to determine if he would in fact receive better service. Only if he were offered a rapid and attractive match would he switch. The act of switching would involve signing the transactions engineered by the competing notary. The client could easily observe the service quality of the initial deal before he switched, and he would not be acting on a promise that could be retracted. It thus appears reasonable to assume an initial period of high-quality service.

With these assumptions, we can characterize the most interesting Nash equilibria of the repeated game described above. Specifically, if the time n that it takes information to decay is longer than one game period, and if (as seems reasonable to assume) both notaries are informed at the beginning of the game, then the infinitely repeated game has three pertinent Nash equilibria:[24]

 I. *Lock-in.* Clients never switch and notaries never share information.
 II. *Periodic Switching.* Clients switch between notaries every $n - 1$ periods. Notaries provide high-quality service only for $n - 1$ periods after being hired. If clients remain too long with the same notary, they receive low-quality service. Notaries never share information.
 III. *Information sharing.* Clients switch after any period during which the notary has failed to share information with a potential rival. In equilibrium, notaries share information and provide high-quality service, and clients are loyal.

Not all the equilibria occur for a given parametrization of the model. For a proof, see appendix 2.

The three equilibria have strikingly different implications for notary-client relationships. The first equilibrium features complete segmentation, in the sense that clients are tied to notaries. The second equilibrium involves switching by clients. The third is one of partial segmentation and of release of information by notaries. Intuitively, the existence of each of these equilibria depends on the client's switching costs. If switching costs are low enough ($R^h - R^l \geq s$), then equilibrium I can be ruled out. Indeed in our model the client can provide information to notaries by moving his business regularly. But he will only want to move regularly if he values high-quality service enough (enough, that is, relative to low-quality service) to warrant paying the switching costs. If the switching costs are high enough, then equilibrium II can be ruled out because the client will never want to transmit information on his own. As for equilibrium III, it exists for all parameter values.

More than one of these simple strategy equilibria will exist for given values of the exogenous parameters. We can use theory, though, to eliminate equilibria that are unlikely. At the extreme ranges of switching costs, only one of the three equilibria seems plausible. If switching costs s are low ($e < s < R^h - R^l$), equilibrium III will prevail. Here, equilibrium II is undone because the hired notary has an incentive to begin sharing information so as to retain the client. The client in turn will fail to switch if the notary begins to share information. Similarly, if s is very

24. These equilibria are not necessarily subgame perfect. In particular, equilibrium II is never subgame perfect. Instead of eliminating equilibria through theoretical refinements, we prefer to examine their empirical implications. We highlight three equilibria with strikingly different implications for the data. There are of course other equilibria. Indeed, the Folk theorem tells us that we can construct equilibria that will span the range between the different equilibria that we have found.

high, notaries are likely to lock their clients in. Equilibrium III will then be undone because the notary knows that if he stops sharing information the client will not carry out his threat of switching.

Although it seems unlikely that switching costs were so high that lock-in was the only robust equilibrium, we do not know enough about the transaction costs of the market to determine in advance which equilibrium was most likely to prevail. We therefore do not rely on theory alone to guide equilibrium selection. We could focus on equilibrium III because it is the equilibrium that maximizes the sum of the payoffs to the different players, as long as switching costs are larger than the notaries' cost of sharing information $(s > e)$.[25] But that would be putting too much faith in the ability of individuals to act for the common good. Indeed, although equilibrium III is supported along a wider range of switching costs than either equilibrium I or II, a priori we cannot tell how Parisians forecast their strategic interactions.

Fortunately the three equilibria we highlight have starkly different implications for the data. Equilibrium I is the simplest. In it, clients are locked in to a single notary, and the notaries never share information. As for equilibria II and III, understanding them requires more detail about the process of information sharing. Here we should think of periods as units of time within which a client will carry out multiple financial transactions. Information sharing is a byproduct of arranging deals with other notaries in a fraction 2α of a client's transactions, and for α of these the client will do business before another notary. In contrast to equilibrium I, we will thus observe defections in a fraction α of a client's records. But the pattern of defections will be quite different for equilibria II and III. For equilibrium III the pattern will be one of regular defection from a favorite notary followed nearly always by a return to him. Equilibrium II, by contrast, will not involve such isolated defections. Instead, clients will switch their allegiance from notary to notary at regular intervals, and between switching their loyalty would be perfect.

Testing the Model

Our model has highlighted three equilibria for the interaction between notaries and clients—three equilibria with very different patterns of behavior. In the first equilibrium, no switching ever occurs, and clients receive low-quality service. Such an equilibrium arises if switching costs

---

25. It is likely that $s > e$ because notaries could economize on the cost of sharing information by exchanging information about many clients in a single meeting.

TABLE 6.4   FREQUENCY OF LOYALTY RATES AND OF THE USE OF OVER TWO NOTARIES BY THE
NUMBER OF A CLIENT'S CONTRACTS

Number of Contracts	Percentage of Clients with Perfect Loyalty	Percentage of Clients with Loyalty $\geq.66$ and <1	Percentage of Clients with Loyalty $\geq.33$ and $<.66$	Percentage of Clients with Loyalty ≥ 0 and $<.33$	Percentage of Clients Using over Two Notaries
2–3	45.4	11.0	43.6	0.0	6.9
4–9	21.3	29.5	39.9	9.3	49.6
10–19	13.0	40.9	35.3	10.9	72.1
>20	3.8	56.6	32.1	7.5	83.9
All clients	39.5	15.7	42.6	2.2	17.6

Source: See text.
Note: All the calculations are restricted to individuals involved in more than one contract. The loyalty rate is for all contracts, as defined in table 6.2. Note that with three or fewer contracts, the loyalty rate cannot be less than 0.33.

(s) are high enough. But since it has the strong feature of perfect loyalty to notaries, it is easily testable, and the data reject it decisively. Indeed, fewer than 40 percent of the clients who appeared in more than one contract remained perfectly loyal to their favorite notary during the twelve months of our sample (table 6.4). On average individuals defected from their favorite notary about 30 percent of the time.

The second equilibrium depends on low switching costs because clients must convey information about themselves to notaries by moving their business regularly. This equilibrium features a run of contracts carried out with one notary, then a switch just before the quality of service is about to decline (or when information begins to decay), followed by a run of contracts with another notary and finally a return to the first notary. Note here that the frequency of switching depends on the minimum time needed for information to decay and quality assurance to waver. Precisely how long it took before information decayed is uncertain, but notaries themselves acted as if their information lost its value within a few months.[26] Whatever the exact time, the second equilibrium has three strong implications for the data. First, if we can observe transactions for a number of periods, then the subgroup of notaries who oversee a particular client's business ought to share it roughly equally. As a result,

26. One sign of how long notaries' information lasted comes from the rules about the clerks who helped prepare contracts and were as well informed as the notaries themselves. There was always a risk that a clerk might depart with valuable information, particularly when a notarial office changed hands. At that point the rules of the notarial corporation required that a clerk not leave for three months—a period presumably long enough to seriously depreciate the value of any information he held. See *Statuts et règlements des notaires parisiens* 1766:33.

clients will not have primary notaries. Second, because keeping notaries informed is costly—it requires switching—a client will only interact with one notary at a time. If the information decay process and the time of quality assurance are similar, then over the long run the client will use only two notaries and will shuttle back and forth between them. Third, because the client bears the costs of keeping alternative notaries informed, he will only employ two notaries.

None of these three implications is consistent with the data. First, clients did not divide their transactions equally among several notaries. More than 55 percent of the clients reserved two-thirds or more of their business for a single notary. Second, individuals did not deal with notaries sequentially. Rather, their interactions with alternative notaries were isolated incidents in runs of repeated business with their favorite notary. Third, a surprisingly large number of individuals consulted more than two notaries (table 6.4).

The third and final equilibrium also requires a low cost of switching because switching is used as a threat, but the process of information sharing is carried out by the notaries and not the clients. As a result, clients remain loyal to a particular notary for most of their contracts, but their defections may be spread out broadly across a number of notaries. Defection here is not the result of an anticipated fall in the quality of service; rather, it is a means to ensure that high-quality service will continue. The resulting equilibrium is the only one of the three that fits what we observe in Paris in 1751.

It also fits what direct evidence there is that notaries shared information. Such direct evidence is rare, because notaries shared the information about clients during informal meetings at which no minutes were kept. Furthermore, they had no obligation to preserve letters from other notaries and notes about clients, unlike their formal records. Where such documents have survived, though, they do demonstrate beyond a doubt that notaries passed information to one another about their clients. When notary Simon Hurtrelle was arranging loans for a client who was buying a government office, for instance, he solicited the names of prospective lenders from Laideguive, a fellow notary. Laideguive immediately came up with a client who could furnish 25,000 livres.[27]

Loyalty to the notary thus has a complex interpretation. Individuals remained loyal because they relied on the notary to transmit information essential to their transactions. The information, our analysis implies, had to flow both within and across notarial businesses. The flows allowed

27. AN Y 18581 (notary Hurtrelle); Voltaire's correspondence with his notary yields an equally persuasive example.

rapid matching of heterogeneous clients and permitted clients to police
their notaries. Information, not custom, thus seems to account for the
rhythm of loyalty and defection.

Implications of our Model

Our model explains one way of resolving problems of asymmetric information in capital markets. This solution emerged in the eighteenth century, and if we move backward (or forward) a century, the tactics for
coping with asymmetric information were quite different. But for the
moment, let us consider the solution at work in Paris in 1751, which
revolved around the Parisian notaries. They put in place an original ar-
rangement for transmitting information, one that defies the simple-
minded contrasts between Gemeinschaft and Gesellschaft, between hierarchies and prices, and between the personal exchanges of ancient
societies and the anonymous markets of today.[28] Indeed, even though a
notary had personal ties to each of his clients, the clients themselves
typically did not know one another. In this context, notaries could have
easily taken advantage of their position. Yet that did not happen, for
the notaries solved the problem. A notary allowed his clients to defect
periodically, in order to give them a credible threat in case he misbehaved. The great virtue of this mechanism was its availability to all social
classes: it protected clients both rich and poor, those with public reputations and those without. It even worked for clients who rarely visited a
notary.

The notaries thus made possible numerous financial transactions that
would never have taken place in a large city like Paris. They owed their
success not only to the contemporary legal framework but to the informal institution of regular referrals that structured their interactions with
clients. For clients, regular referrals provided a credible commitment
that notaries would offer high-quality service. The result was a thriving
financial market, making the notaries' practice of regular referrals a su-
perb example of the sort of informal institution that arises to deal with
problems of asymmetric information.

Similar problems have afflicted many other financial markets, for
even today investors and entrepreneurs rely upon intermediaries such

---

28. There were parallels in Britain, where scriveners and attorneys arranged mortgages
for their clients. Miles (1981) suggests that an attorney negotiated mortgages both within
his clientele and by sharing information with other attorneys. See also Anderson 1969a,
1969b; Melton 1986; and Neal 1994.

as venture capitalists to reduce informational asymmetries. If an intermediary in one of these markets misbehaves, the investors and entrepreneurs may have little recourse, because it is often difficult to demonstrate the misdeeds in court. Here too the intermediary may come to have a significant hold over clients such as entrepreneurs.

With the Parisian notaries, this danger was avoided thanks to information sharing by the notaries, information sharing that permitted competition. That solution—that equilibrium of our game-theoretical model—is really the capstone supporting our entire book. Methodologically, we uncovered it in three steps: by applying game theory, eliminating competing explanations, and bringing quantitative evidence to bear on our theoretical analysis. Such a combination of techniques is rare in history, and it is even unusual for economic historians, who, if they do apply game theory, usually stop before submitting their models to quantitative tests.

But the significance of this equilibrium extends beyond mere methodology. Not only does it explain the notaries' success after the Law affair, but as we shall see, it also reveals why they could not repeat their achievements in the changed institutional environment of the nineteenth century. It is, of course, just one equilibrium among others, just one of the various possible patterns of behavior that would have been rational for the Parisian notaries. It did not characterize their actions in the 1600s, and even in the mid-eighteenth century notaries made abortive attempts to engage in a very different kind of behavior, as we shall discover in the next chapter.

CHAPTER SEVEN

Notaries, Banking, and the Expansion of Credit in Old-Regime Paris

BY EXPLOITING OBLIGATIONS AND REFERRALS, Parisian notaries raised huge amounts of capital from the 1740s on. Their achievements, though, extended well beyond the volume of loans they arranged. They could boast of having opened the city's public and private credit markets to women and to a growing number of lenders from outside Paris as well. They helped families resolve the ubiquitous problems of the life cycle and offered investors a wider selection of credit instruments for their portfolios. Buoyed by their success, some notaries began to swim in new and more hazardous financial waters. They immersed themselves in short-term credit and drifted beyond the broker's role analyzed in chapter 6. It even seemed as if some of them were about to plunge into banking. Beyond simply matching borrowers and lenders, as a broker would, they were tempted to lend out short-term deposits, much like modern banks. The profits from doing so were high, but so were the attendant risks. Indeed, the hazards of lending out short-term deposits swept so many notaries into bankruptcy that the government had to intervene. In the end, the notaries chose to remain brokers, and they by and large sealed themselves off from banking and short-term credit.

Deposits and Bankruptcies

Notaries in Paris could have simply remained brokers of rentes and obligations. After all, for a notary to limit his role to that of a broker had several advantages. In the first place, it absolved him of most risks once loans had been arranged. Apart from a concern for repeated business, the risks were not his but the lenders', and, unlike them, the notary would not suffer if, say, a government crisis caused borrowers to default. Furthermore, serving as brokers for long-term loans was what notaries knew best. Lending out short-term deposits would almost inevitably involve them (at least to a certain extent) in short-term credit, a completely different institutional realm. If we think of the notaries' usual long-term loans as moving financial capital over time, then short-term lending shifted it across space, through bills of exchange payable in another city in two or three months' time. These bills of exchange passed primarily among merchants and were drafted, as we know, without the aid of notaries. Disputes, as when debts were not paid, were swiftly settled by commercial jurisdictions, with legal documentation coming not from notaries but from the merchants' own books. Merchants in such cases did not need either a notary's assistance or his expensive authentic copies, and many notaries no doubt lacked the merchants' or bankers' experience in handling bills of exchange. True, there were other short-term placements, such as the billets of government financiers, but here too the financiers themselves and other financial specialists (bankers, agents de change) could easily outdo the notaries' expertise.[1]

Still, as their long-term lending swelled, a number of the notaries found their coffers filled with deposits. With business thriving, they had more and more cash on hand, cash that could be put to use until a deal was consummated. Often they held the money as a prelude to a long-term investment or major purchase, such as a piece of property or a government office. They might collect it as income from a client's portfolio and then disburse it to pay his bills. And increasingly they received it from clients who were eager for a return on short-term deposits. Whatever the source, though, the funds could be lent out for a profit.[2]

What the deposits meant for investors stands out quite clearly in the financial correspondence of someone like Voltaire.[3] Deeply engaged in the management of his own portfolio (as we might expect of a man who was himself the son of a Parisian notary), Voltaire, we know, dealt initially with a variety of financial specialists, from agents de change to government financiers. Among them notaries figured prominently, particularly

1. For the laws governing bills of exchange, see chapter 1. As for government financiers, Voltaire considered both buying their billets and entrusting them with his money, and to do so he sought out the advice of agents de change. See Voltaire 1953–77, letters 1,240 and 1,245 (18 and 27 March 1737).

2. For a detailed example see "Registre des dépôts par les particuliers chez le notaire Simon Hurtrelle," AN Y 18581 (pièces 4, 6, and 7).

3. What follows is based on a reading of Voltaire's letters to his notaries, hommes d'affaires, and other financial agents, and an analysis of Voltaire's financial transactions in both the 1751 enumeration and a similar enumeration from 1761, which we are currently preparing for use. For more on Voltaire's finances, see Nicolardot 1887; Muller 1920; Kozminski 1929; Donvez 1949.

after 1755, when he came to depend increasingly upon a favorite notary, as in the model of the previous chapter. Naturally, Voltaire relied heavily on notaries for his long-term investments. Even back in 1737, when he wished to put money into life annuities, the name that came to mind was that of a notary, Camusat. He instructed his business agent, Bonaventure Moussinot, to call upon this notary, for Voltaire judged him "more likely than anyone else to place my money in life annuities. . . . If Camusat can invest 15 to 20 thousand livres in life annuities, I am ready."[4]

But Voltaire also used notaries when he wanted to deposit cash and gain a quick return—clear evidence that notaries paid interest on their deposits. To be sure, he had alternatives for his cash, such as placing it with financiers or using it to purchase short-term government debt.[5] Yet notaries were certainly competitive in the market for short-term deposits. A year and a half before Voltaire sought the life annuity, he wanted to "deposit some cash, on a confidential basis, with a notary who is discrete and faithful." Apparently he intended that some of the short-term deposit would pay for the annuity; the rest—since the deposit itself might amount to as much as 50,000 livres—would go for other purposes. The notary who got it could certainly "invest [the money] where he sees an opportunity," but Voltaire let it be understood that he reserved the right to withdraw the money "on the spot" if necessary.[6]

Increasingly common in the eighteenth century, interest-bearing deposits were hardly limited to wealthy individuals like Voltaire. In the 1780s, for example, prosperous tenant farmers north of Paris were leaving money with their Parisian notaries so that it could be invested.[7] The practice had grown so widespread that even the popular press took note. In his enormously successful *Tableau de Paris,* for instance, the hack writer Louis-Sébastien Mercier noted the spread of such deposits with dismay. To him, it seemed part of an alarming revolution that spoiled the notaries with riches and drove up the price of their offices:

4. Voltaire, 1953–77, letters 1,342 and 1,353 (14 and 28 December 1737). See also letter 1,328 (17 November 1738), in which Voltaire asks Moussinot to find a notary who can invest 20,000 livres in rentes viagères. There was a notary Camuset in Paris at the time, but his repertoire for 1737–39 contains no acts concerning Voltaire. Perhaps Voltaire actually meant Camuset but misspelled his name and never ended up using him. Or perhaps he was simply referring to a notary named Camusat in the provinces.

5. Voltaire 1953–77, letters 1,240 and 1,245 (18 and 27 March 1737). Cf. letters 1,353, 1,354, and 1,357.

6. Voltaire, letter 994 (8 March 1736). For the use of the money, which was eventually deposited not with a notary but with a receveur général des finances at Montauban, see letters 1,245, 1,246, 1,353, 1,354, and 1,357.

7. Moriceau and Postel-Vinay 1992:55, 255.

The public has paid for the precocious affluence of these [Parisian] notaries. . . . Fifty years ago, notaries charged for holding money on deposit; today, they borrow it, [paying interest] at 6 percent. The excessive price of their businesses will bring about a revolution in their corporation, which has overstepped its bounds and will be brought down by the reckless extravagance of their wealth.[8]

Once notaries had charged fees for taking money on deposit. Now, Mercier worried, they paid interest and madly rushed about, arranging financial deals and investing the cash in their vaults.[9]

Another eighteenth-century onlooker, the attorney Barbier, painted a vivid portrait of one of these notaries who was so deeply immersed in the deposit business: Antoine-Pierre Laideguive. He ran a highly successful étude in the early 1740s, and it was rumored that in Paris "everyone depends on his étude directly or indirectly because of the quantity of deposits made there."[10] He devoted all of his time to lending the money out and making deals:

His obsession was to make all the deals in Paris. Every morning he ran about the city in a carriage. At noon he granted audiences like a minister. With a sensitive stomach, he dined little, left at 4 P.M. in his carriage to travel all about Paris a second time, returned home, went out again, came back at 11 and ate a chicken by himself.[11]

Precisely how much money Laideguive took in we do not know, but evidence from other notaries who sought out deposits suggests that the sums involved were indeed large.[12] His colleague Simon Hurtrelle took in more than 330,000 livres in deposits in 1735, and although 1735 was certainly a banner year for him, the size of the average deposit was always at least several thousand livres (table 7.1). To be sure, much of the money deposited with notaries was swiftly withdrawn, but the useable balance could be quite high. When the notary Gérard-Claude Bapteste went bankrupt in 1744, his debts mounted to some 1.2 million livres. Of these, some 700,000 were short-term debts, and nearly all of that probably represented deposits or other money borrowed on short-term loans from clients.[13]

8. Mercier 1783–88, 2:34.
9. Mercier 1783–88, 2:31–35.
10. Barbier 1885, 3:496–97, writing in 1744.
11. Ibid.
12. We will analyze Laideguive's operations in forthcoming work.
13. ANMC CXVII 787 (4 December 1751). Hurtrelle kept a running balance of his deposits for several months after he bought his étude in 1734; typically, it amounted to about 10,000 livres.

TABLE 7.1   SIMON HURTRELLE'S DEPOSITS, 1734–35 AND 1754–55

	1734	1735	1754	1755
Gross sum deposited (livres)	127,924	334,980	133,263	49,237
Annualized sum deposited				
(livres)	271,200	—	—	73,855
Duration of deposits (days):				
unweighted average	218	23	81	84
average weighted by size	104	9	51	110
median	2	2	38	119
Number of deposits:				
in list of deposits	11	32	25	15
in minutes	2	15	3	3
in both	1	1	0	0

Source: AN Y 18581, registers 4 and 6; AN MC LXVII répertoires 7 and 8.
Note: Hurtrelle's list of deposits begins on 22 June 1734 and ends on 31 August 1755. The anualized sums deposited project the results of the partial years 1734 and 1755 on to full years. The number of deposits in the list of deposits were those in AN Y 18581; the number in the minutes were those with an acte de dépôt in the répertoire for Hurtrelle's étude LXVII. The duration of some deposits is unknown because Hurtrelle failed to indicate when or if they were returned; these deposits have been omitted from the calculation of durations.

How then was the money on deposit invested? Some, it seems, was placed in bills of exchange or short-term government debt.[14] Some was apparently advanced to clients who wanted to borrow short term, such as Voltaire.[15] And some was lent for longer terms to borrowers who signed obligations.[16] Precisely what the proportions were, though, is difficult to say, for notaries preserved few records of the transactions. The reason, no doubt, was that notaries were not supposed to lend out funds on deposit. They were to leave it in their strongboxes and not touch it. Strictly speaking, lending a deposit out was illegal and necessitated the complicity of both notary and client—hence Voltaire's search for a "discrete and faithful" notary who could pay him interest on a deposit by investing it. As a result, clients who wanted their deposits lent out usually did not receive a notarized *acte de dépôt* (deposit receipt) for the money they gave their notary. Instead they got only his *billet:* a private and non-negotiable IOU, which gave them only a junior and unmortgaged claim to his assets and left no trace in the notarial archives.[17] Those actes de

14. Barbier 1885, 7:195–96.
15. Voltaire, 1953–77, letters D11,193 (5 May 1763); 18,197 (25 January 1775). For examples from Hurtrelle's business, see AN Y 18581.
16. See ANMC LXVII 488 (4 December 1734); AN Y 18581, registre 4 (2 December 1734 and 1 February 1735).
17. Guyot 1784–85, s.v. "dépôt" and "billet"; Mousnier 1979–80, 2:391.

dépôt which did survive in the notarial minutes were apparently quite different. They seem to have been reserved for court cases or for clients who really did just want their deposits kept in the strongbox.

That at least is what notary Simon Hurtrelle's records suggest.[18] When he went bankrupt in 1755, his private papers were seized, including lists of the deposits that he lent out. The deposits on these lists were almost never recorded as actes de dépôt in Hurtrelle's minutes, either at the dawn of his career or on the eve of his bankruptcy (table 7.1). Rather than actes de dépôt, he gave depositors his personal billet. And from the evidence we have, other notaries who lent out deposits did much the same.[19]

From the spread of deposits one might infer that the notaries were in fact shifting out of brokerage and into banking. If so, their entrance into banking was often incremental. They may not have even pooled the deposits that they invested. When Hurtrelle began working as a notary in 1734, he did keep a running balance of his deposits, which might indicate that he was gathering the funds on deposit together before lending it out. The balance disappeared within several months, however.[20] Instead, Hurtrelle seemed to match up new deposits with particular loans in which he himself was now the lender. He was still a broker but now for himself. Thus the widow Robequin's 3,000 livre deposit in 1734 funded an obligation that allowed a young man to purchase a military office. Rather than serve as a broker for a loan from Robequin directly, Hurtrelle gave her his personal billet and then used the deposit to make the loan himself, via an obligation in which his own role was disguised under the name of a straw man, Mouricault. Similarly, Monsieur Le Noir's 30,160 livre deposit in 1735 went for a loan from Hurtrelle to the

18. AN Y 18581, pieces 4 and 6. The same sort of distinction comes out in the notaries' own accounts of the deposit business, which they provided when the Châtelet threatened to regulate deposits in 1764: ACNP box 46 (7 and 18 March 1764).

19. ANMC XXIII 572 (4 January 1751): billet de dépôt déposé of chevalier Charles Jean Locquet de Grandeville, who had deposited 14,662 livres with notary Antoine-Pierre Laideguive on 19 February 1744. Grandeville had received only a billet for his deposit, and Laideguive's *répertoire* (*répertoire* 5 of étude LXV) shows no deposit for Grandeville or his procureur on or near the date of 19 February 1744. When Laideguive went bankrupt later that same year, Grandeville had to leave the billet itself with a notary to establish his claim in Laideguive's bankruptcy proceedings. Similarly, when notary Gérard-Claude Bapteste went bankrupt in 1744, many of his creditors held billets and not actes de dépôts: ANMC CXVII 787 (4 December 1751). Finally, Delaleu, Voltaire's notary, took Voltaire's money on deposit, and yet the corresponding deposit transactions do not appear in the *répertoire* of Delaleu's étude.

20. AN Y 18581, registres 4 and 6.

Marquise d'Armantières, with Hurtrelle's own role hidden once again by the same straw man. Le Noir got his deposit back but only after the marquise had repaid her loan.[21]

Why did notaries move beyond brokerage and engage themselves personally in loans? The only plausible explanation are the profits from the new business it engendered. Clearly, the offer of interest-bearing deposits drew forth funds that were not otherwise available for loans: a client might well entrust even more money to his notary if he knew that his funds could be withdrawn on demand or with very little notice. If the notary had enough cash on hand to satisfy depositors, he could invest the rest and no doubt earn a handsome return. Admittedly, there survives practically no information about what the deposits cost a notary or about what he could earn on the loans that the deposits funded.[22] But the deposits would, at the very least, spare him the expense of searching for funds outside his clientele and of splitting his fee with another notary. The deposits might also attract new clients. Also in favor of their profitability is the testimony of contemporaries like Mercier and Barbier, who linked the wealth of the notaries to the practice of lending out deposits.

Lending out deposits could thus win a notary riches, but it also created a number of problems. To begin with, if deposits were used for short-term loans, they could undermine the equilibrium described in chapter 6 and have perverse effects on a notary's clients. The notary, for example, would have less of an incentive to refer to a colleague those of his clients who were looking for long-term loans. Instead, he could just string them along with short-term credit until they could be matched with lenders from his own étude. He would also have less reason to assure the swift payment of money due his clients. After all, if they were short of cash because payments due them were late, they might ask him for a short-term loan and thus boost his profits.[23]

Worse than such problems of moral hazard were the hazards of lending out the deposits. Profits may have been high, but they entailed con-

---

21. ANMC LXVII 488 (4 December 1734); Y 18581, registre 4 (2 December 1734 and 1 February 1735). The loan to the marquise also involved a contract between the depositor Le Noir and the straw man Mouricault: Le Noir had to bring in Mouricault's declaration when he received his deposit back. We will examine the tactics notaries used to enter banking in forthcoming work.

22. The Marquise d'Armantières apparently paid interest at a 7.8 percent annual rate on her loan from Hurtrelle. That is not extraordinarily high, but the loan was secured with excellent collateral: shares of the Compagnie des Indes on deposit with the notary. See AN Y 18581, registre 4 (1 February 1735, 26 November 1735).

23. For a real example of such behavior, see Voltaire 1953–77, letter 19,576 (16 July 1777).

siderable risk now that the notary was personally engaged in the loan. The danger for the notary was that a major part of his liabilities—namely, his deposits—were short term and could be withdrawn in an instant if a client suddenly needed cash. True, the notary and his clients could decide upon a term for a deposit, but the depositors often specified that they wanted to withdraw their money on demand.[24] If we consider the actual experience of notary Hurtrelle, we see that although his deposits might last for an average of a month or more, the larger ones were usually withdrawn sooner. And so many were withdrawn almost immediately that the median time a deposit remained with Hurtrelle was as low as two days in certain years (table 7.1).[25]

Meanwhile, a notary's assets were not the sort of liquid investments that could swiftly be converted into cash in order to contend with a rush of withdrawals. What counted among the assets here were not just the loans that the notary made with the deposits but his entire portfolio. Unfortunately, much of the typical notary's portfolio was placed in investments such as rentes, offices, and real estate. These investments were what notaries knew best, but they were nearly impossible to liquidate in moments of crisis. For example, seven years after notary Gérard-Claude Baptiste went bankrupt, his creditors were still having difficulty converting his assets into liquid form. Indeed, most of what Baptiste held was real estate, and only one item—his notarial office—could even be assigned a cash value. Despite the passage of seven years, his creditors had amassed only some 0.7 million livres in cash to pay off the notary's 1.2 million livres of debts.[26]

It is true that some notaries put money in the billets of government tax farmers or other negotiable short-term credit instruments, such as the *billets au porteur* or bills of exchange of merchants. But these short-term financial instruments, we should recall, were not the realm of the notaries' greatest expertise. Nor were they even very liquid. They were not listed on a public exchange, and they might be particularly difficult to unload in moments of fiscal or commercial crisis—precisely the moment when clients would seek to withdraw their deposits.[27]

What France sorely lacked here, one might argue, was the equivalent of the Three Percent Consol in Great Britain, a secure and publicly traded government security. With it notaries would have had an easier

---

24. Voltaire 1953–77, letter 994 (8 March 1736); AN Y 18581 (24 January 1735).

25. Some of the very short-term deposits were clearly money in transit that was left with Hurtrelle when transactions were about to close.

26. ANMC CXVII 787 (4 December 1751).

27. Barbier 1885, 7:195–96.

time dealing with withdrawals, for they could have simply sold government bonds from their portfolios.[28] On the other hand, even government securities like the consol could plunge in value during a fiscal or commercial crisis. That was the experience in Britain in 1761 and 1794, for example, and in France in the nineteenth century.[29] Perhaps it was simply too much to hope for a government bond that could easily be sold without a loss during a financial panic. If so, then practically all the notaries could do to prevent bankruptcies would be to hold large reserves of cash. They would have to refrain from lending out most of their deposits and instead simply hold the cash in their coffers. But that of course would have meant a retreat or even an end to deposit lending.

As long as notaries did lend out a large fraction of their deposits, though, and as long as they had no liquid assets to sell in moments of crisis, they risked going bankrupt. Despite Antoine-Pierre Laideguive's brief moment of spectacular success with deposits, he ultimately went bankrupt, as did a number of his colleagues who had immersed themselves in the deposit business. And just a month before Laideguive's collapse, Paris was stunned by Bapteste's failure, notwithstanding his reputation as one of the "most esteemed" notaries in Paris. The cause, apparently, was the sudden withdrawal of a large sum on deposit. According to Barbier, the whole city was frightened by the two bankruptcies in quick succession, which raised grave doubts about notaries. Laideguive's case was particularly troublesome: "Everyone in Paris is dismayed," said Barbier, who specifically traced the bankruptcies back to the profitable business of lending out money on deposit. "They run after deposits, and as their greatest profit lies in investing the [deposited] money, five or six more are likely to fail very soon—notaries who would have stayed afloat without their colleagues' bankruptcies."[30]

Barbier was not the only one alarmed by the rash of failures. Newsmongers took note of notaries' problems in manuscript gazettes that captured and spread Paris's gossip. They trumpeted news of the bankruptcies and of a subsequent wave of notarial suicides, which were perhaps yet another sign of difficulties with deposits.[31] The disasters

---

28. Neal 1990. Although some of France's long-term government debt was traded on the Paris Bourse, it was not homogeneous, nor as secure or as liquid as the British consol. See Velde and Weir 1992.

29. Neal 1990:169–79, 231–57.

30. Barbier 1885, 3:487–88, 496–97 (in 1744); and 1885, 4:5 (in 1745).

31. Bachaumont 1784–89, 27:264–65 (1774); 15:220 (1780); 17:51 (1781); 20:23 (1782).

culminated with the thundering crash of the notary André-Guillaume Deshayes, who absconded in 1764 and had to be hanged in effigy. The hanging marked popular opinion indelibly, in a way reminiscent of other public executions such as that of the would-be regicide Damiens. Publicized at the time, the Deshayes case was still remembered with consternation a generation later. In the 1780s, a lawyer writing in a legal dictionary could remark without hesitation that "everyone knows the death sentence . . . meted out to . . . Deshayes."[32] In the same decade, the popular journalist Mercier still recalled Deshayes with a sense of relief that the disasters afflicting the notaries had passed: "Bankrupt notaries no longer abscond to Holland. They blow their brains out in bed or hang themselves from a drainpipe. One remembers the notary Deshayes, who was condemned to death but, having vanished, was only hanged in effigy." For Mercier, the problem was not just the financial ramifications of the notarial bankruptcies. It was also that they were inevitably tangled up with public opinion and public order. The notaries, Mercier observed, "have made themselves guilty of offenses which concern public order." They had the public trust, held a semi-public office, and played too large a public role for their financial debacles to be a strictly private matter. After all, they were major intermediaries for government loans.[33]

The spate of bankruptcies was not merely some fictional story that gushed forth from sensationalistic journalists like Mercier. There actually were more notaries who failed, particularly in the middle of the eighteenth century. After Antoine-Pierre Laideguive went belly-up in 1744, his embarrassed older cousin Pierre-Louis Laideguive—himself a successful and respected notary—grew worried. As an officer of the notarial corporation, he began to mull over reforms to prevent bankruptcies in the future. He also began to keep a list of notaries whose businesses collapsed. By the late 1750s, his list showed fifteen notaries "who have failed in the last 12 years" (table 7.2).[34] That was 1.25 bankruptcies a year, far more even than during the notorious financial scandals of the early nineteenth century, in the days of Guizot and Balzac. It was no doubt more than Paris had witnessed earlier in the eighteenth century

32. BN F 23717, "Sentence rendue en la chambre criminelle du Châtelet de Paris, qui condamne André-Guillaume Deshayes" (24 February 1764); Guyot 1783–84, s.v. "banqueroute." For evidence that Deshayes's hanging in effigy marked popular opinion when it occurred in 1764, see the *Journal encyclopédique* (March 1764); and the *journal* of bookseller S. Hardy (BN Fonds français 6680, 24 February 1764).

33. Mercier 1994, 2:1458–59; see also Mercier 1783–88, 2:33.

34. For Laideguive's reputation, see Bachaumont 1784–89, 8:296.

TABLE 7.2   CAREERS AND EXPERIENCE OF BANKRUPT NOTARIES, 1731–56

Last Name	First Name	Years of Experience at Bankruptcy	Began Career	Bankrupt and Ended Career
Chèvre	François-Nicolas	5	1726	1731
Laideguive	Antoine-Pierre	12	1732	1744
Bapteste	Gérard-Claude	27	1717	1744
Cornet	Alexandre	4	1742	1746
Champia	Pierre-Hector	1	1746	1746
Julienne	Nicolas	22	1725	1747
Crevon	François	20	1727	1747
Rossignol	Guillaume	2	1747	1749
Gaucher	Pierre-Philippe	3	1746	1749
Ballot	Sylvain	31	1719	1750
Barrier	Gabriel	6	1746	1752
Lemoine	Etienne-Nicolas	8	1744	1752
Boursier	Etienne-Simon	2	1751	1753
Brelut de la Grange	César	22	1733	1755
Hurtrelle	Simon	21	1734	1755
Fourestier	Claude-Pierre	8	1748	1756
Average experience at bankruptcy		12.13		

Source: ACNP, box 46 (unsigned mémoire of Laideguive); Delarue 1786; and the *répertoires* of Parisian notaries at AN MC.

Note: The table is based on Pierre-Louis Laideguive's list of notaries "qui ont manqué depuis 12 ans." Laideguive's list is undated, but it was probably drawn up shortly after the failure of Claude-Pierre Fourestier in 1756. It also includes the earlier bankruptcy of François-Nicolas Chèvre in 1731.

too.[35] Worse, the pace of failures seemed to be accelerating. If Laideguive's list is complete, only one notary went bankrupt in the 1730s, but eight did in the 1740s, followed by seven more in the years 1750–56 alone. The situations grew even worse in the early 1760s with the thundering collapse of the notary Deshayes.

The notaries who floundered were not just financial novices who fell victim to their own inexperience. Some, we shall see, were in fact seasoned veterans of the deposit business, such as Laideguive and Hurtrelle. Furthermore, although bankruptcy did sometimes strike at the onset of a career, it often hit notaries with years of experience (table 7.2). On

35. ACNP, box 41, contains records of notaries who still owed the Company of Parisian Notaries money for taxes and government loans when they surrendered their offices. Seven notaries apparently found themselves in such a situation, the first in 1698 and the last in 1721. If the records are complete and bankrupt notaries always owed the company money, then the rate of bankruptcy between 1698 and 1721 would be only 0.3 per year. It would be even lower if no notaries failed before 1698 and in the 1720s. The records here may, of course, be incomplete. But debts to the company did usually go along with bankruptcy, and the company itself had ample reason to preserve records of notaries who owed it money. See also Limon 1992.

average, a notary who went bankrupt had over twelve years of experience—almost exactly as much as colleagues who remained solvent. That bankruptcy was no respecter of age and experience made it all the more frightening.

It was not only investors who were alarmed. The government itself began to worry and eventually intervened "to reassure the alarmed public."[36] The king's chancellor grew concerned, as did the *procureur général*—the king's representative in the Parlement who kept an eye out for public welfare. So did the Châtelet, the law court to which Parisian notaries were attached. In the wake of the Deshayes debacle, the Châtelet in fact resolved to impose a draconian set of regulations on the notaries. Henceforth, the notaries would have to begin keeping registers showing the state of their strongboxes and all their deposits. Judicial authorities would visit their études periodically to inspect the registers and make sure that deposits were not being misused.[37]

These regulations were not the first attempt to prevent bankruptcies by laws and regulations. After Gerard-Claude Bapteste and Antoine-Pierre Laideguive went bankrupt in 1744, chancellor Daguesseau proposed fixing the price of notarial offices to restrain the recent run up in their cost. His goal, it seems, was to keep notaries from taking on so much debt upon purchasing their offices that they would be drawn into risky business. Here the procureur-général Joly de Fleury agreed. So too did Laideguive's older cousin, the notary Pierre-Louis Laideguive, who was deeply troubled by the bankruptcies that had besmirched his family and his profession. But Laideguive wished to go well beyond fixing prices. To begin with, he wanted to prohibit all deposits, whether they were lent out or not. If clients persisted in leaving money with their notary, they would be unable to pursue him before commercial courts in case he went bankrupt. Their only recourse would be to sue in the slower and more costly civil jurisdictions, and even then they would have at best only a junior claim to his assets. In addition, Laideguive wanted to suppress fifty-three notarial études, so that the remaining notaries would no longer need the deposit business. And as a final measure, he wanted to outlaw the notaries' use of negotiable billets à ordre or lettres

---

36. BN Joly de Fleury 385, fol. 174 (28 February 1764): unsigned letter apparently from the Châtelet to Joly de Fleury.

37. For evidence of the Châtelet's and the procureur général's concern in late 1763 and early 1764, see BN Joly de Fleury 385, fols. 157–74; ACNP, box 46 and Délibérations (4 to 18 March 1764). For the somewhat earlier worries of chancellor Lamoignon de Blancmesnil, see ACNP Délibérations, 7 December 1760. We have not found the Châtelet's arrêté concerning the notaries, which was dated 2 March 1764. But we know of its contents from the notaries' own response in ACNP, box 46 (7 and 18 March 1764).

de change. The penalty for those who issued or accepted such negotiable instruments would be huge: the forfeiture of their notarial offices. True, enforcement might be difficult, but Laideguive would reward clerks who turned in notaries violating the ban. Of course, the effect would be to deprive notaries of one of the few assets that could (at least in theory) be liquidated in a moment of crisis. That would only compound the risks of lending out deposits.[38]

For the moment, Laideguive's proposals came to naught, though they had the support of the directors of the Parisian notarial company. Daguesseau's ideas met a similar fate, despite the assent of Joly de Fleury. But by 1756 further bankruptcies had revived the calls for reform, leading Laideguive to recirculate his proposal. His ideas remained too radical for the judicial authorities, but the debate kept boiling thanks to a disgruntled notarial clerk named Carbon, who had worked for a notary named Lecointe. After Lecointe went bankrupt in 1759, Carbon wrote to the chancellor to complain that the high price of notarial offices was impelling notaries to take risks and pushing them into bankruptcy. The solution he demanded was, once again, fixing the price of offices. Not long thereafter the chancellor himself admonished the notaries for their misbehavior.[39]

Now Laideguive had second thoughts. Abruptly changing his mind, he wrote a memo opposing the very sort of price fixing which he had once supported. Perhaps he and other notaries feared that prices would be fixed low enough to deprive sitting notaries of the capital gains from a recent run up in the price of their offices. In any event, Laideguive now denied that the high price of offices was what tripped notaries up, and he stressed that price fixing was simply impractical.[40] Although he— and apparently his colleagues as well—had reversed course on price fixing, they did at least put into practice one of Laideguive's original proposals. On 9 May 1762 the company of Parisian notaries decided to prohibit notaries from signing or accepting the billets à ordre, lettres de change, and other negotiable instruments.[41] The penalty they adopted

38. BN Joly de Fleury 2148, fol. 355; ACNP, box 46. The key evidence in box 46 is an unsigned and undated *mémoire* and a subsequent letter from Laideguive to a colleague that allows us to establish that the mémoire was written by Laideguive in 1744 in response to regulations proposed by procureur-général Guillaume François Joly de Fleury.

39. ACNP, box 46, letter dated 14 March 1756 to Pierre-Louis Laideguive and Carbon's undated letter to the chancellor; Délibérations, 7 December 1760, a warning from the chancellor about unspecified misbehavior among the notaries.

40. ACNP, box 46: "Observations sur la variation du prix des offices."

41. ACNP Déliberations, 9 May 1762; Patu 1766:38. Why the notaries took this step in 1762 is not clear, but it does not seem that they were reacting to yet another embarrassing bankruptcy.

was essentially what Laideguive had proposed—the loss of the notary's office.

Even if this heavy penalty led notaries to respect the measure, it would still have no effect on the billets simples (IOU's) that undergirded the deposit business. The ban on negotiable instruments did make managing deposits more difficult, but it certainly did not keep the notary Deshayes from floundering in 1764. Nor did it stop the Châtelet from drawing up their own stringent regulations in that same year.

Those regulations, however, frightened the notaries enough that they leapt into action to lobby against the Châtelet's resolution. In a fortnight, they chose a committee to argue against the new rules—Laideguive was one of the members—and approved a brief that the committee sent the Châtelet. In the brief, the notaries stressed that the Châtelet's reforms were too easy to evade. Worse, they would undermine essential public confidence in notaries. A notary who wanted to cheat could simply omit deposits from his register, and he could easily keep his strongbox and register in balance—presumably (though the notaries do not linger over the details) by making unregistered loans. Meanwhile, the constant visits to check on their registers would ruin "the credit and confidence that the public should have in the notaries." Inevitably, the notaries would all come under suspicion, even the honest ones, because of the misdeeds of a few. The result "would utterly destroy the trust that they have enjoyed, trust which links and animates all the dealings they have to be involved in."[42]

In place of the regulations, the notaries favored stronger police powers for the company itself, backed up by severe penalties—as in the Deshayes bankruptcy—for those notaries who did go astray. They did not want the authorities to tamper with their lucrative deposit business, which would vanish if the magistrates started snooping around. Investors would never leave money on deposit (here the notaries made it clear they meant the kind of deposits that were lent out) unless the whole operation was conducted in perfect secrecy. A deposit register would simply scare investors away, since it would "unveil the mysteries of families and fortunes."[43]

To be sure, their brief was self-serving, but the notaries were not being completely unrealistic. They had long defended the confidentiality of

42. ACNP, Délibérations, 4 through 18 March 1764; box 46: "Assemblée du comité tenue en la maison de M. Laideguive" (7 March 1764), and "Mémoire contenant les observations et reflexions de la communauté des notaires au Châtelet de Paris . . ." (18 March 1764).

43. ACNP, box 46: "Mémoire contenant les observations. . . ."

their dealings with clients, and the privacy of their records constituted one of the fundamental liberties of the Old Regime. Clients—especially powerful and privileged ones—simply did not want their financial dealings exposed to public inspection and the possible depredations of the tax collectors. The notaries were also correct in noting the ease with which the Châtelet's regulations could be skirted simply by omitting deposits and loans from the proposed deposit registers. Given the difficulty of enforcing such rules, it was probably better to rely upon the sort of harsh punishment to which Deshayes was sentenced. The threat of execution would then compensate for the difficulty of detecting notaries who ruined themselves and their clients by lending out too much of their deposits.

Finally, the notaries were right to stress the importance of public confidence, for it really was essential to their financial role. Notaries earned that confidence by providing their clients with top-notch service: finding them money, making their investments, selling their assets, and doing it all quickly and appropriately. If a notary's service was unsatisfactory, then his clients could usually just abandon him and take their business to one of his colleagues. The reason, as we know from chapter 6, was that the clients almost always had another notary to whom they could turn. Clients simply had to compare their usual notary's service with what this alternative notary proposed. An investor who wished to put money into an obligation, for example, might simply make sure that the usual notary could arrange a suitable loan more quickly than the alternative notary.

Such a comparison, though, did not suffice when it came to the deposit business. With investments in obligations it might be enough to compare the terms of the loans and the speed with which they could be arranged, but deposits demanded much more information. It was not enough just to consider the interest rates the notaries offered on deposits and the conditions under which the money could be withdrawn. Clients would also want to assess the riskiness of the deposits, and that would require knowing both what the notaries' entire portfolios were and how other depositors were likely to react. At the very least, the clients would have to know how liquid their usual notary's assets were and how much of his funds on deposit were lent out. They would also have to guess whether other depositors would stage a run either on their notary or on other études. Would the depositors panic and demand their cash back? Would the panic spread from other études to their own notary, as confidence in the notaries as a whole was undermined?

Information of this sort was simply not available. To begin with, even if a notary did volunteer to reveal the contents of his portfolio, the information would probably not be credible: why would clients believe a notary who assured them that his assets were liquid and his reserves of cash sufficient? As for discerning the reaction of other depositors, that would be even more difficult. All clients could do would be to seek signs of impending panics or of their own notary's risky dealings in the information spread by café gossip, news sheets, and popular literature.[44] Public opinion of this sort has usually been a subject for cultural history, particularly the history of the Revolution's cultural origins. But more was bruited about in late eighteenth-century Paris than just attacks on the king and political scandal. Parisians also spread financial news, from rumors about government loans to the news of notarial bankruptcies. The news circuits would probably take note if the judicial authorities suddenly inspected a notary's étude—even if the inspection were simply part of new regulations. The news would spread, for although Paris was a large anonymous city, notaries were semi-public figures. Depositors might then rush to withdraw their money, and notaries throughout the city might fail. The whole credit system might then collapse, a disaster for the notaries, their private clients, and the state.

In the end, the notaries won the battle, for the Châtelet's regulations were never imposed. Perhaps the Châtelet was persuaded by their arguments, or perhaps it succumbed to political pressure from what was a highly effective lobby, one that advanced its own money to the state and raised enormous sums for the government from private lenders. The notaries had successfully avoided damaging proposals in the past, such as the contrôle des actes. The Châtelet's regulations were just one more example.

The Châtelet failed to stop notaries from engaging in risky behavior. One can, however, imagine other solutions to this problem. What the notaries needed was either a financial asset that could be liquidated easily, or a lender of last resort who could bail them out. Unfortunately, easily liquidated assets were not on the horizon. The French government offered nothing like the English consol, and even solid government securities like the consol might plunge in value or prove difficult to sell in moments of financial crisis. The same was true of other interest-bearing assets that were supposedly easy to liquidate—the short-term credit of merchants and government financiers. Furthermore, such short-term credit usually lay outside the notaries' grasp because of the segmentation of credit markets. As for a lender of last resort, the Law affair ruled out having a government bank play that role; in any case, central banks did not bail out financial institutions anywhere else in Europe until the last

44. Darnton 1994.

half of the nineteenth century. But conceivably a private institution could step in during crises. It could furnish cash and help balance deposits and withdrawals, as regional banks did in late nineteenth-century German credit cooperatives.[45] Or failing that, it might at least provide clients with insurance for their deposits.

Such an institution was actually proposed, at least anonymously, by someone who claimed to be entangled in the Deshayes bankruptcy. What he suggested was a form of insurance for deposits. The Parisian notaries as a group would back up the deposits. Clients who left money on deposit with notaries would take their billet or acte de dépôt to officials of the company of notaries, and the company would therefore have a reliable way of tracking notaries who courted disaster by excessive deposit lending.[46] This proposal, however, remained a dead letter, probably because it required too much cooperation among highly individualistic études and too much sharing of sensitive business information. Perhaps too some notaries realized that it risked provoking enormous problems of moral hazard, for once clients were insured, desperate notaries had all the more reason to put deposits at risk, much like unscrupulous savings and loan executives in twentieth-century America.

Although the Châtelet did not impose its regulations, it had undoubtedly succeeded in frightening the notaries. They knew they were treading on thin ice with the judicial authorities, who had already hanged Deshayes in effigy and who were threatening equally harsh penalties in future bankruptcies. Meanwhile, their clients were being bombarded with worrisome news about the Deshayes affair in cafés and popular literature. With both the authorities and public opinion in a state of alarm, there were signs that both notaries and their clients were beginning to retreat from the deposit business. Notaries did continue to lend out deposits and even to fail, but after 1764 none of their bankruptcies provoked dramatic intervention by the courts. And by the 1780s, observers like Mercier seemed to suggest that although bankruptcies had not disappeared they had at least subsided.[47] The statistical evidence we have points in the same direction. Though for the period after 1764 we lack anything as complete as Laideguive's list of bankrupt notaries, fewer bankruptcies cropped up in news gazettes such as Bachaumont's *Mémoires secrets,* which usually took note when notaries failed. The *Mémoires secrets* in fact listed only three notarial bankruptcies and two notarial suicides for the years 1762–87. That amounts to only 0.12 bankruptcies

45. Guinnane 1991.
46. BN, Joly de Fleury, 385, fol. 159.
47. Mercier 1783–88, 2:33 and 1994, 2:1458–59.

per year, or 0.19 if we assume that the suicides were also the result of business failures.[48] The *Mémoires secrets* may of course be incomplete, but even if we make generous allowance for omissions, the number involved still seems to be far below the 1.25 bankruptcies per year registered in the years 1744–56. During the rest of the Old Regime, Paris never again witnessed a rash of bankruptcies like that before 1764, and the notaries did not become bankers.

Instead, most of them reverted to their highly lucrative role as brokers of medium- and long-term loans. The resulting division of the Parisian credit market between notaries and bankers had parallels elsewhere in Europe. In the private credit market of seventeenth- and eighteenth-century England, for instance, bankers also tended to specialize in short-term loans, while mortgages were arranged by very different intermediaries, such as scriveners and attorneys. And throughout Europe, it was not until the late nineteenth century that bankers began to make long-term loans and fund them with their short-term deposits.[49] The widespread split between short- and long-term lending derived from the same causes as in France: divisions in the legal system, the lack of a lender of last resort, and the paucity of liquid assets.[50] It also reflected similar informational barriers. In England, for example, scriveners and attorneys were experts in the conveyances and title searches that accompanied land sales and mortgages, and they naturally came into contact with borrowers and lenders. It was no wonder then that they began to match them and arrange loans.[51]

In Paris, the notaries' retreat from banking had some important consequences. In the first place, it removed one source of strain on the notaries' practice of referring business to one another: no longer would a notary be as tempted to advance money to a borrower until he could find a lender in his own clientele. Abandoning deposits also gave added

48. Using an index that covers the years 1762–87 (Bachaumont 1866), we went through the *Mémoires secrets* (Bachaumont 1784–89) and looked for all references involving notaries. We found two bankruptcies and two suicides. To these we added one additional bankruptcy that Foiret (1912:12) found in the *Mémoires secrets*.

49. Neal 1994; Quinn 1994, 1997; Miles 1981; Anderson 1969a, 1969b; Melton 1986. On the difficulties of funding long-term loans with short-term deposits, see Michie 1988 and Gerschenkron 1962.

50. Of course, if highly liquid assets had been readily available in all denominations, then demand for deposits themselves would have been much smaller in the first place. Instead of depositing money with a banker, customers could have held liquid securities in their portfolios and then sold them when they needed cash.

51. Neal 1994:167–68; Miles 1981; Melton 1986. Miles suggests that attorneys shared information with one another in much the same way as French notaries, and Melton shows how a scrivener could move from brokerage to banking.

impetus to the obligation market, which began to surge by the end of the 1760s. For notaries, obligations involved none of the personal risks of the deposit business, and yet they would appeal to clients who did not want to tie up their money in a long-term loan. Such clients might have initially preferred an interest-bearing deposit, but in light of the bankruptcies both they and their notaries might have turned instead to medium-term obligations. There were of course other reasons to favor such loans—notably the government's decision to cut the maximum interest rate on rentes in 1766—and, as notaries honed their skills at arranging obligations, their businesses flourished. The result was a dramatic increase in the value of notarial études after 1760 and a credit market that met the needs of a wider variety of borrowers and lenders than ever before.

Consequences for Borrowers and Lenders

What then were the notaries' accomplishments, beyond arranging scores of loans? Did they open the credit market to new participants? Did they find suitable financial instruments for investors and move savings where it might be needed most, across social, geographic, and generational boundaries? And did the capital they mobilized spur investment?

As far as investment is concerned, most of the sources, alas, fall silent because rentes and obligations do not usually reveal why someone borrowed. Sometimes a reason is given—for instance, when a rente is used to finance an office or to purchase real estate—but even the practice of mentioning offices or real estate is far from consistent. Often all that appears is the laconic phrase that the loan is "for the borrower's affairs."[52]

Nor is there any indirect way to tease out the effect that notarial credit had on investment. Marriages undoubtedly absorbed some of the capital that notaries raised (figure 3.1), because parents borrowed to help newlyweds get established. One might hope to probe the relationship via a regression of the volume of new loans on the number of marriages, but lack of an interest rate series means that we face a system of simultaneous equations with no information about prices, which also affected the volume of new loans. In the jargon of econometrics, the regression of volume of new loans on marriages is just a reduced form equation, and it tells practically nothing about the strength of the real relationship between marriages and new loans.

52. See, for example, ANMC LXII, 203 (12 November 1670).

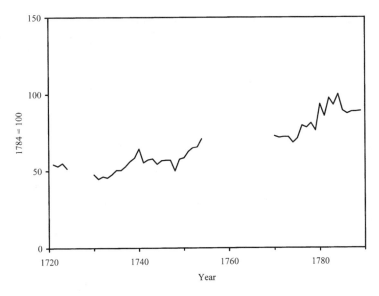

FIGURE 7.1 Index of Annual Firewood Consumption in Paris, 1721–89 (1784 = 100). The index includes firewood only, not charcoal, and it is based on annual averages of all the sources collected in Bourgoin 1969. Years 1725–29, 1755, and 1757–69 are missing.

Similar problems cloud the relationship between notarial credit and investment in buildings. Although rentes were no doubt used to finance many construction projects in eighteenth-century Paris, the rente contracts themselves pass over such matters in silence, and any attempt to uncover the effect of credit on construction investment is stymied by the lack of an interest rate series. Worse yet, there are no series of building permits and no figures for imports of building materials available for Old-Regime Paris.[53]

Yet all is not lost. First of all, we do have the city's consumption of firewood, which ought to have increased as new hearths were built and old residences expanded. Firewood consumption does rise sharply in the late eighteenth century: by 48 percent between 1731–40 and 1771–80, and by 76 percent between 1731–40 and 1781–89 (figure 7.1). The climate does not appear to have cooled, nor was firewood simply cheaper. Some of the firewood did go to industry and commerce, but artisans and manufacturers usually preferred charcoal, which had the

53. In particular, there is nothing like the nineteenth-century series in Chevalier 1950: 110, 291.

added advantage of a declining price relative to firewood itself.[54] Of course, if some of the wood was used by artisans and manufacturers, then firewood consumption would serve as an index not just of residential construction but of industrial investment as well. In either case, there is an obvious parallel between investment (whether in construction or commerce) and the growth of the Paris credit market.

The connection between credit and construction is reinforced by qualitative descriptions of the booms and busts of building in Old-Regime Paris. They tell a story of construction slowing at the end of the Regency (1723) and then picking up again in the late 1750s and 1760s, matching the curve traced by private indebtedness (figure 2.4).[55] In some instances, the link between credit and building is quite clear, because the construction projects were actually financed by the notaries. Such was the case, for instance, for at least part of the development of the Palais-Royal, whose owners—the house of Orléans—issued rentes to fund the construction.[56]

Admittedly, the ebb and flow of building in Paris could have resulted from other causes as well. It might reflect politics and patterns of government spending. Or it might have been driven by architectural fashions and by legal changes that gave contractors and construction lenders stronger claims in bankruptcy proceedings.[57] But if there were no connection between construction and the credit market in Paris, then it would be difficult to imagine what all the private loans went for. Between 1770 and 1789, net private indebtedness in Paris climbed 533 million livres, or 28 million a year. Some of the 28 million may have simply offset higher prices for the goods the loans were meant to purchase, such as buildings, land, and education. (That would be the case, for instance, if borrowers were simply taking out loans to buy the same old buildings but were charged higher prices than previous owners.) A further portion may have passed to the government indirectly, going for government offices or to financiers who then relent the money to the government.

54. The evidence we have about the climate concerns dates of nearby wine harvests, which suggest that the temperature over these years was rising slightly, at least in spring and summer (Le Roy Ladurie and Baulant 1980). While the price of firewood in Paris climbed 54 percent between 1731–40 and 1781–90, the price of charcoal only went up 28 percent (Hauser 1936:150–53). For the preference for charcoal in industry, see Diderot and d'Alembert 1751–76: s.v. "charbon" and "bois de chauffage"; and Isambert 1822, 26:282.

55. Chagniot 1988:241–71.

56. Chagniot 1988:266–68; Barker 1989:185–87, 195; Bercé, Boubli, and Folliot 1988:154.

57. Chagniot 1988:241–71.

But we estimate that at least 12 million remained every year to fund the acquisition of additional private assets: further education, new businesses, or—most likely of all at a time when real estate was the most common asset—more land and buildings.[58]

That, at a minimum, was the real increase in the stock of private assets financed each year through the Paris credit market. If Parisian investors were footing 81 percent of it, as our samples for the years 1770–89 suggest, then they were expending at least 4 percent of the city's after tax income on new private assets.[59] The assets they bought no doubt included some farmland and country estates, but that sort of purchase was more common in the previous century, when the tax regime and the threat of monetary manipulation favored investment in rural property. Besides, choice rural holdings near Paris had been bought up long ago.[60] In all likelihood, the bulk of the new acquisitions were made in Paris itself, and most were no doubt urban real estate—in particular, the buildings produced by Parisian developers.

It may be difficult to estimate precisely the effect that notaries had on investment, but it is much easier to grasp how they affected dealings among the generations. What notarial credit did, quite simply, was to help people cope with the natural variations of earnings and consumption as people aged—what economists call the problem of the life cycle. Consider, for example, the sort of prosperous young man who began his career with a visit to his notary. He might be buying a shop or purchasing a government office. He might be constructing a new residence, or paying what was due to his siblings when he inherited the bulk of his parents' estate. Large expenses of that sort would usually crop up early in a career, before a person had amassed much in the way of liquid savings.[61] The young man would want to borrow, and lenders with the necessary liquid assets within his family might be lacking. Hence, the recourse to borrowing via the family notary.

58. We estimate that price appreciation amounted to no more than a bit over 13 million a year and that at most a sixth of the 28 million went to the government indirectly. For the reasoning behind our estimates, see Hoffman, Postel-Vinay, and Rosenthal 1999, note 33.

59. The income estimate here (230 million livres a year in the 1780s) is from Lavoisier 1864–93, 6:437–39. The fraction of new assets funded by Parisian investors comes from table 7.6.

60. Hoffman 1986, 1996. Parisians did fund improvements (such as better barns) on farms nearer the city, often via loans to tenant farmers. But investments of that sort would eventually be captured by higher land rents and sales prices, which have already been taken into account in our estimates of price appreciation. For examples, see Postel-Vinay 1998; Moriceau and Postel-Vinay 1992; and Moriceau 1994:720–24.

61. For examples, see Sargentson 1966:26–32.

In such cases, the notary would seek a lender from men and women who had amassed savings during their lives and now wanted to invest. Because they had put money aside, these lenders would usually be older, though the motives behind their lending might vary greatly. Those who had no children, such as spinsters and clergymen, might care little about their heirs. They would be more interested in providing for their own old age than in bequeathing wealth to others, and they would probably find a life annuity ideal. It would give them the largest steady income over the remaining years of their lives, because nothing would be left to pass on to any heirs. And it would have the added advantage of continuing no matter how long they lived. Married men, by contrast, would have reason to prefer a rente, particularly if they were wealthy and worried about irresponsible descendants' dissipating their fortunes. Under Parisian law, the rente would protect against such a disaster. It converted cash, which profligate heirs could always squander, into a perpetual stream of income payments that even a generation of spendthrifts could not easily interrupt.[62]

Evidence from the notarial records confirms this picture. Borrowers were indeed relatively young, while lenders turn out to be older. In our detailed samples of loans from the years 1690 to 1788, fully 68 percent of the borrowers were under forty, compared to an estimated 55 percent for the French adult population as a whole during the period 1740–89. Lenders by contrast were far more mature: 78 percent were forty or older, versus only 45 percent of French adults (table 7.3). What the Paris credit market apparently did was to channel money from wealthy older lenders to the state and to younger private borrowers. Consider the funds lent for private credit: 81 percent came from lenders forty or older, and 57 percent went to borrowers under forty.

Practically none of these loans involved transactions between members of the same family or relatives. In our detailed sample of notarial loans, borrowers and lenders were related in only 3.1 percent of the contracts, even if we include relatives by marriage. It is undoubtedly true that relatives made some loans inside their families without recourse to a notary, but the thriving Parisian credit market suggests that families alone could not match all the thrifty women and old men with all the creditworthy youths. Thanks to notaries, such extrafamilial credit transactions were far easier in the eighteenth century.

The notaries also seemed to help each lender find the credit instruments that suited his situation and motives for investing. If he was worried about his heirs, notaries apparently guided him toward investment

62. Giesey 1977.

TABLE 7.3   AGE DISTRIBUTION FOR BORROWERS AND LENDERS, 1690–1788, AND
FOR THE FRENCH ADULT POPULATION, 1740–89

	Number of Contracts (percent)	Funds Lent (percent)	French Adult Population (percent)
Lenders			
less than 40 years old	21	19	54.5
40 to 59	59	47	28.5
60 or older	19	34	17.0
Borrowers			
less than 40 years old	68	57	54.5
40 to 59	25	25	28.5
60 or older	7	18	17.0

Source: Reprinted by permission from Hoffman, Postel-Vinay, and Rosenthal 1992, table 2. The ultimate data source for borrowers and lenders was a preliminary version of the detailed samples described
in table 2.2; it involved over 8,300 loans.
Note: Ages were found for only twenty percent of the lenders and three percent of the borrowers; they
came from two sources: life annuity contracts that mentioned the borrower's age and biographical
dictionaries. The figures for lenders include those who lent to the state, and multiple lenders and
borrowers have been counted each time they appear. We have assumed that all borrowers were over
twenty. It is worth pointing out that Louis d'Orléans, who borrowed several million livres when he was
in his twenties, was excluded from the borrowers' age calculation. Had he been included the borrowers
would have been even younger. The figures for the age structure of the French population as a whole
are estimated averages for 1740–89 for both males and females; by adults, we mean all those aged
twenty or more. Since the age structure of the French population changed hardly at all before 1830,
there is little risk in using the 1740–89 averages for the entire period 1690–1788.

in perpetual annuities. If providing for old age was the issue, they pushed
life annuities. Here the best evidence comes from the difference between investors in rentes perpétuelles and investors in rentes viagères
in the 1751 enumeration, but it does admittedly pose something of an
identification problem. The problem is that there were only 216 government perpetual annuities issued during 1751, versus 3,695 private ones.
There were also more than three times as many government life annuities as private life annuities. Hence in 1751 the choice between perpetual
and life annuities was virtually the same as the choice between private
and government annuities, and it is hard to tell whether a given investor
chose a private rente because he was the sort of person who was likely to
be concerned about his heirs or because he feared government default.

Given the risks associated with lending to the Old-Regime government, we wished to disentangle the issue of perpetual annuities versus
life annuities from that of private versus public loans. What we needed
to test our description of the lenders' motives were more private life
annuities. We therefore added to the 1751 enumeration evidence we
had collected earlier on a large number of life annuities issued in the
next year—1752—by the king's relative, the Duc d'Orléans. We then

employed logit analysis (a statistical technique for analyzing categorical choices, like that between a perpetual and a life annuity) to probe the lender's motives. We estimated two separate logit equations: one for the choice between perpetual and life annuities, and a second for the choice between public and private life annuities.[63] Adding the life annuities from 1752 does mean that our sample is not random, which creates some econometric problems. There are ways of dealing with the problems, though, and of keeping them from affecting the logit results (table 7.4).

Since the logits do therefore seem trustworthy, it is gratifying that they seem to confirm our story. The coefficients are consistent with the notaries' taking into account each lender's motives and guiding him toward the appropriate choice of a perpetual annuity or a life annuity. To begin with, individuals without heirs, such as clerics and spinsters, were much more likely to invest in life annuities rather than rentes perpétuelles, which would be passed on to descendants. So were married women, but they too had reason to be more concerned about old age than about heirs.[64] Widows, on the other hand, clung to perpetual annuities—indeed, more tenaciously than any other investors. The likely explanation has to do with their reason for investing. Typically, it was either because they were managing their children's estate or because they were rich, for only prosperous families left their women resources to manage. In either case, they had more of a motive to worry about their heirs than did unmarried women or even married women, who could assume that children would be taken care of out of their husbands' estates. Finally, wealthy men in the Parisian elite also showed a strong attachment to perpetual annuities. Although the contracts do not reveal whether they actually had children, it is reasonable to suppose that most of them did and that they wanted to give their children money for dowries, for government offices, and for a luxurious train of life. They were therefore willing to sacrifice what were in fact higher expected returns on the life annuities to protect their families' capital.

As for the choice of private or government life annuities, it turns out that clerics, the male elite, and women of all types (single, married, and

63. We also considered a more complicated multinomial logit equation for the choice among perpetuals and the two types of life annuities. Because the results were similar, we report only the binary logits, which are easier to interpret.

64. The funds for their investment might come from their dowries, which were supposed to provide for their support in old age, or joint savings with their husbands, who would presumably take primary responsibility for the heirs. Contemporaries, it should be noted, were aware of the link between life annuities and the lack of heirs; see, for example, Mercier 1783–88, 1:229–32.

TABLE 7.4   BINARY LOGIT EQUATIONS: CHOICE OF ANNUITIES BY LENDERS IN 1751

Dependent Variable	Choice of Perpetual rather than Life Annuities		Choice of Government Life Annuity rather than Private Life Annuity	
	Coefficient (*T*-statistics)	Expected Change in Probability of Choosing Perpetual Annuity for One Unit Change in Independent Variable	Coefficient (*T*-statistics)	Expected Change in Probability of Choosing Government Annuity for One Unit Change in Independent Variable
Independent Variables				
Constant	−0.08 (−2.26)		0.99 (16.82)	
Membership in elite	0.16 (2.46)	0.04	−1.02 (−10.05)	−0.22
Clergy	−0.90 (−8.30)	−0.21	−0.54 (−3.88)	−0.12
Married women	−0.58 (−7.64)	−0.14	−0.42 (−3.85)	−0.09
Single women	−0.77 (−12.25)	−0.18	−0.24 (−2.56)	−0.05
Widows	0.41 (5.24)	0.10	−0.42 (−3.24)	−0.09
Number of cases	8197		3998	
Percentage of cases in which dependent variable = 1	51.23		67.66	

Source: See text.

Note: The dependent variable is 1 for the choice of a perpetual annuity rather than a life annuity and for the choice of a government rather than a private life annuity. All the explanatory variables except the constant are dummy variables. The residual category consists of men who are neither in the elite nor clergy: overwhelmingly men of what we called the middling sort. The sample used to estimate the two logits was constructed by adding data on 646 rentes viagères privées sold in 1752 to evidence from the 1751 enumeration. It was therefore not a random sample, and to get consistent estimators, we had to weight each observation via the method of Manski and Lehrman 1977. The weight for each observation was calculated by taking the frequency of the value of the dependent variable for the observation in an underlying population relative to its frequency in the particular sample we had constructed by adding the data from 1751 and 1752. The frequencies of the dependent variable values in the underlying population we in turn estimated by using our counts of credit contracts for the years 1746–56. In the end, this weighting had practically no effect on the logit results. *T*-statistics in parentheses.

widowed) preferred private life annuities to government ones, even though they both promised similar nominal returns. Their preference confirms that in the eighteenth century government bonds were far from a safe investment. The only group fond of government life annuities (and their fondness was only relative to the other groups) were the re-

maining lenders—essentially the middling sort of merchants and professional men. Their penchant for government life annuities may have reflected their own considerable assets. They were wealthy enough to take
on some risk, but unlike the elite they were probably not already overbur-
dened with government bonds or with assets whose value might rise and
fall with the government's fiscal health. They did not have government
offices, whose value could suffer when the government faced financial
difficulty, and unlike government financial officers, they probably were
less likely to own the even more precarious short-term government
IOU's. Nor were they likely to have invested indirectly in the government—as many nobles did—by lending money to government financiers. For them, a government life annuity might have seemed risky, but
its return would probably not be correlated with the return on the rest
of their portfolio. It was thus worth taking the risk that government life
annuities posed, particularly since they bore a high return. That notaries
sold them such investments thus makes considerable sense.

Although private life annuities were therefore favored by most lenders, they were always in short supply. Few private borrowers operated on
a large enough scale to issue them: in statistical terms, few borrowers
were large enough to benefit from the law of large numbers. Clearly,
the state had an advantage here because it borrowed such enormous
sums. With demand running strong among the numerous investors who
worried about their income in old age, it is hardly surprising that the
government turned to public life annuities to finance more and more
of its deficit. It could hardly compete against private perpetual annuities,
given its tarnished history as a borrower. Switching to life annuities,
though, offered the state a practical way to raise funds with few private
competitors, albeit at a higher cost. It was also a way to tap funds provided by a new set of lenders, who could not rely on family (or pensions
either, obviously) for support in old age. As we know from chapter five,
the Parisian notaries (along with bankers) bore a major responsibility
for selling the state's life annuities to these new lenders.

One might argue that lenders actually chose the appropriate investment or annuity on their own, not because of some advice they had
received from their notary. Perhaps they did, but it was still the notary
who located the annuity that matched their desires. He rendered the
appropriate investment possible, just as he made possible a transfer of
funds between generations that escaped the limitations of familial bequests. How else can one explain the unusual life annuity contracts that
were assembled for particular clients, if the notary himself was not putting them together? In 1761, one client, Nicolas Piault, got nine government annuities, each one of them contingent on the life of a different

seventy-year-old.[65] Given the terms of the annuities, Piault was guaranteed a high return for a short time span, but putting his contracts together required locating nine people nearly exactly seventy years old. It was highly unlikely that Piault found the seventy-year-olds on his own. One of them came from as far as Auvergne; others appeared again and again in similar contracts in the same étude. Obviously, the notary was crafting the contracts, both for Piault and other clients. He did not need a Genevan banker to show him how to take advantage of government annuities.[66]

Such feats were not the only accomplishments which Parisian notaries could boast about. What they could be proudest of was their success in arranging transactions across the boundaries of gender, geography, and social class. Without them, credit would have stuck to the channels of family, neighborhood, and profession, and scores of possible transactions would never have been made.

Not that borrowing and lending were suddenly possible for everyone. As today, borrowers and lenders came disproportionately from the social elite. There were occasionally more modest borrowers such as Pierre Quiet, a wigmaker from the parish of Saint Paul, who in 1751 received 2,000 livres from another wigmaker, Benoit Caldero of the parish of Saint Gervais. But wigmakers were hardly paupers, and Quiet could back up his loan with considerable collateral: a barbershop worth some 2,900 livres.[67] However, most of the parties to loans occupied more elevated rungs on the social ladder. If we restrict ourselves to the years 1730 through 1788, when information on professions is most illuminating, then 64 percent of private borrowers were nobles and officers, whereas in Paris as a whole—to judge from Daumard and Furet's reading of marriage contracts in 1749—under 9 percent of the city's lay adult population consisted of such members of the elite (table 7.5). The ranks of

65. Such life annuities should not be thought of as retirement contracts; rather they were investments more akin to futures contracts. In a futures contract, one person may promise to deliver 100 barrels of oil at $21 a barrel three months hence. If the price rises, he loses; if it falls, he gains. In effect, he is betting that the price will fall. In the case of our life annuities, the state offered to pay an annuity that reflected the life expectancy of a particular age class (here individuals 70 and above). The investor was thus betting on the life span of an individual. If the "life" lasted longer than expected, he won. If the "life" ended sooner, the state won. By selecting healthy seventy-year-olds (the youngest individuals in the age class), the investor was pushing the odds in his favor, and the state was the victim of adverse selection. By making nine separate bets on nine individuals, he was reducing the variance of his return. The investor could in fact bet on any life, so long as he could establish the person's age; life annuity contracts were even taken out on the life of the king.

66. ANMC IX 708 (January-February, 1761). For the Genevan bankers, see Lüthy 1959–61, 2:464–559.

67. ANMC CXV (October 1751).

TABLE 7-5 THE SOCIAL CLASS OF LENDERS AND BORROWERS, 1730–88

When Borrower's Class Is		Percentage of Lenders or Funds Lent From					Percentage of All Borrowers or of Funds Borrowed	Percentage of Paris Marriages
		Nobles and Officers	Church	Trade and Finance	Crafts, Domestics, and Other Occupations	Women		
Nobles and officers	N	46.0	6.9	29.8	7.2	10.0	63.6	8.6
	F	68.7	6.0	18.4	2.0	4.5	85.0	—
Church	N	35.5	6.4	33.8	11.3	12.9	3.7	0
	F	62.2	4.8	22.9	2.6	7.4	2.2	—
Trade and finance	N	25.1	3.9	50.1	10.4	9.9	20.1	13.8
	F	35.1	3.4	49.9	5.5	5.4	8.4	—
Crafts, domestics, and other occupations	N	21.0	0.0	21.0	44.4	13.5	9.8	77.6
	F	38.4	0.0	17.1	17.5	6.8	2.6	—
Women	N	37.2	0.0	34.8	16.2	11.5	2.6	0
	F	68.5	0.0	14.9	11.0	5.5	1.1	—

Any class of private borrowing	N	38.7	5.4	33.4	11.8	10.4	45.7
	F	65.1	5.6	21.1	3.3	4.8	67.7
State borrowing	N	26.6	5.7	48.5	6.3	12.8	54.3
	F	54.2	9.0	26.9	3.2	4.6	32.3
All borrowing, state and private	N	32.1	5.6	41.7	8.9	11.7	
	F	61.6	6.7	23.1	3.3	5.3	
Total number of loans for each class of lender		1,166	204	1,511	321	425	
Total value of loans for each class of lender		19,269	2,103	7,202	1,036	1,669	

Source: Adapted from Hoffman, Postel-Vinay, and Rosenthal 1992, table 1; the table is based on a sample of 3,627 loans. The data on marriages come from Daumard's and Furet's (1961, 10–19) analysis of Parisian marriage contracts in 1749.

Note: N is the percentage of the number of individuals who fall in a given category, F is the percentage of funds lent, and total values are in thousands of livres. Although we could have adopted a more detailed system of social classification, we used the one here in order to make comparisons with the data in Daumard and Furet 1961. The table omits contracts in which the borrowers and lenders were males for whom no occupations were given in the loan contracts. It also excludes loans to Louis d'Orléans, who borrowed about five million livres in the sample. The category of women here comprises only those who could not be classified in a social group using a husband's occupation; they are mostly spinsters and widows. The trade and finance category includes merchants, financiers, notaries, and other professions, and bourgeois de Paris.

the borrowers reached to the very pinnacle of noble society to include figures such as the colossally wealthy duc Louis d'Orléans, who took on over five million livres of debt in our sample alone during the 1750s, chiefly by selling life annuities. Also numerous among the borrowers were merchants, financiers, notaries, and *bourgeois de Paris* (essentially prosperous city dwellers who were not noble). The groups seriously underrepresented were those lower down the social ladder, such as artisans and day laborers. In 1730–88 only 10 percent of the borrowers in our sample were artisans (including masters) or wage earners—a group that formed perhaps 78 percent of the city's lay adult population. Of course, such a result is hardly surprising, for artisans and wage earners generally lacked the collateral to borrow long term. They might be able to arrange obligations, but most likely they would have to turn to other intermediaries such as pawn shops to borrow.

As could be expected, most lenders also came from the ranks of the wealthy, for only they had the money to lend. In 1730–88, for example, 39 percent of private lenders were nobles and officers, while 33 percent were merchants, financiers, notaries, and bourgeois—moneyed groups far more prominent among lenders than among borrowers (table 7.5). To be sure, it was becoming much more common for prosperous servants and wage earners to lend to the government via the life annuities that notaries sold. But they still played only a small role in lending, as did artisans. In a sense, then, the credit market shifted funds within the wealthy elite, with a net flow from merchants, bourgeois, and financiers to the state and to officers and the nobility. The notaries thus made possible the movement of capital among groups who lived in different neighborhoods, held different assets, and did not regularly socialize with one another—most notably, from the merchants and bourgeois to the officers and nobles.[68]

Beyond releasing credit from social ties, the notaries also opened the investment market to a growing number of women and non-Parisians. It was the private credit market that witnessed the influx of women, not the market for government loans. Indeed, in the government market, the percentage of lenders who were female did not rise at all in the eighteenth century, and the same was true of the fraction of funds lent

---

68. Unlike some of the financiers, the merchants and bourgeois did not necessarily have recurrent business dealings with the officers and nobles. Nor did they typically marry their daughters to the nobles' or officers' sons. See Chagniot 1988:323–31 and Daumard and Furet 1961:74–75, who show that 85 percent of the wives of *officiers civils nobles* come from families of *officiers civils, officiers militaires*, or *nobles sans profession*.

to the state by females.[69] In the private market, by contrast, the number of female lenders rose substantially: from under 12 percent in 1662 to 20 percent or more in 1740 and 1780 (table 3.6). The increase would have been even more dramatic had it not been for the rise of the obligation, which women shunned. If obligations are excluded, so that only private rentes and viagères remain, then women jump from 14 percent of the lenders in 1662 to 32 percent or more after 1740. The fraction of the total funds for rentes and viagères that women provide climbs as well, though not as much. The reason was that women tended to make smaller loans. That tendency, and their aversion to the thriving market for obligations, kept women from boosting their share of the funds lent out in the private credit market as a whole—the market not just for rentes and viagères, but for obligations too. One might worry, of course, that the growing number of women is a chance result, but a statistical analysis argues to the contrary: women really did lend more frequently in the eighteenth century.[70]

It would be tempting to explain the increase in the number of female lenders by legal changes or by a shift in attitudes. Perhaps women with money to lend were suddenly delivered from the obligatory financial tutelage of spouses and male relatives. Or perhaps it was a revolution in male attitudes toward women, with husbands and fathers allowing women to invest on their own. There are no signs, though, of a legal revolution that suddenly gave women control of property in the eighteenth century. Nor was there any radical shift in attitudes that would have freed more women to lend: despite Enlightenment criticism of social conventions, the philosophes did not really question the status of women in society.[71] Furthermore, if the rising number of women lenders could in fact be traced back to changes in laws or attitudes, then more women would have bought the government's perpetual and life annuities too. Government loans were certainly riskier than many private ones,

69. In our detailed samples of loans, 30 percent of the government's lenders were female in 1690–99 and 26 percent in 1700–09, versus only 21 percent in the 1770s and 1780s. The percentage of funds lent by women does not increase either, and a more sophisticated statistical analysis, which takes into account the preferences certain women had for rentes viagères, also undercuts the idea that women entered the public market in larger numbers.

70. The evidence comes from a logit analysis of the odds of getting a female lender, conditional on the year of the loan and on the type of loan made. The relevant logit coefficients are large and all highly significant.

71. This is the opinion of Hufton 1996:435, who suggests (58–59, 108–109, 511) that there was no change in the legal regime either.

but if women were liberated from financial tutelage and permitted to invest, then more women should have bought government loans than in years past. As we know, that was not the case.

A more plausible explanation would be to trace the change in women's behavior back to the notaries, who provided female investors with information. As far as government loans were concerned, such information was probably not so important. The risks and advantages of each government loan would have been public knowledge, at least in the wealthy households of Paris. Women with money to invest could put their savings in government loans without their notary's help, although his assistance would have certainly made the task easier. Lending to a private borrower, by contrast, would have been far riskier for most women. It would have been hard for them to find borrowers, at least outside their families. Furthermore, many female investors would have lacked the professional ties that could reveal a borrower's creditworthiness. They would be unable to tell whether a borrower would repay and unable to pressure him if he fell into arrears. But once they could consult their notary, private lending would be far easier. He could seek out investments for them and tell them which borrowers were creditworthy. The women would in turn choose the appropriate sort of loan for their circumstances, but like other investors, they would depend on their notary.

It was not just female lenders who gained access to the Parisian credit market via notaries. Investors from outside the city did too, and once again notaries bore responsibility for opening the credit market. In the early eighteenth century and before, private lenders were particularly likely to hail from Paris. Roughly 90 percent of them resided in Paris in 1662 and 1690–1710, and they furnished over 90 percent of the funds lent out (table 7.6A). It was particularly rare for non-Parisians to lend to private borrowers within the city. Less than 4 percent of all loans fell into that category in 1662, and in many of these the lender actually came from the city's suburbs or the surrounding region.[72] The state did somewhat better in attracting non-Parisian lenders, but it is clear that the private market did not yet mobilize capital from afar.

Only after the Law affair—and then only with some hesitation—did capital slowly begin to flow from the provinces into Paris. By the middle of the century, provincial loans to Parisians constituted well over 10 percent of the capital pool—far more than the 3 percent back in 1662

---

72. By surrounding region, we mean the Seine-et-Marne and the former department of the Seine-et-Oise.

TABLE 7.6   RESIDENCES OF BORROWERS AND LENDERS, 1662–1789

A. Loans to Private Borrowers

Residence of		1662		1690–1710		1730–49		1750–69		1770–89	
Lender	Borrower	F	N	F	N	F	N	F	N	F	N
Paris	Paris	77	64	83	76	74	74	63	62	72	67
Paris	Elsewhere	14	29	7	10	10	9	3	4	9	11
Elsewhere	Elsewhere	6	3	2	2	5	4	1	4	3	5
Elsewhere	Paris	3	4	9	11	11	13	33	31	17	17
Total Parisian lenders		91	93	90	86	84	83	66	66	81	78
Total Parisian borrowers		80	68	92	87	85	87	96	93	89	84

B. Loans to the State (same periods as in part A)

Lender's residence	F	N	F	N	F	N	F	N	F	N
Paris	—	—	84	80	75	71	60	78	63	42
Elsewhere in France	—	—	14	19	13	15	39	21	19	24
Foreign	—	—	4	1	12	14	1	1	18	34

Source: Detailed samples of loans described in table 2.2.
Note: N is the percentage of the total number of loans in a given category; F is the fraction of funds lent. Paris means the city only, not the surrounding region.

(table 7.6A). Indeed, by 1750–69 such transactions amounted to a third of the funds lent, involving 31 percent of the lenders.

Clearly, by mid-century notaries were hunting for capital outside of Paris. Why, though, did they only begin to do so after the Law affair? One reason was the Law affair itself, which multiplied financial contacts between the provinces and Paris, as debtors repaid old debts and speculators sought new loans. Yet another reason derived from changes in the government's own borrowing. The crown was now marketing loans like the viagères, which had a broader appeal and were more widely held than older state debt. To sell them, notaries had to seek out new sources of funds. They began to branch out of their Parisian clienteles, reaching first to the provinces and eventually (with the help of bankers) to lenders abroad. By the 1770s and 1780s well over half the state's creditors were foreigners and provincials. Parisians still contributed over 60 percent of the money, but they were a minority among the purchasers of long-term government debt (table 7.6B).

The same picture of credit stretching into the countryside emerges from the 1751 inventory of notarial contracts. The crown borrowed little that year, so the inventory is practically silent about government borrowing. But it does reveal the residences of private borrowers and their lenders, and of parties to notarial contracts in general (figure 7.2). If we first trace the individuals who appeared in notarial contracts in general in 1751—not just loans, but any document preserved by Parisian notaries—we find them not just in Paris but throughout the Paris basin. If we turn our attention to an analogous map of the borrowers and lenders in 1751, certain differences emerge. Inhabiting the rich northern half of France, the borrowers and lenders lived closer to Paris than the average party to a random notarial contract—what one might expect given the difficulties of enforcing credit agreements at a distance. Still, notarial credit extended remarkably far, reaching many clients who lived over one hundred kilometers from Paris. The Parisian notaries were thus moving large sums of capital across France for long-term loans.

Here, historians may be surprised. Mesmerized by fabled banking houses, they have perhaps exaggerated the importance of bills of exchange as the sole means to move capital in the past. Clearly, bills of exchange were the mechanism to convey funds over long distances, but turning the flow of funds into long-term investment (or at least into the purchase of durable assets) required notaries.

In fact, the geographical range of notarial credit was broader than the 1751 enumeration suggests, for 1751 lacked the loans to the state that attracted foreign investors. To appreciate the extent of foreign lending requires a look at a similar inventory for the year 1761 (figure 7.2).

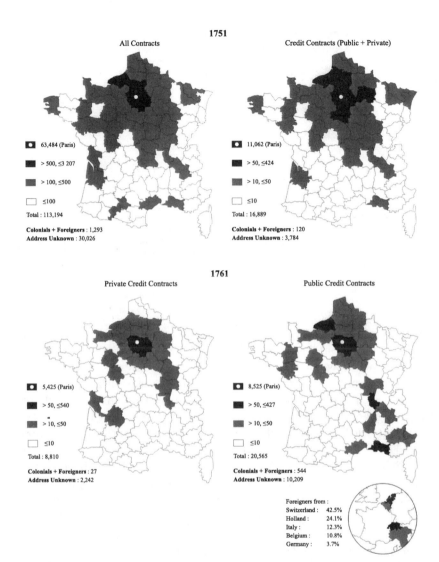

FIGURE 7.2 Residences of Individuals in Notarial Contracts, 1751 and 1761. For 1751, the one map shows the residences of the parties to all notarial contracts that year; the other displays the residences of parties to credit contracts. Since there was little government borrowing that year, the residences are primarily those of borrowers and lenders in private credit contracts. For 1761, one map shows the residences of borrowers and lenders in private credit contracts; the other, residences of the state's lenders. In all four maps, individuals are counted each time they appear in a contract. The source for the maps are computerized inventories of Parisian notarial records in 1751 and 1761; for a description of these inventories, see Hoffman, Postel-Vinay, and Rosenthal 1999, note 26.

TABLE 7.7   CHOICE OF CREDIT INSTRUMENT AND RESIDENCES OF BORROWERS AND
LENDERS PRIVATE BORROWERS ONLY, 1662–1789

	Both Lender and Borrower in Paris				Borrower in Paris, Lender Outside			
	Obligations		Rentes		Obligations		Rentes	
Period	*F*	*N*	*F*	*N*	*F*	*N*	*F*	*N*
1662	69	56	82	73	8	6	1	2
1690–1710	77	76	85	80	7	11	10	12
1730–49	66	72	75	74	8	13	12	13
1750–69	74	80	61	57	23	9	35	36
1770–89	78	73	57	60	13	15	25	19

Source: As in table 7.6.
Note: *N* is the percentage of the total number of loans in a given category; *F* is the fraction of funds lent. Rentes include both private perpetuals and viagères. Note that there are still other obligations and rentes that do not fall into our categories: loans in which the lender resided inside Paris and the borrower outside, or loans in which parties lived elsewhere. Our residential categories are therefore not exhaustive.

The analogous map for that year—when the state borrowed heavily—reaches into much of western Europe. As in 1751, private lenders did not just come from Paris itself. The state's creditors, though, came from even farther away—in particular, from foreign countries.[73]

With the notaries spinning a web that linked savers living miles from Paris, the city's credit market began to change. Back in the middle of the seventeenth century, Paris had been a net lender of funds to the outside world. The money that left the city went primarily to borrowers in neighboring communities and to a narrow circle of rich provincials. In the eighteenth century, Paris switched roles. It became a net borrower, a transformation that was in large measure the notaries' accomplishment. They were now selling more and more perpetual and life annuities outside of Paris (table 7.7). Although these instruments were traditional, they appealed to the investor outside Paris who worried about his retirement or his heirs. An investor might be able to arrange a similar loan locally, but if he relied on the Parisian notaries, he would benefit from their financial contacts in Paris and from their extensive information about borrowers and the risks they posed. Increasingly, the investor bought his rente perpétuelle or viagère through a Parisian notary, and that is what brought capital to Paris.

Meanwhile, the other available credit instrument, the obligation, remained primarily a transaction among Parisians, though its function had changed. Back in the seventeenth century, the obligation had provided

73. Riley 1973.

legal notice that informal debts were in arrears. As such, it was a favorite legal weapon for the provincial supplier whose Parisian customers were late in paying their bills. It served a similar purpose in the arsenal of the Parisian landlord who was bent on consolidating his claims on rural debtors. By the second half of the eighteenth century, though, the obligation was transformed. The notaries, as we know, had fashioned it into an attractive instrument of medium-term credit, one far more flexible than perpetual or life annuities. Since it did involve less initial screening than annuities, it meant that either the lender or his notary had to do more monitoring after the loan was made. That made it much more attractive when both lender and borrower were based in Paris, for even if the notary took care of the monitoring, it would be easier for him to report to a lender who lived in Paris.[74] It is no wonder then that the obligation remained predominantly a loan among Parisians (table 7.7).

The Expansion of Credit and the End of the Old Regime

The Parisian notaries thus managed to raise money from the provinces and even (with bankers' help) from abroad. Although they remained brokers of loans—their unhappy experience with deposits taught them not to do otherwise—they still mobilized huge amounts of capital. They did so by playing upon the information they held and by offering lenders a variety of attractive credit instruments. Along the way, they opened the Parisian credit market up to women and provincial investors, and the funds they amassed helped pay for land and buildings, for offices and businesses purchased by the young, and for the frequent deficits run up by the government in the late eighteenth century.

With all this capital flowing into Paris from afar—particularly, for the government's loans—there is one final question that naturally arises: why did the crown not simply repudiate its debts when a financial crisis struck in 1788 and touched off the French Revolution? After all, the monarchy had defaulted repeatedly in the past—most recently under the financial minister Terray in 1770. One would think that bankruptcy would have been all the more attractive in 1789 because foreigners and politically weak provincials now held a considerable amount of the government debt. They were presumably an inviting target for a selective

74. The 1761 inventory lends support to this argument, for lenders in obligations in 1761 tended to live closer to Paris (thirteen kilometers) than did lenders in private rentes and viagères (twenty kilometers). Weighting the distances by the number of times an individual appears leads to similar results.

default. Such reasoning may of course seem a bit Machiavellian, but similar thoughts had occurred to Colbert and many of his successors.[75] And the same thinking had guided the crown's actions only seventeen years earlier, in the bankruptcy of 1770.[76]

Yet as we know, there was no such default in 1789. The usual explanation is that the monarchy's creditors were too numerous and too powerful—so powerful that bankruptcy would have been a political disaster.[77] Yet as we will show in chapter 8, such an argument is untenable. In 1789 the crown's creditors were less cohesive than they had ever been, making the financial incentives for default greater than ever before.

Why then did the monarchy not follow the identical path in 1789? Several reasons come to mind, and they all involve a debate over constitutional reform. The debate grew in intensity in the last two decades of the Old Regime as writers made repeated appeals to public opinion. The opinion that mattered here was that of the enlightened public. It spoke out in many places: in salons, clubs, and crowded cafés, but perhaps even more so in the bound volumes of great philosophes and the cheap pamphlets and libels of popular journalists. The term public opinion itself may seem amorphous, but it had grown common in French literature both high and low in the late eighteenth century.[78] Ministers like Necker and Calonne appealed to it. The police watched over it. And it had become an arbiter—perhaps *the* arbiter—of political decisions, something unthinkable a century before.

Although public opinion was divided over constitutional issues, it seemed to be united in its opposition to default. Default was branded despotism—a withering indictment in the late eighteenth century.[79] The link between despotism and default was forged initially in reaction to the state bankruptcy engineered by Law, whom Montesquieu called "one

75. Hoffman 1994:246–47.

76. Marion 1927, 1:248–56; Flammermont 1888–98, 3:ix–xi. In the early stages of the 1770 default, when the Parlement of Paris was a threat, Terray spared the *rentes sur l'hôtel de ville*, which filled the portfolios of the court magistrates and other powerful Parisians. See also Bosher 1972 for Terray's default on the short-term debt.

77. The best presentation of this argument can be found in White 1989:566.

78. We looked for the phrase "opinion publique" in the University of Chicago's ARTFL electronic database of French literature, which includes a wide variety of writing, from the works of the High Enlightenment to pamphlets and diaries. In the 349 texts from the years 1600–99 (roughly 15 million words), "opinion publique" appeared only two times, and it cropped up only nine times in the 167 texts (9 million words) from 1700–49. We found it 143 times, though, in the 269 texts (16 million words) from 1750–89. For recent discussions of public opinion, see Baker 1990; Chartier 1991; Darnton 1994; and Furet 1981. For an example—the journalist Mercier—see Baker 1990:187.

79. Darnton 1994:211–16, 242–46.

of the greatest promoters of despotism yet seen in Europe." It was bolstered by the rhetoric of the magistrates in the sovereign law courts, who told the king he had to honor his debt contracts. The link grew stronger still in the wake of Terray's bankruptcy in 1770 and the subsequent coup by chancellor Maupeou, who dissolved the sovereign courts and sent the magistrates into exile. In print, Terray's default was denounced as "intolerable despotism," while Terray himself was condemned for working hand in hand with the hated Maupeou.[80] When bankruptcy was suggested again in 1787–88, pamphleteers were quick to pounce upon the "despotism" of such proposals and to remind readers of the terrible evils wrought by Law and Terray. The major sovereign law court, the Parlement of Paris, also jumped in, burning a journal that had proposed default. By then bankruptcy was all too thoroughly tarred with the brush of despotism. It is thus hardly a surprise that the National Assembly banned any mention of the subject in 1789.[81]

In addition, default could not be separated from the bigger controversy over constitutional reform. In the pamphlet literature of 1788 and 1789, discussion of default and fiscal affairs was dwarfed by attention given constitutional matters.[82] Even the authors who concentrated on the fiscal crisis could not avoid constitutional issues.[83] The reason was simple. If the crown's fiscal problem was settled without any change in the constitution, then the king would simply get more money to spend, either from a default on his debts or from a permanent tax increase. But he could then squander the money on foreign wars, while the opportunity for political reform would be lost. The trouble was that once the king got the money there was simply no way to tie his hands, at least under the Old-Regime constitution. The only way out of the dilemma was constitutional reform, and as contemporaries well knew, the fiscal crisis gave them a powerful lever for prying a new constitution out of the monarchy's clutches. For many, it was therefore better to prolong the fiscal crisis and fight instead over the shape of the constitution.

80. Norberg 1994:253–98; Kaiser 1991; and [Coquereau] 1776. The quotation from Montesquieu is cited in Norberg (280). Admittedly, the Parlement of Paris acquiesced in the default of 1770. Furthermore, the magistrates in the Parlement did not fling charges of despotism at ministers, and they would probably have been happy with any default that singled out groups like financiers. Still, the magistrates did argue that the king should keep his word and honor his legitimate debt contracts. The best example here is the Parlement's remonstrance of 9 August 1763, which is discussed in Norberg (287). See also Flammermont 1888–98, 2:360–410.

81. [Brissot de Warville] 1787; White 1989:566–67; Kaiser 1994:300–42.

82. Norberg 1994:297–98, 379.

83. See, for example, [Brissot de Warville] 1787:17–23, 41–45.

That, rather than a choice between taxes or default, was the real issue at the outset of the French Revolution. Solving the fiscal crisis would have to wait, and so would any default or tax increase. In the end, the fiscal crisis would be resolved, but the resolution would bring notarial credit to its knees, along with scores of investors who had placed their savings in notarial loans.

Since the ultimate fate of notarial credit was thus bound up with politics, one might ask whether the flourishing capital market in late-eighteenth-century Paris was itself the result of the monarchy's having finally learned to respect public opinion in matters of finance. Did the private credit market thrive in eighteenth-century Paris because the crown was now committed to listening to public opinion and paying its own debts? In other words, did confidence in the public debt buoy up private lenders?

Such an argument has been made for the Glorious Revolution in England, but it does not fit Old-Regime Paris.[84] The upturn in private lending in Paris began before public opinion arose as a political force, and the private credit market prospered long before opinion turned against government default. Indeed, private lending increased despite repeated defaults by the state in 1759 and 1770. And it continued to grow even though the interest premium on government bonds revealed a sizeable and continuing risk of government default. No, the success of capital market in Old-Regime Paris cannot be traced back to a commitment to pay government debt. Its causes, we know, lie elsewhere: an expanding economy, a stable currency, new credit instruments, and above all else skillful financial intermediation by Parisian notaries.

84. North and Weingast 1989.

CHAPTER EIGHT

Micro-Economics and Macro-Politics: Credit and Inflation during the French Revolution

AFTER REACHING A PEAK in the 1780s, the long-term credit market suddenly collapsed, brought down by the devastating inflation of the French Revolution. The inflation, which wiped out over 99 percent of the currency's value between 1789 and 1795, was not the only radical change that shook the credit market in these years, for the Revolution remade many formal institutions.[1] Yet the inflation does deserve our attention, both because of the impact it had and because of the neglect it has suffered at the hands of scholars. Historians have by and large ignored it in recent years, as their attention has shifted to topics such as public opinion and political ideas. Economists, it is true, have stepped into the breach with analyses of the revolutionary government's finances and its monetary policy. But their models suffer from serious defects, because they neglect politics and overlook a great deal of individual behavior.

Here our data from the private credit market sheds new light not just on the inflation itself but on the entire course of revolutionary politics. All we have to do is to apply a simple economic model to our data and pay close attention to the course of political events. (Readers unfamiliar with the Revolution may wish to consult the chronology, table 8.1). We begin by discussing one of the best recent macroeconomic accounts of the French Revolution. We next introduce the evidence from the private credit market and discuss what our own economic model implies about the behavior of private borrowers and lenders. We then examine the inflation's political roots and its economic consequences.

What we learn is that politics and monetary and fiscal policy were

1. For the magnitude of the inflation, see Crouzet 1993:576.

TABLE 8.1   CHRONOLOGY OF KEY REVOLUTIONARY EVENTS

Political Events	Monetary Events
Estates General (May–July 1789)	
Constitutional Assembly (July 1789– October 1791)	Assignats authorized (December 1789)
	(Real Bills Regime, 1790–92)
	First assignats issued (January 1791)
Legislative Assembly (October 1791– September 1792); Declaration of war (April 1792)	
Trial and execution of Louis XVI (December 1792–January 1793)	
Convention (September 1792–October 1795)	
Terror (September 1793–July 1794)	*(Legal Restriction Regime (during the Terror))*
	(Hyperinflation, August 1794–1796)
Directory (October 1795–November 1799)	End of the assignats (February 1796)
	Bankruptcy (September 1797)

Note: Sargent and Velde's monetary regimes appear in italics.

inseparable during the French Revolution. The revolutionary government ran an enormous deficit, but rather than raising taxes or defaulting on government debt, it printed paper money—the assignats—thereby unleashing inflation. The choice was a political one, for maintaining a deficit turned out to be a means to achieve political goals that a variety of political actors pursued. These goals, which ranged from the shape of the French constitution to the whole nature of society, took precedence over choosing a particular solution to the government's financial problems. It is therefore impossible to tell whether a key political actor supported a particular solution to the government's fiscal woes (having tax-exempt nobility pay taxes, for example) simply by asking whether he would escape its costs. The reason is that the solution might bring the revolutionary political crisis to an end and rule out desired political reforms. Ultimately, the political incentives made inflation appealing, and many of the political actors put up with it in the hope of getting the sort of government and society they wanted.

The inflation was thus inextricably bound up with political change. That insight was certainly clear to many contemporaries, although they differed greatly among themselves about precisely how the inflation would work itself out. In the end, the inflation proved an expensive way to keep the government afloat. It imposed heavy costs on society, particularly on groups that were politically and economically vulnerable, such as women and the elderly. And it etched into everyone's mind the terrible economic risks that could be expected whenever governments were unstable.

Beyond its consequences for France, the revolutionary inflation can also teach historians an important lesson. It is a lesson that should prove useful for all historians, even those (in cultural history, for example) who would normally pay little attention to inflation or to anything smacking of economics. The lesson is this. If we ask which individual suffered most from the inflation, we find groups (such as women, the elderly, or government bondholders) that were torn by conflicting interests and unable to mobilize politically. The same holds, though, for many other groups that the typical historian invokes when doing political and cultural analysis, whether he or she is writing about the French Revolution or any other topic. Rarely does the historian ask whether these groups were divided or able to rally for political action, and he or she may therefore greatly exaggerate their political impact.

A Macroeconomic Model of the Revolution

For scholars who have tried to account for the Old Regime's financial crisis and the inflation of 1790–96, explanations have usually centered on economic incompetence or political corruption. For François Crouzet, for example, the Old Regime systematically mismanaged its finances, and in his view corruption was the root of the problem. The financial crisis of 1787–88 was thus hardly surprising. For Florin Aftalion, the confiscation of the estates of the church was such a flagrant violation of property rights that for the public nothing seemed safe from the revolutionaries' demand for revenues. As a result, after 1789, the revolutionary government had nothing to lose from inflation. It had already ruined its reputation as a defender of property rights and money—in the language of economics it had lost its credibility—and it thus faced no costs from inflation.[2]

In a recent paper, Thomas Sargent and François Velde break with these traditional interpretations. Because their work fits the evidence about money stocks, inflation rates, and the government's finances, it certainly represents a step forward. But at the same time, it fails to address a number of key questions: how individuals behaved, for example, or whether they anticipated the repeated changes in monetary policy during the Revolution. Here our evidence from the private credit market can provide the answers.

For Sargent and Velde, the monetary and fiscal policies of the period were fashioned by individuals with considerable economic sophistica-

2. Crouzet 1993; Aftalion 1987.

tion, sophistication that in turn influenced policy decisions.[3] In their view, the Old-Regime financial ministers had long been aware of the "unpleasant arithmetic" of public debt and had tried to manage the king's finances as best they could, even though taxation failed to keep up with increases in expenditures. The revolutionaries themselves also knew well (from the very moment that the issue of assignats was contemplated) how difficult it was to manage a system of paper money. According to Sargent and Velde, the revolutionaries presided over three different monetary regimes between 1790 and 1796—three different periods of monetary history, each with its own money and rate of inflation:

> The first period ends late in the summer of 1793, and is characterized by growing real balances and moderate inflation. The second period begins and ends with the Terror. It is marked by high real balances . . . and roughly stable prices. The fall of Robespierre in late July 1794 begins the third of our episodes, in which real balances decline and prices rise rapidly. We interpret these three episodes in terms of three separate theories about money: a 'backing' or 'real bills' theory, . . . a legal restrictions theory, and a classical hyperinflation theory.[4]

When Sargent and Velde speak of real balances, they simply refer to the real value of the money that people hold—real in the sense of what goods it will buy. When they invoke the Terror, they mean the period of revolutionary dictatorship between the late summer of 1793 and the summer of 1794. When they talk of a "real bills" regime, they mean that the new currency is backed by an equal amount of real resources. As a result, people hold the new money, and it does not create inflation. Finally, their monetary regime of legal restrictions is one in which the government forces private parties to hold large balances of money. Thus immobilized, the money does not create inflation until it is released into the system, and at that point inflation takes off.

The story told by Sargent and Velde neatly organizes the chronology of public finance, monetary emissions, and the inflation rate. It is also consistent with the declarations of the revolutionary government. Yet that is but one test of their theory, for their macroeconomic data offer few clues as to how individuals perceived the financial turmoil during the Revolution. Here our data from the private credit market allow us to view the financial course of the Revolution from the perspective of

3. Sargent and Velde 1995.
4. Sargent and Velde 1995:498–500.

private actors. To take but one example, if the real bills monetary regime had taken root in the minds of Parisians, then the private credit market should show no signs that people expected future inflation.

There is a second problem with Sargent and Velde's macroeconomic model as well: they pay little attention to the transitions between their monetary regimes—in effect treating the transitions as if they had been unanticipated.[5] Yet monetary policy can be profoundly influenced by expectations. If, for example, people expected that the revolutionary government would inflate the assignat in the future, then they would get rid of their paper money, causing prices to rise even before the government presses started to print more assignats. The revolutionary government (or any government for that matter) can only carry out its monetary or fiscal policy if people find the policy credible and unlikely to change. Otherwise, people will react in a way that may undermine the policy. Such worries are particularly likely during Sargent and Velde's first two monetary regimes (real bills and legal restrictions). Here again the data from the private credit market yield important information. In fact, the data from the private market suggest that anticipating the end of monetary regimes was the central monetary problem of the French Revolution.

Our Model of Borrower and Lender Behavior in the Private Market

Private credit contracts can thus help us go beyond Sargent and Velde's macroeconomic model. In particular, the private contracts can actually tell us whether individuals anticipated the changes in monetary policy during the French Revolution. All we need do is combine the evidence from the private contracts with a simple economic model of what private borrowers and lenders were doing. But in constructing the model, we must take into account legal rules and other institutional constraints.

The first rule that we must keep in mind is that medium- and long-term debt contracts were all denominated in livres, the unit of account. Their value therefore depended directly on the monetary policy.[6] The same was true for the assignats. The inflation of the Revolution thus had

---

5. Sargent and Velde 1995:501 n. 38, and 508.

6. Loan contracts denominated in sacks of wheat were illegal under the Old Regime, and although they occasionally cropped up in the countryside in the early nineteenth century, we found none of them in Paris during the Revolution. For rural examples, see AD Vaucluse, Actes Civils Publics, L'Isle-sur-Sorgue, 1807; and AD Aube, 4Q3794, 195 (1822).

enormous redistributional consequences in the private credit market. And because the parties to such contracts had much to gain or lose, their behavior tells us a great deal.

Two other institutional details are important as well. Interest rates were legally capped at 5 percent and not indexed so that prices provided no escape from inflation.[7] Furthermore, the types of contracts that borrowers and lenders had at their disposal—rentes and obligations—gave borrowers and lenders very different rights when it came to repaying loans, a legal distinction of great importance for our data. With the rentes, as we know, it was borrowers who controlled the repayment. They, and they alone, decided whether and when a rente should be reimbursed. With obligations, by contrast, lenders could demand repayment by a given date or even on short notice. The reason has to do with the duration of the obligations. When initially drawn up, the obligations specified a date when the loan was due, but by the 1780s most obligations remained outstanding beyond this initial date. That could only happen if the lenders agreed to extend the loans, perhaps by using payment schedules that notaries had devised. By extending an obligation bit by bit, a lender could determine its duration precisely. And once the initial due date had past, he could even force immediate repayment, for the extensions would typically be verbal or not notarized, and the only document with any legal force would be the original loan contract. It is true that borrowers could often reimburse obligations early if they wished, but they could not delay repayment indefinitely in the hopes of gaining from inflation, as they could with rentes.

The distinction between rentes and obligations may seem a strange legal quirk, but for our purposes it is actually a godsend, for it allows us to disentangle the way people were thinking about the two major monetary problems of the revolutionary era, accelerating inflation and monetary stabilization. (Here, as in chapter 4, stabilization means that the government abandons the livre and requires borrowers to repay even their old debts in a new and more valuable currency. Stabilization will therefore frighten borrowers and delight lenders.) If people generally expect inflation to accelerate, then lenders will want immediate repayment, whereas borrowers will prefer to wait before reimbursing their loans. The lenders will force borrowers to pay back their obligations but they will be unable to do the same with rentes. As a result, we will see obligations repaid, but not rentes. On the other hand, if monetary stabilization is in the offing, borrowers will rush to reimburse both kinds of loans,

---

7. While the decree of 3 September 1789 legalized interest-bearing term debts, the legal ceiling on interest remained 5 percent until July 1796.

and lenders will by and large not be able to stop them. We will consequently see both rentes and obligations paid back.

It is worth emphasizing that inflation and stabilization created two separate problems for borrowers and lenders. One involved estimating the future inflation rate; the other, the likelihood of monetary stabilization. Both phenomena could redistribute money and cause losses. The effect of inflation was perhaps the easiest to understand, for it simply shifted wealth from lenders to borrowers, who repaid their debts in cheap assignats. But stabilization (such as the transition from the livre to the franc after 1796) would also redistribute wealth. Precisely how much would depend on the details—for example, how contracts in livres were valued in francs.

Borrowers and lenders could not ignore these two problems during the Revolution. History itself reminded them, for the consequences of France's previous experiment with paper currency—the Law affair— were well known.[8] As we saw in chapter 4, private borrowers who had reimbursed their debts during Law's inflation had prospered, with those repaying latest enjoying the greatest gains. Some debtors, though, had missed the occasion. Clearly timing had been essential.

The Revolution posed an analogous problem for borrowers. Each passing month reduced the real value of their debts, but at any moment the state might stabilize the currency and raise the cost of repayment. Such concerns were hardly trivial. When the currency was finally stabilized in July 1796 the government chose to revalue outstanding private debts at their historical cost.[9] Repayments already made with assignats were legal and final, but unreimbursed loans taken out before the assignat were given the same silver value they had back in 1789. Outstanding loans from the assignat period—1790–96—were assessed according to a set of regional depreciation tables, which were supposed to reflect local inflation rates.

Given these rules, a borrower who took out a loan in the 1780s could repay it in 1795 for less than 1 percent of the original principal. If he waited another year, however, he would once again have to pay the full

8. For references to Law in parliamentary debates, see *Archives parlementaires* 1862, 10: 681–89, 12:602–11; 13:54–55, 63; 18:530–56.

9. The currency was not officially stabilized until 4 February 1797 when the last of the paper currencies was demonetized. By the end of 1795, however, private transactions were only occurring in metallic currency. Even before the assignats were abandoned there was discussion about how to value outstanding contracts (Caron 1909:iv–xiii). The original report was issued in April 1795, but the final decisions were not made until June 1797. In modern times, only Argentina in 1986 has tried to implement such a scheme, without success; see Heyman and Leijonhufvud 1995.

principal. Although this stabilization benefited debtors, it was in fact less generous to them than the practice common today—appraising contracts at the final and most depreciated value of the old currency. And what counted most was guessing the time of the stabilization exactly. Borrowers who paid off their debts just before the stabilization profited the most.

Appendix 1 models the decision borrowers faced. In the model, the borrower's decision to repay depends on four variables: inflation in the past; the probability of stabilization, which brings inflation to a halt; expected inflation in the future if stabilization fails; and the size of the debt. All other things being equal, the probability of repayment increases with past inflation, the probability of stabilization, and the loan size. However, the probability of repayment declines as expected inflation in the future rises. Intuitively, what the borrower must do is opt between a sure gain by repaying immediately and the possible return from waiting. The return from waiting equals the expected gain from future inflation less the losses in the case of stabilization. Inflation in the past boosts the profits from immediate repayment; hence higher inflation in the past makes immediate repayment more attractive. Future inflation offers the possibility of additional gains and makes waiting appealing. Stabilization, of course, hurts borrowers, so a high probability of stabilization makes them want to pay back their loans.

Lenders faced the opposite problem, and one could construct an analogous model for their behavior. If stabilization seemed imminent, they would obviously want to delay repayment, but there was little they could do, since borrowers could repay rentes at will and whatever obligations were past their initial maturity.[10] The prospect of inflation, though, would induce lenders to force repayment of their obligations as quickly as possible.

The evidence from the private market can also disclose whether individuals agreed or disagreed about the financial course the Revolution was likely to take. If repayments were broadly dispersed and relatively insensitive to current events, then beliefs about the course of the Revolution varied significantly because individuals solved the repayment problem differently. Conversely, if repayments were concentrated around salient events, actors must have shared similar beliefs about coming monetary transitions.

It is entirely possible that individuals did not come to share the same

10. During the Revolution, obligations often contained clauses banning early repayment. Although the enforceability of the clauses was not clear, they still serve as evidence that lenders anticipated that borrowers might want to repay just prior to a stabilization.

beliefs about monetary transitions. After all, the Revolution was a rapid sequence of unparalleled events. Forecasting its course was difficult, and it is not surprising that individuals reached different conclusions about what the political and financial future would hold. Some may have interpreted the coming of war as a sign that the deficit would worsen and that assignats would depreciate. Others may have believed that the Revolutionary armies would win quickly, making the war brief and profitable. Still others may have thought that the war would be lost quickly and the monarchy restored to its full powers. And all the while there were unforeseen events intervening, jarring forecasts and keeping them from converging. In such a situation the past could not be used to inform the proximate future. And with no mechanism to aggregate information— no market on which everyone could buy and sell bets about the currency—it might take a long time for people to reach agreement about what was going to happen.[11]

In other words, lenders and borrowers need not have had the same expectations about future inflation and the probability of stabilization. The broader the range of reasonable expectations, the more variation we would see in the graph of repayments. The borrowers who believed that inflation would accelerate and that stabilization was way off in the future would wait to reimburse their rentes and obligations, while those with opposite beliefs would rush to repay. A similar logic would apply to lenders and obligations, and as a result the spread of reimbursements for both rentes and obligations will tell us how divergent beliefs were.

Our model thus has a number of important implications for the behavior we should observe in the private credit market during the Revolution. Testing these implications, though, requires financial series more detailed than those described in chapter 2. In particular, we need enough data to distinguish the different effects of inflation on obligations and on rentes, for the repayment of the rentes reveals what borrowers expected, while the reimbursement of obligations can tell us compar-

---

11. What happened in Paris is hardly unusual, for there is abundant evidence that markets work poorly during inflation. Part of the explanation for such poor performance is that under high inflation information aggregation fails. See Heyman and Leijonhufvud 1995. The fact that people might have different forecasts or make large forecasting errors does not mean, however, that rational expectations fail. The concept of rational expectations is premised on the idea that individuals will make optimal use of the available information to forecast the future. In the case of the Revolution, individuals might make optimal use of what they knew, but that information could vary greatly from person to person because there was no mechanism to aggregate information. Furthermore, it was difficult for people to update their forecasts on the basis of unfolding events because the events themselves were unique. Forecasting errors would therefore be large.

atively more about lenders. If either set of repayments bunch up around salient revolutionary events, then the borrowers (or the lenders) must have shared beliefs about changes in monetary policy. On the other hand, if they spread out and remain unperturbed by revolutionary events, then such beliefs must have varied greatly from individual to individual. We have put these detailed financial series together—the process is described in appendix 3—and beyond unveiling the expectations of borrowers and lenders, they also shed considerable light on the redistribution that the revolutionary inflation imposed.

The Private Credit Market and the Course of Inflation

With the implications of our model in hand, let us examine the evidence from the private credit market and see what it says about the course of the revolutionary inflation. We focus on the repayments, not only because they reveal so much about expectations but also because they outstripped new loans and thus dominated the movement of private indebtedness. We analyze the data from the private market in three steps. We first lump all the repayments together and next contrast the reimbursement of rentes and the reimbursement of obligations. We then summarize what the private market says about the three key monetary regimes sketched by Sargent and Velde.

If the repayments are lumped together, what stands out right away is the surge of repayments in 1791 (figure 8.1). This surge, which continued into early 1792, raises questions about the "backed" currency at the heart of Sargent and Velde's first monetary regime—the "real bills" regime, when the revolutionary money, the assignat, was backed by land. As the wave of reimbursements suggests, not everyone was convinced that the assignat would be a stable monetary regime, and people began to act on their suspicions about the assignat over two years before Sargent and Velde's transition to a second monetary regime, that of legal restrictions. Admittedly, the repayments could have reflected fears of an impending stabilization or concerns about the issue of more assignats in the future, which would set off inflation. As we shall see, though, it was fear of inflation that apparently set off the reimbursements, inflation that the backed currency was supposed to avoid.

By late 1792 repayments declined, only to rise again early in 1793. This second increase predated by several months Sargent and Velde's monetary regime of legal restrictions during the Terror, raising further questions about the true end of the real bills regime. During the Terror itself (September 1793 to July 1794) repayments actually dropped, al-

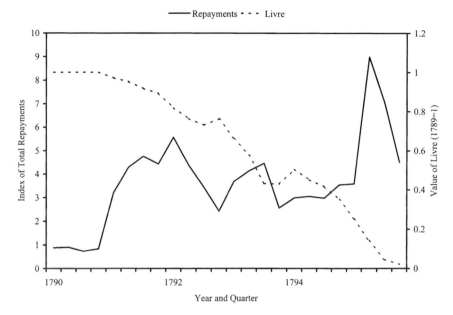

FIGURE 8.1 Total Loan Repayments and Inflation in Paris, 1790–95. The graph shows total loan repayments by year and by quarter, beginning with the first quarter of 1790, along with the rate of inflation. The base (which equals 1) of the index is the average number of repayments per quarter from 1785 through 1789.

though they remained higher than they had been in the 1780s. Perhaps the legal restrictions (and ultimately the threat of the guillotine) made it difficult for borrowers to pay off old loans in order to take advantage of the more than 50 percent decline in the livre's value. Or perhaps some borrowers foresaw the hyperinflation that would follow the Terror.

The end of the Terror did not immediately ignite the hyperinflation, which came more than ten months later. But it did set off a third wave of repayments. What is startling about the third wave is that it peaked in June 1795, a full nine months before the assignat inflation ended in February 1796.[12] Borrowers thus anticipated inflation, but they repaid too soon. Had they waited a few more months, they could have repaid their debts at nearly zero cost.

The pattern of repayments is even more telling if we disentangle obli-

12. The inflation did not stop completely until February 1797 when other forms of paper money were eliminated. From the perspective of the private credit market two other dates mattered: in November 1795 individuals were no longer required to receive repayment in paper money and in July 1796 individuals were released from specifying contracts in units of currency (Crouzet 1993:422).

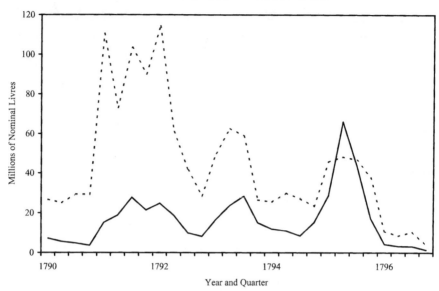

FIGURE 8.2   Rente and Obligation Repayments in Paris, 1790–95

gations from rentes (figure 8.2). Doing so is not easy. The problem is
that when the notarial indexes mention a repayment (a quittance) they
do not reveal whether it was a rente or an obligation that was being
repaid, or even some other kind of debt. We therefore collected quarterly samples of original rente and obligation contracts to see how important each was in the stream of total repayments.[13]

What strikes the viewer immediately in figure 8.2 is that the initial
burst of repayments in 1791 and early 1792 consisted almost entirely of
obligations. There was a much smaller increase in rente reimbursements, but that probably had very little to do with borrowers' expectations. Instead, it probably resulted from the abolition of the traffic in
government offices. Before the Revolution, most government officers
bought their posts. In August 1789, though, the National Assembly abolished the practice and decreed that the offices would be repurchased
by the state.[14] The problem was that many of the officers had financed

13. Together rente and obligation repayments never total more than 60 percent of all
repayments. Hence the series of rente and obligation repayments can move independently.
For the samples of repayments from rente and obligation contracts, see appendices 3
and 5.

14. *Archives parlementaires* 1862, 1st ser., 9:337–78.

their posts by borrowing, typically using rentes, with the offices themselves serving as collateral. When the state bought the offices back, the
collateral therefore vanished. With other rentes, the disappearance of
the collateral would not obligate the borrowers to repay, but it did in
this instance.[15] The officers therefore had to reimburse their creditors
earlier than expected—a rare and exceptional instance in which borrowers were actually obliged to pay back rentes.

Whatever the reason for the reimbursement of rentes, it was dwarfed
by the repayment of obligations, a clear sign that lenders feared inflation. If it had been borrowers who were rushing to pay back their loans—
say because they expected imminent stabilization—then the repayment
of rentes would have jumped as high as obligations, but that never happened. Clearly, the lenders dreaded inflation, even though the assignats
were still fully backed by church property in 1791. By the end of 1792,
though, their fears had been realized. The assignats in circulation now
exceeded the value of church lands. The assignats had lost 30 percent
of their value, and so had the lenders' loans, all of which were nominal
claims. Worse yet, the government showed no signs of printing fewer
assignats in the future. To avoid losses, the lenders forced repayment of
the only loans for which they controlled the duration—the obligations.
Their strategy made eminent sense, and since rentes were not being
repaid (save when dictated by the repurchase of government offices),
borrowers seem to have shared the view that inflation was in the offing.

Thus neither borrowers nor lenders acted as though they believed
that the real bills regime would ward off inflation. Their doubts emerged
as early as January 1791, a full two and a half years before the end of
Sargent and Velde's real bills regime. Despite all that sophisticated political observers said about the backing of church lands, the public anticipated inflation—and ultimately the failure of the backed currency—
and did so well before the assignats exceeded the value of the backing.

They realized that the assignats needed fiscal discipline to succeed,
and they must have suspected that the necessary discipline (a tax increase and lower expenses) was an unlikely outcome. According to sophisticated financiers like Dupont de Nemours, the public knew of the
unpleasant arithmetic of monetary issue and were unlikely to accept
further assignats without expecting inflation.[16] If the National Assembly
shared this knowledge, the revolutionaries' pronouncements must be
interpreted in one of two ways. The first is that government officials were

15. For an example, see ANMC, LXX (December 1791), the reimbursement of a
40,000 livre rente that had as collateral the office of *trésorier de France en Guyenne*.
16. Bergasse 1789; Dupont de Nemours 1790.

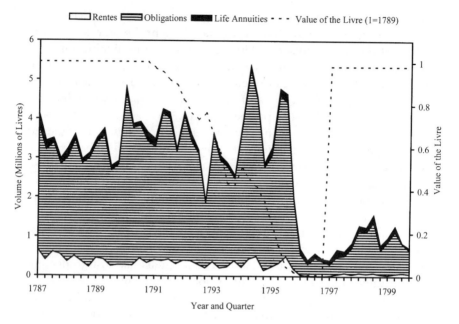

FIGURE 8.3 Volume of New Loans in Paris, 1787–99. The volumes of new rentes, obligations, and life annuities are plotted along with the value of the livre by year and quarter, beginning in the first quarter of 1787.

sophisticated but extremely optimistic about the course of the Revolution. Alternatively, they were trying to fool the public, but their deception began to fail in 1791.

What of Sargent and Velde's next regime, the regime of legal restriction, from the late summer of 1793 to the summer of 1794? What do repayments reveal about it? Even before this period began, the trial and execution of Louis XVI (December 1792–January 1793) had unleashed a new wave of reimbursements, which did not abate until the onset of the Terror in September 1793 (figure 8.1) These repayments included some rentes but even more obligations (figure 8.2). As a result, the stock of outstanding obligations dropped more than the stock of rentes, even though the few new loans being made were predominantly obligations.[17] (See figure 8.3 for the volume of new loans.) That more obligations were being repaid suggests that some lenders anticipated higher inflation, a reasonable fear since inflation was in fact accelerating. But the repay-

17. Between the first and the third quarter of 1793, the stock of outstanding obligations fell from 107 million livres to 38 million, a decline of 64 percent. During the same period, the stock of rentes fell only 18 percent, from 268 million livres to 220 million.

ment of rentes implies that some borrowers were afraid as well. To judge from their actions, they apparently dreaded the return of silver currency and stabilization, perhaps after a collapse of the Revolution itself. They therefore began to reimburse their rentes. Even so, many rentes still remained outstanding, a sign that other borrowers had quite different expectations about the future.

The Terror itself forced people to revise their expectations. The volume of new obligations began to grow again (figure 8.3), while the reimbursement of rentes and obligations fell (figure 8.2). The stock of outstanding obligations even began to rise, as did the value of the livre. The political controls must have convinced some lenders that inflation had been mastered. They therefore stopped forcing repayment of obligations and even granted new loans. Unfortunately, they did not anticipate the hyperinflation that would follow the Terror. As for borrowers, some of them may have foreseen the hyperinflation and hence decided to take out new loans. But they had stopped expecting stabilization.

The end of the Terror in July 1794 did not immediately change monetary and fiscal policy. The government's financial policy still remained in the hands of Cambon, who had been in charge under the Terror. It is no surprise then that the repayments of rentes and obligations remained stable until Cambon's ouster in the spring of 1795. His fall, though, touched off a debate over the legal status of the assignat, a debate which even witnessed proposals to deny assignats status as legal tender. Had such a proposal become law, creditors would no longer have had to accept assignats at their face value; they would instead receive a bundle of assignats that reflected the damage done by inflation.

Although the proposal failed (for fear that it would completely destabilize the currency), it did set off a final rush of repayments in the spring and summer of 1795 (figure 8.1). Because both rentes and obligations were involved (figure 8.2), borrowers must have expected imminent stabilization. It could not have been lenders' fears of inflation, for in that case only obligations would have been repaid.[18] The borrowers correctly inferred that the assignat's legal status was soon to be altered and rushed to get rid of assignats. Inflation soared, and reimbursements rose to nine times their prerevolutionary average, remaining at a near record level through the end of the summer of 1795. Only at the end of 1795 did repayments finally collapse, with most outstanding debts now extinguished.

18. The rise in new loans (figure 8.3) suggests that lenders too expected stabilization—hence their willingness to make new loans to borrowers whose expectations were apparently not so dire.

In this third of Sargent and Velde's monetary regimes, the borrowers anticipated stabilization but they did so imperfectly. Inflation rates persisted at nearly 50 percent per month well into 1796. Had borrowers correctly anticipated the continuing inflation, they would not have rushed to repay their contracts in early 1795. Rather, they would have waited until October when the livre was at a mere 5 percent of its original value. Only a quarter of the debtors who repaid during the hyperinflation waited that long, and their repayments constituted a mere 7 percent of all the reimbursements during the Revolution. Although most debtors did anticipate the end of the assignats, they did not correctly guess the exact moment of stabilization, and many of them repaid their loans too early. Once again, beliefs about the financial future were quite dispersed.[19]

The evidence from the private market implies that we have to move beyond the macroeconomic model of Sargent and Velde. Private individuals behaved in ways that are inconsistent with their model. Both borrowers and lenders seemed to foresee the end of the real bills regime well before it was supposed to be over, and some of them at least anticipated other monetary transitions too, though their forecasts were far from perfect. Their expectations about the financial future could at times differ greatly from individual to individual—in 1793, for example, when some borrowers predicted stabilization but others did not. Such heterogeneous expectations are perhaps understandable, given the complexity of the problem Parisians faced. To arrive at a decision about debt, they had to juggle past inflation, nominal contracts, and guesses about future inflation, the probability of monetary transition, and the likelihood of different stabilization schemes. It must have been like wandering through a strange house in the dead of night, an excursion inevitably fraught with mistakes and accidents. Yet perhaps we exaggerate the difficulty of the problem. Unlike us, Parisians had long experience with nominal debt contracts. And the lesson from John Law's system had not been forgotten. The assignats may have created a labyrinth for debtors

19. It is no surprise that beliefs about the financial future were quite dispersed, if only because the Convention and the subsequent assembly, the Directory, passed contradictory legislation. These laws were surely taken as signals of what might happen, but they could not be used to predict the future with any accuracy. As early as the spring of 1795, the Convention debated using a sliding scale to deflate assignat contracts. In April 1795 it made clear to the public that the use of assignats was soon to be limited. The Convention and thereafter the Directory passed two laws limiting the use of depreciated assignats in private credit. The first, in July 1795 (25 messidor, an III), had little effect, but the second one in November (12 frimaire, an IV) signaled the end of redistribution in private credit (Caron 1909:v–xxv; Marion 1927, 3:293–311, 343–49).

and creditors, but experience and the memory of the Law affair provided them with Ariadne's thread. As a result private actors seem to have had similar approaches to the inflation, but the political and economic turmoil allowed them to maintain a wide distribution of beliefs about when the financial crisis would end. Their behavior is therefore consistent with a simple model of debt management and with very dispersed beliefs about the future.

The Causes of Inflation

To understand the causes of the revolutionary inflation, we have to turn to politics, for politics and monetary and fiscal policy were inseparable during the Revolution. The reason was simple: the chief actors in the financial drama were also deeply engaged in the struggle for political power. The king, and after him the revolutionaries, made decisions about domestic and foreign policy that in turn affected the budget. They did so knowing that their political decisions had financial consequences. And as the evidence from the financial markets demonstrates, the public was also aware of the link between politics and the government's financial and monetary policy.

Although the revolutionaries realized that money creation was a tempting way to increase the government's resources, they knew that it could touch off inflation and have unpleasant consequences.[20] Why then did they resort to it—rather than to a tax increase or a default—to close the government's yawning deficit, a deficit that had opened up at the end of the Old Regime?

One possible answer to this question comes from yet another important macroeconomic model of the revolutionary inflation, which argues that the Revolution was essentially a fiscal battle over paying the bill for the Old Regime's financial collapse.[21] The battle pitted taxpayers against the government's creditors, neither of whom wanted to pick up the onerous tab. The taxpayers wanted to avoid a tax increase, while the creditors wanted to escape the alternative, a government default. Each side believed that the other might be the first to throw in the towel and pay the bill. Each was therefore willing to endure inflation and the other costs of postponing fiscal adjustment in the hope that the other side

20. See "La pensée économique pendant la révolution française," *Actes du colloque international de Vizille*, 6–8 September 1989, which appeared in a special issue of *Economies et Sociétés*, série Histoire de la pensée économique 24 (1990).

21. White 1995; Alesina and Drazen 1991.

would be the first to concede. The result was a lengthy war of attrition, which lasted until the restoration of the monarchy in 1814.

Although it may seem promising, we do not agree with this second macroeconomic model either. In its place, we would stress a very different battle—a battle over politics. Fiscal policy loomed large in this battle, not because the Revolution was a financial war of attrition but because fiscal policy was a weapon in the larger political debate. That debate shifted over time from a struggle over parliamentary versus absolute monarchy to the relationship between church and state, to relations between center and provinces, and finally to the choice of republic versus monarchy. But throughout it, fiscal policy remained a useful political tool for players ranging from the king down to revolutionary clubs. They supported or opposed fiscal measures (and monetary policies too) in order to further their own political agendas, not because they would end up paying higher taxes or suffering losses in a government default. For some of them, it would be self-defeating to solve the government's financial problems, for a large deficit could be a means of extracting political concessions. Politics could even make the inflation worth enduring. Political actors might in fact put up with it in order to remain in power or to get the sort of government and society they wanted.

Although the political battle began with the monarchy's abortive attempts to get a permanent tax increase out of the law courts (the Parlements) in the second half of the eighteenth century, it came into clearest focus in 1789 when the crown convened the Estates General—a body drawn from the clergy, nobility, and the third estate. The monarchy hoped that the Estates would prove pliable and grant a permanent tax increase. One might even assume (on the basis of something like the war of attrition argument, for example) that the representatives of the third estate and their allies would have readily done so if the higher taxes were imposed upon the tax-exempt clergy and nobility. But such an argument ignores the political issues. The members of the third estate and their allies understood that the power of the purse was an important political weapon, and they used it to their advantage. Their goal was to institutionalize a national assembly that would meet regularly. Their opponent, the monarchy, had clearly demonstrated its aversion to such powerful consultative bodies. The crown had not summoned the Estates General since 1614, and only a crippling shortage of cash had persuaded Louis XVI to convoke them in 1789. The members of the third estate and their allies knew that if they granted a permanent tax increase the king would no longer need the assembly. He might send the representatives home or use force against the assembly.[22] Keeping the assembly alive would mean putting off a permanent solution to the government's fiscal problems.

It is thus not surprising that the Estates enacted only stopgap fiscal measures and gave no serious thought to granting the king his fondest wish, a tax increase. In fact, the revolutionaries made sure that the crown could not legally raise revenue on its own by outlawing the myriad of uneven Old-Regime taxes.[23] The National Assembly (as the Estates were called after June 1789) devised the most complex and protracted scheme of tax reform imaginable: the new fiscal regime would rest on a land tax requiring a detailed survey of France. Such a survey was deemed essential to a fair tax assessment, but it promised to take decades to complete.[24] While the process of land-tax reform was spun out, a representative assembly could be institutionalized. The assembly opted for such a reform precisely because it had political bite. By worsening the deficit, it made the crown dependent on the assembly. Further, the assembly quickly enacted a set of reforms that increased the short-term public debt by nearly one billion livres, leaving the monarch with a stark choice between either default or constitutional change. The National Assembly was not trying to coax bondholders or taxpayers into footing the bill for the crown's debts. Rather, it was trying to force the king into accepting the assembly as a permanent representative body.

Until late in 1792, therefore, politics and fiscal policy simply cannot be divorced. True, it was no longer necessary to constrain the government's revenues, once the king was finally deposed in August 1792. But now tax revenues no longer kept pace with expenses, for the radicalization of the Revolution swelled the deficit, forcing the revolutionaries to print even more assignats. Perhaps the worst financial blow was France's war with Austria. Despite the celebrated victory at Valmy in September 1792, the revolutionary armies experienced at best mixed results on the battlefield, as expenditures mounted. Meanwhile, on the home front the state faced provincial revolts that impeded tax collection.[25] Both the war and the domestic troubles, it should be stressed, resulted from political decisions taken by the revolutionaries. The Legislative Assembly voted

22. Sutherland 1986:63–68, 82–85.

23. Taxes were declared illegal on 17 June 1789, less than two months after the Estates were convened and the very same day (hardly a coincidence) that the Estates renamed themselves the National Assembly. The new taxes were enacted in a series of edicts in 1790, culminating in the law of January 1791 (Crouzet 1993:94, 120).

24. The cadastre was not completed until 1850: Herbin and Pébereau 1953:24.

25. Sutherland 1986:ch. 5.

for war on 20 April 1792, and it was a series of domestic reforms that prompted the provincial revolts. And the revolutionaries who made these decisions also controlled the printing presses that were churning out assignats. The economy simply could not escape the consequences of radicalization and war: deeper deficits and more inflation.

In this situation, which lasted from 1792 to 1795, printing money provided the central government with the means of survival. The revenue that printing money brought in—what economists call the inflation tax—suited the unstable revolutionary governments perfectly. It required no bureaucracy of tax collectors and no significant consultation either. It was—both then as now—perfectly attuned to the needs of a weak government, because opponents could do little to prevent its collection.[26] The revolutionaries opted for the inflation tax not because they had something to gain from inflation. Rather, they did so because the inflation tax was really their only fiscal instrument if they wanted to stay in political power and fight a war. Not until 1796 did victory on the battlefield allow the government to secure enough revenue from conquered territories to stop the printing of money and return to a specie currency.

At bottom, then, fiscal and monetary policies were always weapons in a larger political battle. But one might still ask how large a budgetary adjustment was needed to solve the government's financial problems. If it was small, particularly early on, then the king might have been able to fix the problems—at least temporarily—without summoning the Estates General and without compromising his political authority. He could have done so by defaulting on enough of the state's debt to eliminate the deficit, which ran to about one hundred million livres a year. That would have meant reneging on about half of the long-term debt, or an equal amount of the short-term debt. The king would have wiped out the deficit until the next war broke out; however, without a permanent tax increase, he could still not compete militarily with his major military rivals.

Would the state's creditors have resisted such a move? The war of attrition assumes they would. So too does the argument that a default would have been a political disaster simply because the state's creditors were numerous and powerful.[27] In France, though, many bondholders had little political clout. To begin with, some 30 percent of the long-term debt was held by foreigners—principally Swiss, Dutch, and Italian investors.[28] Repudiating their bonds would have reduced the state's long-

26. The same is true today: Cukierman, Edwards, and Tabelini 1992.
27. White 1989.
28. See chapter 7.

term obligations by some half a billion francs or more and cut the deficit in half. If royal officials had ferreted out the holdings of foreigners in the short-term debt, another few tens of millions might have been eliminated.[29] A selective default on foreigners would have been very attractive, at least in the short run, though half the deficit would still remain.

Since a default on foreigners alone would not have eliminated all the deficit, French holders of government debt would have had to suffer as well. In contrast to the Law affair, the magnitude of the default on French bondholders could have been quite small. In 1788 the debt stood at about four billion livres. If we assume that most of the government debt yielded some 8 percent (for payments of 320 million livres in annual interest, of which 220 million went to French debt holders), then the king could have balanced the budget by repudiating the foreign debt completely and cutting interest payments on the debt held by French subjects to 6 percent. A default of this magnitude—complete elimination of the foreign debt plus the reduction of interest payments on the domestic debt—was small by historical standards, and it would have brought the state's finances back into balance at the end of 1788. Furthermore, the French bondholders would still be receiving a higher rate of interest than investors in British debt and more than they could earn in the private market.

Politically, however, such a default was impossible, for by 1789 it would have been considered an unacceptable act of despotism.[30] Furthermore, the revolutionaries quickly made matters worse by adding another billion livres to the debt by the end of 1789.[31] Balancing the budget would have now required a 40 percent cut in interest, an amount that was no longer small by historical standards.

A short-term solution to the deficit was thus briefly within reach at the outset of the Revolution. But it was not adopted, chiefly because control of the deficit was not the end of the political process, but a means. For opponents of the crown, the deficit was the critical tool influencing the distribution of power. As for the crown itself, it never contemplated default because that solution only yielded a temporary reprieve. A complete default on the debt would only have secured about 220 million livres annually, enough to fight another small war like the

29. It is unlikely that any of the foreign investors' governments would have taken action against France. The only cost of such a default, then, would be diminished access to international credit, which would have been important only if France were to engage in another war.

30. See chapter 7.

31. The increase in debt came from the central government's assumption of other institutions' debts and from the abolition of the venality of government offices.

American War of Independence but perhaps not enough to defeat England.[32] Serious competition with England, which the king desired, required raising taxes. For the monarch the problem was that the elites were unwilling to raise taxes without securing political concessions.

By focusing on political actors in Paris such as the king and the Estates General, we perhaps lay ourselves open to the charge that we are neglecting taxpayers and government bondholders. Since they were not directly involved in the political battle—so the argument might go—their behavior would have reflected not politics but the losses and gains from particular fiscal and monetary policies. They would therefore have acted in exactly the way that the macroeconomic model of the war of attrition predicts, and they might even have tried to pressure political actors to adopt favorable fiscal and monetary policies. If they were effective interest groups, they could conceivably have pushed the political actors into waging the war of attrition by proxy.

The taxpayers and bondholders, though, were not unified and effective interest groups, and their behavior was not likely to have fit the predictions of the war of attrition model. To take but one example, consider the elite, who held much of the government debt. They should therefore have mobilized against default and for tax increases. Although they did oppose default, they were also vocal opponents of tax increases, for they would obviously be the ones to pay once taxation was extended to the privileged.[33] Whatever the outcome, they would bear the burden. It is no wonder that they did not behave the way that the war of attrition predicts.

Of course, the exact burden that the elite would bear if taxes were increased depended on how much the rates would shift for those already paying taxes. In general, the debate over taxes in 1787 and 1788 divided those favoring an unchanged tax base from those who, like the king and the third estate, argued for its extension. Yet precisely because the fiscal issues involved both changes in the tax base and in the tax rates, the individuals who would pay increased taxes could not present a united front against government bondholders, and the division in their ranks would rob these "taxpayers" of their effectiveness as an interest group.

Similar rifts split the government bondholders. By the end of the Old

32. A complete default would have liberated resources to the extent that the crown had a primary surplus. In the 1780s the crown was running a deficit of about 100 million livres and faced interest payments of about 320 million livres. Canceling the debt would therefore have released about 220 million livres.

33. Egret 1962:93–97, 130–37; Markoff 1996:80–82, 170–71. The privileged did often renounce tax exemptions. But as Markoff notes, that was usually only a clever rhetorical strategy, for they would then qualify their renunciation in a way that would keep their tax burden small.

Regime, they too were quite diverse.[34] Many of them, for instance, already paid taxes themselves or would do so if taxes were raised. Given such divisions in their ranks, they would have been unlikely to unite behind a program of higher taxes.

Casting the battle over government policy in terms of bondholders versus taxpayers also neglects other groups who had major stakes in the debate over fiscal and monetary affairs. One such group consisted of borrowers in the private credit market. In the short run, they favored inflation because it would have allowed them to repay their debts at a fraction of the anticipated cost. But they were too diverse to unite either. Private borrowers came from every social class, from princes of the blood down to peasants in the remotest corners of France. What set them off from lenders were age and gender. Borrowers were more likely to be young or male, while lenders were older or female. Inflation could thus cut across individual families. And in a society where family ties were paramount, it would have been difficult for borrowers (or lenders too for that matter) to lobby for any particular monetary or fiscal measure.

In any case, the political actors who fought over and ultimately determined monetary and fiscal policy looked at much more than economic impact when they chose the particular measures they favored. Inflation was part of a larger battle over political power and the shape of institutions, not fiscal readjustment. At first, the political actors fought over the constitutional rules that would govern politics in the future. It was no surprise, for example, that the first assembly named itself the *Constituante* or Constitutional Assembly. Later in the Revolution, the nature of society came under debate. The political actors here were not taxpayers and government creditors, who were in any case too diverse and too unorganized to be effective pressure groups. Rather, they were the king and the various legislative and constitutional assemblies. They also included the revolutionary clubs, the Paris commune, the counter-revolutionaries, the Committee of Public Safety, the Directory, and the army. These political actors faced issues much graver than the burden of fiscal adjustment. At the beginning of the Revolution, for instance, members of the Estates General opposed a rapid solution to the country's fiscal problems, for fear that it would leave power in the hands of the king and reduce the pressure for constitutional reform. And after elections in April 1797, a counter-revolutionary minority in the Assembly was willing to "wreck any financial reform" that the executive—the Directory—proposed.[35] This minority wanted to undermine the Revolu-

34. See chapter 7.
35. Sutherland 1986:299.

TABLE 8.2   THE REVOLUTION AND REDISTRIBUTION IN THE PRIVATE AND
                  GOVERNMENT CREDIT MARKETS: ESTIMATES FOR FRANCE AS A WHOLE

	Government Debt	Notarized Private Debt
Outstanding in 1789	Less than 4,800	More than 4,170
Repayments 1789–96	Less than 900	More than 7,200
Default in 1797	2,600	0
Outstanding in 1797	1,300	Less than 50
Estimated redistribution	2,850	1,675

Source: For government debt, the sources are Sargent and Velde 1995, table 1; *Annuaire statistique de la France, 1926* (1927:156); and Marion 1927, vol. 3. For the private credit market, the figures are derived from our estimates of outstanding private debt during the Revolution in Paris, which are extended to France using our survey of 1780; for details, see appendix 3 and chapter 10.

Note: All the figures are in millions of livres. Redistribution in the public credit market equals the amount of the default plus the losses on government debt repaid in depreciated currency during the Revolution. The losses were calculated from the change in value of the livre between 1789 and the date when government bonds were repaid. Such repayments included assignats paid to holders of offices in 1790–91, which in nominal terms were on the order of 750 million (Sargent and Velde 1995). Since these repayments stopped in 1792, the losses were at most 225 million even if we exaggerate them by assuming they were all made in 1792.

   Redistribution in the private credit market was estimated by assuming that the rate of private repayments in Paris applied to rest of the country. Although that may lead to an overestimate in provinces where civil war prevented repayments, it probably causes an underestimate in regions where the maturity of debt was short. The estimate comes from the difference between the real value of a debt when it was contracted and the value of the assignats used to pay it off. This procedure underestimates the losses suffered by creditors because it is not clear what creditors could do with their funds. The longer they waited to reinvest them the more they lost.

tion, and postponing fiscal adjustment was once again a means toward that end. If there was any war of attrition during the French Revolution, it was therefore fought over politics, not fiscal adjustment. The penalties for losing were enormous: they ranged from exile and loss of power to imprisonment and even the guillotine. The returns for winners were equally dramatic. Faced with such political incentives, the political actors in the Revolution willingly bore the costs of postponing fiscal adjustment. They did so in order to get and preserve the sort of government they wanted—a government that would favor their interests in the future.

The Long-Term Impact of the Inflation

The French Revolution redistributed huge sums of money. In 1797, the state defaulted on two-thirds of its debt, a loss of 2.6 billion livres to the government's creditors.[36] Meanwhile the revolutionary inflation cost lenders in the private market 1.67 billion livres more (table 8.2), as the stock of private debt dropped to nearly nothing. The evidence from no-

36. Marion 1927, 4:55–69.

tarial records demonstrates that the most serious harm was inflicted upon women, the elderly, and other investors of relatively modest means. They, not the wealthy, were the real victims of the revolutionary inflation. Nor was their loss the only damage that the inflation did. It convinced investors to expect inflation whenever governments were unstable, thereby contributing to a depression that gripped the long-term private credit market for decades.

Calculating the redistribution in the public market is relatively straightforward. It is simply the amount of the government default in 1797, plus any principal that the government repaid in devalued money, but such repayments were relatively small (table 8.2). For the private market, however, the calculation is more difficult. There the losses came when borrowers repaid loans in depreciated assignats. In the calculation, careful attention must be given to the chronology, for until the end of 1794 the value of the assignat was not trivial. There is another complication as well. If creditors used the assignats they received in repayment to purchase goods or real assets, they could reduce their exposure to further inflation losses.[37] During the Terror, though, the market for goods broke down, making it more difficult to dispose of assignats. Taking into account the collapse of real markets would surely increase the size of the losses. Yet even without such refinements, half of the value of private rentes simply evaporated, while obligation losses amounted to a quarter of the value of the debts outstanding in 1789. While these losses to repayments were large in either case, the lenders who held obligations clearly fared much better than those who held rentes. The institutional structure of the private market thus had clear implications for the gains and losses from inflation.

Compared to these losses, the revenue raised by printing money was small. The revenue—the inflation tax—came to less than half a livre for every livre that was redistributed. Even if we remove from the calculations the default on two-thirds of the public debt because it was in fact disconnected from printing the assignats, the redistribution still remains large relative to the inflation tax. In order to raise some two billion 1789 livres by printing assignats, the revolutionary governments provoked losses of a nearly equal magnitude within the private credit market.[38]

What then were the consequences of the inflation and the redistribu-

37. Individuals who used the assignats that they received to purchase property seized from the church did very well, because the property was purchased with a fractional down payment and an installment plan that allowed early repayment.

38. White (1994:230) points to an inflation tax of roughly two billion livres, or a bit under half the sum of total redistribution in table 8.2 (2,850 million livres from government debt plus 1,675 million from private debt).

tion in the public and private credit markets? Many lenders, obviously, were worse off: in the language of economics, their welfare had suffered. One might argue that the lenders were wealthy and could thus bear the losses from inflation and government default. But many of them were of relatively modest means, such as the numerous domestic servants in Paris who invested their retirement savings in the credit market.[39] They might suddenly be facing retirement without any income and yet be too old to work. The situation might be similar for women and for elderly investors in general: they could not find employment to compensate for what they had lost. The inflation and the redistribution had interfered with their plans for retirement and probably also with transfers of wealth from savers to their children and heirs—what economists call intergenerational transfers. Some individuals did of course profit from the inflation and redistribution, but it is highly unlikely that they would somehow compensate for all the losses by making better use of the money they had won.

The inflation was particularly hard on the modest investors. Our model of loan repayments predicts that smaller loans were more likely to be reimbursed late in the inflation and thus to impose an even greater loss on the lenders, who received assignats that had depreciated even more.[40] And that is exactly what happened during the Revolution. People who lent small sums of money were reimbursed late (because of the fixed costs of reimbursement) and thus lost more to the inflation tax than large-scale investors (table 8.3). Since it was modest investors who tended to make these small-scale loans, the conclusion is inescapable: the inflation tax was highly regressive.[41]

Paris bore more than its share of the losses here. Contracts in which non-Parisians repaid Parisians were nearly twice as frequent as those in which Parisians reimbursed non-Parisians. Because Parisians were net creditors to the rest of France, they felt the burden of the inflation keenly, even though the inflation was more a product of politics in Paris than politics elsewhere in France.

Beyond these welfare effects, the inflation also changed individuals'

39. Roche 1981:83. A number of domestics showed up in our loan samples; in table 7.5 they are lumped together with craft artisans and other occupations.

40. Because of the transaction costs of reimbursing loans, borrowers in our model will only choose early repayment for loans above a certain size. Smaller loans will be less likely to meet this condition and hence they will tend to be repaid late in the inflation. For details, see appendix 1.

41. The data in table 7.5, for example, imply that lenders who were craftsmen made loans that averaged roughly 3,200 livres, while loans from nobles and officers were much larger—some 16,500 livres on average.

TABLE 8.3   SIZE OF PRIVATE RENTES REPAID BY PERIOD

	Nominal Value (thousands)		Real Value (thousands)		Number of Obs	Real Value of the Livre (1789 = 1)
	Mean	Median	Mean	Median		
1790.1	52,479	5,000	52,479	5,000	15	1
1790.2	9,868	4,750	9,868	4,750	17	1
1791.1	26,487	8,000	25,427	7,680	41	0.96
1791.2	11,950	9,000	10,755	8,100	11	0.9
1792.1	6,772	4,000	5,282	3,120	59	0.78
1792.2	4,120	2,000	3,049	1,480	5	0.74
1793.1	6,342	3,375	4,059	2,160	50	0.64
1793.2	11,394	4,200	4,900	1,806	97	0.43
1794.1	10,343	3,121	4,965	1,498	27	0.48
1794.2	7,246	1,800	2,681	666	28	0.37
1795.1	9,589	4,000	1,630	680	279	0.17
1795.2	7,287	3,165	291	127	95	0.04

Source: Our detailed sample of Parisian repayment contracts for the Revolution. For details, see Archival Sources.

Note: 1790.1 means January through June 1790; 1790.2 means July through December 1790, etc.

expectations about the financial future. Although economists suggest that unanticipated and isolated bouts of inflation should not affect expectations, this logic does not apply to the Revolution. Individuals did not perceive the revolutionary inflation as a unique event but rather as a lesson about political economy. The inflation of 1791–95 was a historical experience forever joined with political turmoil and monetary instability in the minds of the French people. Like the Law affair in the 1710s, the inflation of the Revolution had a lasting effect on expectations.

It did so in a number of ways, all of which reduced the level of financial intermediation in Paris for several decades at least. If the inflation had been taken as an isolated event, the market might have recovered as quickly as it had in the 1720s. But the reverse occurred. The lessons the inflation taught were learned well, and nearly permanently. The first lesson was that, given the stabilization enacted in 1796, outright repayment of loans had been the wisest course especially for those who had waited until 1795 to do so. For borrowers, properly anticipating stabilization was critical.

The second and more important lesson was that there existed a deep connection between political and monetary stability. The inflation of the Law affair had occurred during an unstable regency. During the Revolution, inflation followed political turmoil. Parisians, and the French more generally, understood that political crises could lead to inflation. As long as contracts remained nominal with fixed interest rates, inflation would redistribute wealth. As chapter 9 will show, these expectations devastated notarial credit and provoked a shift to short-term lending.

———

The historian François Furet has contrasted two starkly opposed approaches to the study of the French Revolution. One, that of the nineteenth-century historian Jules Michelet, is narrative, emotional, and "marked by an intuitive grasp of men's souls and actors' motives." The other, pioneered by the early social scientist Alexis de Tocqueville, is abstract, analytical, and measures the "gulf between the Revolution's outcome and the revolutionaries' true intentions."[42] In our study of the revolutionary inflation, we have combined elements of both approaches by linking political events to a microeconomic model of borrowers' behavior and to an economic analysis of the gains and losses from government monetary and fiscal policy.

Much can be gained from such a combination. Not only does it shed new light on the inflation—a subject neglected by historians—but it also illuminates the whole course of politics between 1787 and 1814, from the Revolution's origins to the very tactics that the revolutionaries employed. It even raises important questions for cultural historians, who usually have little interest in economic history. Our approach reveals, for example, that Parisians swiftly shed Old-Regime financial habits once the Revolution was under way. In the short run they simply reacted to new risks and to the availability of new financial instruments. In the long run, however, the Revolution changed their whole psychology.

Our approach also teaches a lesson about historiography, whether of the French Revolution or any other subject. Historians routinely assume (usually for a priori reasons) that groups of people are the key to historical analysis. But they rarely ask whether the groups were divided or able to act politically. Their a priori reasons usually seem sufficient. Thus Marxist historians invoked the bourgeoisie to explain the French Revolution, taking for granted that the bourgeoisie formed a cohesive political force. More recently, cultural historians, inspired by Jürgen Habermas, have spoken of the public or of the public sphere. What they have in mind, at least for the French Revolution, is a rather amorphous group of informed readers, who participated in revolutionary political debates.[43] The trouble with such groups, though, is that they are torn by conflicting interests and ideals and unable to mobilize politically. We

42. Furet 1981:14–16.
43. See, for example, Chartier 1991.

discovered as much when we asked who lost the most to the revolutionary inflation. The individuals who suffered the worst losses, such as women, the elderly, or government bondholders, were neither unified nor able to act as a political force. Much the same is true of groups in general. Individuals typically have diverse interests and wants, and even if they all share the same political goal, it does not mean that they can work to achieve it. Until scholars learn to pay closer attention to the competing interests that tug at individuals, the history of the Revolution will remain suspect.

Unlike Michelet and Tocqueville, who concerned themselves with politics, we focus on economic behavior, at least initially. But we also stress that monetary and fiscal policy cannot be separated from revolutionary politics. Monetary and fiscal policy was a means to stay in power and to achieve political goals. Politics must therefore be taken into account in explaining why the Revolution's political actors ultimately chose inflation, for they did not do so simply to avoid higher taxes or losses to default. Politics is in fact important for understanding any of the fiscal and monetary policies adopted during the Revolution. Even the Estates General's failure to solve the fiscal crisis back in 1789 was a tactic designed to extract constitutional concessions from the crown.

The neglect of political motives is one of the flaws of the war of attrition, one of the recent macroeconomic models that have been devised to explain the revolutionary inflation. The war of attrition has other flaws as well. It focuses on unified interest groups of taxpayers and government bond holders, but as we have argued, taxpayers and bondholders are unlikely to have behaved in the way that the war of attrition assumes. The two groups overlapped and they were hardly unified. And the whole model overlooks other parties who also had a stake in monetary and fiscal policy, such as private debtors and the king.

The other recent macroeconomic account of the revolutionary inflation—that of Sargent and Velde—also has limits. Although their model explains the pattern of public finance and monetary emission, they fail to account for the wide variety of individual behavior that we unearthed thanks to the data about repayments in the private credit market. Those data call into question their whole approach, which, at bottom, tries to compress all sorts of individual behavior into a model of a single person's action—a so-called "representative agent." As the repayments demonstrate, individual borrowers and lenders did not agree about the financial and political future. The repayments (and no doubt their expectations about the future too) were simply too dispersed to reduce their behavior to a model of a single representative agent.

Sargent and Velde also miss evidence that individuals attempted to predict the course of government fiscal and monetary policy. The predictions were never perfect, and there was considerable disagreement about what would happen. Still, the transitions from monetary regime to monetary regime were—to a certain extent—anticipated.

To account for the differences in expectations and behavior, we must conclude that information could not be aggregated easily during the rapid inflation of the Revolution. The decentralized credit market in revolutionary Paris simply could not quickly bring individuals to a common expectation about the political and economic future. Although such a failure may seem disappointing, markets in other countries too have failed to aggregate information under rapid inflation.[44] The divergent expectations in revolutionary Paris are thus neither unique nor surprising.

The Revolution imposed three enormous losses on the Parisian economy: the government default of 1797, the inflation tax, and the damage done to private lenders when their loans were repaid in worthless assignats. Each loss totaled about two billion francs. The default was certainly not a consequence of the inflation; rather, it was the financial conclusion to the political crisis of 1789. The reimbursement of private loans, though, was a direct result of the inflation, for it could never have occurred without the proliferation of the assignats. The evidence from the private credit market thus completely changes our understanding of the revolutionary inflation and its consequences. The inflation (and the government default too, for that matter) was hardly an efficient way to raise money. Indeed, for every livre the inflation tax raised, private investors suffered a one-livre loss. The victims it left in its wake were not just wealthy investors. They included Parisian domestics and other modest investors, who endured particularly harsh treatment. Women and the elderly also suffered, and they would not find employment to compensate for their losses.

The French Revolution taught investors to fear inflation whenever governments were unstable. Their fear took a lasting toll on the economy. Indeed, once forged during the Revolution, the link between political instability and inflation influenced investment decisions at least until the 1870s. Ironically, the efforts Parisian investors took to avoid inflation proved unnecessary, for the political parties in power in France stuck to a fixed specie currency from 1803 on.

44. Tomasi 1990, 1993; Palerm 1990.

CHAPTER NINE

The Long-Term Financial
Consequences of the Revolution

DURING THE FRENCH REVOLUTION, the gyrations of the assignat had demonstrated that inflation was closely tied to political instability. And because private interest rates had been fixed, lenders had suffered the most severe losses. It was a lesson that they—and the public—would long remember. Nonetheless, after the currency was finally stabilized, the state made every effort to convince the public that inflation would never occur again. It created a new currency, the *franc*.[1] It reworked the national debt and forsook borrowing for a long while.[2] These and other smaller steps, it was hoped, would assure the public that severe inflation would never return. But in the first half of the nineteenth century the public was not prepared to forget the bitter lesson of the assignat, even though the monetary regime established in 1797 proved quite stable, enduring until the First World War with little change.[3]

Political regimes in the postrevolutionary era proved much less resilient. The trouble was that four major factions vied for power in France throughout much of the nineteenth century. Two were descendants of the Old Regime (Legitimists and Orleanists), while the two others were products of the Revolution (Bonapartists and republicans). At one extreme, the Legitimists wanted to restore the Old Regime's political and economic order. At the other, the republicans threatened to eliminate nondemocratic institutions in postrevolutionary France. With the four major factions locked in an enduring struggle, and with Parisians (though not all French people) willing to pull their support from any one of the groups when it was in charge, political crises regularly struck

1. Marion 1927, 4:185–249.
2. Bordo and White 1991.
3. Flandreau 1995.

France, political crises that stirred up both financial and institutional uncertainty.

It is true that the political crises of 1814, 1815, 1830, 1848, and 1851 did not overturn property rights and that the transfer of authority often occurred almost overnight. Nonetheless, lenders still feared a prolonged crisis that could annihilate their investments. The ongoing political battles continued to frighten them, for as the Revolution of 1789 had demonstrated, a new regime could, within a few short months, shift from benign neglect to preying upon financial instruments. All it took was a significant drop in fiscal receipts—which did occur in 1848. Although in the end these political crises left most lenders unscathed, it was not until the 1850s that the psychological connection between political instability and financial crisis was finally broken.[4] In the first half of the nineteenth century, credit markets were thus clouded by the continuing threat of political instability and its dire financial consequences.

What did that mean for Parisian notaries? They had thrived as financial intermediaries during a long period of political and financial stability in the eighteenth century. In the politically turbulent nineteenth century, though, they never succeeded in rebuilding their business. Each time a political upheaval engendered a financial crisis, the notaries stumbled, and their role in capital markets diminished.

Meanwhile, other financial intermediaries such as bankers gained at the notaries' expense. Although they faced the same risks of political and financial instability, they seemed better able to surmount the crises. And because they eventually took the notaries' place, the Parisian credit market as a whole did not suffer. Indeed, Paris actually increased its hold over long-term credit in France.

Why then did the Parisian notaries fall behind? One might think that they were simply obsolete. Their lending practices (so the argument might go) were ill suited to a world of political and financial risk. At the same time, they just could not mobilize enough capital for what was now an industrializing economy. On closer inspection, though, neither criticism seems valid. The notaries were not outmoded, and the true causes of their decline must lie elsewhere.

This chapter begins by analyzing the problem that the Revolution and political instability had posed for investors and financial intermediaries. It also looks at the Parisian notaries' response to this problem—the creation of the prorogation. We next examine the notaries' decline and

4. The war of 1870 and the siege of Paris did lead to a financial crisis. As in 1848, the government's credibility was sorely tested by massive withdrawals from savings banks, but once again the state weathered the crisis without changing monetary policy.

estimate the effect that the Revolution and political instability had on their business. We then turn to the city's other financial intermediaries and note how their success in surmounting the crises of the nineteenth century spared the Parisian capital market and actually increased the city's control of long-term lending. We close by considering why the notaries lost their place at the top of the long-term credit market.

Financial Change in a World of Scarce Credit

After the monetary turmoil halted in 1797, fear of inflation caused a severe problem both for financial intermediaries and for individuals who wanted to borrow. Solving the problem meant modifying the entire financial system, but such a change was difficult to accept, for it meant the intermediaries would bear greater risk during political crises. Nonetheless, despite all the risks involved, the Parisian notaries did take a step toward the necessary solution by devising a new financial instrument, the prorogation, which should have helped them recover their dominant role in the long-term credit market.

The essence of the problem was a mismatch between the preferences of the lenders and borrowers. Lenders, for their part, wanted to be able to withdraw their funds whenever they feared political instability might unleash a monetary crisis. Borrowers, by contrast, preferred long-term loans to short-term credit. Indeed, they did not want to have to interrupt their plans simply because their loans were unexpectedly not renewed, and when loans funded investments (such as construction) that only generated revenues upon completion, they had to have loans that would last long enough for the projects to be finished.[5] Exactly how much long-term credit would be available thus depended on the ability of intermediaries to reconcile the mismatched preferences of borrowers and lenders: the borrowers sought long-term loans; the lenders wanted the opposite.

Although one could imagine many ways of dealing with the mismatch, no satisfactory solution emerged in Paris until the 1850s. Back in the late eighteenth century, the bilateral credit market might have overcome the mismatch if notaries could have found enough short-term lenders to assure the renewal of loans. But the bilateral market (in which notaries acted only as brokers) never revived, for reasons explained in the next chapter.

Faced with the mismatch, many financial intermediaries were tempted

---

5. Examples of such projects would be agricultural improvements, transportation projects, or the construction of multistoried buildings.

to draw upon short-term money to fund long-term debt. Doing so simply involved selling short-term notes or accepting short-term deposits and then using the cash to make long-term loans. It did, however, entail a great risk for the intermediaries: namely, that deposit holders would unexpectedly demand their money back, or that the intermediaries themselves would suddenly be unable to peddle their short-term notes. The risk, in the language of economics, was both idiosyncratic and systematic. It was idiosyncratic in the sense that an individual depositor might unexpectedly make a large and atypical withdrawal. It was systematic in the sense that a political crisis might drive all depositors to remove their funds and cause the entire short-term loan market to dry up.

This risk was one with which intermediaries could scarcely contend. One obvious solution—reserves—often proved insufficient to meet unexpected withdrawals, and another—mutual insurance—was practically nonexistent. A large-scale bill market would have certainly helped, by giving intermediaries liquid assets that could be sold to meet withdrawals. But such a market never developed, because the Paris stock exchange was too small and because legal distinctions between personal and commercial debt limited the use of bills. Of course, even a broad and thriving bill market would not have protected against the systematic downturns that struck credit markets during political crises. In such crises, even normally liquid bills would be of no help, for they too would decline sharply in value and be difficult to sell.[6] The only thing that would have assisted intermediaries here was a lender of last resort, but the Bank of France and the treasury lacked the resources to cope with anything larger than isolated incidents. The financial fallout from political crises was simply beyond their reach.

Borrowers therefore simply learned to make do without true long-term credit. Some garnered medium-term funds through a notary. They hoped that their lender would extend their loans when they came due or that they would be able to find a new source of funds. Such makeshift solutions would not work, however, in a liquidity crisis. Borrowers could also turn to the short-term market run by bankers and sell short-term notes. There, the hope was their notes could be placed on the market regularly.[7] But again the borrowers were at the mercy of a liquidity crisis. The problem, at bottom, was that both strategies forced borrowers to assume risks that had little to do with the intrinsic profitability of their investment projects.

6. Lévy-Leboyer 1964.
7. Gille 1959:57, 149.

As for lenders, because they believed that inflation might return, they demanded terms different from those that had prevailed under the Old Regime. In the years immediately following the inflation, interest rates varied freely, and contracts were occasionally indexed in the countryside. The short supply of credit, because of the fear of inflation, kept interest rates on obligations above 10 percent per year in many regions. In Paris, notaries acknowledged that interest rates exceeded 12 percent in 1797 and 1798. After 1799, rates fell to 9 percent, then to 8 percent in 1802, later returning to near 9 percent in 1805. Interest rates stayed at that level until 1807, when the state brought back the traditional cap of 5 percent. Except for qualitative information of this sort, though, it is difficult to track interest rates in Paris, because they were rarely reported in the contracts. As a 1806 report from the corporation of notaries noted:

> Each notary has had the pleasure of witnessing loans at 5 percent. But these instances were only rare examples. We [Parisian notaries] nearly always removed from the contracts any stipulation of a rate above 5 percent: the parties reached a separate agreement on this point. Indeed the notaries thought that it was their duty not to transmit to posterity the knowledge and example of something that in this respect was only the result of transitory circumstances.[8]

Whether notaries continued to sanction informal agreements about interest rates after 1807 is unclear, but the high interest rates until 1807 probably reflected a dramatic shortage of credit. Some observers, such as the nineteenth-century American scholar and diplomat A. D. White, argued that credit had shriveled up in France because the Revolution permanently reduced savings rates and thus the supply of capital.[9] It is impossible to tell whether the savings rate actually declined, but it does seem that the supply of financial capital dropped. Indeed, during the Revolution, financial balances must have fallen simply because they had little value; they may not have returned to their 1789 levels for quite some time. Furthermore, there is every reason to believe that supply of credit, rather than demand, dried up.[10] The Revolution might have temporarily reduced demand for credit but it did not eliminate it. Entrepreneurs and business people still needed to borrow, and families still needed to redistribute resources over time.

8. Cited in Poisson 1990:145.
9. White 1896:65.
10. An institution like the Banque Territoriale only offered loans at rates above 10 percent. The loan contracts are in ANMC, LXXXVIII, 917 to 931. See Bergeron 1978: 112–13.

Once the 5 percent cap was reimposed in 1807, intermediaries could vary only three other features of debt contracts to alleviate lenders' fear of inflation: collateral, contract size, and duration.[11] Additional collateral could be required by a lender to limit losses in case of a default, but it would do little to offset the risk of inflation.[12] As for smaller contract size, it could facilitate portfolio diversification and thereby protect against default too. It could also reduce exposure to inflation by giving a lender a mix of loan maturities. In the bilateral markets of the early nineteenth century, though, diversification of this sort imposed additional transaction costs because of the fixed fees of private debt contracts, and in the long run contract size did not play an important role in cutting exposure to inflation.

Duration, the third variable of credit contracts that intermediaries and creditors could control, was the only one that really alleviated anxieties about inflation after 1797. Lenders had learned a simple lesson: individuals who had held their financial assets in obligations prior to 1789 fared much better than those who had held them in rentes. (Keep in mind that lenders could not prevent borrowers from reimbursing their loans some time between 1790 and 1795.) Indeed, 90 percent of the obligations that had been outstanding at the end of 1789 were reimbursed by the end of 1792, when the currency was still worth more than half of its value. In contrast only 40 percent of the rentes outstanding in 1789 had been reimbursed that early. On the basis of this experience, creditors concluded that long durations were a danger in times of political instability.

Not surprisingly, in the years following 1797 lenders refused to make long-term loans. In the first decade after the inflation ended, most debts lasted less than two years. As public confidence in the monetary regime increased, lenders began to make longer loans (table 9.1). Meanwhile, notaries made it possible to extend the actual duration of obligation loans beyond what was specified in the original contract. The terms of each obligation included a date at which the debt was supposed to be repaid, but lender and borrower could agree to extend it. This practice (which was common in the short-term debt market) became customary for long-term debts in after 1830. Notaries drew up a *prorogation* contract, allowing the lender to extend his loan without losing control of his

11. For short-term loans, the 5 percent interest-rate cap was of little importance because inflating the capital sum provided an easy way to increase interest rates. For longer term loans, discounting created problems of moral hazard and was not used much.

12. Postel-Vinay (1998) shows, however, that collateral requirements increased with political uncertainty, and particularly so for smaller debts, where the redistribution had been most intense during the Revolution.

TABLE 9.1   DURATION OF NOTARIZED OBLIGATIONS IN PARIS

Period	Number of New Prorogations over Number of New Obligations (percent)	Fraction of Loans Due Extended by Prorogations (percent)	Initial Duration of Loans (years)	Actual Duration of All Loans (years)	Estimated Duration with Prorogations (years)
1780–89			4.20		
1790–96			4.02	3.03	
1797–99			2.00	2.00	
1800–09	4.8	6	3.52	4.14	4
1810–19	17.4	13.7	3.90	4.47	4.55
1820–29	17.5	15.7	4.24	5.53	5.45
1830–39	33.4	24.8	4.69	6.83	6.98
1840–49	40.5	32.4	5.60	7.82	8.28
1850–59	48.5	28.1	5.50	6.35	7.11
1860–69	21.4	21.4	5.50		

Source: See appendix 4 and chapter 2.

Note: Initial duration is the unweighted average duration of obligation contracts taken from two sources in the indexes to the notarial records: (1) summaries of original loan contracts, and (2) summaries of prorogations when they gave how long the original loan had been outstanding. In the case of prorogations we excluded all durations greater than ten years, because it was likely that these had already been extended once. Actual duration is the average duration from quittances. Finally, estimated duration with prorogation is our estimate of duration taking into account the effect of prorogations. Here we assumed that, when used, the prorogations extended loans for a term equal to the initial duration. Only initial durations are available for the 1860s because we stopped collecting data in 1869.

capital. This contract, with flexible initial durations and the possibility of prorogation, increased the availability of credit. It allowed each lender to invest for a period that reflected his confidence in the monetary system and the borrower. It also permitted him to reevaluate his loan decision on the basis of information acquired after the loan contract was signed. If a borrower performed properly and the political regime seemed stable, the debt could be extended. From the borrower's perspective, of course, the contract structure was less desirable than a long-term loan, but it did broaden access to credit. It also lowered transaction costs by making it unnecessary to drum up new lenders who could fund a loan renewal. And it placed the borrower at an advantage over alternative debtors in periods of crisis. By the time his loan came due, he had accumulated a credit history with his lender, whereas new borrowers had no such informational advantage. After all, if a crisis erupted, a lender would not want to compound the systematic risk by adding uncertain new borrowers. If the lender kept funds in the financial market at all, he would renegotiate outstanding debts rather than make loans to new borrowers.

The prorogation contract was the most significant innovation in no-tarial credit in the nineteenth century. It had much less of an impact, though, than the eighteenth-century obligation, for it added flexibility to only one dimension (duration) of the relationship between lenders and borrowers, whereas the obligation had also relaxed the constraint on interest rates. Nonetheless, the prorogation did matter because it became extremely prevalent. By the 1840s, nearly a third of all loans that came due were extended via prorogation agreements (table 9.1). By the 1850s, prorogations were half as numerous as new debts, and by the 1840s, debts lasted almost eight years. Overall duration more than doubled between 1805 and 1850, and that growth can be divided about equally between the increase in initial maturity and the growing popular-ity of prorogations.

With the prorogation, the Parisian notaries succeeded in adapting the obligation to the new political and economic environment. Isolated examples in fact suggest that some of the notaries were using the revital-ized obligation to mobilize capital for a variety of economic purposes. From January to December 1852, for example, the notary François Da-guin drew up seventy-three separate loan contracts for François Louis Alfred Pioche, represented by the banker Opperman.[13] Pioche was a partner in Pioche and Bayerque, a banking firm in San Francisco with a branch in Paris.[14] Thanks to the loans Daguin arranged, Pioche man-aged to raise some 320,000 francs from men and women living in Paris, Orléans, Tours, and other cities of northern France. Though the precise purpose of these loans is unclear, they may well have gone to San Fran-cisco, where Pioche and Bayerque played a key role in the development of public utilities.[15] And that was not all that Daguin did. Soon after, in March 1853, he raised one million francs for the Forges de Châtillon. The metallurgy firm, already one of France's largest, merged with other producers in 1854 to become the country's leading iron and steel pro-ducer.[16]

The Parisian notaries could therefore have played a central role in nineteenth-century credit. Indeed, as the examples suggest, some no-taries were competing directly with more 'modern' forms of financial intermediation. The notaries had at their disposal the prorogation, which should have helped them contend with the major problem facing

13. ANMC étude CXVII Re 21, 1852.

14. San Francisco City Directory, 1861. ANMC, CXVII Re 21, 1854.

15. Cross 1927; Armstrong and Denny 1916:46–51.

16. ANMC étude CXVII, Re 21, 1853. See also Gille 1968:130–55. In 1853, the same year they borrowed under the auspices of Daguin, the Forges de Châtillon also issued some six million francs of bonds on the stock market.

financial intermediaries: the fact that borrowers preferred long-term loans, while lenders wanted to be able to withdraw their funds on short notice, whenever political instability threatened to create a credit crisis. The prorogation was not a complete solution to the problem, but it meant that the notaries were just as prepared to deal with it as any other financial intermediary. After all, the other intermediaries had no special institutions that could step in during liquidity crises; in particular, there was no lender of last resort. The prorogation should have helped the Parisian notaries regain their role in the long-term debt market, but as we shall see, that never happened.

Notarial Credit in Paris, 1797–1869

Instead of recapturing their old role, the Parisians notaries ended up on the margins of financial intermediation. As the level of private indebtedness demonstrates (figure 2.4), notarial credit grew slowly and fitfully in the nineteenth century. True, the French Revolution had created long-lasting problems for all financial intermediaries, but for the Parisian notaries, the difficulties seemed insurmountable. Each nineteenth-century political crisis knocked them for a loop.

In 1797 the value of outstanding private loans was negligible—no more than a mere 132 million francs. Most older debts had been repaid during the inflation, while loans contracted during the Revolution were now worth only a fraction of their nominal value. Nonetheless, financial recovery began aggressively. Although notarial credit would never fully recover from the Revolution, by the 1830s it had emerged from the abyss where it had been plunged by the inflation. By the 1810s, the number of credit contracts had risen to about half of what it had been in the eighteenth century, while the volume of new loans amounted to some 70 percent of the Old-Regime level. In the 1840s, the stock of outstanding debts peaked at 60 percent of its prerevolutionary record. Although long-term debt rose again in the 1860s, the increase was not the notaries' doing. Rather it was the newly formed Crédit Foncier de France (CFF) that was responsible. On their own, the Parisians notaries never restored long-term lending to eighteenth-century levels.

As table 9.2 and figure 9.1 show, postrevolutionary lending was conducted almost entirely via obligations. By 1830, 95 percent of all funds were loaned via obligation contracts; perpetual annuities had almost disappeared. Once it was possible to specify interest rates in obligations, there was essentially no reason to sign perpetual annuities any more. Meanwhile, the notaries' life annuities had been replaced by annuity

TABLE 9.2   NOTARIZED CREDIT CONTRACTS IN NINETEENTH-CENTURY PARIS

Decade Beginning	Average Number of Contracts per Year			
	Perpetual Annuities	Obligations	Life Annuities	Other Contracts Relating to Credit
1780	2051	4832	1529	10,994
1790	858	4060	564	19,128
1800	157	6606	505	19,838
1810	22	4848	380	14,479
1820	24	4313	378	14,737
1830	2	3832	222	17,362
1840	7	4498	190	17,767
1850	4	3294	116	15,006
1860	1	4441	113	14,108

Source: Our estimates of numbers of contracts for Paris; for details, see chapter 2.
Note: The other contracts relating to credit include *quittances, transports, mainlevées,* and *prorogations.*

contracts sold by insurance companies.[17] Since nothing prevented borrowers and lenders from signing life and perpetual annuity contracts in the nineteenth century, we must assume that they simply preferred to use obligations. One consequence of their reliance on obligations, though, was an increase in transaction costs, and the higher transaction costs in turn made financial investments arranged by notaries less attractive, even with prorogations.

In addition to the prorogation, two other new loan contracts also appeared, but these innovations did not expand the notary's role as a financial intermediary, for he did little more than draw them up. The first new instrument was the notarized credit line *(ouverture de crédit),* which bankers began giving clients in the 1820s. It proved particularly important for entrepreneurs in the countryside, because they could use it to issue notes payable in Paris. Yet notaries did little to arrange such contracts. Usually, they provided neither the capital nor the information about the borrower. Moreover, though individual credit authorizations could be quite large—several surpassed 100,000 francs—as a whole notarized credit lines were never a quantitatively important affair. Bankers issued them to a small number of clients, and the loans were typically of brief duration.

The second innovation was the CFF loan, which provided the first modern, fixed-interest-rate mortgage. Because we devote chapter 11 to

17. See Courtois 1873; Bresson 1825.

☐ Private Perpetual Annuities ☰ Obligations ■ Private Life Annuities ⊞ Crédit Foncier de France ☐ Credit Lines

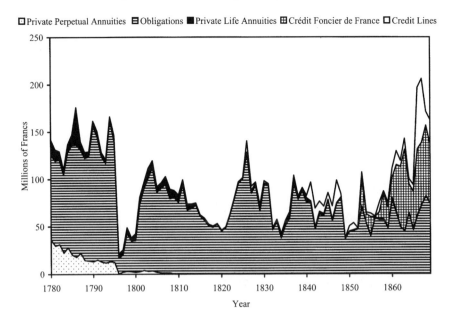

FIGURE 9.1   Volume of New Loans by Type of Contract, 1780–1869

the impact of the CFF, we only point out here that it swiftly came to dominate the Parisian mortgage credit. By 1869, the CFF was originating nearly half of all new notarized loans, and more half the outstanding notarized loans in Paris had been arranged by the CFF. As with the credit line, though, the notaries had little or nothing to do with CFF lending.

The notaries' role looks even weaker if we consider lending per capita. As table 9.3 shows, all the per capita indicators declined in the nineteenth century. Between the 1780s and the 1860s, the number of notarized credit contracts per person fell by nearly 80 percent. By the 1860s, the typical Parisian was using his notary to borrow only one fifth as much as his great grandparents would have done eighty years before. Outstanding debt per capita fell even more sharply. One might of course argue that the drop in these per capita figures simply reflected the rapid increase in the Paris population. But in a city, population growth is capital intensive, and it demands more lending for housing and infrastructure.

Clearly, the Parisian notaries had failed to recover their Old-Regime preeminence; worse yet, their financial dealings proved particularly likely to founder during political turmoil. Beginning in 1808, notarial credit slipped into the first of three major phases of decline reflected in all of our indicators. Each decline was touched off by a political crisis.

TABLE 9.3   PER CAPITA NOTARIAL DEBT IN PARIS

Decade Beginning	Paris Population	Number of Contracts per 1000 People	Per-Capita Annual Volume of New Loans		Per-Capita Private Indebtedness	
			Notarial Credit	Credit Lines and CFF	Notarial Credit	Credit Lines and CFF
1780	600,000	14.02	230.0	0.0	1,572.5	
1790	547,000	10.02	107.8	0.0	466.7	
1800	580,000	12.53	162.0	0.0	651.4	
1810	713,000	7.36	98.2	0.0	631.3	
1820	750,000	6.25	112.0	0.0	526.8	
1830	866,000	4.68	84.3	21.2	563.0	
1840	1,053,000	4.45	64.6	10.5	508.7	
1850	1,174,000	2.90	46.0	13.5	425.6	31.0
1860	1,866,000	2.66	42.9	35.4	244.0	175.9
Benchmark Dates						
1780	600,000	14.98	239.6		1,408.3	
1807	580,000	12.41	179.1		867.7	
1840	936,000	5.18	88.9		542.6	
1869	1,850,000	2.78	54.3	34.5	262.3	306.5

Source: As in table 9.2, except for the population, which comes from Charlot and Dupâquier 1967 and Chevalier 1950.

Note: All monetary figures are in constant silver francs per person.

Unlike the Old Regime, when political crises were generally transitory, political ferment in the nineteenth century spelled long-term trouble for notarial credit.

The first long decline began in 1808 and did not end until 1823, a full eight years after the Bourbon restoration. Outstanding debt levels declined by nearly half. Though not all events register in the series, the political causes of the crisis are beyond doubt. Notarial credit suffered from uncertainty over the fate of the Empire, which increased with the invasion of Spain in 1806 and of Russia in 1812. May 1814—the month of Napoleon's first abdication—saw the second smallest volume of new loans in the entire century. His short-lived return during the Hundred Days of 1815 only aggravated matters by demonstrating that the Bourbons had at best limited political support.

Throughout the next three decades, notarial credit in Paris echoed the political scene. The brief revolution in 1830 cut down notarial credit for a second time: between 1830 and 1834 the volume of new loans was halved again. The July monarchy then saw a steady growth in notarial lending, which peaked in 1848 when outstanding debts reached 554 million francs. When the 1848 revolution ushered yet another period of political uncertainty, the volume of new loans fell for the third time, dropping from 82 million francs in 1848 to 37 million in 1849.

One can tighten the link between notarial credit and political crises by examining the duration of notarial loans. The collapse of Napoleon's empire, for example, shortened loan maturity dramatically: between 1810 and 1819 the initial duration of loans (in other words, the duration specified in the original loan contract) dropped from 59 to 32 months. Similarly, initial loan durations fell sharply (from five years to four) after the Revolution of 1830, and the same thing happened in 1848, with initial durations sliding from six years to five. Political turmoil also affected the renegotiation of loans. In 1830–31 and 1848–51, for instance, prorogations grew more common. On the whole, the response to political crises was mixed. On the one hand, as the drop off in new loans suggests, lenders retreated from the credit market. At the same time, confidence declined, shortening the initial period duration of loans that lenders specified in the loan contracts.

Yet lenders also used prorogations to extend their loans both during and after crises. They no doubt granted the extensions to avoid forcing debtors into default at a time when their collateral assets were of little value. As we noted above, the extensions were natural responses to increased uncertainty.[18] The prorogations grew more common during political crises, and as a result, the actual duration of loans usually remained relatively long, even though the initial durations were shorter.

Political crises thus had a permanent effect on notarial credit, and the crisis that mattered most was the Revolution. To assess the impact it had on notarial markets, we estimate how notarial credit would have evolved had the Revolution never occurred. Since the Revolution altered nearly every financial institution, such counterfactual estimation may appear foolhardy, but it is the only way to gauge the effect the Revolution had on notarial credit.

Fortunately, we have access to several sources of information that permit a variety of counterfactual scenarios. For simplicity, we focus on the outstanding debt series and consider two imaginary scenarios. The first is the most extreme: it imagines what would have happened to notarial credit without a Revolution. The second examines what would have happened if the Revolution had been merely a transitory shock, which affected the level of indebtedness but not the growth rate of lending. We

---

18. In the case of liquidity crises, lenders had little incentive to strategically call in their mortgage loans because under French law debtors were the residual claimants of the loans. Given the delay necessary to have the collateral auctioned, lenders could not hope to recover their funds quickly.

make these extreme assumptions in order to highlight the impact the Revolution actually had. Throughout we rely on simple linear trends so that the analysis will be transparent.

We begin by estimating how private indebtedness would have grown, had per capita debts remained at the levels they reached in 1780 (table 9.4, estimate 1). Because the Parisian population grew faster after 1810 than before 1789, lending should have accelerated after the Revolution. This estimate in fact suggests that by 1869 private indebtedness should have been nearly three times larger than it had been in 1780 and some 2.4 times bigger than it actually was, even with the Crédit Foncier. We arrive at a similar estimate if we assume that indebtedness were to continue along the linear trajectory of growth begun in the eighteenth century (table 9.4, estimate 2).[19] Even if we ignore the CFF's lending, notarial credit should have been four times greater in 1869 than it was in reality.

These first two estimates totally neglect the Revolution. They also probably overstate the role of inflation on the collapse of private credit because the Revolution eliminated the sale of public offices, an important source of demand for private loans. Since the buyers of the offices often financed their purchases via private loans, the sale of offices boosted private borrowing. Still, one should not go overboard and overstate the impact of eliminating the sale of offices. Although indebtedness might have dropped temporarily, there is no reason to believe that the growth of lending would have slackened. Furthermore, although the price of some offices was rising, it is unlikely that office sales fueled the tremendous surge of private lending in the eighteenth century.

Let us now consider the consequences if the Revolution had only been a transitory shock that reduced the level of private indebtedness but not its growth rate. To do so, we use four different benchmarks for the new and lower level of indebtedness and four different assumptions about the subsequent growth of lending. We start with the outstanding level of debt in 1797 and let indebtedness rise at the rate at which it expanded from 1726 to 1789 (table 9.4, estimate 3). That allows us to imagine what lending would have been like had the Revolution merely cut indebtedness back to the level of 1797 but not disturbed its rate of increase. Our second estimate takes the same level of indebtedness but applies the growth trend from 1798 to 1807 in order to judge how the credit market might have developed if Napoleon's demise had not interrupted what appeared to be a process of rapid recovery (table 9.4, esti-

19. Because notarial credit grew exponentially under the Old Regime, our assumption of a linear trend yields a very conservative estimate for the level of indebtedness.

TABLE 9.4 INDEXES OF LONG-TERM PRIVATE INDEBTEDNESS AFTER THE REVOLUTION: COUNTERFACTUAL ESTIMATES

| Year | Actual Indebtedness | | Counterfactual Scenario and Estimate | | | | | |
| | Notaries Alone | Notaries and CFF | If There Had Been No Revolution | | If the Revolution Were a Transitory Shock | | | |
			Estimate 1	Estimate 2	Estimate 3	Estimate 4	Estimate 5	Estimate 6
1780	100.00	100.00	100.00	100.00	100.00	100.00		100.00
1800	23.32	23.32	98.77	133.17	28.80	23.32		
1807	59.58	59.58	103.70	137.05	40.52	38.84	59.58	19.12
1840	60.10	60.07	165.43	196.37	95.95	111.61	181.11	78.51
1869	57.40	124.38	308.64	242.13	144.72	175.76	711.22	149.07

Source: As in table 9.2, except for the construction index, which comes from Chevalier (1950).

Note: All numbers in the table are indexes with 1780 = 100. As explained in the text, the counterfactual scenarios use linear extrapolation to estimate what notarial credit would have been under different assumptions. The estimates thus all involve evaluating a linear expression $a + bx$ and then dividing the result by the actual level of private indebtedness in 1780 to create the index. Here a is the initial level of debt, x is the variable used for extrapolation, and b is the slope of the extrapolation line, which determines how fast indebtedness grows.

In the scenario of no Revolution (estimates 1 and 2), a is the actual level of private notarial debt in 1789. In the other estimates, it is lower, as would be the case were the Revolution a transitory shock. For estimates 3 and 4, a is the actual level of debt in 1797, and for estimate 5, it is the actual level of debt in 1807. For estimate 6, which is an index of rural debt, a is the actual level of indebtedness in the countryside in 1780; it is estimated using a sample of rural markets described in chapter 10.

For estimate 1, b is per capita indebtedness in Paris in 1789, and x is the change in the Parisian population since 1789. For estimates 2 and 3, b is the rate of increase of private indebtedness between 1726 and 1789, and x is the time that has elapsed since 1789. For estimate 4, b is the rate of increase of indebtedness between 1797 and 1808, and x is the time elapsed since 1797. For estimate 5, b is the ratio of indebtedness to the value of Chevalier's construction index in 1807, and x is the increase in this construction index. Finally, in estimate 6, b is 1, and x is the estimated increase in outstanding debt in the countryside.

mate 4). A third estimate starts with the level of debt in 1807 and assumes that lending rose in parallel with construction in Paris (table 9.4, estimate 5). Finally, our fourth estimate relies on a growth rate derived from evidence about provincial lending in 1780, 1807, 1840, and 1869 (table 9.4, estimate 6). For these years, we used population figures to aggregate lending in a set of rural and urban markets. We then estimated the trend of non-Parisian lending and checked our results for plausibility against evidence collected by the state after 1840.[20]

Despite starting with widely different assumptions, all four of our estimates exceed the actual level of indebtedness by a wide margin. All the series in fact suggest that the credit market would have regained its Old-Regime level by 1850, if the Revolution had been merely a temporary shock. And by 1870, notarial credit would have mobilized twice as much capital as it had in 1789. Yet in reality notaries in 1870 were raising barely half the capital they had back at the end of the Old Regime.

It would take the arrival of the Crédit Foncier for long-term lending to boom again—particularly, the sort of long-term lending that financed construction. And when the long-term market did revive, notaries were no longer the key intermediaries. One can see as much by examining figures for imports of building stone into Paris, which serves as an index of construction in the city.[21] One glance at the figures demonstrates that notaries were no longer funding Parisian construction, as they had done under the Old Regime. The trend in the construction series is simply nothing at all like the path of private indebtedness.

In our counterfactual scenarios, the estimates that end up closer to reality are all ones that reduce the level of lending to take into account the effects of inflation. Ignoring the Revolution and its inflation leads to big errors.[22] Arguments that inflation worked as a lump-sum tax and had no persistent effects must thus be rejected.[23] The Revolution had a dramatic and permanent impact on notarial credit in Paris and, as we

20. For the estimation procedure, see chapter 10.

21. Chevalier 1950. Admittedly, this series does overstate the growth in demand for long-term credit, for public construction was important yet it was not financed by notarial credit.

22. In table 9.4, estimates 3, 4, and 6 end up closer to the actual level of indebtedness than estimates 1, 2, and 5. Estimates 3, 4, 5, and 6 all start from a lower level of indebtedness, unlike estimates 1 and 2, and only estimate 5 veers wide of reality.

23. The argument that the inflation had little distortionary effect is an implication of Sargent and Velde's (1995) approach because they assume that monetary transitions are treated as exogenous by the public. As we have shown in chapter 8, such an assumption seems ill suited for studying the Revolution itself. If we are correct, it does not fit the Revolution's long-term consequences either.

show below, it had an enduring—though not permanent—effect on financial markets as a whole.

Notarial credit was therefore both unstable and slow to grow in nineteenth-century Paris. After the Revolution, major political crises spelled trouble for the notaries, who seemed unable to overcome adverse political events. As a result, they never regained their Old-Regime role as major financial intermediaries.

The Paris Financial Market in the Nineteenth Century

If notarial credit had been stagnant throughout the eighteenth century, historians would not be surprised. Such long-term stagnation would have simply confirmed the widespread belief that it took universal banks and a thriving stock exchange to mobilize long-term capital. But the golden age of notarial credit under the Old Regime forces us to rethink such assumptions. The key question to ask is how other financial intermediaries dealt with the financial risks and political turmoil. After all, the notaries were far from alone in providing financial services in nineteenth-century Paris, and their competitors, such as bankers, also had to overcome the adverse effects of political upheavals. Did the other financial intermediaries fare as badly as the notaries?

Let us first consider the intermediaries who floated the public debt or who were engaged in other forms of long-term lending in which the state was involved. These "public" intermediaries included savings banks, municipal pawn shops, and the stock brokers and investment bankers active on the official stock markets. Although there was only one savings bank, pawn shop, and stock exchange in Paris, there were others in the provinces, and over the course of the century their numbers grew. The public intermediaries did not include the notaries, for the notaries had lost their role in selling government debt and they played little or no role in any of these financial organizations.

How then did these public intermediaries fare? Like the notaries, they all seemed vulnerable to political crises. To take the example of public debt, government bond prices fell dramatically in 1830 and 1848, and during these periods of political instability the government found few takers for its new debt issue, a development that must have made life difficult for the bankers who peddled state debt.[24] As for the savings banks, they were driven to default in 1848, when depositors withdrew nearly two-thirds of their funds, forcing the state to come to their res-

24. Priouret 1966:101–20; Gille 1967, 2:42–46.

cue.[25] Similarly, the municipal pawn shop in Paris was forced into default in the Napoleonic era. And private issues on the bourse suffered in two ways during political crises: securities disappeared (30 percent in 1830 and 10 percent in 1848), and prices fell (by 20 percent in 1830 and 40 percent in 1848). Politics thus left a heavy mark on the public intermediaries, as it had on the notaries.

Unlike notarial credit, these public forms of lending all managed to recover and go on to rapid growth in the nineteenth century. Despite reverses in 1830 and 1848, the public debt grew ninefold between 1815 and 1870, even though the yield on government bonds was falling from above 6 percent to 4.3 percent. The deposits in savings banks grew between 1815 and 1870: from nothing at all to 54 million francs in Paris and 711 million in France as a whole. Although what happened to France's pawn shops is unknown, in the Paris shop, the number of pawns multiplied almost threefold, and the value of loans rose even faster. And the Bourse went from listing a handful of nongovernmental securities in 1815 to more than two hundred in 1869, thereby expanding from a market restricted to government debt to include many private issues. Apparently, political uncertainty did not stop the public intermediaries from recovering. Nor did it prevent the nineteenth century from being a period of rapid financial development.[26]

The last and most important set of intermediaries to consider are bankers. Unfortunately, there is little systematic evidence about banking in nineteenth-century Paris. Unlike notaries, bankers were under no obligation to preserve their financial records. And the family firms that dominated banking protected their proprietary information and the privacy of their clients. It is thus impossible to recover quantitative evidence about their business, such as the amount of lending they did or the interest rates they charged.[27] The only evidence that does shed light on the relationship between banking and political uncertainty is the number of bankers active in Paris.

We concentrate our attention on the bankers listed every five years starting in 1805 in the *Almanach du Commerce*.[28] The list of bankers highlights both the instability of the profession and its growth (table 9.5).

Turnover was almost always about one-third between each five-year cross section, and the link between political crises and turnover is obvious. Of the 213 bankers active in 1841, 164 had opened their businesses

25. Priouret 1966:109.

26. *Annuaire statistique de la France* 1966:494; Lepetit and Hoock 1987; De Wateville 1850:5; Dupin 1844; Danieri 1987; Deschodt 1993; Bresson 1825; and Courtois 1873.

27. Gille 1959; Lévy-Leboyer 1964.

28. Lists in the official almanach tell a similar tale.

TABLE 9.5   SURVIVAL OF BANKERS IN PARIS

Year	Number of Bankers According to Almanach Officiel	Almanach du Commerce	Average Bank Age (years)	Turnover	Bankers New to List	Bankers Exiting a Second Time
1800	72		6.1	0.45	76	0
1805	55	110	8.4	0.64	27	0
1810	42	92	11.8	0.36	12	1
1815	41	61	15.7	0.38	35	0
1820	50	94	6.4	0.41	58	1
1825	139	141	6.5	0.26	79	4
1829		154	7.1	0.37	65	2
1835		121	10.5	0.56	53	1
1841		213	8.6	0.32	131	5
1845		193	10.0	0.43	72	6
1850		173	12.3	0.42	62	10
1855		207	10.0	0.47	135	6
1862		334	9.6	0.47	215	0

Source: *Almanach Officiel* (1800–29), *Almanach du Commerce* (1805–65).
Note: The numbers from the *Almanach Officiel* are the average number of bankers for the five years beginning with the year in question. Since the *Almanach Officiel* stops in 1828, the 1825 figure is an average for 1825–28. The numbers from the *Almanach du Commerce* are those reported for the single year in question. Bank age is the average number of years existing banks had been open in the year in question. New to list is simply the number of bankers who have appeared since the previous year in the table. To calculate turnover, we first sum the number of bankers who are new to the list and the number of old bankers who have disappeared since the previous year in the table. We then divide this sum by the total number of bankers in the year in question. Exit a second time is the number of bankers who disappeared since the previous year and who had disappeared once before.

after the Revolution of 1830. Of the 226 bankers in 1855, only 65 had been continuously operating since before 1845, and 135 had started after 1850. It is thus clear that the Revolution of 1848 brought major changes to the banking industry. By 1855, only a small core of 22 banks had survived for a long time. These 22 firms had been in continuous operation for at least 25 years, with three dating back to the Old Regime (Mallet, Hottinger, and Delessert). Alongside them were a large number of short-lived banks, which came into existence when the government seemed stable and then disappeared during political crises. A quantitative measure of the connection between banking and political stability can be gleaned from the relationship between rente yields and the number of bankers. The correlation between the yield on government rentes and the number of bankers is −0.51, suggesting that banking expanded when the public had confidence in state finances and shrank during periods of doubt. Regression analysis confirms that the connection is not simply a trend effect.

In the long run, however, the political crises finally ended, and the

TABLE 9.6   DEBT IN FRANCE AND PARIS AT MID-CENTURY

		Paris	Rest of France	Share of Paris
Municipal pawn shops (Monts de Piété)	Number of loans in 1847	1,570,000	2,830,000	0.36
	Value of loans in 1847 (millions of francs)	27	21.9	0.55
Savings banks (Caisses d'Epargne)	Number of accounts in 1843	161,000	483,000	0.25
	Value of deposits in 1847 (millions of francs)	278	80	0.78
Public debt	Number of holders of 5 percent rentes in 1836	104,083	16,179	0.87
	Value of 5 percent rentes in 1836 (millions of francs)	1,764	159	0.92
Notarial credit	Number of loans in 1840	4,803	632,000	0.008
	Value of loans in 1840 (millions of francs)	83	768	0.09

Source: Monts de Pieté: De Wateville 1850. Caisses d'épargne: Dupin 1844. Public debt 1837: Mavidal and Laurent 1862, 2d. ser., 117:493–94. For notarial credit, see chapters 2 and 10.
Note: The public debt data do not break out private and institutional holders. We can check our estimate of notarial debt against the government's reports for the 1840s (Martin du Nord 1844:3; Conseil d'Etat 1850; Allinne 1978:23).

bankers grew ever more numerous. Their numbers rose steadily, surpassing two hundred by 1840 and three hundred by 1862. Then, under the Second Empire, joint stock and corporate banks finally blossomed. Meanwhile notarial credit was shrinking, though notaries still competed with the bankers, at least until 1848. Indeed, as we shall show in chapter 10, the notaries attempted to enter the short-term debt market, while bankers moved into the mortgage market. Both groups were trying to integrate short- and long-term credit, but until the 1850s their efforts failed. But on balance, the bankers were more successful, because they expanded their investment banking and commercial and personal lending.

Although scant sources make a complete picture of credit markets impossible for Paris, two facts are quite clear. First, financial markets and their intermediaries were badly shaken by political events. But among the intermediaries, only the Parisian notaries seem to have been unable to overcome the financial risks created by political uncertainty, and as a result, notaries declined in importance relative to other intermediaries, especially bankers. While in 1815 only the national debt mobilized more capital than notarial credit, by 1869 notarial lending had fallen to fifth place behind the national debt, private issues on the Bourse, the Crédit Foncier, and the savings banks.

———

Political uncertainty caused problems for financial intermediaries in the nineteenth century, but it did not slow Paris's rise as a financial center.[29] Indeed, thanks to the efforts of financial intermediaries other than the notaries—in particular, bankers—most Parisian capital markets witnessed steady if not rapid growth in the first half of the nineteenth century. The national debt grew fivefold from the 1810s to the 1850s, and the Bank of France's short-term portfolio grew even more.[30] By the 1850s, the capital invested in railroads, an unknown business in 1810, surpassed all the capital raised by Parisian notaries.[31] Though a large fraction of the funds came from the provinces, lending in the middle of the nineteenth century still remained concentrated in Paris (table 9.6). Although the city comprised less than 3 percent of the population, it dominated nearly all forms of credit, from the municipal pawn shops to the stock exchanges. The only exception was notarial debt, which was languishing.[32] Outside of Paris, there were simply no financial intermediaries who could raise capital on the scale that the state and railroads demanded. Even when local groups made major investments into a particular railroad project, the bonds were listed in Paris.[33]

Meanwhile, the Parisian notaries stagnated and faltered. Why then did they lose their grip on long-term lending? One might argue that their lending practices were simply too antiquated to cope with the political and financial risks. But the notaries actually had devised a new financial instrument—the prorogation—that was ideally suited to risks of

29. It is therefore likely that the growth in the share of financial assets in total wealth that Daumard (1973) discovered during the July monarchy continued through the Second Empire.

30. *Annuaire statistique de la France* 1966:520.

31. Dupont Ferrier 1925:241. The same was true for the Caisses d'épargnes: see Priouret 1966:460–61.

32. *Archives parlementaires* (1862, 2d ser., vol. 118) and Grosskreuz (1977:110, n. 1) show that the investors in the canal enterprises from 1820 to 1848 were mostly Parisians, with 70.5 percent of the funds coming from Paris or the surrounding department of the Seine et Oise. See also Tudesq 1966:656–64; Gilles 1965:111–17, 121; Lévy-Leboyer 1964:660, 678. One should note, however, that these estimates cannot be firmly established for the nineteenth century, for evidence about the public debt burned up in 1870, and the records of the *agents de change* remain closed to historical researchers.

33. Tudesq 1964:656.

lending in the turbulent nineteenth century. Outmoded business practices therefore do not seem to be the cause of their decline, particularly
since other financial intermediaries had nothing better to offer. None
of them had mutual insurance or access to a lender of last resort.

Alternatively, one might claim that the notaries succumbed to economic change. Industrialization, so the argument might go, demanded
a new breed of financial intermediaries. After all, the notaries typically
put together bilateral loans; the parties to their loans were most often
a single borrower and a single lender. If they could only arrange small-
scale transactions of this sort, they could never have financed France's
industrial expansion, for it required capital from a large number of different sources.

Although such a line of reasoning may seem plausible, it too collapses
on closer inspection. Even under the Old Regime, we know that notaries
in Paris frequently acted as underwriters for private or semi-private enterprises that demanded substantial amounts of capital. Mobilizing the
funds for industrialization was certainly not beyond their reach.[34] As we
shall see, the explanation for the notaries' decline lies elsewhere. In part,
it was state regulation and the creation of a national lien registry. And
in part it was the structural problems that afflicted notarial credit.

---

34. Parisian notaries, for instance, raised two-thirds of the capital needed by the Estates
of Burgundy for canal construction in the 1780s (Potter and Rosenthal 1999). For other
examples see chapter 7.

CHAPTER TEN

Institutions and Information
after the Revolution

"Roguin has absconded. . . . For five years he had been messing around with his clients' money, and why? For a mistress. . . . All the rogue's property is mortgaged to the hilt."[1]

IN BALZAC'S 1837 NOVEL *César Birotteau,* the notary Roguin swindles his Parisian clients and runs off with their money. As his behavior suggests, notaries no longer inspired universal confidence in nineteenth-century Paris. While some certainly took their clients' affairs to heart, others leapt into dangerous speculation and went bankrupt as a result. The whole business of being a notary was disrupted, with some études briefly booming and others collapsing as they lost clients. Rarely did any of them remain at the top for long. And all the while, the notaries faced increased ruinous competition from bankers and other financial intermediaries.

The origins of the instability lay with legal and administrative reforms that affected what both notaries and their competitors did. The most important of these changes was the creation of the *hypothèques,* a system of registering liens and real estate transactions. The system was not used much in the countryside, but it was utilized heavily in Paris, where it made public the sort of information that notaries kept to themselves in the eighteenth century. Public availability of this information incited Parisian notaries to steal one another's clients, and it opened the door to competition from intermediaries such as bankers. In the end, the whole notarial business was destabilized.

The hypothèques also prevented a return to the sort of cooperation that had characterized the notaries' behavior in eighteenth-century Paris. In other words, the hypothèques blocked a return to the game-

1. Balzac, *Histoire de César Birotteau* (Paris: Garnier, 1964), 231–33.

theoretical equilibrium of chapter 6, an equilibrium (or expected pattern of actions) in which notaries shared financial information with one another and clients were assured of good service. With the end to this equilibrium, nothing prevented notaries from abusing their clients, and some, like the fictional Roguin, did exactly that, usually by speculating with their clients' money and then going bankrupt. Notarial bankruptcies mounted, frightening away clients and provoking legislation in 1843 that barred notaries from engaging in banking or financial speculation.

The legal changes thus furnish yet another reason why the Parisian notaries slipped from their Old-Regime preeminence. Out in the countryside, by contrast, hypothèques were seldom used, and rural notaries managed to restore cooperative behavior. But in Paris notaries practically disappeared from the credit market. Other financial intermediaries did take their place in the city, but certain clients found it much harder to get loans—home buyers, for example, and entrepreneurs.

We begin the chapter with the hypothèques and the other institutional changes that disturbed the notaries' businesses. We next see what effect the hypothèques had, particularly in Paris, where they intensified competition, destabilized the notaries' business, and accelerated their decline. We then turn to the long-run consequences for the Parisian notaries: bankruptcies, the loss of clients, and the legislation of 1843—additional factors all driving the Parisian notaries out of financial markets. We close with the impact on clients: without Parisian notaries to arrange loans, some borrowers were deprived of credit.

The Institutions of Nineteenth-Century Credit

New legislation during the Revolution and the Empire had immense consequences for medium- and long-term credit. It affected the kind of private debt contracts that could be drawn up, and it imposed taxes and fees on notarial documents. And it created a new system for registering notarial records, especially those involving liens and real estate transactions.

Let us begin with private debt contracts. Although the revolutionaries were primarily concerned with public finance, they did not neglect private debts. They quickly abolished usury laws, allowing private term debts to bear interest, provided the interest did not exceed a 5 percent ceiling for personal debt and 6 percent for commercial debt.[2] By permitting

---

2. *Archives parlementaires* 1862, 1st ser., 9:337–78.

interest rates in all contracts, revolutionary reforms made rentes obsolete, thereby continuing a trend that had begun under the Old Regime. The obligation became the standard contract at the beginning of the nineteenth century, as notarial manuals noted:

> [Rentes contracts] were common before the law of October 1789 which ended the prohibition on interest: since then, one hardly sees private rentes any more. The reason is simple: when one lends money for a limited term, one can get the same interest as with a rente. It is therefore more convenient to use the first means, which allows the lender to recover his capital at the stipulated time . . . if he decides to do so. In contrast, rente contracts, which give the debtor the right to free himself when he wants, take away from the creditor the right to demand the repayment of his capital, so that, in this respect, rente contracts handicap the lender.[3]

Why would a lender resort to a rente, when an obligation would now let him state an explicit interest rate and also control payment of the loan?

Not that all the laws governing debt had changed. The legal distinction between personal and commercial debt survived the Revolution intact, and it continued to keep the notaries away from banking. Under the law of personal property, which applied to private persons, debtors were sheltered from both repossession and imprisonment for debt. By contrast, commercial debtors (such as merchants and anyone who issued paper money) enjoyed far less protection.[4] Notaries ended up specializing in debt that fell under the law of personal property, while bankers organized capital movements governed by commercial law. Since intermediation in each market required different kinds of information, it is not surprising that two distinct financial intermediaries evolved.

The most important reform of the Revolution and the Empire was the creation of the hypothèques, which registered liens and real estate transactions.[5] If they were used, the hypothèques would, for the first time, make information about collateral public. It is true that the Old-Regime monarchy had already taken steps in this direction, creating a registry for liens on public offices and government rentes in the seven-

---

3. Massé 1827:72–73.

4. *Archives parlementaires* 1862, 2d ser., vols. 117 and 119.

5. The reforms began with the law of messidor, an III and continued under the Consulate and the Empire. See Baron Grenier 1824; Flour de St-Genis 1889; Vilar-Berrogain 1958; and Massaloux 1989.

teenth century and starting another registry system for real estate in the 1770s. However, neither of the earlier systems was particularly popular.[6]

Here the hypothèques marked a true improvement. In contrast to the monarchy's efforts under the Old Regime, the government was now willing to spend the necessary money, including the funds needed to create and link together a loan survey—the hypothèque registries—and a land survey—the *cadastre*. While the cadastre allowed individuals to determine property boundaries and to track property ownership, officials of the local hypothèque offices used it and the hypothèques registration to assemble registers of loans, borrowers, and liens. These linked registers disclosed what local land had been pledged as collateral. They also revealed credit histories, at least for those of a borrower's loans which were backed by mortgages on local real estate.

The advantage was that loans registered with the hypothèques were granted special treatment in noncommercial default proceedings. The only requirement—beyond the payment of fees—was that the loan collateral had to be real property. Using the hypothèques also necessitated the services of a notary, but now any notary in France could get a summary of the liens on any piece of property in the country.[7] The information was publicly available, in contrast to the Old Regime, where it had been the preserve of a small number of notaries. It would also be reliable, provided that most lenders registered their loans with the hypothèques. If they did not do so, then the reports from the hypothèques would obviously be incomplete and of much less value.

The problem was that many lenders chose not to use the hypothèques.[8] Why would a lender not register loans with the hypothèques? To understand why, we need to consider in greater detail the advantages and disadvantages that the hypothèques had for an individual lender. Obviously, one advantage was that the lender acquired information about the borrower's credit history, information that was reliable if the hypothèques were widely used. Another advantage was the special treatment accorded registered loans in noncommercial default proceedings. In a default, if a loan had been registered and the borrower later took on additional debt, then the holders of this additional debt were not

6. See chapters 1 and 3.

7. Although the hypothèque records were open to the public, only notaries had the necessary expertise to use them.

8. Precisely how many is impossible to say, but if the fraction of unregistered liens was anything like the fraction of unregistered land sales, it was very large. In the middle of the nineteenth century, for example, only half the land sales for over 1,200 francs were registered, and only some 12 percent of sales under 600 francs. See Martin du Nord 1844, 3:528–29; Wolowski 1848:119; Conseil d'Etat 1850:296.

repaid anything until the lender with the registered debt was satisfied. In other words, the hypothèques generally gave a lender seniority over all subsequent debt.[9]

With these advantages came certain disadvantages. In the first place, the lender had no seniority over debt taken out before he had registered his loan with the hypothèques, and in some instances, registering his loan would even reduce what he would expect to be paid in case the borrower defaulted. Second, the fees for registration and for the notary might offset any expected gains from the hypothèques, making them a losing proposition for many lenders. That in turn would reduce the value of the hypothèques for all, by making the credit histories less reliable and by undercutting the security that registration provided in cases of default.

Let us consider the lender's decision in greater detail, beginning with the somewhat complicated process of events that took place when a borrower defaulted. If a borrower could not pay, his loans would be ordered chronologically, according to the date of the hypothèque for registered loans and the date the loan was contracted for other debts. The borrower's collateral and other assets would first be used to pay off any unregistered loans taken out before the first registered loan. If the assets did not suffice to do so, the holders of these unregistered loans would each receive an amount proportional to the nominal capital of their loans. If there were assets left over, they would then go to reimburse the holder of the first registered loan. Any remaining assets would then be used to pay off unregistered loans between the first and second hypothèque, with the holders of the unregistered debt all receiving an amount proportional to the nominal capital of their loans. If they were paid off, any funds remaining would reimburse the holder of the second hypothèque, and the process would continue.

Although the procedure may seem complicated, it created a clear risk for a lender who was pondering whether to register a loan. If the borrower already had a number of outstanding debts, then registration might leave the lender with nothing in a default. That could happen if the borrower's collateral and other assets proved insufficient to pay off the outstanding debts. In that case, not registering the loan would actually leave the lender better off in a default, for his loan would be lumped together with older unregistered debt, and he would then receive the same amount as the holders of this older debt. Registering the loan would give the lender nothing. Not registering did risk diluting the lend-

9. There were only three exceptions to this rule. Women's dowries and money owed to the state and to estates of minors were senior to all other debts.

er's claim if the borrower took out more unregistered loans, but it is clear the lender could decide not to register. It would all depend on how much outstanding debt the borrower had and what the value of his assets and collateral were. The lender could get the information needed to make the decision from the hypothèques, but only if the borrower's outstanding loans were registered.

We can think about this problem in an abstract way. If registration is the general rule, then each lender will demand it. Indeed, registration provides valuable information and helps secure loans. But if few lenders register their loans, then it may not pay for any single individual to require registration. In that case, information about borrowers will continue to be transmitted informally. As a result, use of registration may turn out to depend on historical accidents, and shifts from an equilibrium with little registration to one with universal registration may occur in a number of ways.

One way would be if a lender knew he was the first person to lend money to a borrower and was willing to make a large loan. In that case, registration would have real value for the lender because it would give him a senior claim on the borrower's collateral. The size of the loan would matter, though, because a small loan would almost certainly be reimbursed in bankruptcy proceedings. And once this initial lender required registration, later lenders would have the same incentives. Large pieces of real estate would then enter the files of the hypothèques after sales by mortgage.

Lower hypothèques fees would also trigger an increase in registration, by cutting the cost of the information. Because the bulk of the fees were fixed, an increase in average loan size or loan duration would boost registration too. Here one obstacle to lower fees were the charges that the notaries themselves imposed for recovering information from the hypothèque registers. Since the hypothèques were an alternative to the notaries' own informal knowledge, the notaries might have wanted to price searches in the hypothèques in a way that discouraged registration. Otherwise they might end up like many rural notaries, who could no longer charge high fees once the hypothèque system freed information from their control.[10]

Not surprisingly, the costs of hypothèques in particular, and state-imposed fees in general, were heavily debated in the nineteenth century. The debate focused on two issues: (1) Whether loans would end up not being notarized because of heavy fees. These fees included the notary's own charges, plus stamp and enregistrement taxes that were now levied

10. Wolowski 1848:120–21.

on all notarial transactions. (2) Whether the additional fees charged for the hypothèques would keep loans from being registered even if they were notarized. The fee schedules were regressive, both for notarization and for registration with the hypothèques. During the parliamentary debates over reforms of the hypothèques after 1830, it was argued that a borrower who wanted to take out a one-hundred-franc loan for a year would have to pay 5 francs for a notarial contract, 1.65 francs for the enregistrement tax, 1.3 francs for the stamp tax, and 3.67 francs for the hypothèque. The transaction costs would amount to 11.62 francs, nearly 12 percent of the loan. It is no wonder therefore that reformers argued for lower fees on small loans.[11]

The one-hundred-franc example is of course something of an exaggeration since most loans were larger and hence faced proportionately less in the way of fees. But we can draw a more accurate picture of transaction costs of the hypothèques and notarization. The notary's own fees can be recovered from reports filed with the ministry of justice starting in the mid-1860s. The reports listed average fees and average transaction sizes, thereby providing little information about small transactions. For 96 notaries who filed complete reports, the linear estimates suggest that on average they charged 1.3 percent of the value of a credit transaction, including a fixed fee of 0.3 francs. If we break up the sample to focus on the smaller transactions, though, it becomes clear that the fixed fees were much larger in markets with small loans. For markets in which average loan size was less than 800 francs, for instance, the fixed fees reached 3.2 francs. The fees declined as loan sizes increased. For notaries whose typical transactions exceeded 5,000 francs, loan fees averaged only 0.63 percent of the capital.[12]

As for the other fees charged for notarization, the enregistrement tax was proportional and decreased over time (1.1 percent of the value of the loan before 1851, 0.55 percent after). Hypothèques fees also decreased during the nineteenth century. More precisely, they were relatively inexpensive at the very beginning (0.25 francs per page according to the law of 11 March 1799), but jumped to one franc in 1810. It is only in 1855 that they were reduced to 0.5 francs per page.[13] Because a simple loan contract might take only one page, the hypothèque fee schedule was nonlinear. Even so, there were limits to the varia-

---

11. For the hypothèque costs, see Allinne 1978:42. Other sources suggest that fees may have been somewhat lower (Bigo 1947:48), but the authors may well have had larger transactions in mind, in which fixed fees were negligible.

12. AN BB[10] 1625, 1634, 1636, 1637, 1645, 1652, 1661, 1675, 1678, 1680.

13. *Bulletin des lois,* Law of 21 ventose, an VII; decree of 21 September 1810; Ordonnance of 1 May 1816; Law of 23 March 1855; and decree of 24 November 1855.

tion since all loans had to be assessed for at least one page at the beginning and one at the end of the contract. Taking into account these limits and setting the stamp tax at what it was worth in the 1840s, we can construct a fee schedule that represents the cost of notarizing loans and of registering them as a function of their size and duration (table 10.1).[14]

The table displays what would have been charged for loans of various sizes in several sorts of credit markets—in the countryside, in Paris, and in other French cities. We have also included the fees on the hypothetical one-hundred-franc loan that was the focus of political debate in the 1830s and 1840s. Even with a more realistic fee structure, the cost of notarizing and registering the one-hundred-franc loan doubled the annual interest charge that small borrowers faced. Because few borrowers could bear such cost, it was no wonder that few small loans were notarized.

It is equally clear from the table that the cost of the hypothèques was a pittance compared with the total for the notary's fees, stamp taxes, and the enregistrement tax. That was true in particular for the large loans that typified urban credit markets. Indeed, for loans above one thousand francs, the hypothèques imposed far less of a burden than the enregistrement, and for cities, the hypothèque costs were trivial.

The argument so far has been a purely logical one: it rests on the incentives created by the fees for notarization and for registration with the hypothèques. But there is actual evidence that the fees discouraged the registration of small loans. It comes from samples of notarized loans that we collected in Paris in 1806, 1820, and 1840 (table 10.2). They demonstrate that registration did generally rise with loan size. The pattern of increasing registration with loan size grew particularly pronounced as registration grew more and more common. By 1820, only 13 percent of the loans under one thousand francs were registered, compared with 74 percent of loans over ten thousand francs, and in 1840 the pattern was even more pronounced.

The evidence also suggests that registration was far more common in Paris than out in the countryside. We know that loans in the countryside were much smaller on average, and samples demonstrate that rural borrowers were just as sensitive to the fees for notarization and for registration with the hypothèques.[15] If we assume that rural borrowers were as

14. Allinne 1978:42, citing Martin du Nord 1844, gives a total stamp tax cost of 1.3 francs but does not tell when it was paid. We divided the tax into 0.87 francs paid when the loan was taken out and 0.43 francs when it was repaid.

15. For the smaller loan sizes in the countryside, see table 10.3. For evidence about rural sensitivity to the fees, see Postel-Vinay 1998:152–63, especially figure 3.

TABLE 10.1   ESTIMATED ANNUAL COST OF AN HYPOTHÈQUE LOAN: TYPICAL EXAMPLES CIRCA 1840

	100-Franc Loan	Typical Loans in Countryside		Typical Loans in Cities Other than Paris		Typical Loans in Paris
		Small	Big	Small	Big	
Loan size (francs)	100	235	700	3,685	9,000	20,000
Duration (years)	1	1	2	3	3	5
(1) Fixed notary fee (francs)	3.2	3.2	0	0	0	0
(2) Variable notary fee (percent of loan size)	1	1	1.4	1.3	0.7	0.7
(3) Enregistrement tax (percent)	1.1	1.1	1.1	1.1	1.1	1.1
(4) Stamp tax (francs)	0.9	0.9	0.9	0.9	0.9	0.9
(5) Hypothèque fee (francs)	1	1	2	2	4	8
Fixed costs (1 + 4 + 5) (francs)	5.1	5.1	2.9	2.9	4.9	8.9
Variable costs (2 + 3) (percent)	2.1	2.1	2.5	2.4	1.8	1.8
Total cost per year (percent)	10.80	6.41	2.19	1.24	0.93	0.55
Total cost per year without hypothèque registration (percent)	9.30	5.77	1.97	1.21	0.91	0.54

Source: See text.

Note: All percentages shown are relative to the loan size.

TABLE 10.2   HYPOTHÈQUES REGISTRATION IN PARIS, 1806, 1820, AND 1840

Loan Size (francs)	1806		1820		1840	
	Number of Loans	Percent of Loans Registered	Number of Loans	Percent of Loans Registered	Number of Loans	Percent of Loans Registered
1–1,000	3	0	8	12.5	1	0
1,001–5,000	55	38	23	82	16	25
5,000–10,000	16	50	16	69	15	40
10,000–50,000	10	50	27	74	27	78
Over 50,000	2	50	0	—	2	100
Total	88	40	74	69	61	54
Total capital	1,095,818	67	848,656	76	953,214	72

Source: All surviving loans in ANMC, études IX, XXI, XXVII, XLIII, LXII, and LXX during the years 1806, 1820, and 1840; in CXVII during the years 1806 and 1840; and in LXXVIII, CXI, and CXV during the years 1820 and 1840.

likely to pay for registration as the Parisian borrowers in table 10.2, then we can use an 1841 government survey of loan sizes to estimate the fraction of rural loans that were registered with the hypothèques.[16] All we have to do is to take each 1840 registration rate in table 10.2 and multiply it times the number of rural loans of the corresponding size. We then add the figures up to get the total number of rural loans that were notarized, and a similar calculation gives us the total fraction of funds that were lent via registered loans.

If we do the calculation, we find that 16 percent of rural loans were registered with the hypothèques. The registered loans in the countryside accounted for no more than 34 percent of the money lent out. The contrast with Paris is striking, for according to our samples, 54 percent of loans were registered in Paris by 1840, representing 72 percent of the money lent out (table 10.2). The difference may actually be greater than our estimate implies, for our use of registration rates from table 10.2 may well exaggerate rural use of the hypothèques.[17]

The fee structure thus worked against registering small loans with the hypothèques. Overall, this bias in the fee structure was more a matter of economics than of policy. The fixed fees which inflated the cost of registering small loans in fact reflected the numerous tasks that officials

16. Martin du Nord 1844:3; Wolowski 1848:120–21; Conseil d'Etat 1850:285. We verified the results of the 1841 survey using a more detailed survey undertaken in 1890: Archives du Ministère des Finances, B 38930.

17. The 16 percent presented in the text is an overestimate because for any given loan size the propensity to register was lower in the countryside than in Paris. The reason was that rural notaries had preserved their local informational advantage; they therefore offered competitive informational services that reduced the need to register loans.

had to perform, regardless of loan size. They had to open registers upon the initiation and termination of every loan contract, and the cost of doing so did not vary with the capital lent. Small loans were therefore nearly as time consuming to administer as large ones.

The legal and administrative reforms during the Revolution and Empire affected the credit market in a number of ways. They made it possible to include an explicit interest rate in all loan contracts, and as a result, the obligation became the standard contract for medium- and long-term loans. The reforms also imposed fees and taxes on notarial credit, and most important of all, they created a system to register liens and real estate transactions, the hypothèques. The hypothèques revealed the status of a borrower's collateral to the public and thus had the potential to break the notaries' hold on information that was crucial for lending. But for that to happen, the hypothèques had to be used extensively, for otherwise they provided lenders with little real security.

One of the obstacles to using the hypothèques were the fees and associated costs of having loans notarized. Because the fee structure favored the registration of large loans, the hypothèques were more likely to take hold in areas where large loans were common, in cities such as Paris or in regions where property holding was concentrated. It was there that the hypothèques flourished, making information about borrowers available to the public. But loan size, as we shall see, was not the only factor dictating the success of the hypothèques. Their future also depended on the fate of older, informal sources of information about collateral—information of the sort the Parisian notaries held.

Paris and the Provinces

After the Revolution, two distinct systems of long-term credit developed in France. The first arose in sections of the country, such as the countryside, where few lenders used the hypothèques. There notaries rekindled the sort of cooperation that we encountered back in eighteenth-century Paris. They retained key information about collateral, but they shared it with one another and with their clients.

In Paris, by contrast, a very different system arose. Lenders there did rely on the hypothèques for medium- and long-term loans, and, as a result, the city's notaries lost their informational advantage and could never restore the equilibrium of cooperation and information sharing that had prevailed in the eighteenth century. In Paris, the system of hypothèques drove the notaries to compete with one another for clients, and it opened the door to competition from financial intermediaries such as bankers as well. The competition in turn drove notaries to take risks, provoking bankruptcies and instability in the notarial business. In 1843 the government finally intervened and barred the notaries from engaging in banking and financial speculation.

Here it is worth recalling what the old equilibrium of cooperation and information sharing had amounted to back in eighteenth-century Paris. For our purposes, the equilibrium meant that Parisian notaries cooperated with one another, by referring clients to one another and by sharing information about the clients' affairs. Notaries chose to cooperate (that is, to share information and refer clients) because failure to do so would have cost them access to their colleagues' information and clients. If a notary failed to cooperate—if he defected from the equilibrium—his colleagues would punish him.

Given such an equilibrium, let us imagine what happens when the hypothèques make information available about a fraction of the borrowers. The borrowers whose loans are registered with the hypothèques will take out bigger than average loans. They will thus be attractive clients for any notary, and because their collateral and credit dealings are registered with the hypothèques, any notary will be able to offer them service. He will not have to wait for a colleague to refer them to him and to share information about them. He will consequently be tempted to defect—tempted in other words to steal these clients from his colleagues instead of waiting for referrals—because the losses from defection will no longer be so severe. He will lose future referrals and information sharing from other études, but he will gain access to all the attractive clients whose dealings are recorded with the hypothèques. He will also be able to make matches that are almost as efficient as those he would have made had he cooperated, provided that registration is widespread. And finally, if he defects, he can take advantage of clients who do not register their transactions. He can simply stop sharing information about them and then charge them higher fees. Since their dealings will not be public knowledge, they will have difficulty switching études.

As more and more notaries defect, the hypothèques will grow all the more attractive. When notaries stop cooperating, the hypothèques will become the only way to tell whether someone is a reliable borrower, and, for many clients, they will also be the only source for the information that allows clients to change études. Only the hypothèques will give clients a way to seek out a better notary and avoid getting abused.

Defections by notaries thus have clear consequences for cooperation and for the privacy of information. What keeps cooperation going is the private information notaries hold and share. Every time a notary defects, the value of this private information will fall. The notary will not be deterred by the potential loss of clients, for those clients who register their debts with the hypothèques do not care if the notary cooperates, and the others will quickly be locked in and unable to switch études. The defections will thus push clients to use the hypothèques, if only to avoid getting locked in with an abusive notary.

The argument so far has a number of implications for credit markets, particularly when it is combined with what we know about the effect of the fees charged for notarizing and registering loans. The first implication is a hypothesis about the difference between Paris and the countryside: in the countryside, where the hypothèques did not catch on, notaries should have retained a more prominent role in credit than they did in Paris. It remains a mere hypothesis, though, rather than a firm prediction, because one can imagine the notaries remaining important in Paris even if the hypothèques were widely used.[18]

The other implications are predictions that follow logically from our argument. Three in particular can be tested against evidence that we have; they all concern markets like Paris, where use of the hypothèques was common: (1) In such markets, large loans should have come to predominate over small ones, as the hypothèques replaced older sources of information about borrowers. (2) The notarial business should have become unstable, for with the hypothèques, large clients no longer needed to remain loyal to their usual notary, and their disloyalty would force him and other notaries to compete with one another. (3) Notaries would consequently try to provide new services to retain their clients. In particular, they would have engaged in the risky practice of banking, driving up the number of bankruptcies.

To test our hypothesis that notaries retained a more prominent role in rural lending, we would ideally like to determine the fraction of loans that were actually notarized. That we cannot do since we lack data on unnotarized loans. But we can at least see whether the volume of notarized loans was increasing in the countryside—increasing, that is, relative to Paris. To do so, we gathered data on notarized loans in thirteen rural credit markets in 1780, 1807, and 1840. We collected similar evidence for the provincial cities of Avignon, Dijon, and Rouen, and we of course already had such evidence for Paris. What we sought for each market were the volume of new loans, the average loan size, and the loan durations that were recorded in the original debt contracts. We

---

18. If use of the hypothèques intensified competition and the competition in turn drove down notarial fees, then notarial credit might have expanded. Indeed, it could conceivably have grown even if other financial intermediaries were entering the Parisian credit market.

also fashioned a rough estimate of the outstanding notarized debt in each market by multiplying the size of each loan by its duration (table 10.3). We call this rough estimate the steady-state outstanding debt (SSOD), for in a credit market which does not experience growth, the stock of outstanding debts will on average equal the volume of new loans times their duration. Although the whole procedure may seem unreliable, it does lead to a figure for the volume of new notarized loans in France as a whole that comes very close to government reports.[19]

If we can trust the SSOD estimates in table 10.3, notarized debt grew much more rapidly in the thirteen rural markets than it did in Paris in the years 1780–1840. As expected, mean loan sizes in 1840 are much smaller in the countryside too. We can in fact sharpen the comparison between Paris and the countryside by calculating average per capita SSOD for the thirteen rural markets and then multiplying it times France's total rural population. That gives us SSOD estimates for the countryside as a whole in 1780, 1807, and 1840, which we can use to estimate the growth rate of rural notarized debt between 1780 and 1840 (table 10.3). If we believe the figures, in the countryside as a whole, notarized debt was increasing 1.2 percent annually, while in Paris it was falling 1.27 percent a year—all strong evidence in favor of our hypothesis.

We can use the SSOD for Dijon and Rouen to estimate SSOD for cities other than Paris. Once again, we relied on per capita SSOD to extend the figures from Dijon and Rouen, and we can of course calculate a growth rate for notarized debt in cities other than Paris. In these cities, loans were larger in the countryside, and, as in Paris, notarized debt grew more slowly than in the countryside (table 10.3). Finally, if we sum up the SSOD figures for Paris, for other cities, and for the rest of France, we can calculate total outstanding notarized loans for all of France in 1780, 1807, and 1840. We can derive analogous figures for the volume of new notarized loans in these years, and we can combine our estimates with official tabulations for 1869 and 1890. When we do so, we see that notarized debt in Paris declined relative to the rest of the country (table 10.4). The decline is particularly pronounced if we remove loans of the Crédit Foncier de France (CFF) from the totals. It was heavily involved

19. The government reported that in 1840 some 519 million francs of new notarized debt was registered with the hypothèques (Conseil d'Etat 1850). It was also estimated that 37 percent of notarized loans were not registered in the period 1841–45 (Allinne 1978: 23). If the same percentage applied to new loans in 1840, then the volume of new notarized loans as a whole—both registered and unregistered—would be 825 million francs in 1840. Our own data (table 10.4) suggest that the number was about 851 million, which is quite close.

TABLE 10.3 OUTSTANDING NOTARIZED DEBT IN SELECTED MARKETS: SSOD ESTIMATES

Market	1780 (thousands of francs)	1807 (thousands of francs)	1840 (thousands of francs)	Mean Loan Size in 1840 (francs)	Growth Rate 1780–1840 (percent per year)
Paris	1,167,000	389,000	541,000	20.0	−1.27
Other cities					
Rouen	52,826		27,904	10.0	−1.06
Dijon	9,250	3,680	14,640	11.0	0.77
Avignon		1,385	5,058	1.4	−0.18
Average for French cities					
Rural markets					
Maubeuge	2,031	569	3,834	1.9	1.06
Château-Thierry	1,247		3,713	2.2	1.84
Tréguier	529		996	1.8	1.06
Bar-sur-Seine	296	424	1,147	1.5	2.28
Rugles	248	41	548	1.2	1.33
Nuits-St Georges	230	60	478	0.8	1.23
Montbard	209	85	758	2.0	2.17
L'Isle-sur-la-Sorgue	2,204	110	529	0.6	−2.35
Salon	364		376	0.7	0.05
Privas	496	228	701	1.2	0.58
Lasalle, St-Jean-du-Gard	100	77	674	0.9	3.23
Apt	1,055	335	1,174	0.9	0.18
Orange	241	656	1,472	0.6	3.06
Average for rural markets					1.20

Source: For Paris, see chapter 2. For the other localities, the source is the local Contrôle des Actes for 1780 and the local Enregistrement des Actes Civils Public for 1807 and 1840. The population figures used to devise the urban and rural growth rates were taken from Lepetit 1988:450–54 and Sicard 1987.

Note: SSOD is a rough estimate of outstanding debt; it equals the value of new loans times their initial durations. The debt here is all notarized. The average urban SSOD growth rate was derived by calculating per capita SSOD for Paris, Rouen, and Dijon and then weighting these per capita SSOD figures by the 1836 population of French cities of roughly the same size to get SSOD for all French cities. In the calculation, Paris was given its own population as a weight; Rouen was given the population weight of roughly the same size to get SSOD for all French cities. In the calculation, Paris was given its own population as a weight; Rouen was given the population weight of Lyon, Marseilles, Bordeaux, Toulouse, Rouen, Nantes, and Lille; and Dijon was given the weight of the remaining French cities. Since the rural markets all had nearly the same population, the average rural SSOD growth rate was calculated by simply taking an unweighted average of SSOD in all thirteen markets.

TABLE 10.4   VOLUMES OF NOTARIZED LOANS AND SSOD ESTIMATES OF NOTARIZED DEBT: PARIS AND FRANCE, 1780–1890

	1780	1807	1840	1869	1869	1869	1890	1890	1890
Volumes									
Type of loan[a]	1	1	1	1	2	3	1	2	3
Paris	143	104	97	169	64	105	140	76	64
Rest of France	250	276	754	919	32	882	832	67	765
Total	393	380	851	1,083	96	987	971	143	828
Parisian share (percent)	36.3	27.3	11.4	14	66	9.4	14.4	53.1	7.7
SSOD									
Type of loan	1	1	1	1	2	3	1	2	3
Paris	1,167	389	414	1,004	565	439	1,598	1,216	382
Rest of France	2,690	476	2,072	4,941	531	4,410	4,895	1,072	3,823
Total	3,857	866	2,486	5,945	1,096	4,849	6,493	2,288	4,205
Parisian share (percent)	30.3	44.9	16.7	16.8	51	8	24.6	53.1	9.1

Source: For 1780, 1807, and 1840 the source is table 10.3. For 1869 and 1890, it is Allinne 1978:23; 1984:20, fig. 10. The population figures used in the calculations are as in table 10.3.

Note: All value in millions of francs. SSOD is defined as in table 10.3. Figures may not add up due to rounding error. For this table, the figures in table 10.3 were used to derive per capita loan volumes and SSOD estimates for the French countryside; they were then multiplied by France's rural population to get estimated loan volumes and SSOD for rural France as a whole. Similar estimates were made for Paris and for the other cities of France via the population weights utilized in table 10.3.

a. 1 = all loans, 2 = CFF loans only, 3 = non-CFF loans.

in Paris real estate lending in the second half of the nineteenth century, but although its loans were notarized, we shall see that it was the CFF and not the notaries who actually arranged the loans.

The data thus support our hypothesis that notaries retained their prominent role in rural credit markets, even as they declined in Paris. But what about the other implications of our argument—the three predictions about Paris? The first prediction is that public information from the hypothèques will cause large loans to predominate in Paris, and sure enough data on loan sizes bears the prediction out (table 10.5). As the table demonstrates, the distribution of loan sizes shifted steadily to the left over the course of the nineteenth century. Loans smaller than five thousand francs diminished in importance, with loans under one thousand francs practically disappearing by 1840, even though they still represented far more than one year's income for a skilled worker. Loans over twenty thousand francs, by contrast, accounted for an increasing percentage of all loans and an even greater fraction of all funds loaned. Apparently, even the growing middle class found it harder and harder to borrow through a notary.

The next prediction (that competition born of client disloyalty would destabilize the notarial business in Paris) is hard to test directly. But as the Parisian notaries well knew, the successful études in the nineteenth century were those that attracted clients. The clients moved to find notaries who could carry out the transactions that they desired. Innovators saw their business boom as new clients flocked to their études.[20] This mobility broke with the pattern of behavior that prevailed among clients in the eighteenth century, and it did seem to destabilize the notaries' businesses. The best evidence for the instability comes from our decennial counts of loans in forty Parisian études.[21] If we examine the counts, the turnover among the études arranging the most loans is striking, with few notaries able to keep their position for long. A total of twenty-two études—over half the sample—appeared among the five études with the highest number of loans at least once between 1800 and 1869. And twenty-three études fell to the bottom of the list at least once. Further, ten études managed to make it both to the top five and to the cellar at least once. Although counts of loans are not identical with business profits, the whole pattern does seem to fit what we had predicted.

20. Hoffman, Postel-Vinay, Rosenthal 2000.

21. The counts include all loans in the ten études we sampled from plus similar figures from thirty additional Parisian études. We undertook the counts every ten years in the nineteenth century in order to check that our original ten études were representative; for details, see chapter 2.

TABLE 10.5   SIZES OF NOTARIZED LOANS IN PARIS

	1780	1800	1810	1820	1830	1840	1851	1860	1869	CFF 1860	CFF 1869
Smallest loan	0.18	0.1	0.1	0.1	0.1	0.1	0.1	0.1	0.3	2	0.8
Largest loan	400	360	1,000	734	500	1,000	300	300	1,650	3,500	2,000
Median loan	6.2	6	5	6	8	10	9	10	12	30	35

Source: Samples of notarized loans from our ten original études and the thirty additional études that we used to check our ten for representativeness. For the études involved, see chapter 2.

Note: All values are in thousands of francs. The data for the decades prior to 1860 take in all notarized loans. For 1860 and 1869, CFF loans are reported separately in the last two columns.

As for the third prediction—that Parisian notaries would delve into banking and go bankrupt—it deserves some elaboration. The argument is simply that, if registration was important, notaries would provide new services to keep clients loyal. In particular, they would have offered banking services to their clients, which would involve the notaries' taking deposits or borrowing short term from potential lenders. Doing so would attract a supply of capital at a time when, as we know, lenders preferred short-term commitments. And with a greater supply of capital, a notary would be better able to serve borrowers, who could easily switch to other études now that the hypothèques had made credit histories public information. The trouble, though, was that notaries then faced the risk of bankruptcy whenever liquidity crises erupted, and, as we know, such crises struck frequently in the nineteenth century.

Although we might have missed a few bankruptcies between 1825 and 1852, we have found at least twenty-five of them, far more than occurred in any other period of similar length.[22] The only other instance of such a rash of bankruptcies occurred in the mid-eighteenth century, before notaries realized that banking was dangerous. As in the eighteenth century, the immediate triggers of bankruptcy varied, but the fundamental cause always involved banking. As a banker, the notary would take in money via short-term liabilities—either deposits or short-term loans from clients. He would then use the short-term money to fund loans. The whole process might leave no trace in the notarial archives: that would be the case if both the deposits and the loans that the notary made were informal and not notarized. Alternatively, the notary might draw up one set of obligations for the clients from whom he borrowed short term and another set of obligations for the loans he funded as a banker. In either case, the notary risked bankruptcy. It could hit him when his own investments failed to perform. Or it could strike when a liquidity crisis caused clients to demand their deposits back.

In the end, the Parisian notaries' venture into banking failed. It was

22. Among Parisian notaries, the number of bankruptcies by five-year period was as follows: one in 1815–19, none in 1820–24, four in 1825–29, seven in 1830–34, three in 1835–39, three in 1840–44, seven in 1845–49, one in 1850–54, one in 1855–59, none in 1860–64, one in 1865–69. The bankruptcy information here comes from an exhaustive search through (1) all the files at the ACNP for notaries whose first name started with the letters A, B, or C; and (2) all the dossiers at the Ministry of Justice (AN BB[10]) for notaries who died or left the profession in the years 1825–28, 1830–31, 1840–41, and 1846–51. This search procedure yielded information about 158 of the 170 instances in which a notarial business changed hands in the years 1825–52. We followed a similar procedure to seek bankruptcies in 1855, 1857, 1860, and 1865–69, but we found only two. Our bankruptcies include destitutions and forced resignations.

TABLE 10.6   RESIDENCE OF BORROWERS AND LENDERS BY PERIOD

Year	Lenders from Paris (percent)	Borrowers from Paris (percent)	Both from Paris (percent)	Number of Loans in Sample
1800	72	67	48	46
1806–10	83	73	61	358
1820	80	71	59	120
1840	82	78	65	230
1851	82	81	67	1548

Source: For 1800, 1806–10, 1820, and 1840, all loans from the ten standard études described in chapter 2. For 1851, we used a computerized enumeration of all notarial acts in 1851 that has been prepared for the Archives Nationales.
Note: This table omits foreigners who never amounted to more than one or two individuals in each sample.

hardly their fault, for as we explain in chapter 9, no institution yet existed that could cope with the idiosyncratic and systematic risks inherent in banking. But in the end, the notaries who dabbled in banking went belly up so often that they frightened away clients. As Balzac's *César Birotteau* suggests, the bankruptcies struck the popular imagination, and many individuals simply did not feel that they could safely place their savings with notaries. As we know from chapter 9, notarial credit itself stagnated. Furthermore, the notaries seemed to have great difficulty attracting new clients, as they failed to create business practices that could compete with other financial intermediaries. Perhaps that is why they stopped bringing in larger and larger numbers of clients from outside Paris, thus reversing the trend of greater geographic openness that had begun in the eighteenth century. Of the transactions that the notaries did arrange, more and more involved contracts in which both parties came from Paris (table 10.6).

Notaries went belly up outside of Paris too, but the failures in the countryside did not seem as threatening as those in the city. It was in any case the bankruptcies in Paris that pushed the government to intervene in the 1840s and bar the notaries from banking and financial speculation. The government's legal reforms were supposed to apply to all of France, but they were only enforced in the capital—evidence of the difference between Parisian and provincial credit markets and a sign that bankruptcy was an integral part of this difference. Initially, the government tried to rely on administrative institutions that had been created under the Empire. In particular, it pushed the notaries' own *chambres de discipline* (the oversight committees of the local notarial organizations) to do more policing of wayward notaries. The chambres were staffed by senior notaries and were responsible for investigating reports of wrongdoing and for keeping track of what notaries did. They could reprimand or fine notaries who strayed from the right path, or even force them to resign.

In Paris, the key task of the chambre was to keep notaries out of banking and financial speculation. As the state's attorney *(procureur du roi)* said to the public prosecutor *(procureur général)* with authority over the Parisian chambre:

> The Parisian notaries must undoubtedly be saddened that a number of their colleagues have set such a dismal example in recent years. They should know that the government is firmly resolved to put a stop to this indulgence which, if it were to last, could no longer be excused. . . . The chambre de discipline is therefore invited to exercise the most rigid oversight over those notaries within its jurisdiction who, like the notaries Lambert and Lemaire, would stray from their duty and participate in speculation unbecoming to their station.[23]

In addition, each time a notarial office changed hands, the chambre was required to investigate both the outgoing notary and his successor thoroughly. It was also supposed to standardize accounting procedures in order to facilitate periodic audits of the notaries.

Before the Revolution, the Parisian notarial corporation had only limited power to police its members; the law of ventose, an XI (March 1803), which created the chambres de discipline, had certainly made the task easier. Yet individual notaries still had no incentive to monitor one another's behavior because they were not liable for one another's debts. Without incentives, the Parisian notaries proved unwilling to watch their colleagues' behavior, despite all the government's entreaties. Although they did screen new entrants into the corporation, once a notary was admitted he was allowed to do pretty much as he pleased. As for the chambre, it only acted after problems arose; it never took steps to prevent bankruptcy. Typically, it arranged for out-of-court settlements of complaints against notaries, or it used its powers to exclude notaries after they misbehaved. It did tax the notaries to settle claims against colleagues who had done wrong, but the tax still did not give individual notaries an incentive to watch what their fellows were doing.

In the end, all the efforts of the chambre failed to prevent notarial bankruptcies in Paris. And after the Parisian notary Jacques-François LeHon went bankrupt in 1841, in a crash the likes of which had not

23. AN BB[10] 846 (10 May 1831).

seen for more than half a century, the government decided to act.[24] In 1843 it passed a law that prohibited the sort of financial dealings that carried a risk of notarial bankruptcy. Specifically, the law stated that notaries were forbidden:

To participate in any stock market speculation, commercial operations, banking, discounting, or brokerage.
To speculate on . . . transfers of debts.
To invest in their name money that they have received on deposit, even if they pay interest.
To serve as cosigners or bondsmen, in any capacity, for loans that they have drawn up. . . .[25]

The law thus ruled out deposit banking and speculation in the stock market and in the short-term credit market. It also made it illegal for notaries to take a personal position in investments. In short, it drew a clear line between banking and what the notaries had traditionally done, a line that the notaries were not supposed to cross.

Despite all the problems with LeHon and other failed notaries, it is worth noting that the bankruptcies remained isolated incidents. They by and large did not cluster during liquidity crises or periods of political turmoil, save for 1848–51. Fewer than one in ten of the notaries went belly up, for instance, during the worst liquidity crisis of the nineteenth century (1828–33). And of the twenty-six notarial bankruptcies between 1820 and 1852, fewer than one-third occurred during the severe credit crunches after the 1830 or 1848 revolutions. As for the notaries who failed, they turn out to be little different from their colleagues if we consider the amount of time they had been in office, the cost of their études, the number of acts they drafted, and the number of loans they arranged. The only thing that apparently distinguished them was their penchant for engaging in risky business dealings.

The 1843 law passed in response to the bankruptcies was applied primarily in Paris. In the provinces—and in particular in the countryside—it was largely ignored, and there notaries continued to dominate rural credit for the rest of the nineteenth century. The law thus contributed to the different paths that lending took in the city and in the countryside, but it was not the only reason for the divergence. The major cause was the hypothèques. They were little used in the provinces, allowing nota-

24. LeHon left liabilities of roughly 5.7 million francs, while his assets amounted to only 3.3 million. Although the notarial corporation made up some of the difference, the uncovered liabilities were enormous.
25. *Bulletin des lois du royaume de France* 1843:6.

ries to retain control of medium- and long-term lending. But in Paris, registering loans with the hypothèques was common. The registration drove Parisian notaries to compete with one another for clients, and it opened the medium- and long-term credit market to bankers and other intermediaries. The competition in turn pushed the Parisian notaries to take risks and to flirt with bankruptcy. In the end, the hypothèques prevented the notaries from cooperating and sharing information with one another, as they had in the eighteenth century.

By making public the information about collateral, the hypothèques thus hastened the notaries' decline in nineteenth-century Paris. If the Parisian notaries had retained their hold over information about collateral, then bankers could not have entered the medium- and long-term credit market. The notaries would not have competed with one another, and they would have maintained their preeminence as financial intermediaries.

Long-Term Consequences for Notaries in Paris

The hypothèques were not the only reason for the decline of the Parisian notaries, for the rash of bankruptcies also had a role to play. With so many notaries failing between 1825 and 1852, investors grew wary of notaries and chose to invest their funds with other financial intermediaries. The bankruptcies frightened off borrowers and other clients too. Unlike bankers who fell under the swift justice of the commercial code, notaries were government officers, subject only to the authority of their peers and of the Ministry of Justice. When they failed, the court proceedings were slow, and it took a long time to recover money that had been entrusted to their care. True, the notarial corporation might intervene and reimburse a bankrupt notary's creditors, but it was not obliged to do so.

Unfortunately, clients had no way to keep the notaries from engaging in behavior that carried a risk of bankruptcy, at least before the law of 1843. Back in the eighteenth century, the equilibrium of information sharing ensured that notaries would treat clients fairly well, but in Paris the equilibrium was now gone and impossible to reconstruct. The only alternative for clients was to leave their notaries for other financial intermediaries, and the loss of clients meant a diminishing role for the notaries in Parisian credit markets.

The notaries' shrinking role in credit markets actually made it easier for the government to pass the 1843 law restricting their financial dealings. As long as the Parisian notaries had dominated medium- and long-

TABLE 10.7   AVERAGE PRICE OF ÉTUDES, AVERAGE REVENUE, AND AVERAGE VOLUME OF LOANS
FOR NOTARIES IN PARIS

		Revenue		No CFF		CFF Included	
	Price	Observed	Estimated	Volume of Loans	Share of Revenue (percent)	Volume of Loans	Share of Revenue (percent)
1815–24	245	28.9	42.8	540	8.5		
N	19	20	171				
1825–34	364	41.1	45.2	725	10.7		
N	33	22	141				
1835–44	428	59.3	53.5	630	8.1		
N	48	95	176				
1845–54	381	58	56.9	527	6.2		
N	35	124	136				
1855–64	452	69.2	68.6	593	4.9	987	8.5
N	16	98	100				
1865–69	540	75.2	75.2	714	5.3	1365	10.3
N	24	25	49				

Source: AN BB[10] and ACNP. The volume of loans are taken from our own estimates described in chapter 2.
Note: Prices are in thousands of francs. Prices, revenues, and volume of loans are all averages per étude; *N* denotes
the number of cases. To construct the estimated revenue in the table, we took fees for a sample of notaries in 1866–
69 and used them to infer revenues from credit for the other years. Observed revenue is what the notarial corporation
reported to the government after auditing exiting notaries' books. Many notaries did not report their revenue—
particularly early on—but they did not indicate the fees they paid. Since some notaries reported both, we could derive
a relationship between fees and revenue and use it to estimate revenue for all the notaries.

term credit, they would not have become the targets of such legislation
because it risked crippling credit markets. But once they had left borrowing and lending behind, the government could rein in their financial
dealings without any risk of disturbing the market.

Why, though, did the notaries not fight the edict of 1843? There were
several reasons. First of all, by 1843 credit accounted for only a small
fraction of the notaries' revenue. Earnings from credit fell from more
than 11 to 5 percent of their revenue between 1820 and 1870 (table
10.7). Giving it up was no longer a great sacrifice. In addition, the Parisian notaries must have known that engagement in the credit market
endangered their business outside of credit. Involvement in the credit
market meant competition for clients, which in turn entailed banking
and the risk of bankruptcy. But the bankruptcies cast a cloud over all
notaries, even those who had retreated from the credit market. Their
reputation was at risk even in noncredit dealings, where being a faithful
agent for clients still mattered.

The problem, in short, was that the bankruptcies threatened to undermine the notaries' entire business. By 1843, the bankruptcies had been
a regular feature of the Parisian financial landscape for nearly two de-

cades, and when LeHon failed in 1841, the notaries not wrapped up in banking probably welcomed the government's intervention. With credit playing a diminishing role in their business, they had nothing to lose from sacrificing credit, and they in fact had everything to gain in other areas of service if their reputations could be spared.

There was one final reason for supporting the 1843 legislation: lending no longer drew upon the other services notaries provided. That had not been the case back in the eighteenth century, when the notaries carried out three important and interrelated functions: arranging long-term credit, serving as real estate brokers, and providing families with important legal records over the course of the life cycle, such as wills, marriage contracts, and probate documents. The information notaries needed to arrange loans and peddle real estate came from drafting the legal records, for doing so revealed who wanted to lend, who had collateral, and who wanted to buy or sell real estate. But in the nineteenth century, the hypothèques eliminated the synergy among the three functions, leaving notaries with little reason to remain in control of long-term credit.

On the whole, the Parisian notaries fared well in the nineteenth century, despite their exit from the credit market. The value of études did drop somewhat after the 1843 law was passed, but as table 10.7 and figure 1.1 demonstrate, prices quickly recovered, and ended up in 1870 having nearly tripled since 1810. Despite the high price of offices, notaries were receiving a handsome reward for their efforts. The typical notary's revenue still ran to about 13 percent of the price of his office, and if the notary could finance his office at 5 percent, his gross revenue amounted some forty-five thousand francs a year, a high wage in nineteenth-century Paris. Although he had to pay rent and salaries to his clerks, he still made immensely more than factory workers, who typically earned about four hundred francs a year. Other indicators of the notaries' economic well being abound. The taxes they paid to the government nearly tripled during the period, while the average number of acts they drew up increased by 40 percent for formal contracts (minutes) and 10 percent for the less formal brevets. Clearly, the Parisian notaries continued to prosper long after they had withdrawn from credit.

In the nineteenth century, the typical Parisian notary faced much stiffer competition both from his colleagues and from other financial intermediaries. The competition was so ferocious that it drove the notaries to take great financial risks. Some went bankrupt, and the notarial business as a whole was destabilized in Paris. Clients fled, eroding the notaries' business. In 1843 the government moved to put a stop to the situation by cutting the notaries off from financial speculation altogether.

The competition and the bankruptcies it engendered both contributed to the notaries' decline. The ultimate cause of the competition, though, lay with the legal and administrative reforms of the Revolution and Empire—specifically, the hypothèques. Where they were used, as in Paris, the hypothèques made information about collateral public. The public information about collateral put an end to the notaries' informational advantage, and it opened the door to competition from other intermediaries like bankers. It also incited the notaries to fight with one another for clients. It thus blocked a return to the eighteenth-century equilibrium we uncovered in chapter 6: the equilibrium of cooperation and information sharing, in which notaries referred clients and assured them of good service. In the countryside, by contrast, the hypothèques never had such success, and there notaries continued to dominate medium- and long-term lending, by sharing with one another the information that they controlled. But in Paris that was no longer the case.

In Paris, a new legal institution—the hypothèques—thus proved to be a boon for bankers but a bane for the notaries. In the language of economics, the hypothèques complemented what bankers did but served as substitutes for the equilibrium of information sharing by notaries. The hypothèques thus teach a general lesson about institutions. They do so because they provide a ideal example of what we have called a formal institution—namely, explicit rules enforceable by law. The equilibrium of information sharing, by contrast, is an equally ideal example of what we have called an informal institution—namely, implicit rules that are not enforceable by law. Bankers' dealings with one another would also be an informal institution. The formal institution of hypothèques was thus a substitute for one informal institution (the notaries' equilibrium of information sharing) and a complement for another (the bankers' practices). Hence formal institutions need not replace informal ones. Depending on the context, they can also spur them on.

The hypothèques and the other institutional changes of the Revolution and Empire did more than just accelerate the notaries' decline. They also affected society as a whole, for the notaries' retreat from the credit market did not simply shift lending to other financial intermediaries. It also had the effect of redistributing funds among potential debtors. Unfortunately, we have only limited information on the distribution of financial assets and liabilities in the Paris population.[26] Nonetheless,

---

26. Daumard 1963:484–85.

TABLE 10.8   LOAN SIZE DISTRIBUTION IN NINETEENTH-CENTURY PARIS

Loan Size (francs)	Municipal Pawn Shop		Savings Bank		Notaries	
	Number of Loans	Value	Number of Accounts	Value	Number of Loans	Value
0–500	10,180	25,562	101,294	14,900	157	58
501–1,000	734	550	28,276	20,100	284	256
1,001–5,000	492	1,722	44,171	77,000	1,364	4,591
5,001–20,000	30	870	0	0	2,220	62,332
20,001–99,999	0	0	0	0	936	36,304
100,000 and above	0	0	0	0	127	24,249
Total	11,436	28,704	173,741	112,000	5,088	127,792

Source: Watteville (1850), Dupin (1844), and, for the notaries, our own samples for 1840 and 1851.
Note: Value is in thousands of francs.

we can analyze information published in the 1840s for the Paris savings bank and the municipal pawn shop. If we combine this information with our own data about the remaining notarial lending, we can see the consequences of the notaries' demise. For small loans (under one thousand francs), the savings bank and pawn shop seem to have replaced the notaries without difficulty. At these levels the notaries were providing a trivial amount of credit in the 1840s, but other financial intermediaries were available (table 10.8).

For loans over five thousand francs, the notaries remained important (table 10.8). One might therefore argue that their exit from lending deprived large borrowers of credit, but such an argument neglects the other intermediaries that these big borrowers could turn to. They could seek loans from bankers, who arranged private placements via *sociétés en commandites*—and made substantial advances to private firms or private individuals.[27] And at the largest scale, entrepreneurs could turn to the Bourse to fund their projects—provided, of course, they received government approval.

It was in the intermediate range (one to five thousand francs) where the notaries' decline put the biggest squeeze on credit. Notaries remained important here: in the 1840s, the notaries were arranging three times more loans at this level than the municipal pawn shop and offering loans with much longer durations. During the nineteenth century, loans of this intermediate size slipped from a half to a quarter of all notarized credit contracts, as though the borrowers were being pushed out of the market. The problem for borrowers at this intermediate level was that they had no alternative sources of funds for loans lasting beyond a few

27. Gille 1959:52–76.

months. Even for shorter terms, lenders like the municipal pawn shop made few loans in the one- to five-thousand-franc range. Private bankers might have taken up the slack, but they did yet not make long-term loans directly, and the sums involved were too small for the bankers to arrange private placements, even though they amounted to several years' wages for a skilled worker.

Individuals with savings of one to five thousand francs had far more opportunities to enter the broad financial market than a borrower seeking a loan at this level. After all, they could leave their funds with the municipal pawn shop, open an account at the savings bank, buy stocks and bonds, or deposit their money with a banker. It thus appears that a particular segment of demand for credit went unfulfilled—the demand for intermediate-sized loans. The notaries' decline kept small-scale entrepreneurs from using real estate as collateral for business ventures, because their loans were too small to pay the fees for a notary and a hypothèque. The decline also made it harder for the middle class to purchase housing. That left Paris a city of tenants, and it also hobbled entrepreneurship, because many firms started with a loan to an entrepreneur who pledged real estate as collateral. As a result, Paris may have actually had too few small firms, not too many. And the unfulfilled demand would be an impetus for one final reform of mortgage credit—the creation of the Crédit Foncier.

CHAPTER ELEVEN

The Rise of the Crédit Foncier

THE NINETEENTH CENTURY was marked by continuous agitation for financial reform. Cries for change in the financial sector came from nearly all sides. Some argued that listing requirements for the French stock market were too restrictive, others that the absence of large universal banks reduced the growth of industry.[1] Still another camp maintained that agriculture's performance was seriously undermined by the high cost of credit in the countryside. Finally, real estate developers agitated for improved urban mortgages. Only two groups sat on the sidelines: bankers and notaries. Both benefited from the institutional setup that prevailed before Louis Napoleon's coup in 1851 and the subsequent establishment of the Second Empire. Bankers dominated lending in Paris and to a lesser extent in other cities, while notaries held sway in the countryside.

With the change in regime in 1851, the institutional equilibrium began to evolve. Napoleon III was committed to a program of economic expansion that included building railroads, real estate development in Paris, and industrialization. These goals required new mechanisms to mobilize capital. Railroads therefore received subsidies; industry secured the assistance of the Crédit Mobilier, a large investment bank; and real estate and agriculture were to be served by the Crédit Foncier de France (CFF). Unfortunately, Napoleon's program was undermined by the Crédit Mobilier's bankruptcy and by the CFF's reluctance to lend in the countryside. The problem for the two new organizations was that they could not easily overcome their disadvantage in information relative to existing financial intermediaries. Because the Crédit Mobilier never learned to do business within its informational and financial constraints, it collapsed. The CFF did respect these constraints, and it ultimately prospered. But its success came at a cost: it extended loans to only to a small, rich minority.

---

1. Dupont-Ferrier 1925; Gerschenkron 1956.

To assess the impact of the CFF, we first review its financial history. We then explore the impact of information constraints on CFF lending. Next we analyze notaries' responses to the rise of the CFF and reexamine the politics of credit under the Second Empire (1852–70). We close the chapter by arguing that, except in Paris, the CFF was a complement to, rather than a substitute for, notarial credit networks. It assisted them but did not replace them.

The Crédit Foncier

The establishment of the Crédit Foncier followed a number of unsuccessful private and public initiatives to increase the supply of long-term mortgage credit. Dating back to John Law at least, numerous reformers had agitated for the creation of lending organizations that would use land as collateral.[2] In the nineteenth century, two such projects ended in dismal failure. Both the Banque Territoriale, and the Caisse Hypothécaire were private efforts to create a national long-term credit bank.[3] These banks had been unable to overcome the twin problems of an unstable real estate market and of political uncertainty.[4] The only remedy to these problems was to create an organization that would have the size and scope needed to diversify risks both across projects and over time.

The Crédit Foncier was founded in 1852 as a regional mortgage bank with only moderate government supervision.[5] By the end of the decade, officers appointed by the government had taken control of the bank and revised its statutes, and the state had implicitly guaranteed its bonds. The officers, who served very long terms, clearly used the bank to further the government's economic policies, but they also displayed great concern for keeping the bank profitable. Their revisions to the CFF's statutes extended the bank's role in long-term credit to the entire country. Under the Second Empire, the CFF was the only financial organization in France that was allowed to float bonds on the stock exchange to fund a mortgage portfolio. Although there were scores of other mortgage brokers in the provinces and even in Paris, they had to rely on traditional sources of funds. Further, with other mortgage brokers, savers and debt-

2. The first projects for such a land bank dated back to the seventeenth century; see Perrot 1992:195–216.

3. Gille 1959:136–37, 293–369.

4. Lescure 1980:6.

5. For more details on the early history of the CFF, see Allinne 1983 and Dupont-Ferrier 1925.

ors were almost always locked into bilateral contracts denying them the benefits of risk pooling.[6] It is thus not surprising that the CFF quickly became the largest mortgage lender in France.

In the next decade, the CFF also acquired a monopoly over the sale of municipal bonds.[7] It simultaneously expanded its short-term lending and branched into financial and monetary speculations. These other activities proved to be both remarkably profitable and controversial, at times overshadowing its mortgage lending, but it is the mortgages that are the focus of our analysis. Since the CFF did little mortgage lending in the countryside, many scholars argue that it was more interested in speculation and in the politically important rebuilding of Paris than in the mortgage business.[8] Yet the CFF's actions were understandable. Its failure to make more mortgage loans in rural areas probably resulted from difficulties in screening loan applicants. Indeed it took several decades for the CFF to acquire a network of branches sufficient to cover all of France. Until then, it could only reach those borrowers who could come to one of its branches and who had the kind of real assets that made lien verification easy—essentially, owners of large compact estates.[9] Meanwhile, it was making mortgage loans in Paris; indeed, it quickly became the dominant mortgage lender there. But the expansion of its mortgage business in Paris depended on solving informational problems.

One other obstacle for the CFF were the limits placed on the interest rates it could charge on its mortgages.[10] It had to cover its administrative costs and make a profit on the difference between the cost of its capital and the interest it charged borrowers, and all the while there were limits to the interest rate it could demand. It is thus hardly surprising that, as interest rates rose from 1854 to 1857, the number of loans issued by the CFF fell dramatically. The state was slow to liberalize the CFF's lending rules, and, as a result, the bank did not start to issue more loans until much later in the decade. Yet despite these initial difficulties, the

6. Pooling for the lender increases liquidity and decreases risk. For the borrower, it allows for longer expected loan terms because loans are no longer subject to the idiosyncrasies of a single lender.

7. Allinne 1983:75–80.

8. Allinne 1983:87–90.

9. The mean size of estates put up as collateral for the CFF between 1852 and 1869 was nearly seventy-five hectares (Archives du Crédit Foncier, Procès verbaux du Conseil d'administration, Autorisations de prêts 1854, 1857, 1860, 1863, 1866, 1869).

10. Until 1857 the CFF could charge no more than 3.6 percent interest, and total annual payment—including amortization over 50 years—was capped at 5 percent (Allinne 1983:32, 38).

CFF remained profitable and by the 1860s it had become the largest private financial institution in the country.[11]

The financial structure of the CFF was designed to limit risk and to avoid liquidity crises. By statute, the CFF could only lend one million francs at most to any given person or corporation, reducing the risk associated with concentrated investments.[12] It also limited its loans to 50 percent of the assessed value of the collateral, like most other mortgage lenders. Finally, the CFF's mortgages were thirty- to fifty-year installment plan loans, whereas other lenders offered only four- to eight-year mortgages with balloon payments.[13]

The structure of its loans assured that even borrowers with temporary cash flow problems could make their payments, thereby reducing defaults far below what other intermediaries could anticipate. In traditional notarial transactions, defaults were usually provoked when lenders unexpectedly demanded reimbursement of their principal. That was the cause, rather than a borrower's inability to make the interest payments. With the CFF's arrangements, for the first time, such short-term crises could easily be avoided.

To fund its mortgages, the CFF issued long-term notes.[14] Its notes were general obligations and offered a guarantee based on the pool of its loans rather than any specific mortgage. The CFF was thus functioning as mortgage pooling institution, something that neither the Banque Territoriale nor the Caisse Hypothécaire had achieved.

While the pooling of loans was supposed to reduce risk, the public was not initially eager to hold the CFF's bonds, and its shares performed poorly. To grow, the CFF needed to raise capital, and to do that it had to tighten its links to the government, which would reassure investors. The CFF found a way out of this dilemma when the state altered its structure in a series of steps. First, the state allowed its receivers general (tax agents) to collect funds for the CFF.[15] No other private firm used

11. The Caisse des Dépôts was a much larger financial institution, but most of its capital came from the legal requirements that savings banks and local organizations hold their funds in accounts at the Caisse. Thus its funds came more from legislative fiat rather than from voluntary placement (Priouret 1962).

12. This restriction was quickly ignored, and by the end of the 1850s loans larger than one million francs occurred regularly.

13. For the duration of mortgages arranged by notaries and other lenders, see table 9.1. In the provinces, the average initial duration ranged from three to six years in the following markets: Privas, Vauvert, St Gilles, La Salle, Tréguier, and Château-Thierry. The sources here are the Actes Civils Publics registers of the Enregistrement.

14. The notes were initially marketed either by the institution or by the borrower.

15. Allinne 1983:30–34.

TABLE 11.1   NEW CFF LOANS BY PERIOD

Value by Quarter	First Quarter of 1853 through Second Quarter of 1855	Third Quarter of 1855 through Second Quarter of 1860	Third Quarter of 1860 through Fourth Quarter of 1869
1. Total volume of new loans (millions of francs per quarter)	21.95	18.78	36.79
2. Total volume of new CFF loans (millions of francs per quarter)	5.61	2.94	14.93
3. Average CFF share (percent)	25.28	15.67	40.58
4. Minimum CFF share (percent)	0.05	0	13.11
5. Maximum CFF share (percent)	51.99	72.83	66.72

Source: Our standard samples of ten notaries; for details see chapter 2.

the government's fiscal agents as intermediaries, and the privilege of doing so gave the CFF an implicit government guarantee. The notion that the state would protect the bank's investors was given a further boost by the increased role of government agents in the administration of the CFF. As a result, it sold so many bonds that by the late nineteenth century it had become the biggest nongovernmental issuer of debt in France.

Access to capital allowed the CFF to grow rapidly. By the mid-1860s, it was making nearly half of all mortgage loans in Paris. By 1869, its portfolio included nearly two-thirds of all outstanding mortgage debt in Paris. The CFF grew in three phases. It began making loans in January 1853, and between then and the spring of 1855 it accounted for a quarter of all mortgage loans in Paris (table 11.1). After this first phase of expansion, the CFF's business slackened in the late 1850s, with its market share dropping to some 15 percent of all mortgage loans—this despite the state's liberalization of its lending constraints. Finally, in the 1860s, the CFF's growth resumed and steadied, with lending rising from three million francs a quarter to nearly fifteen million francs a quarter in the 1860s.

To explain the variation in the CFF's lending, one might be tempted to invoke the cost of the capital it raised. This explanation would seem all the more appealing because of the constraints on what the CFF could charge on its mortgages.[16] The cost of the CFF's capital was close to the interest rate on government bonds. The CFF's bonds were rated nearly

16. In the mortgage market, the CFF was essentially a regulated monopolist, limited to charging the costs of its funds plus a markup to cover its administrative expenses. Since it was a price taker as a borrower, one could easily imagine a simple model in which its lending was completely determined by its cost of capital.

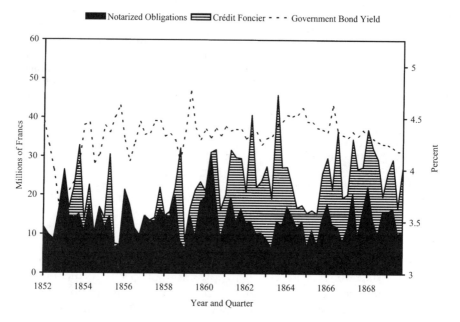

FIGURE 11.1 Interest Rates and the Volume of Notarized Loans in Paris, 1852–70

the equivalent of government bonds, and since the CFF's debt issues were too small to influence significantly the interest rate that the state paid, it is reasonable to assume that the government bond rate was statistically exogenous as far as the CFF was concerned. (Exogenous here simply means that officials at the CFF took the government bond rate as a given that they could not affect. It permits us to use simple ordinary least squares regressions to study the effect of the interest rate on the CFF.) We can therefore simply regress the CFF's lending on the government interest rate to see how much of the variation in lending can be explained by the cost of the CFF's capital.

The regression reveals that the relationship between CFF lending and the interest rate on government bonds was weak. It could well be a statistical fluke (the *T*-statistic is only 1.70 with 66 degrees of freedom).[17] And even if we trust the coefficient, it explains only 4 percent of the variation in the CFF's lending. A graph of the interest rate and CFF lending drives the point home: the relationship was feeble at best (figure 11.1).

17. With a Cochrane-Orcutt correction for serial correlation, the results are:
Crédit Foncier Lending $= 67.7 - 13.1^*$ Government Bond Yield
$$(33.4) \quad (7.7)$$
Standard errors are in parentheses; $n = 68$, $R^2 = 0.04$, and Rho $= 0.48$ (standard error of 0.10).

The same was true of notarized loans. They too bore only a weak relationship to interest rates.[18] True, private credit did plummet when the government bond yield shot up in 1848, and it recovered in 1852 when government yields declined. However, the link between loans and interest rates stops there. In all likelihood, what was driving notarized loans was less interest rates than long-term changes in financial practices. Less and less was being lent by notaries in Paris, and the interest rate did not vary enough to account for this decline.

If interest rates cannot explain the CFF's lending, what then was the cause of the drop-off in the CFF's mortgage business from 1855 to 1859? To answer this question, we must turn from statistics to history and consider two misfortunes that befell the CFF in the late 1850s, two misfortunes that reined in the bank's lending. First of all, in 1857 the government refused to authorize any bond or stock issues.[19] This drastic measure sharply curtailed the CFF's lending because it could only make loans if it could issue bonds. Then, in 1858 and 1859, misfortune struck again in a sharp economic contraction that dramatically reduced the demand for mortgages.[20] It was not until the beginning of 1860 that business picked up again.

Thereafter the CFF enjoyed easy access to loan funds and a long queue of clients, at least in Paris. By 1869, it was mobilizing twenty-four times the capital of the most active notary in the eighteenth century and twenty-eight times that of the largest notary in the nineteenth century. The CFF was also offering loan maturities that were six to eight times longer than standard nineteenth-century notarial contracts. Somehow, the CFF had completely changed credit in Paris. Again, interest rates do not account for its stunning growth or for the changes it had wrought in the Parisian credit market. As we shall see, the actual explanation lies elsewhere.

Information and the Destination of Loans

The CFF did have obvious advantages that played a large role in its success. Because of its size, it could make bigger loans than notaries, and its size also allowed it to diversify its loan portfolio more than other lend-

18. Obligation Lending $= 18.7 - 8.7^*$ Government Bond Yield
$$(18.9) \quad (4.4)$$
Standard errors are in parentheses; $n = 68$, $R^2 = 0.001$, and Rho $= 0.21$ with a standard error of 0.16.

19. Gille 1967, 2:197.

20. Lévy-Leboyer and Bourguignon 1985:329.

ers, thus cutting the idiosyncratic risks of its lending. Yet another factor
in the CFF's favor was its ability to lend money out for longer terms,
which appealed to borrowers. It could do so because it was able to raise
money itself in the long-term market and because its novel loan terms
reduced the risk of suffering a liquidity crisis.[21]

By themselves, however, these advantages could not guarantee the
CFF's success. If they had, then the CFF would have triumphed every-
where in France, for size and ability to make long-term loans would have
worked just as well in the French countryside as in Paris. The CFF,
though, was far more successful in Paris than in the countryside. In 1869,
for example, it made about 38 percent of the new mortgages in Paris,
but only 3 percent in the rest of France. In that same year, it held an
estimated 56 percent of the outstanding notarized debt in Paris, but
only 11 percent in the countryside (table 10.4). This dramatic difference
between city and countryside suggests that the CFF faced an additional
problem, a problem that size and loan terms would not solve. That problem was one of information—the information needed to select borrowers—and the CFF only solved it in Paris.

The CFF began with no information about borrowers—no informational capital in the language of economics. Worse yet, it had to compete with financial intermediaries, including the notaries, who had
accumulated a great store of informal information about potential
borrowers. The CFF, therefore, faced what economists call a serious lemons problem.[22] If its competitors took full advantage of their information, they would skim off the low-risk borrowers for themselves, leaving
the CFF with the dubious ones that other lenders had turned down.
Simply charging such borrowers higher interest rates would actually ag-
gravate the problem, for the best borrowers would not have paid the
high rates while the worst borrowers (those with no alternatives) would
have done so willingly.[23]

To succeed, the CFF had to overcome the lemons problem; in other
words, it had to limit its informational disadvantage. That meant lending
in areas where it had a comparative advantage in information. In particular, the CFF had to offer loans to borrowers for whom the informal information of the notaries and its other competitors was of little value. It

---

21. Falling interest rates did create difficulties, though. When interest rates dropped,
borrowers tried to renegotiate their loans, but the CFF found it difficult to redeem its own
bonds.

22. Akerloff 1970.

23. Stiglitz and Weiss 1981.

also had to offer loans that other lenders would find very difficult to fund even if the borrowers were trustworthy.

One way for the CFF to do this was to require that all of its loans be registered with the hypothèques administration. While the hypothèques were far from perfect, they did reduce informational asymmetries dramatically—in particular in regions where registration was frequent. As we know from the previous chapter, use of the hypothèques rose over the course of the nineteenth century. By the time the CFF began lending, there was therefore a population of borrowers whose credit histories were publicly available—a novelty that the CFF's predecessors had not enjoyed. Relying on the hypothèques of course pushed the CFF to lend in Paris, because it was there, as we know, that registration was most common. And in the countryside, the CFF favored loans secured by large parcels of real estate because they too were more likely to be registered than other rural loans.

The second part of the CFF's strategy was to focus on loan contracts that were more desirable than those proposed by traditional financial intermediaries. That meant bigger loans and longer loan maturities than other mortgage lenders offered. As a result, the CFF ended up concentrating on the largest borrowers in France.

If we examine data on loan sizes, we can see whether the CFF pursued this two-pronged strategy of focusing on registered loans in Paris and on big borrowers in the countryside (table 11.2). The table reveals the sizes of CFF and non-CFF notarized loans, both in Paris and in rural France. (Here rural France is defined to be all of the country except for Paris and the five most urbanized departments.) In the countryside, we do not know the distribution of loan sizes for non-CFF loans in the 1850s and 1860s, but an 1890 government survey of all mortgage lending prob-

TABLE 11.2   DISTRIBUTION OF LOAN SIZES: CFF AND NON-CFF LOANS

	CFF				Non-CFF		
	Paris		Rural		Paris		Rural
	1850s	1860s	1850s	1860s	1850s	1860s	1890s
Mean (1,000 francs)	97.4	77.9	41.9	36.9	20.2	30.1	2.7
Median (1,000 francs)	40	35.5	14.5	12	10	12	1.1
Standard deviation	117.4	157.1	77.2	75.4	32.9	82.8	

Source: For Rural CFF enumerations, Archives du Crédit Foncier (Procès verbaux du Conseil d'administration, Autorisations de prêts 1854, 1857, 1860, 1863, 1866, 1869); for Paris CFF and Paris Non-CFF, the ten études that we have followed and the thirty others that we have examined for comparative purposes; and for Rural 1890s, Archives du Ministère des Finances B 38930. For details about the études, see chapter 2.

ably indicates what loan sizes for the whole rural market were some thirty years earlier.[24]

In the countryside, the median loan made by the CFF in the 1850s was at least thirteen times larger than the median loan in the rural market as a whole in 1890. The size difference confirms that the CFF was seeking out the large-scale borrowers in the countryside, whose loans would of course be more likely to be registered with the hypothèques. In Paris the median loan made by the CFF was also big: four times the size of the median non-CFF loan in the 1850s. But the size gap between CFF and non-CFF loans was smaller in Paris than in the countryside, although Parisian loans as a whole were of course much bigger than rural mortgages. In Paris, the CFF made loans within the top three quartiles of the loan distribution; in the countryside, it made only giant loans, in the upper tail of the distribution. That difference between Paris and countryside, though, fits what we know about the hypothèques in Paris. Hypothèque registration was common there, and if the CFF was focusing on registered loans in Paris, we would therefore expect a relatively wider range of loan sizes in the capital than in the countryside. Our argument about the CFF's strategy thus seems confirmed. The bank was at some informational disadvantage relative to other intermediaries in Paris, but thanks to the public information in the hypothèques that disadvantage was limited.

The CFF did reduce its informational disadvantage slightly by the end of the 1860s. The ratio of the median of the CFF loans to the median of the non-CFF loans fell from thirteen to eleven in the countryside and from four to three in Paris. For the CFF to reach beyond such mammoth loans would mean establishing regional offices to manage local information, but that did not occur before the end of the century.[25]

Rural notaries therefore found it easy to coexist with the CFF. Indeed, the bank offered loans that were so large that they were beyond the means of most notarial credit networks in the countryside.[26] Adapting to the CFF was thus straightforward. Because the rural notaries had a comparative advantage in local information about smaller borrowers, they left the small number of large loans to the CFF and retained the high-volume, small-scale credit for themselves.

The CFF therefore did not end up with all the untrustworthy borrow-

---

24. Because loan sizes probably increased between the 1850s and the 1890s, the 1890 numbers are likely to understate the difference we are trying to capture.

25. Allinne 1983.

26. Because big rural loans could have been negotiated in provincial cities, it would be interesting to know how financial intermediaries in cities outside Paris dealt with the CFF.

ers. In other words, it solved the lemons problem that could have thwarted its growth. It did so by focusing on particular borrowers and thereby dividing up the credit market in a way that prevented notaries from taking advantage of their information to skim off the desirable borrowers. The CFF's strategy was to target Paris and the biggest borrowers in the countryside. In rural areas, the CFF's loans were so much larger than the notaries' that it did not have to fear being left with dubious borrowers. In Paris, its mortgages were sizeable too, but not that much bigger than the loans arranged by Parisian notaries. What kept the Parisian notaries from exploiting the situation was the hypothèque registration, which was so widely used that it offset the notaries' informational advantage. Whatever lingering edge the notaries had must have been small, for the CFF continued to profit from Parisian real estate lending. If the CFF had failed to resolve the lemons problem, it would never have made such money. But with the lemons problem out of the way, it could thrive on its strengths: its ability to weather liquidity crises, the low cost of the funds it raised, and the size and duration of the mortgages it offered.

The CFF and Notaries in Paris

In Paris the CFF's arrival was dramatic, for the bank overwhelmed the business of other mortgage lenders. Since neither notaries nor the CFF have left a direct record of this competition, we must deduce how they adapted to each other. How did the Parisian notaries adjust to the CFF? Did it diminish their role in the credit market? Did it create any new business for them? We begin this investigation by examining the traditional part of notaries' affairs: loans drawn up by notaries that did not involve the CFF. (Henceforth this traditional business will also be referred to as non-CFF lending.) We will then turn to the loans issued by the CFF itself. Because all these CFF loans were notarized, the notaries did collect some fees from them, and, as a result, we close by considering how the bank distributed its business across notaries.

As far as the non-CFF lending is concerned, the Parisian notaries failed to benefit from Haussmann's rebuilding of Paris or from the financial boom under the Second Empire. On average, their new loan business after 1852 was 16 percent below what it had been in 1830–48. And although their non-CFF lending did rise 8 percent between 1860 and 1869, the CFF's new lending increased by more than 300 percent in the same period.

The Parisian notaries were clearly unable to compete with the CFF,

and after 1860 they progressively abandoned their own credit brokerage
to other financial intermediaries in the neighborhoods of the Chaussée
d'Antin, the Bourse, and the Place Vendôme—the northwestern quad-
rant of the city that was its financial center. We begin to see the other
intermediaries in the notarial records, where they appear as recurrent
lenders, arranging loans themselves and only turning to the notaries to
draft the contracts. In our samples for 1860 and 1869, many of the loans
were made by such repeat lenders.[27] Finding lenders who made many
loans was not itself a new phenomenon. What was novel was that the
repeat lenders were now financial intermediaries rather than simply
wealthy savers. They put together their own loans and merely used the
notaries to draw up the contracts.

A number of them were bankers. Among the ten études we followed
in our samples, two in particular became dependent on bankers for loan
intermediation. In one instance, it was the Callaghan family bank, which
played a very important role in étude CXI after 1850. In another—étude
LXII—it was the Mallet bank. Long associated with the étude, it became
the dominant provider of loans under the Second Empire. Like the CFF,
these bankers and other financial intermediaries were unlikely to demand informational services from notaries, other than access to the hypothèques registers. In other words, even in their traditional financial
transactions, the notaries were providing fewer and fewer informational
services.

The notaries' role in the credit market may in fact have suffered even
more than our evidence suggests. The reason is that we may well underestimate the role of bankers in the non-CFF lending, for we cannot identify most private bankers in the notarial records. Many lenders may have
actually been bankers, but the meager information about professions
in the nineteenth-century notarial documents does not reveal that fact.
Bankers had made only limited inroads into long-term mortgage lending before the CFF was created. But once the CFF was functioning, it
may have encouraged other financial intermediaries to encroach upon
the notaries non-CFF lending.

27. In étude CXV, in the 1860s we find the Banque Geofroy, and a man named Blanke
who identifies himself as a banker. In étude CXVII, two individuals named D'Aguin and
Nicolas Guiard each appear repeatedly as lenders, though they only identify themselves
as propriétaires. In étude XLIII, Leroy Rosset, maison de banque, is the short-term credit
supplier. Etude IX featured Armand Guillaume, propriétaire, as an important lender. Often the parties to contracts only identified themselves as "propriétaires" (owners of real
assets). That is why we have not broken down lending in the nineteenth century by profession or social class. The only way to determine class or profession is to match names and
addresses with city directories, a time consuming task offering little reward for this project.

Although we cannot say much about the professions or social classes of borrowers and lenders, we do have considerable information about loan sizes, and it reveals a great deal about how the Parisian notaries adapted to the CFF. Although loan sizes plummeted after the Revolution, by 1840 the size distribution in Paris had returned to what it had been back in 1780, albeit with half as many loans as before.[28] In 1780 contracts greater than 150,000 francs constituted a quarter of the funds loaned. By 1840 a quarter of the funds were again being lent in contracts greater than 150,000 francs. Loan sizes then increased rapidly after the credit contraction of 1851. By 1869, a quarter of the funds in non-CFF lending involved loans larger than 200,000 francs.

That result is surprising, because one might have expected that in order to compete with the CFF the Parisian notaries would have focused their business on small loans, where they had the greatest advantage relative to the big bank. With small loans, the notaries' informal information would remain valuable, and hypothèque registration would be too costly for the CFF. But the distribution of loan sizes shows that the Parisian notaries were shedding smaller borrowers. By 1869, loans smaller than two thousand francs represented only 6 percent of all new notarial loans, versus 10 percent under the July Monarchy.

While loan sizes increased, the number of loans shrank, yet another sign that access to credit was severely restricted and available only to a smaller and smaller fraction of the population. The arrival of the CFF did not open access to long-term credit either.[29] The total number of loans rose, but the population was increasing much faster. Increasingly, credit in Paris was concentrated among borrowers and lenders.

Although the Parisian notaries were abandoning their traditional business of loan brokerage, they still had a role to play in the CFF loans. The CFF did not need their informational services, but it could use them to draft loan contracts and to do the necessary research in the hypothèque bureaux. How then did the CFF distribute this business among notarial études?

We can tell by examining what happened to the ten études that we have followed and the thirty others that we have sampled every ten years for comparative purposes. If we look at 1860 and 1869, the period of the CFF's steady growth, we immediately notice a contrast between what the CFF did in 1860 and what it did nine years later. In 1860, the CFF's

28. The average number of new loans in the 1780s was 8,343 a year, while in the 1840s it was 4,804.

29. After 1860, the CFF did begin making loans under two thousand francs, but they accounted for less than 1 percent of its portfolio.

business tended to be concentrated in a smaller number of études. Several études did no CFF business at all in 1860 (III, XXVII, XXXIV, XCII, CXI), and four others drew up only one loan (II, XIX, XVII, XLIII).[30] In 1869, by contrast, all of the forty notaries recorded at least two CFF contracts, and most études drafted between four and ten. Having initially concentrated its business in the hands of a small number of notaries, the CFF was progressively spreading out.[31]

In Paris, the CFF was thus extending its lending business to more and more notaries, and through them reaching more and more clients. Meanwhile, the number of loans authorized by the CFF doubled between 1860 and 1869. The bank's rapid growth left non-CFF lending in the dust and boosted outstanding private debt to levels unknown since the late eighteenth century. While non-CFF debt grew by some 8 percent between 1860 and 1869, outstanding CFF loans increased a phenomenal 446 percent. By 1869, CFF debt represented 56 percent of all long-term debt. The bank had expanded so rapidly that long-term private debt in Paris finally managed to surpass (though only slightly) the peak of the 1780s (figure 2.5). The CFF had indeed changed the face of mortgage credit in Paris: the stagnation of the nineteenth century was over.

One might presume that the Parisian notaries would have fought the Crédit Foncier, much as the Rothschilds opposed the new investment bank, the Crédit Mobilier.[32] From James Rothschild's point of view, the Crédit Mobilier was a direct competitor.[33] Although the Crédit Mobilier might increase overall lending by making the financial system more efficient, it was likely to take business away from the traditional financial intermediary for government and industry—the Haute Banque, which Rothschild helped to lead. Rothschild's opposition to the new institution was therefore understandable.

The Parisian notaries, though, did not behave like Rothschild. They acquiesced in the workings of the CFF and were easily co-opted. The appointment of Antoine Hailig, a retired head of the Paris notarial corporation, as the first chairman of the CFF's board of directors was a clear sign of how easy it was to gain the notaries' assent.[34]

The reasons for the notaries' acquiescence are easy to understand.

30. In the case of étude XLIII, the loan was actually authorized in 1859, but the capital was not delivered until 1860.

31. Back in 1853, the CFF had limited its dealings to even a smaller number of études, for in that year nearly half of the notaries drafted no CFF loan contracts.

32. Gille 1967, 2:184–204.

33. See for instance the bidding wars among different financial groups for underwriting Spanish bond issues (Gille 1967, 2:286–90).

34. Allinne 1983:31.

True, there were some reasons to oppose the CFF. The bank's loans brought the notaries smaller fees because the loans lasted so long that there were no renegotiations or prorogations. And because the CFF used the hypothèques, it did not need the notaries' informal information. Yet the notaries more than offset these losses thanks to the increased number of loans the CFF made, loans that were all notarized. The CFF even attracted borrowers from the countryside since many rural proprietors came to the capital to negotiate mortgages. The revenues from the CFF more than compensated for the end to loan brokerage.

The Parisian notaries abandoned the financial market to the CFF for pragmatic reasons as well. The government had banished them from banking in the 1840s.[35] To compete with the CFF, the notaries would have had to reenter banking, an enormous institutional change that the government would have vetoed. After all, it considered the notaries to be not market makers but public servants who were charged with drafting private contracts.[36] And the notaries themselves would have had a difficult time shouldering the risks that competition with the CFF would have entailed, for they lacked all the organizational advantages that allowed the CFF to ride out liquidity crises. For the notaries, the possibility of going head to head with the CFF had been ruled out long before the bank opened in 1852. Instead of battling the CFF, the notaries returned to scrivening, a role they had given up in the early eighteenth century.

A Concluding Contrast: The Countryside

The history of credit markets in the rest of France sometimes follows that of lending in Paris, while at other times it goes off on a different path. The growth of lending in the eighteenth century and the catastrophe of the Revolution were both national phenomena, which varied a bit from region to region in their intensity but not in their direction. In contrast, the nineteenth century saw credit markets diverge in Paris and the rest of the country. In Paris, financial instability made it impossible for notaries to reconstitute their traditional system of lending; long-term credit stagnated until the creation of the Crédit Foncier. In the provinces, by contrast, the effects of the Revolution were largely erased by 1840.

After the Revolution, the steady expansion of credit outside of Paris continued to depend on well-established local credit intermediaries

35. See chapter 10.
36. Woloch 1994:331–32.

such as the notaries. None of the national banks were eager to open provincial branches—except in the largest cities—until at least the 1880s. It required considerable government pressure, for example, to get the Bank of France to open a branch in every prefecture after 1880.

Why did the Parisian banks shun the countryside? It was because they could not form stable cooperative relationships with local credit interme- diaries. Without such cooperation, the Parisian banks were shut out of local credit. They could not turn to the hypothèques for information about borrowers, because the hypothèques were rarely used. The only information about borrowers and collateral was in the hands of local intermediaries—provincial bankers and notaries. The Parisian banks ei- ther had to co-opt local credit intermediaries or face the dire conse- quences of funding projects rejected by better informed local competi- tors—the lemons problem again.

Why national lenders did not link up with the local notaries or acquire other local sources of information remains a puzzle, yet for this study the issue is of little importance, for mortgage lending continued to grow in the countryside even without modern banks. Towards the end of the nineteenth century, France was thus divided into three distinct financial areas: Paris, where corporate and commercial banks dominated; provin- cial cities, where local banks competed with local intermediaries; and finally the countryside, where notaries and other traditional intermediar- ies reigned supreme. The continued vitality of these traditional interme- diaries depended upon the fact that they had the advantage in acquiring and managing information. Institutional change could not offset their informational advantage, and it took time for corporate organizations to acquire the necessary informational capital and to overcome prob- lems of adverse selection and moral hazard. The obstacles were not acci- dents of French history. Indeed, they are common to financial develop- ment around the globe.

Conclusion

Two Centuries of Credit

LIKE THE HAND-PAINTED PANORAMAS that fascinated Parisians in the nineteenth century, our research offers unexpected perspectives on the city and, beyond, on the wider world. We do enjoy one advantage over panoramas, though, in that we can focus our perspective both across time and society. In particular, we have painted a picture of credit markets in Paris between 1660 and 1869 that highlights the importance of notarial credit. In this conclusion we revisit the data while emphasizing the long-run viewpoint that they allow. The data lead us to stress five substantive and methodological points. First, lending was widespread in Paris even though financial institutions at the time looked nothing like what economists and historians have grown to expect. Second, to study the development of financial institutions, historians and social scientists must quantify, do so over long spans of time, and analyze the financial activity in a market framework. Third, secondary markets or political reform, though important, are at best sufficient conditions for financial expansion. Fourth, if scholars are to understand the development of financial intermediaries' networks, then they must study the spatial distribution of information. Fifth, the past course of events that people remember and deem relevant—history in our sense of the word—has had rich and complex effects on the evolution of European financial markets. Indeed historical circumstance must be considered separately for each locality, region, or country; for the whole financial system; and for each network of financial intermediaries.

Perhaps the most telling fact about the abundance of credit in Paris can be gleaned from the years just preceding the French Revolution. Notarial credit in Paris then stood at a secular peak (figure C.1). Notaries arranged two hundred thirty livres of long- or medium-term private credit and ninety-three livres of public credit for every child, woman, and man in Paris, an amount that exceeded the yearly wage of an unskilled worker. This remarkable achievement was long neglected by his-

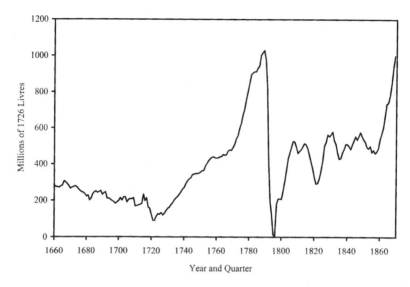

FIGURE C.1 Private Outstanding Notarial Debt in Paris, 1660–1870

torians of financial markets because it was based on a set of institutions that the Revolution condemned to oblivion. Yet during the Old Regime, notaries had created an informal network capable of mobilizing capital for a broad variety of activities. They raised loans to finance the public debt, the purchase of government offices, the construction of canals and real estate, and mundane family events like marriages. By the second half of the eighteenth century they had drawn a surprisingly diverse population into the credit market. To be sure, the political and financial elites were well represented, but one could also find domestics preparing their retirement, foreigners attracted by the generous terms of government debt, single women placing their savings in the hands of notaries, and scores of other individuals involved in the business of everyday life. Parisian notaries were capable of mobilizing such vast sums of money for both private and public borrowers because they had become very effective at transmitting information between lenders and borrowers. It in fact appears as though most parties to loans had little interaction with one another prior to their exchange of capital. Notaries, therefore, stood at the center of a financial system that provided the key ingredient to match borrowers and lenders: information.

As we turn away from 1789 and look further back into the past, we can see that credit had long been a feature of French life. In the earliest years for which we collected data, notarial lending per capita still averaged seventy-eight livres a year, while outstanding debt came to five hundred livres for each Parisian.[1] Credit was common in Europe by 1660, and no doubt long before 1660 as well.[2] Although loans were often made in the seventeenth century, they depended on an information system that was quite different from that of the 1780s. Indeed, borrowers and lenders seem to have relied much more on personal information than on any intermediaries, and the notaries were often just scriveners, drawing up contracts but doing little else. It was not until the beginning of the eighteenth century that they became deeply involved in intermediation.

Perhaps because the credit market lacked good middlemen, private indebtedness under Louis XIV remained less than a third of what it would become in the 1780s. Yet the lack of intermediaries was not the only reason for the stagnation in seventeenth-century credit. The economy was depressed and savers were reluctant to hold financial assets because of the uncertainties that hung over financial markets. The greatest risk came from the government, for in the seventeenth and early eighteenth centuries the crown frequently intervened in credit markets in ways that directly and indirectly taxed financial instruments. The government's most pernicious policy was its habit of tinkering with the unit of account, which undermined the value of debts that were to be repaid. Between 1670 and 1726, the crown sliced off some 40 percent of the livre's silver content, and with each devaluation lenders watched their financial returns plunge. Although they did not abandon credit markets entirely, they did shun new investments.

In the same period, the government issued the bulk of its obligations in a short-term market dominated by financiers and bankers. Although notarial records contain government debt contracts prior to 1720, most of these represent consolidation of old debts, not new debt issue. As in the case of private credit, therefore, notaries only played a limited role in the placement of government debt, and usually they just drafted the contracts.

The Regency of 1715–23 marked the climax to the government's attack on capital markets. Rapid inflation driven by the issue of paper money and stringent controls on interest rates were followed by a sweeping renegotiation of the public debt. At the same time, private borrowers

1. The figures here are in 1726 livres.
2. It was not the lack of credit that prevented us from pushing the quantitative series back another hundred years. As Schnapper (1957) documented, rentes perpétuelles were already widespread in the sixteenth and early seventeenth century. The cost of assembling a representative view of financial activity in Paris, however, is then much larger than later. In particular, notarial archives are not as well preserved before 1660, so a different enumeration technique would be necessary.

used the inflation to write off half of their debts. The short-run effect of this crisis was a crippling lack of confidence in financial assets—the levels of lending of the 1700s would not be matched again until the mid-1730s. In the longer term, the crisis was a juncture between two financial systems in Paris, that of the seventeenth century based on personal connections and that of the eighteenth century dominated by long-term notarized credit. The notaries, though, managed to pass through the crisis unscathed. They had not been systematically involved in short-term government debt or credit prior to 1720, and as a result they suffered little from the government default. Indeed, they actually gained invaluable lists of clients when the government consolidated its debt in 1722–23, because they drew up all the new debt contracts.

From the 1730s and 1750s, a cooperative information system developed and lending grew quickly. At the same time, notaries attempted to use their control over long-term debt to enter deposit banking. The financial crisis of the Regency had weakened bankers and heightened the competition for short-term deposits between bankers and notaries. Some notaries thought it profitable to extend their business into the realm of short-term credit. Their effort, though, had little success—its most visible consequence being an unprecedented rash of bankruptcies. Frightened notaries retreated from deposit banking and focused their attention on long-term credit for the remainder of the Old Regime. As a result, financial intermediation during the later eighteenth century was divided between different networks. In the Parisian system that came about after the Regency, bankers, financiers, and government officers such as *receveurs généraux* and *fermiers généraux* dominated the short-term and inter-regional credit market, while notaries were key in the long-term market. Although this pattern of segmentation held in general, it did break down at the margins, where bankers played an important role in bringing foreign investors to the public debt market and notaries offered short-term credit to some rich households. The complementarity of the networks is highlighted by the long-term cooperation of certain notaries with banking houses. The Mallet bank, for instance, worked with étude LXII and the LeCoulteux bank with étude CXV, and, in both cases, the cooperation endured through changes in the ownership of the notarial office and the titular head of the family banking house.

From a peak in the 1780s, indebtedness in Paris plunged into an abyss during the Revolution. Between 1790 and 1795, borrowers extinguished most of their debts at a fraction of the capital's original value because the Revolution was largely financed by inflation. The revolutionary paper currency, the assignat, was denominated in livres and legal tender, so borrowers could take easy advantage of its rapid loss of value to pay off their old debts. Although historians have paid considerable attention to what happened to public debt during the Revolution, the impact of inflation on private credit has been utterly ignored. Yet, we have shown that the consequences of inflation on private credit were as severe as those involved in public debt. Therefore, it was not just holders of government obligations who suffered, but all creditors. Longer-term lenders suffered more than short-term lenders because they were generally repaid late in the inflation.

Because long-term creditors came from all walks of life, our findings suggest several amendments to the political economy of the Revolution. Some have argued that the inflation was precipitated by conflicts between different social groups (tax-exempt creditors versus taxpayers, for example) over who should bear the cost of solving the state's financial woes. But one can not simply oppose the goals of privileged (and thereby tax-exempt) state creditors to those of the masses of taxpayers who were too poor to save. Indeed, creditors and debtors were far more broadly dispersed in society. Inflation did redistribute resources from the old to the young, from women to men, and from cities to the countryside— but none of these cleavages has a relevant political echo on the fiscal side.[3] At the beginning of the Revolution, the enfranchised population was actually a net creditor to the state and to the rest of the nation. In other words, the revolutionaries of 1789 had little interest in promoting inflation or government default—yet they were the ones that precipitated the crisis.[4] Pitted against a king who held a very strong hand, these revolutionaries realized that precarious public finances were their most powerful weapon in a battle not over finance but constitutional reform. They may have been willing to bear the personal cost of inflation and redistribution to gain the upper hand against the crown.

The Revolution was a chasm both for institutions and for the Parisian credit market. Between 1789 and 1815 the state created new mechanisms for furnishing information to creditors, a change that made it impossible for Parisian notaries to recreate the cooperative network of the eighteenth century. The information publicly available through the hypothèques increased competition among notaries and between types of intermediaries. Because of the competition, bankers attempted to enter long-term credit, while notaries tried to serve as bankers. Both at-

3. Until more research is completed on provincial financial markets, the question of the relationship between indebtedness and political action remains open.

4. As many scholars have noted, the proposals for tax reform that were bruited about at the end of the Old Regime all proposed to reduce tax exemptions and therefore to tax those who were potentially the monarchy's most important creditors. See Marion 1927, 1:399, 432–42; Aftalion 1987:11–47; Egret 1962.

tempts failed, as numerous bankruptcies demonstrate, and by the 1840s the Paris market was again segmented, this time into an ever greater number of financial systems. Long-term private debt was still largely the domain of notaries. Bankers controlled short-term credit, the under-writing of publicly traded long-term securities, and the secondary market of certain securities. Stockbrokers offered a secondary market for the most visible securities—notably French government bonds—and tended to work in close alliance with bankers. The government-backed Banque de France discounted selected short-term bills, while other para-public institutions like the municipal pawn shop and the Parisian savings bank offered opportunities for small borrowers and small savers.

Because the Parisian notaries could not recreate their network, notar-ial credit in the capital stagnated, even as every other indicator of lend-ing in France was growing rapidly. The notaries' failure, in this case at least, did not reflect the rise of an alternative network for long-term credit. Borrowers had to make do with the limited amount of mortgage credit available in Paris or turn to short-term sources of finance. It was not until a hybrid organization—the Crédit Foncier de France (CFF)— was created in 1852 that mortgage credit increased substantially. The CFF used an implicit government guarantee to market long-term bonds to the public. To avoid problems of adverse selection (i.e., getting stuck with bad borrowers) it restricted its loans to clients who met stringent informational conditions—in effect, the richest men and women in France. In return the borrowers received thirty- to fifty-year loans when five years was the norm in the notarial market. In Paris, the CFF relied on mortgage registration with the hypothèque bureaus to reduce prob-lems of adverse selection. Further, the large size of its loans cut the cost of its reliance on the hypothèques. It is no surprise then that the CFF quickly became a forceful competitor to notaries. By 1869, the CFF had captured more than 50 percent of mortgage credit in Paris, and long-term notarized credit, which includes CFF loans, returned to levels not witnessed since the end of the Old Regime.

The changing role of notaries in Paris after the Revolution had much to do with the state's perception of what services they should render. During the eighteenth century, Parisian notaries were major intermedi-aries for public long-term debt. The crown, therefore, had to think twice before intervening in their affairs for fear that it would lose its access to savers. In the nineteenth century, however, the state relied on bankers and the stock market to meet its borrowing requirements, dramatically reducing the political clout of Parisian notaries. It is no surprise that French governments tightened the regulation of the notaries and evicted them from the short-term credit market in 1843. For the major concern was no longer the notaries' role as financial intermediaries but rather their reputation as drafters of legal contracts. In the countryside, however, notaries remained key intermediaries, and there the government conveniently avoided implementing the new regulations.

Defense of Our Methods

Our research rests on two key methodological decisions: a quantitative approach and the analysis of credit using economic theories of imperfect markets. These choices were motivated by our realization that credit was widespread and a far broader phenomenon than simply investment.[5] Without discounting the economic importance of investment or the connection between investment and credit, we began our research aware that credit encompasses a broader set of activities. Credit as a form of intertemporal trade can of course be motivated by a variety of desires (e.g. investment, insurance, life cycle smoothing). In early modern societies, it is often impossible to divorce these different motives because the accounts of families and firms were inextricably intermeshed. How, for example, would one classify a mother's borrowing to purchase a position for her son in 1709, a year of famine? It is also clear that credit contracts, which we focus on, are not the only means for moving resources across time. There were therefore some limitations to what our data could tell us. Yet by relying on quantitative methods we believe we have made considerable headway.

The virtues of quantification in the social sciences in general need not be reviewed here. When studying the notaries' activity, quantification must be tackled in two separate ways. First, we can only quantify what the notaries did by relying upon statistical procedures, for the very abundance of their archives rules out any exhaustive enumeration. Second, quantitative estimates allow us to carry out comparative analyses, which are one of the essential tasks of the historian. That Louis d'Orléans raised two million livres in 1752–53, for example, is of little meaning unless we know what a typical individual might borrow and what aggregate lending was like in those years.[6] Our appreciation is further deepened if we can say whether such large-scale borrowing by individuals was restricted to a decade in the eighteenth century or whether it

5. By credit here, we mean financial transactions divorced from other transactions. There were many other forms of intertemporal trade, such as apprenticeships, reinvestment of profits, and mortgages given out by sellers.

6. For Louis d'Orléans's borrowing in 1752–53, see ANMC étude CXV.

was widespread for long periods of time. More generally, our claim that notarial credit was central to the Parisian economy and to French society rests on the very magnitude of lending in the seventeenth century and on its spectacular growth in the eighteenth century. It is Parisian notarial credit's quantitative importance that made it priceless. Thus this volume is in fact a plea for more quantification over the long run.

Why long-run quantification? Because short-run analyses often overestimate the long-run importance of some institutions. Short-run analyses suffer from the same problems as comparative research with small numbers of cases. Either can lead to the false impression that certain institutions are necessary for growth. To take one example, some scholars have been surprised at the slow use of land titles and loan registration systems in developing countries, despite the fact that lenders seem to use them without fail in developed societies.[7] Yet these same scholars forget that such titling registration was largely unavailable in Europe prior to 1800. Further, as we show, the use of such systems diffused slowly in France and in a manner that had more to do with the structure of land ownership than with the demand for information. In the long run, the public information system (hypothèques) did become the informational foundation for capital markets, but that was not the case prior to 1850. Measuring the role of the hypothèques prior to 1850 tells us little about its long-run consequences, nor does the evidence of its widespread use late in the nineteenth century tell us much about the conditions under which it diffused.

Studying institutions over the long run forces us to confront the issue of how they changed. Because the institutions that matter for credit are often formal institutions created or enforced by the state, we have to consider rulers' motivations. Although political economy is not the focus of this volume, its findings are of direct relevance to at least one important issue in comparative politics. Institutional analysis often makes the state a hollow shell devoid of its own motivations while giving center stage to institutions and pressure groups. The example of France suggests that the state's agents can play an important and independent role in choosing the structures that aggregate individuals into pressure groups. Further, the state's agents often judged any institutional change by its impact on tax revenue. Consider the Parisian notaries, for example. They were essential to government borrowing under the Old Regime. It is no surprise, therefore, that they were among the most protected of all office holders in the seventeenth and eighteenth centuries. Neither their numbers nor the value of their offices changed, and they

7. See Ensminger 1997 and the references therein.

were able to avoid heavier taxes. Provincial notaries, by contrast, fared far worse at the hands of the government. In the seventeenth century, their numbers were multiplied to meet the crown's financial needs.[8] And by the early eighteenth century, they had to pay a variety of taxes on the contracts they drafted.

The Revolution dramatically reordered this equilibrium. At first it appeared that all notaries would be on same footing because after 1792 the same regulation applied to all French notaries. Yet in practice the state viewed Parisian notaries differently from their provincial counterparts. Reversing the pattern of the Old Regime, the Parisian notaries became more closely regulated than their colleagues in the provinces, who were by and large left to their own devices, with the state intervening only to reduce their numbers slowly. One might ascribe this shift to changes in the political cohesion of Parisian notaries, but that was not the case.[9] Indeed, except for a brief period during the Revolution, Parisian notaries have been a well-organized group since at least the sixteenth century.[10] In fact, to the present day, they have maintained a structure separate from that of all other French notaries. What had changed was the attitude of the state. Royal policy had favored the Parisian notaries in the eighteenth century because they placed so much government debt. When bankers took on that role after the Revolution, the Parisian notaries lost their importance as financial intermediaries for the state.

A similar argument can be made for periods of crisis. That interest groups mattered in the Revolution is hard to deny—after all, within a couple of years of the calling of the Estates General, well-defined political factions had emerged. Similarly, during the early Regency the aristocracy managed to push through a reduction in the taxes that it found most onerous.[11] Yet one should not leap to the conclusion that the course of financial crises can be explained by interest group politics. Instead, one should again focus on the interaction between an independent executive and elite parties. In both episodes the crown's opponents chose to worsen the state's finances. They did so even though they stood to lose personally in case of a state default. The reason they were willing to let the situation deteriorate was that they wanted to pressure the crown and permanently reduce its financial independence. Both these attempts proved disastrous for credit markets, as chapters 4 and 8 have detailed. But if the aristocracy failed to wrest political control from the

8. Gaston 1991.

9. There is also little evidence that provincial notaries became significantly more powerful politically.

10. Limon 1992:24–28.

11. Marion 1927, 1:65.

crown in the 1710s, in 1789 the revolutionaries succeeded. These two financial crises were thus not indicative of opposing interests that divided the French population as a whole. Rather, they were marks of the political weakness of the political actors who opposed the crown. Had they wielded more power, the links between fiscal and constitutional reform would not have been as strong. Though such an argument may appear to stray far afield from financial history, the data we collected on credit markets and on their participants prove crucial to distinguishing between the different hypotheses here.

Our approach, which combines data collection with institutional analysis, allows for comparisons absent in most other institutional economic history.[12] By taking on the unglamorous task of counting, we succeed in evaluating the importance of different institutional arrangements over time—we now know, for instance, that the fraction of Parisian loans featuring personal links fell by more than a third between 1660 and 1770. More importantly, our quantitative approach gives scholars studying the boundaries between formal and informal institutions the opportunity to make telling comparisons: would it not be interesting to know what the same statistic would be for eighteenth-century London, fifteenth-century Florence, or nineteenth-century Berlin? Systematic quantification has one further value, for it liberates us from the shackles of theories that typically require that all actors behave in identical ways. Reputational or clientele models, for instance, assume that informal channels are (economically or politically) efficient and therefore that all transactions will occur within the nexus of personal links. The data for France soundly reject such uniformity and argue instead that the goal of quantification is to discover the variety of mechanisms that permit transactions to occur.

As we noted in the introduction, the limits of our quantification derive principally from the sources we used. We do not claim to have encompassed all kinds of credit in Paris. Indeed, our sources only allow us to quantify notarized debts. We know that there was always at least one large financial network where loans were not notarized. Although we have tried as much as possible to situate notarial credit in its broader context, we have been hampered by the absence of good sources on other intermediaries. The quantitative dimensions of bankers' activities, to cite one example, are shrouded in mystery. Conclusions about any financial intermediary or any financial network depend on the context that one supplies for the analysis. That is obvious, but it is a lesson often forgotten. Take for example the ballooning of mortgage lending in the

---

12. North 1981, 1990; Greif 1994.

last half century of the Old Regime. It appears to verify George Taylor's argument that the French were overly invested in noncapitalist wealth prior to the Revolution.[13] Yet the link between our evidence and Taylor's thesis is radically weakened by the lack of any standard of comparison. Two such relevant comparisons come to mind. First, were the British any less likely to hold bonds? One doubts this because their public debt was a much larger fraction of GDP than that of the French, and mortgages were equally ubiquitous on both sides of the Channel. Second, no one has bothered to attempt to quantify the amount of capital placed in variable return investments in Old-Regime Paris. Such contracts, though not as frequent as rentes or obligation contracts, also abound in notarial archives.[14]

The rise of the Crédit Foncier provides a second example of why it is important to embed financial intermediaries in their context. In Paris, the CFF's outstanding loans grew at more than 21 percent per year between 1853 and 1869. If we ignore notarial credit, then the CFF's arrival becomes nothing short of miraculous.[15] If we include it, then Parisian mortgage lending grew at the rapid pace of 6 percent per year between 1853 and 1869. But if we go back to the peak years of borrowing under the July Monarchy, then the growth of mortgage debt falls to a more modest 4 percent per year. That was still twice as fast as the economy, but it is clear that focusing on the CFF alone exaggerates its contribution dramatically.[16]

In collecting our data, we have had to take into account the effect that the state has on the structure of financial markets. Doing so has obliged us to collect a variety of additional evidence. That was one reason why we gathered data on the social and geographic origins of borrowers and lenders, for we wanted to know whether the state's fiscal and monetary policies aimed to hurt or to benefit particular social groups. Similarly, under the Old Regime, the monarchy clearly favored the Parisian notaries over their provincial counterparts, and if one did not know better, one might believe that the surge in lending in Paris after 1730 could be explained by additional privileges that the Parisian notaries had suddenly gained. As we know, the true explanation for the boom in lending lies elsewhere: lending took off in a period of nearly complete institutional

13. Taylor 1962, 1967.

14. Quantifying real estate transactions, *sociétés* (joint stock companies), and *associations* (partnerships) would certainly complement our study by linking our findings to business dealings in general.

15. That, however, is what the standard sources tend to do, beginning with Bigo 1925 and Dupont Ferrier 1947.

16. Lévy-Leboyer and Bourguignon 1985; Allinne 1983.

stasis for notaries and their primary competitors, bankers. Explaining the boom of course requires additional evidence too, evidence that we begin to explore in chapter 6 and will pursue further in a future book.

Beyond quantification, our other key methodological decision was to rely on recent economic models of imperfect markets. That, no doubt, is more controversial. Many historians may judge it crudely anachronistic and will question the relevance of the models of imperfect markets for a period that predates most classical economics and obviously neoclassical economics too. From their perspective, the market is an improper metaphor for transactions that were driven by traditional factors such as custom, power, or clientelism.[17] Yet as we have seen, traditional factors fail to explain the historical case that we have considered. The example of Paris in fact demonstrates that markets can be powerful metaphors, provided that one does not straitjacket them into perfect loci for transactions.

To be sure, we have had to be very selective in our reliance upon theory, for, as we discuss in chapter 6, many models of behavior are underspecified, including both game-theoretical models of reputation and more sociological models of clienteles.[18] Such models have the weakness that, once the empirical pattern of transactions is known, one can always construct a game-theoretic model that will be consistent with it. On the other hand, standard models are likely to be uninformative because they are either too broad or too inflexible to deal with specific historical situations. In particular, it seems unlikely that individuals were constrained in their borrowing and lending by their clientele relationships because the credit market was remarkably broad even in the seventeenth century and would get broader still after 1720. The behavior of lenders throughout our period is in fact consistent with the argument that they were principally concerned with preserving their capital and earning interest. Though this thesis is far from novel, historians have been shy of taking advantage of its implications.[19] The financial concerns of early modern Parisians were thus not remarkably different from our own. What changed over time was the context within which they made their saving, lending, or borrowing decisions. We do not mean that the market treated every person in the same fashion or that personal connections were unimportant. Rather, we argue that phenomena such as discrimination or anonymity can be studied using the tools of economics.

17. Dessert 1984; Fontaine 1994; Hoffman 1996:47–48.

18. For a recent example, see Carruthers 1996.

19. Ehrenberg (1922) made much the same observation early in the century; Robert Forster (1960, 1971, 1980) has taken the issue up repeatedly.

Our research still leaves open the question of how individuals who were new to Paris established a connection with a notary. But it does show how important it was for any Parisian to enter into the information nexus of at least one notary.[20]

We generally emphasize the importance of reducing transaction costs for the development of markets.[21] The particular transaction costs that matter for credit markets are those that relate to the aggregation and dissemination of information. Indeed, credit involves promises, and those who offer capital today in return for promises of future repayment are concerned with weeding out bad risks as well as keeping track of their debtors' activities. Selecting partners to reduce risk or monitoring their fortunes are both informationally intensive activities. The cost of these activities clearly depends on the institutions of the credit market and on the availability of information through other channels. Thus what may appear as a form of social segmentation of credit in the seventeenth century can readily be interpreted as market interaction where identity matters because it helps resolve problems of asymmetric information. In this perspective, it is not necessary to attribute the increased lending in the eighteenth century to some passage of the Rubicon between early modern and capitalist societies. We can simply embed that evolution within a process of market development.

Similarly, one need not ascribe the lack of variation in prices to non-market lending. However tempting, the hypothesis that credit circulated through social as opposed to market channels is rejected by the evidence. Rather, in markets heavily burdened by transaction costs, parties in general (and intermediaries in particular) relied on information to discriminate among potential borrowers. This fact offers little surprise to economists who have established that in the absence of perfect information, it is difficult for financial markets to function properly.[22] Specifically, debtors who have little or no intention of repaying their loans are unlikely to withdraw their loan applications if interest rates rise. What do they care if interest rates double? They do not intend to pay either interest or capital. Prices (interest rates) therefore cannot allocate capital to borrowers with the best projects. Credit markets were priceless for good reasons.

20. Furthermore, the readiness of people in eighteenth-century France to sue for slander at the slightest offense to their reputation shows how fragile this form of information was. Their efforts to preserve their reputations are certainly consistent with the notion that it was easier to destroy one's credit than to establish it.

21. This approach dates back at least to Smith (1776) and crops up more recently in the writing of North (1981, 1990) and North and Thomas 1973.

22. Stiglitz and Weiss 1981; see "Institutional Change in the Long Run" below.

The Evolution of Financial Markets

Many scholars have attempted to find a set of necessary or sufficient conditions for capitalist development. Among the explanations that recur most often is one that focuses upon the development of a large and anonymous market for money. The historiography of financial markets is therefore tightly bound up with the historiography of capitalism. Both literatures have emphasized the period after 1850. The major exception is England, where financial capitalism is often traced back to the Glorious Revolution.[23] In both cases, our long-run approach provides a salient contrast to these received views.

First, since credit was so abundant in late-eighteenth-century Paris, arguments about the development of capitalism must be divorced both from the rise of capital markets and from industrialization. If one believes that capitalism involves large-scale credit in a depersonalized market, then capitalism has to have arisen long before the nineteenth century.[24] Similarly, scholars who equate capitalism with industrialization must accept that the growth of manufacturing need not have anything to do with long-term credit institutions.[25] Credit appears to have been a fundamental part of all European societies for ages: it can be found long before industrialization. More generally, financial markets cannot easily bear the enormous burden that economic history has placed upon them. Their role in investment has been exaggerated—even in the nineteenth century—while their social impact has been underplayed. Participating in credit markets was neither the road to ruin or to riches. Rather, it was often part of individuals' and families' strategies to sustain or increase their wealth.

On a different plane, we also argue that large-scale credit markets antedated key technological and institutional changes. On the technological side, notaries, in Paris at least, were involved in arranging large-scale transactions long before the advent of railroads or big industry.[26] If technological change is related to physical capital, it may have required the development of new financial markets, but technological change did not create credit. Further, the capital requirements of railroads or private firms in the nineteenth century were often no larger than the borrowing requirements of provincial estates or aristocratic

23. See Dickson 1967.

24. The development of long-term credit markets in England and France favored public finance and real estate, rather than manufacturing or trade.

25. See Gerschenkron 1962 and, for an exception, Lamoreaux 1994.

26. Given the early rise of large-scale public finance markets, the one area where technological change may have mattered to credit markets may be warfare. See Braudel 1966.

households, whose demand for credit was easily satisfied by Parisian notaries prior to the Revolution. The argument that the durability of industrial capital required the rise of a centralized secondary market is also suspect. Indeed, notaries offered informal and decentralized services that were not too different from the curb markets paralleling formal stock markets at the end of the nineteenth century.[27] We are not arguing that banks and stock markets played only a minor role in sustaining growth after 1850, but rather that these financial innovations improved and furthered a process that had already begun more than a century before.

The customary focus on the financial intermediaries that came to dominate after 1820 is therefore misplaced.[28] Until the nineteenth century, they simply could not compete with more "traditional" intermediaries in long-term credit. That is likely to have been true all over Europe. Again, we do not want to deny the important role of bankers either before or after the Revolution; instead, we simply want to stress that credit markets were usually segmented. To take the examples of England and France, both countries had several sets of intermediaries before large-scale banks came into being late in the nineteenth century. In England, scriveners and attorneys played much the same role as notaries in France, for they too arranged mortgages.[29] London's bankers corresponded to Paris's bankers and financiers, who cashed or issued short-term and interregional bills. Each country thus had a mortgage market and a bills market.

Because of different legal traditions and because much of the information necessary to carry out intermediation accrues historically, scholars have been willing to believe that different networks arise in different places and support very different amounts of financial activity.[30] Yet the very abundance of credit throughout France (and especially in Paris) suggests it is time to reexamine European financial history, in order to understand how capital markets functioned both during and after the preindustrial period. The reexamination will likely reveal that lending has flourished under legal traditions as different as Roman, customary, and common law and that no single legal tradition has the advantage in nurturing credit, at least before the late eighteenth century. Specific legal systems may of course have influenced the relative importance of different types of contracts or different intermediary networks, but even that more limited role needs to be established empirically.

27. Potter and Rosenthal 1997b; Davis and Cull 1994.
28. Taylor 1962, 1967; Gerschenkron 1962.
29. Anderson 1969a, 1969b; Habakkuk 1994; Miles 1981.
30. Neal 1997.

Similarly, the state has privileged one or another form of intermediation at different times, but the impact of this policy may have been muted as far as credit is concerned. The reason is that there were persistent limits to the effectiveness of the networks that mediated long-term and short-term debt. As a result, multiple networks of credit specialists were able to coexist, despite state policy. Until further quantitative evidence is collected to create a solid basis for comparison, we cannot determine how the state's financial policies or longstanding legal traditions affected the development of credit markets.

The state, of course, has long been accorded a significant role in financial development. Some scholars, like Larry Neal, view state borrowing as a driving force behind the growth of capital markets. Others, like Douglass North and Barry Weingast, put the accent on the state's role in securing property rights and deemphasize its direct effect.[31] While Neal emphasizes how the secondary market drew an increasing volume of capital into London, North and Weingast stress how representative assemblies and commitment mechanisms for the state's debt encouraged financial transactions. That all of these institutional innovations furthered financial development is beyond dispute. But the case of England alone cannot resolve whether they were necessary or sufficient conditions for the growth of capital markets. The answer requires evidence from other countries, and although Paris is not all of France, the city does give us a natural laboratory to examine these issues.

Our work on Paris in fact casts doubt on these hypotheses. The growth of lending in the eighteenth century took place without any of the institutional innovations highlighted by Neal, North, and Weingast. In Old-Regime Paris, the government did not consolidate its debt, and it defaulted repeatedly. Relatively little public debt was traded on a secondary market, and there was no representative assembly. Nonetheless, the private credit market thrived, and therefore the institutions that figure so prominently in the work of Neal, North, and Weingast cannot be necessary conditions for financial development.

They cannot be sufficient conditions either. Nineteenth-century Paris had representative assemblies and a consolidated government debt that was traded on a secondary market. Furthermore the governments of the period stood behind their debt. All the institutional innovations mentioned above were therefore in place, but the credit market failed to achieve steady growth. By themselves the institutional innovation could not guarantee financial development. The relationship between capital markets and institutional innovations is actually more complex than the

---

31. Neal 1990; North and Weingast 1989.

literature on England alone would suggest. To understand why requires a closer look at the historical role played by specific political and financial changes. It also requires that we pay close attention to the costs and benefits of institutional innovation.

The substantive financial divergence between England and France in fact occurred after the speculative bubbles of the 1720s rather than before—long after Britain had become a parliamentary monarchy. By the 1740s, the English crown marketed primarily one kind of bond—the consol—whose interest rate varied over time.[32] In France, by contrast, the monarchy decided to forego the gains associated with this sort of publicly traded, consolidated debt, in return for the benefits of issuing loans with a variety of interest rates and risk levels.[33] Britain had one debt instrument, the consol, which was publicly traded, and France had a variety of instruments, few of which were publicly traded. While offering investors a palette of bonds, the French crown frequently carried out partial defaults that cut either capital or interest in varying amounts depending on the issue that a bond was part of, the size of the holder's portfolio, and whether or not the debt had been traded after issue. And because the monarchy did not consolidate its debt, it could also offer life annuities, which were in high demand during the Old Regime. As we noted in chapter 5, the crown understood quite well that investors preferred to be able to sell their financial assets. But in its eyes, though, the value of a formal secondary market was much reduced. Its incentives to allow public trading in its most risky debt were particularly low, for trading would allow expectations about default to become public knowledge. That did not prevent the rise of several active secondary markets for short-term and long-term bonds, mediated by bankers or notaries. Compared with Britain's stock exchange, though, these markets were limited.

The different strategies of the two countries reflected different fiscal realities rather than different attitudes towards debt. Eighteenth-century France shows that even states without effective representative institutions can make abundant and long-term use of credit markets. Europe's absolutist monarchs, however, faced definite constraints on their ability to raise taxes, which in turn affected their ability to borrow. Because they had severe difficulties in raising new taxes, absolutist monarchs preferred to issue state-contingent debt to finance war. ("State contingent" here simply means that repayment of the interest and principal would

32. At issue, however, savers were often offered lotteries or discounts to make investing more attractive.

33. To be sure, a small amount of the French debt was publicly traded, but these were the safest securities that the state had to service. Others were traded but there was little publicity about prices. See Velde and Weir 1991, 1992.

depend on the future state of the monarchy's finances.) From our perspective, effective representative assemblies have few direct implications
for credit markets, but they do tend to be linked to high tax rates.[34] High
taxes in turn allow high levels of debt. In periods of political stability,
representative institutions in early modern Europe generally tried to
avoid default, because default liberated the crown from its budget constraint and hurt the representatives' pocketbooks. But in periods of political stress—in particular between the crown and the elite—representative institutions were not unduly concerned with default.

In France both the state and private parties were more active in long-
term credit after 1726 than ever before, even though the institutional
structure was largely unchanged.[35] As time passed, however, it became
clear that the financial environment was more stable after 1726 than it
had been before 1713. The monarchy kept the value of the unit of account fixed in silver until the Revolution, and its value with respect to
gold was changed only once in more than six decades.[36] Usury laws were
also left alone except in 1766. In contrast, the rise of representative
institutions in 1789 provoked the most massive financial instability that
the country had ever witnessed. Nonetheless, the revolutionaries, when
discussing monetary institutions, steadfastly refused to give up any sovereignty in monetary policy: representative institutions do not necessarily
lead to commitment. The creation of a stable system of public finance
is thus the result of a much more subtle political equilibrium than North
and Weingast suggest. Furthermore, the rise of financial markets does
not depend on a society's arriving at such a political equilibrium.

Nineteenth-century France also shows that de jure stable public finance practices do not guarantee the rapid diffusion of credit. During
this period, even though the unit of account's value remained constant in
terms of gold and silver, government debt was being paid with exacting
precision, and lenders' interests were carefully protected, individuals were
not convinced that these favorable practices would endure from one political regime to the next. In fact the public associated political instability with
the risk of financial chaos. The fear of inflation was felt far more severely
by private borrowers than by the state. Capital markets therefore remained
segmented, and bilateral transactions continued to predominate.

The development of a credit market does require that the state reduce
aggregate uncertainty—by providing a stable legal setting. That will typi-

34. Hoffman and Norberg 1994.
35. Although our series of government debt crests in the early eighteenth century, the
peaks reflect consolidations, not new borrowing by the state.
36. Marion 1926, 1:375–76.

cally involve fixing the value of the unit of account and not varying usury laws, but little else.[37] The French example also shows that changes in state behavior need not be enshrined in formal legal documents to be effective. The decline in aggregate uncertainty in the eighteenth century allowed notaries to develop their informal system, and lending grew. In contrast, government enforcement of creditors' property rights seems unimportant, at least in the early stages of financial development. Indeed, during these early stages, intermediary networks are likely to rely primarily on informal mechanisms to enforce contracts, and the growth of credit after 1730 in Paris testifies to the effectiveness of such mechanisms. The rise of a public system of information can increase the efficiency of financial markets, but it can also disrupt the functioning of informal networks of intermediaries.

Paris as a Capital

The instability of financial markets in Paris over time is mirrored by the instability in the spatial reach of the capital's intermediaries. For a given network, at least, periods in which Paris grew in importance were followed by periods in which its role declined. Because of the importance of these spatial variations, we have begun new research to better understand the position of Paris in the French credit system. Based on the data we have collected for Paris and a few provincial markets, we can offer some tentative conclusions on the city's financial relations with the rest of the country.

Initially, financial markets were segmented spatially. Networks of intermediaries were largely an urban phenomenon, and the rise of lending in Paris was part of a process of centralization that began as early as the 1740s. By centralization we mean that Paris accounted for a growing share of all lending over time. Since we lack solid information on provincial lending before 1780, we cannot say how intense this process was. But further research may allow one to quantify the extent of financial centralization under the Old Regime. Over the long run, however, the rise of Paris as a financial center is unmistakable.

On another level, the sophistication of financial markets must be in part a function of a city's wealth. Indeed, intermediaries are unlikely to make investments in information gathering unless they anticipate significant demand for their services because most of their investments will

---

37. A stable legal setting does not imply that courts have to be fair or cheap, but simply predictable.

turn out to be sunk costs. Let us consider the problem of such costs in the specific context of the notaries' business. Although some of a notary's sunk costs are requirements for exercising his legal functions, others must be assumed if he is to act as a financial intermediary. The sunk costs that every notary has to bear involve legal training, the capital costs of document preservation, and some form of crude record keeping, which are required to draw up sound legal documents and retrieve contracts in cases of litigation. If a notary becomes a financial intermediary, though, he must control his information in a wholly different way—each client must have a file that must be kept up to date.[38] Further, he must collect information on contractual activity that does not pass through his own office. Both the management of this information and its collection are largely sunk costs. For client files to have value they must be kept current, whether or not the clients are soliciting the notary's services. To be sure, if the notary is also an intermediary in the real estate market, then adding credit represents a marginal investment. But at the very least, then, the discussion of sunk costs must encompass all his intermediary activities as a whole. And for Paris, we must add yet another level of sunk costs—those involved in the organization and maintenance of the informal information network. As a result, the high degree of intermediation in Paris was the result of an organizational breakthrough that created a different information system. Yet that information system could only arise in a large urban center, where intermediaries anticipated high levels of demand for their services. The link between the anticipated demand and the intermediaries' investments in turn opens up a fascinating question, the question of the relationship between financial development and urban development. The data we have begun to collect for the nineteenth century suggest that the relationship was both rich and complex.

Cities are linked into urban networks and so are their financial systems. In this volume, we have privileged long-term credit and intermediary networks within Paris. But many inhabitants of the capital had provincial investments. As a result, they faced two different problems. First, they periodically needed to redistribute their income between the capital and the countryside to meet expenses. Second, they could decide whether to lend or borrow in more than one market.[39] The short-term market

38. Most of the nominative files have been lost, although a few survive at the National Archives. See, for instance, ANMC étude XXIII, VII, X and XV in the 1780s; and XXXI in the mid-nineteenth century.

39. Pierre Daniel Bourrée de Corberon offers a good example of this interregional arbitrage. His family was active in financial markets in Paris in the 1750s and 1760s (ANMC, XCII). In the 1750s through the 1770s, he also invested some 350,000 livres in

(which, for lack of data we have neglected) allowed individuals to consume rural incomes in Paris or to receive payments in outlying areas from their Parisian investments. The mechanisms that allowed individuals to arbitrage across regions have yet to be tracked. Yet the interregional flow of funds was essential for the rise of Parisian notaries, for it mobilized vast amounts of capital. It provided funds for the government, facilitated migration to and from Paris, and made possible the transfer of funds between the capital and the provincial estates of urban dwellers.[40]

Borrowers from the provinces rarely came to Paris to raise money. That is one sign that as far as information was concerned there were strong economies of scale related to distance. (Here, economies of scale simply means that bigger loans entailed lower informational costs—the costs of checking the provincial borrower's collateral, for example.) Yet another sign of the economies of scale in information was the stark difference between the lenders who made loans to the state and those who lent to private individuals. The notaries only reached a broad geographic range of lenders (not just Parisians but lenders in the provinces and foreign countries too) when they arranged loans for the state, for when the state borrowed, both Parisians and non-Parisians possessed the same information. With loans to private individuals, by contrast, the credit market remained local or at most regional. If a wealthy eighteenth-century farmer near Paris might invest money with his Parisian notary that was lent out to private borrowers, his counterpart in Normandy did nothing of the kind, even though he was only some one hundred kilometers further away from the capital.[41] And this situation did not change much after the Revolution.[42] If private credit became centralized in Paris, it was thus not really because the residents of the provinces did more and more of their borrowing and lending there. Rather, it was because wealth was concentrated in the city and because the increasing investment in government loans by foreign and provincial investors released more Parisian funds for private credit.

If we talk about the centralization of credit, we have to take into account all the various lending networks and situate the loans that notaries arranged beside alternative sources of funds. The Revolution either de-

Estates of Burgundy bonds via notaries in both Paris and Dijon. Finally, he appears in thirteen contracts lending some 3,300 livres in the tiny parish of Corberon, in the Baillage of Nuits St Georges (AD Côte d'Or, C 4583, 4588, 4597, 4618, 4640, 4667; and C 9838–9877; ANMC XCII 639, 640, 698).

40. For examples involving aristocrats who consumed rural income in Paris, see Dewald 1987 and Forster 1980.

41. Moriceau 1994:721–22; Moriceau and Postel-Vinay 1992:55, 255.

42. Grosskreuz 1977.

stroyed or severely damaged most financial networks. As a result, the process of financial centralization was temporarily interrupted. It eventually resumed, but not for notarial credit, which dropped off more in Paris than anywhere else. While notaries elsewhere were recovering their financial role, in Paris they gradually ceased putting together loans. They stopped being major loan brokers, even though by the 1830s the capital was gaining a growing share of other financial dealings according to all our evidence.

The result was a striking contrast with the countryside, where notaries retained their importance as loan brokers. The contrast was accentuated by the rise of the CFF, for it soon dominated mortgage lending in Paris but not in the countryside. As chapters 10 and 11 argue, the differences between the countryside and Paris can by and large be explained by the different demand structure for loans in these two areas. These different demand structures explain why "modern" credit intermediaries arose first in Paris and diffused only slowly through the countryside.

Our evidence therefore runs counter to the argument that the traditional forms of financial intermediation were less efficient than the ones which arose in the late nineteenth century. The argument rests on two assumptions. The first is that political and cultural constraints prevented the creation of banks and other "modern" financial organizations in the distant past. The second is that these "modern" intermediaries are efficient given any structure of demand or supply of credit. Plausible though they may seem, both these assumptions are hard to sustain.

The problem with the first assumption is that political and cultural constraints often had much less effect on financial intermediation than did the techniques used to accumulate, manage, and distribute information. In France, it was informational constraints that determined much of the structure of financial intermediation. Political and cultural constraints mattered, to be sure, but they were not decisive. Bankers, for example, faced fewer political and cultural constraints than notaries, but they still did not dominate the entire credit market. Indeed, in most regions they were unable to match the notaries' access to information about real estate assets. And because the lack of this information carried the risk of making loans to untrustworthy borrowers, the bankers severely restricted their long-term rural lending.

By themselves, though, information techniques will not necessarily determine which network of financial intermediaries triumphs over the others. Other factors matter, notably demand and supply conditions. Most scholars ignore them because of the second assumption above, but that is a mistake. The reason is that each society is endowed with different assets, and the assets are distributed among the society's members in different ways. Depending on how concentrated the wealth is, an information technique may turn out to be more efficient because it can be used on a larger scale. The distribution of assets will also affect who participates in credit markets and what debt contracts are used. To be sure, in some instances information constraints will be so restrictive that they will dictate the structure of financial intermediation, regardless of the society's endowments. If credit contracts are extremely expensive to arrange, for example, then bilateral transactions will prevail, and lending will be rare. On the other hand, if the cost of intermediation is low and remains so regardless of the number of transactions, then we may end up with a single universal intermediary who arranges all credit transactions, or instead credit may become fully decentralized, with agents arranging their own deals and having no need for financial intermediaries. Most societies, though, will not have information techniques that lie at these extremes, and the financial system will respond both to endowments and to the cost of information. That raises a natural question: which has more influence on the history of financial institutions, endowments or information?[43]

Institutional Change in the Long Run

The evolution of notarial credit raises questions about two different theoretical approaches that have attracted considerable attention in economic history. Both approaches give history considerable influence on institutional development and economic growth, though for rather different reasons. The first approach is path dependence. Championed by Brian Arthur, Paul David, and Douglass North, it argues that chance events have enduring effects on markets. In this approach, the institutions governing market transactions are characterized by increasing returns: the transaction cost associated with a set of institutions declines as the number of transactions increases. Further, changing these institutions involves negative externalities: individuals make sunk investments based on an institutional structure, and the value of these investments falls when change occurs.[44] In other words, once the institutions are in place, they tend to rule out other forms of market organization.

43. Davis and Gallman 1997.

44. Arthur 1989; David 1985; North 1993. Arthur emphasizes the lock-in effects of increasing returns, which may lead inferior technologies to dominate because of chance events. David followed a similar line of reasoning early on, but more recently he has emphasized that path dependence need not entail severe lock-in effects. North has argued that the network externalities associated with institutions create path dependence effects and that these can have important economic consequences.

The second approach, the economics of imperfect information, says little about history directly.[45] Nonetheless, economic historians have come to recognize the importance of institutions that deal with information asymmetries.[46] One reason to believe that history plays a role in such institutions derives from the distribution of wealth in a society. The distribution of wealth directly affects the demand for loans as well as the transaction costs of lending. As a result, specific institutions evolve in each society to cope with the contractual difficulties resulting from its wealth distribution. Since the distribution of wealth in the present reflects the distribution of wealth in the past, the specific institutions depend on the past.

In the case of financial markets the two approaches meet, because in this case path dependence is driven by the difficulty of coping with asymmetric information. After all, in financial markets, the increasing returns that are required for path dependence lie in the accumulation, storage, and distribution of information about the demand and supply of capital. And in large financial markets, profits can be made from creating a structure to manage information, since some individuals will not be fully informed. Once adopted, however, the information structure may be difficult to dislodge. The old structure will have a built-in advantage because of the information it has accumulated, and the builders of any new structure will have to acquire all that information on their own. Information will also cause the negative externalities inherent in institutional change. If financial intermediaries do not know which new information structure will prevail, then they will avoid investing in any of the new alternatives, for fear that their efforts may not be rewarded. Instead, they will prefer to stick with the existing structure because information can readily be shared among themselves and with law courts. As a result, an information structure may prevail long after it has ceased to be optimal for a society. The only real opportunity for change will come from extraordinary events, like the French Revolution, which dramatically reduce the value of intermediaries' information stocks. Such accidents level the playing field and make institutional change possible.

Although path dependence is theoretically attractive, its economic significance has yet to be demonstrated. Indeed there are few cases (if any) where initial decisions about an institution (e.g., a technical stan-

45. Hart 1995; Stiglitz and Weiss 1981; and, for an application of the issue to long-term change, Legros and Newman 1996. The role of history in the evolution of business firms, however, has received significant attention from theorists like John Sutton 1991.

46. See Temin 1991.

dard) seem to have had a significant impact on the economy.[47] Here, our evidence provides an unusually good test of the theory for two reasons: it allows us to examine the long-term impact of institutional change, and it encompasses significant breaks (the Regency and the Revolution) that open the door to institutional change.

For Paris at least, the record offers at best mixed support for the argument that institutions create significant path dependence in financial markets. Here we must make a distinction between the financial sector as a whole and particular financial networks. At the aggregate level, the case for path dependence in financial markets falters because the conditions are never met. Indeed a key condition is that the economies of scale in information be large enough that a unique set of institutions and organizations dominate. In Paris, however, there were always several networks competing to provide financial services, and lenders and borrowers were never faced with a single set of institutions. As a result, institutions did not get locked in, and intermediaries waxed and waned depending on their efficiency at providing financial services.

Some form of path dependence does seem to apply, though, within particular networks of financial intermediaries. The notaries' dominance of long-term private credit, for instance, was sandwiched between two historical accidents—historical accidents that were independent of the competition between financial intermediaries in the private credit market. The Parisian notaries began their ascent as financial intermediaries because the repeated government defaults at the end of Louis XIV's reign gave them unparalleled access to information about investors. They continued to prosper until the Revolution devalued their information stock and dramatically changed the rules of government finance. In Paris at least, the notaries were unable to adapt to the institutional legacy of the Revolution, and their business waned relative to bankers. Thus, the history of Parisian notaries underscores the importance of path dependence at the level of a particular network.

In the provinces, where notaries dominated long-term credit with little challenge until the end of the nineteenth century, path dependence may well have been even more pronounced. Evidence that supports this argument can be found in the spatial segmentation of information in rural credit markets.[48] As a result, there were clear limits to the geographical dispersion of loan portfolios and equally clear limits to the size of

47. David (1985) presents the argument; Liebowitz and Margolis (1990) demonstrate its limits.
48. Postel-Vinay 1998.

loans. Because local financial intermediaries by and large possessed local information, rural savers were offered little opportunity to invest in "modern" sectors of the economy. On the other hand, this picture of provincial credit overlooks the connections between the countryside and towns. Rural credit markets regularly drew funds from towns, which themselves were connected to larger cities. This picture also ignores the rich who served as go-betweens linking the provinces and Paris. It remains to be seen when and where these connections among different markets operated and when and where they did not.

In Europe as a whole, there were clear limits to path dependence at the aggregate level. Throughout the continent, intermediaries assisted in the exchange of capital between lenders and borrowers. Yet, save for exceptional situations, no intermediary was able to monopolize a given market. Each credit market had multiple intermediaries, because no single intermediary had enough information to serve all the possible clients. Each jurisdiction, for example, typically had a number of notaries. Furthermore, each market usually supported several kinds of financial intermediaries, each focusing on a specific form of credit—a sign of the limits to the economies of scope for financial networks. In some cases bankers competed with notaries, in others lawyers competed with merchants. Whatever the fate history imposed on a particular intermediary or group of intermediaries, alternatives always existed at the regional level. That is why a historical catastrophe could bring down a particular financial network and yet not have the drastic long-term consequences that one might expect.

Nonetheless, within each country's financial system, and more appropriately for us within regions, financial networks evolved in ways that were complex and dependent on past events. In Paris in particular, financial intermediaries sank large investments into information management, investments that were based upon a specific legal and economic environment. It appears that these investments created the conditions of path dependence: members of a network shared and accumulated information in a manner that could not easily be undermined by institutional change. In effect, the investments supported cooperation; in the language of economics, they were commitment devices. The commitment problem was serious because (as Oliver Williamson has argued in other circumstances) the intermediaries—in our case notaries—could not draw up legally enforceable contracts to share information.[49] Because of their investment in this information system, the notaries often resisted institutional change, just like other financial intermediaries.

49. Williamson 1975, 1985.

Their conservatism was warranted, as chapter 10 shows, because changes in the institutional environment destabilized their cooperative arrangements and reduced their informational advantages over their competitors.

Here it is important to know what the limits were to particular financial networks, and, within each network, what the limits were to the size of financial firms.[50] Two factors furnish the answer: government policy and private innovation. Both factors affected what service intermediaries provided and therefore how information was distributed to potential clients.

Unfortunately, neither government policy nor private innovation can easily be understood within the framework of economic theory. Most economic models of asymmetric information in fact take the information available to members of an economy as fixed. The models then attempt to structure the relationship between individuals in ways that minimize the impact of this asymmetry. The models focus on complex price schedules, rationing, and other responses, but they rarely consider investment in information.[51] The implicit assumption is an untenable one: namely, that individuals consider the information they get about potential trading partners as fixed. The assumption is untenable because individuals can make choices about the information they release or acquire. In nineteenth-century France, for example, people could choose whether to use the registers of the hypothèques to advertise their credit rating or to research the history of potential borrowers. How private innovation in information gathering and distribution affects particular trading networks is nearly uncharted in economic theory, yet empirically such phenomena were quite common.[52] Consider, for instance,

50. Those limits cannot be assumed ex-ante. Indeed, there are numerous examples (the Rothschilds in nineteenth-century France, J. P. Morgan and Company in late nineteenth and early twentieth-century America, or Drexel Burnam Lambert in the 1980s junk bond market) that show how individual firms can capture a large chunk of the market. The repeated failures of urban financial intermediaries to penetrate rural areas suggests that there were limits to scope that were not overcome until the twentieth century.

51. Yet it has long been known that these investments can have a large payoff. For an example, see how the substantive conclusion in Stiglitz and Weiss (1981) essentially vanishes when borrowers can be sorted into discrete classes, as is shown by Riley 1987.

52. Economists most often neglect this issue because, given a level of asymmetric information, one can most often devise an optimal contract (one in which all participants behave as though there was full information). The optimal contract apparently solves the economic problem because resources are efficiently allocated. Yet, because the more informed party typically earns a rent (a share of the surplus) for his information, other parties may want to invest in information. It is true that the investment in information need not lead to any change in aggregate output. It can be socially wasteful but privately profitable, because it reduces the more informed party's rent.

the rise of a new technology that demands capital, such as railroads in nineteenth-century Europe. At first, a well-established financial network with its traditional techniques (in this case notaries) cannot gather the information relevant to deciding which projects using the new technology should be funded. But the technology also creates profit opportunities for intermediaries who can properly resolve the informational gap between entrepreneurs and savers. That in part explains the rise of Paris's investment banking establishment—the so called Haute Banque. It remains to be seen whether new industries of this sort require the creation of new financial intermediaries or whether their capital needs can be met through existing financial institutions.

One might therefore interpret the French Revolution in one of two ways: first (following Marx and many others) as an event that liberated France from Old-Regime institutions, or second as a catastrophe that forced institutions to evolve in a dramatic way, a way that was not consistent with the slowly changing French economy. In the case of financial markets, it seems that the Revolution did little to liberate France, for it had a negligible impact on the institutions of rural credit markets, and it left Paris facing problems until the 1850s.

The Revolution did not signal the end to priceless markets. Efforts to rationalize institutions could not overcome the credit market's thirst for information. The ability of intermediaries to manage information depended critically on the nature of the financial assets. If information about debts was broadly available, intermediaries could easily use variation in prices to equilibrate the market. But for heterogeneous debts— and these are the ones relevant to the private credit market—prices could not do so, because each debt (each bond if you will) had to be priced separately. To base debt transactions on prices, private credit markets would have required huge amounts of information. The alternative was for private debt markets to rely directly on information to discriminate among potential borrowers. Intermediaries focused their efforts on acquiring information about borrowers and made little effort to vary interest rates to reflect either a borrower's specific risk or aggregate credit conditions. Potential borrowers therefore competed on the basis of their collateral and reputation rather than on the expected value of their projects. Though one may bemoan the loss of efficiency entailed by such markets, the huge amounts of capital that notarial credit mobilized made these markets positively priceless.

Appendix 1:
A Model of Debt Repayment
under Temporary Inflation

AFTER THE BOUTS of inflation in 1719–20 and 1790–95, the state had to decide how to stabilize the currency and how outstanding debt contracts would be valued—in particular, private contracts signed before and during the inflation. The state's decision had obvious consequences for financial portfolios. Furthermore, expectations of when and how the stabilization might be carried out were central factors in the process of reimbursement that we analyze in chapters 4 and 8.

History suggests three possible transition schemes when a state decides to stabilize its currency after an episode of inflation:

1. The state could ignore the inflation and value all old currency contracts at the pre-inflation value. That was the policy of the 1720s.
2. The state could index contracts by the "real" or gold value of the old currency when the contracts were signed. That was the policy in 1796.
3. Finally, the state could choose the terminal value of the old currency to value all old currency contracts. That is the modern policy.

Because different transition rules might be employed, private actors faced uncertainty about both when and what stabilization might bring.

Since the transition rules had a profound impact on the value of credit contracts, debtors and creditors had to adjust their financial positions to reflect their changing expectations about the likelihood of and structure of stabilization. We used the historical policies to construct a simple model describing the behavior of debtors during the inflation. Our simple two-period model allows us to derive the comparative statics results that matter for our substantive analysis.

We consider first a single borrower who has a debt of N units of account. Assume that there are two periods, with period 1 lasting from time 0 to time 1, and period 2 from time 1 to 2. At time 0, there is an unexpected change in the unit of account, which is devalued by inflation to a level d_1 by time 1 ($0 < d_1 < 1$). At time *1*, the borrower can either repay his debt at a real cost of $Nd_1 + c$ (c here is a transaction cost required to bring the funds to his creditor who is not eager to be reimbursed), or he can simply service the loan.[1] Between time 1 and time 2 the government decides with probability p to stabilize the currency. If no stabilization occurs, inflation will diminish the value of the currency by an additional fraction d_2 ($0 < d_2 < 1$). If the government does stabilize the currency, it will also chose a rule that values the borrower's debt contract at historical cost N.[2] If no stabilization occurs (probability $1 - p$), the debt will be worth $Nd_1 d_2$. For simplicity and without loss of generality we assume that the borrower must pay off the debt at time 2 and that he need not pay the transaction cost c, because the lender has no reason to object to repayment or no way to delay it. The borrower has a discount rate of δ. It follows immediately that borrowers employ the following rule:

if $N[(-d_1 + \delta(d_1 d_2) + p\delta(1 - d_1 d_2)] \geq c$, the debt is repaid in time 1

if $N[(-d_1 + \delta(d_1 d_2) + p\delta(1 - d_1 d_2)] < c$, the debt is carried to time 2.

Notice that $[(-d_1 + \delta(d_1 d_2) + p\delta(1 - d_1 d_2)]$ is decreasing in d_1 and increasing in d_2 and p. Thus, if the depreciation of the currency (d_1) has gone far enough by time 1, the borrower will repay, otherwise he will carry the debt forward and repay at time 2.

The existence of a deterministic rule in the two-period borrower model implies that the solution to the multi-period problem will also feature a threshold depreciation beyond which the borrower repays.

---

1. The fixed cost of repaying debt contracts during the inflation can be justified because borrowers had to carry out an "offre" procedure. A quasi-judicial proceeding, the offre allowed a borrower to reimburse a recalcitrant creditor or his agent. The offre required the intervention of a notary, and its cost did not really depend on contract size. If repayment costs had been proportional to loan size, there would be no variation in time repayment rates by size of contract.

2. In a two-period setting the historical and nominal value of debts is the same, so there is no difference between the 1720s rule and that enacted during the Revolution. Private debts contracted before the inflation began dominated the debt stock at all times. For those debts the two rules are the same, so we neglect the vintage effects that would come about by having more than two periods of inflation. We also neglect the case where the government chooses the modern rule, since the debtor has no incentive to pay his debts off early.

Thus the dynamic problem is an analogue to the two-period problem where, given an inflation or depreciation schedule and a probability of stability of transition, the optimal time to repay is decided by the depreciation that has already occurred. It is easy to show by induction that the same comparative statics results will apply in such a dynamic setting.

The model can be extended to incorporate borrowers who may face liquidity constraints. This more complex case features a borrower with a fixed real (and thereby growing nominal) income to devote to debt service. His income initially may be too small to allow him to repay his debt. In that case, he will repay at a time equal to the larger of (1) the time he would take in the unconstrained repayment decision and (2) the time when depreciation has raised his nominal income enough to allow him to reimburse his debts.[3] Adding this feature to the model suggests that changes in repayment rates will undercount the number of people who would like to repay their debts, particularly in the early stages of inflation.

Three comparative statics results from the simple borrower model are of relevance to the economic analysis of the French Revolution:

1. Given d_1, d_2, p, c, there exist a threshold loan size N such that only contracts at least as large as N will be repaid. (N increases with d_1 and c, and decreases with d_2 and p.)
2. Increasing the probability of stabilization (p) increases the probability the borrower will repay his contract at time 1.
3. An increase in the expected devaluation in period 2 (a fall in d_2) decreases the likelihood that the borrower repays at time 1.

The second and third comparative statics results argue that debtors' expectations of stabilization are crucial in determining the optimal time to repay: expectations of accelerating or persistent inflation diminish the incentives to repay. If a monetary system is likely to endure, debtors will delay repayment regardless of the inflation rate—assuming of course that they can chose whether or not to reimburse their creditors. Empirically, this suggests that the repayment rate of rentes was correlated with increases in the expectation of a monetary transition that would "revalue" nominal contracts downward.

---

3. One might imagine that individuals could borrow to repay their debts—an attractive option given the transition rule adopted in 1797—but in our case the decline in lending limited that option.

Appendix 2:
Equilibria for the Second
Sourcing Game

WE CAN DESCRIBE actions in each period via a triplet *(A, B, C)*. Here $A = 1, 2$ identifies the broker whom the client hires. $B = 0$ (1) if the broker offers low- (high-) quality service. $C = 0$ (1) if the broker does not share (shares) information. The incumbent broker (broker 1) has a strategic choice over quality, and the alternative broker (broker 2) does not.

We can summarize the information situation at the beginning of any period with a pair (i_1, i_2) where i_j is 1 if broker j is informed or 0 if he is uninformed (while strategies may depend on history, payoffs in each period do not). The period payoffs are sketched in table A2.1, with the payoffs of the incumbent broker first, those of the other broker next, and the payoff of the client last. Given the information, there are five possible outcomes corresponding to the five rows of table A2.1.

In a repeated game, a strategy for the client is simply a probability of choosing a broker, a probability that depends on all past moves in the game. A strategy for the chosen broker is a function that maps the past and the client's action into probabilities of sharing information and providing high-quality service. An important part of the history of the game involves how much information has been shared. In a repeated game, we must face the fact that information decays: A broker has less information at time $t + i$ than at time t unless he receives new information. To simplify the analysis, we examine a simple information structure where brokers are either informed or uniformed, and the cost of informing an uninformed broker is $(F - f)$. However, we do allow brokers to share information: an informed broker can reliably share his knowledge with another broker in a cross-clientele deal.

TABLE A2.1   PAYOFFS TO THE THREE TYPES OF STAGE GAMES

	Information								
	(0, 0)			(1, 0)			(1, 1)		
	Broker	Broker	Client	Broker	Broker	Client	Broker	Broker	Client
(1, 1, 1)	$\pi^h - e$	0	$R^h - F$	$\pi^h - e$	0	$R^h - f$	$\pi^h - e$	0	$R^h - f$
(1, 1, 0)	π^h	0	$R^h - F$	π^h	0	$R^h - f$	π^h	0	$R^h - f$
(1, 0, 0)	π^l	0	$R^l - F$	π^l	0	$R^l - f$	π^l	0	$R^l - f$
(2, 1, 1)	0	$\pi^h - e$	$R^h - F - s$	0	$\pi^h - e$	$R^h - F - s$	0	$\pi^h - e$	$R^h - f - s$
(2, 1, 0)	0	π^h	$R^h - F - s$	0	π^h	$R^h - F - s$	0	π^h	$R^h - f - s$

In the repeated game, histories at time t involve five vectors, Q_{1t}, Q_{2t}, K_{1t}, K_{2t}, and Z_t. Here $Q_{1t} = (q_{i1}, \ldots, q_{it-1})$ is defined as follows ($i = 1, 2$):

$q_{ij} = 0$ if broker i was not hired in period j of the repeated game,
$q_{ij} = 1$ if broker i was hired in period j and offered low-quality service, and
$q_{ij} = h$ if broker i was hired in period j and offered high-quality service.

$K_{1t} = (k_{i1}, \ldots, k_{it-1})$, where k_{ij} is the number of periods for which broker i's information in period j would last provided he receives no information. If $k_{ij} < 0$, the broker is informed at time j; if it is 0, he is uninformed. $Z_t = (z_1, \ldots, z_{t-1})$, where z_i is 1 if information was shared in period i and 0 otherwise.

For the sake of simplicity, we limit ourselves to the cases where information decays in either one or two periods. Extending the model to more than two periods is straightforward but provides little further insight.[1] Let us begin with the case where information decays quickly: a broker is uninformed if he has not interacted with his client in the previous period or received information in the previous period. It is easy to show that provided $F - f$ is large enough, in the resulting equilibrium clients never switch and only low-quality service is provided.[2]

Now let us turn to the more interesting case of two-period information decay. Assume further that both brokers are informed at the outset. We consider only the extreme types of equilibria (the ones that lead to the minimum and maximum social payoffs). The Folk theorem shows that there exist equilibria such that any payoff in between these two can be attained.

To find the socially inefficient equilibria we assume that incumbent brokers follow a strategy of only providing low-quality service and transmitting no information. Then clients must decide whether or not they want to switch among brokers. Two cases arise.

First, if $R^h - R^l \leq s$, then there exists a Nash equilibrium where the

---

1. It is easy to show that slower information decay processes lead to equilibria that are qualitatively similar to those obtained with the two-period information decay process.

2. Suppose neither broker is informed at the beginning of play. It then pays for a client to inform a broker ($R^l - F < 0$), but the broker has no incentive to share and it never pays for the client to change brokers ($R^l - f < R^h - F - s$). If both brokers are informed, the client still picks one and gets locked in. If only one broker is informed, the client will interact with him alone. The point is that the client is the prisoner of the first broker he interacts with, because information decays too quickly to allow for switching at low cost. Since the client cannot credibly threaten to switch, he cannot force the first broker he hires to share information.

client switches every period, he receives high-quality service, and he carries out the task of keeping the alternative broker informed. Brokers in this case are passive. If the client should deviate from the equilibrium strategy and rehire the incumbent, then it would pay for the incumbent to provide low-quality service because he would know the client would not want to switch in the next period $(1 + 1/r)(R^h - R^l - s) < F$.

Second, if $(R^h - R^l) < s$, then the client will not switch on his own. So if the brokers each have a strategy of providing low-quality service and offering no referrals, then the client's best response is to accept whatever service the incumbent notary offers. This equilibrium features brokers who never share information and provide low-quality service and clients who are perfectly loyal.

The social optimum occurs when clients use a dismal strategy: they abandon their broker permanently whenever he has not provided high-quality service or transmitted information in the previous period; otherwise, they continue to rehire him. Provided r is small enough, the incumbent broker's best response is to provide high-quality service and share information. The reason is that if the broker provides low-quality service the client will desert him and he will lose π^h in per period profits forever. The loss is greater than the difference in profits in the short term $[(\pi^h - e)/r\pi^l]$. The broker's best strategy is to provide high-quality service and transmit information. The client's strategy is an optimal response, yielding a Nash equilibrium.

Appendix 3:
The Outstanding Debt Series
in Periods of Crisis

The Law Affair

For our analysis of the Law affair, we realized that using variation in the quittance rates for rente contracts signed during the period would underestimate the rate of repayments. The problem was particularly acute for contracts signed in the three crisis years of 1718, 1719, and 1720. Because the nominal volume of lending was extremely high, errors for those three years had potentially significant (and long-lasting) effects on the outstanding debt series. We therefore made two corrections based on the information that we collected.

First, we corrected for the fall in the real value of debt contracts. As table A3.1 shows, interest rates were falling rapidly during those three years; a rente contract signed in 1720 thus had a low value in 1727 after the legal interest rate had returned to 5 percent. For ease of comparison we therefore deflated volumes of rentes by the ratio of the mean interest rate charged to 5 percent. This gives debts capitalized with a 5 percent rate of return.

Repayment rates during this period were extremely high and varied depending upon when the rente had originally been signed. For instance, some 74 percent of rente contracts signed in 1718 contained a marginal indication that they had been repaid by the end of December 1720, but only 7 percent of the rentes from 1720 had been repaid by the end of the year. We therefore needed to adjust the repayment rate depending on the vintage of the contracts. We followed a simple procedure. For debts dating to before 1718, we used the quittance rate to obtain a repayment rate in the fashion detailed in chapter 2 (here the

TABLE A3.1   INTEREST AND REPAYMENT RATES FOR LOAN CONTRACTS SIGNED
DURING THE LAW AFFAIR

	Vintage of Loan Contract		
	1718	1719	1720
Interest rate (average weighted by loan size in percent)	4.75	4	3
Share of vintage repaid in 1718 (percent)	40		
Share of vintage repaid in 1719 (percent)	7.2	15	
Share of vintage repaid in 1720 (percent)	37	29	7
Share of outstanding at beginning of 1721 (percent)	26	56	93

Source: A sample of twenty percent of the loan contracts and quittances drawn up in études XXVII, XLIII, LXII, LXX, LXXVIII, CXI, and CXV in 1718–20.

quittance rate varies relative to the average of 1706 through 1710).[1] For debts from 1718 to 1720, we used the rate of repayment obtained from the marginal annotation made by notaries in the original contract when it was repaid (see table A3.1). Although these annotations are abundant, there was no legal requirement that all repayments be made this way, so we obviously understate the rate of repayment of these contracts.[2] Yet despite this obvious bias, we arrive at a drop of 40 percent in the outstanding debts—enough to demonstrate that the Law Affair had a considerable effect on private markets (table A3.2).

The Revolution

During the Revolution, we faced a problem that was different from that of the Law Affair. Here the difficulty was the difference between the repayment of obligations and rentes. Two different factors are likely to have created difference in the rate of repayments of rentes and obligations. First, with an average duration of five years, nearly all the obligations outstanding in 1789 would have come due by 1794.[3] And because

1. Variations in the base repayment rate have a small impact on the resulting outstanding debts provided that one uses a base which stops short of 1714. After then quittance rates are quite volatile and high so that including them in the base would lead to a lower rate of repayment during the Regency and in particular during the Law affair.

2. One could gain further precision by matching quittance contracts to original contracts. Such matching, though, would require a complete enumeration of all contracts, an enormous task that did not appear warranted.

3. While half the obligations drawn up in 1789 would have come due by 1794, a far greater proportion of the obligations from 1788 or before would have matured by then.

TABLE A3.2 OUTSTANDING DEBT AND DEBT REPAYMENT DURING THE LAW AFFAIR
(DEBT CONTRACTED BEFORE 1718, MILLIONS OF LIVRES)

Year and Quarter	Repayment of Debt s from before 1718	Outstanding Debt by Loan Vintage				
		Pre–1718	1718	1719	1720	Total
1717, fourth qtr.		162				162
1718, first qtr.	3.62	158	3.62			162
1718, second qtr.	4.85	154	8.35			162
1718, third qtr.	6.77	147	16.12			163
1718, fourth qtr.	5.39	141	20.69			162
1719, first qtr.	8.43	133	19.00	12.03		164
1719, second qtr.	9.58	123	18.40	24.47		166
1719, third qtr.	9.14	114	17.30	33.19		165
1719, fourth qtr.	12.57	102	16.30	41.76		160
1720, first qtr.	16.76	85	13.40	37.59	11.74	148
1720, second qtr.	21.26	64	11.00	33.83	19.29	134
1720, third qtr.	18.09	46	8.98	30.45	25.98	114
1720, fourth qtr.	7.43	38	7.37	27.40	28.77	102

Source: As in Table A3.1.

Note: For the vintages prior to 1718 the repayment rates are estimated in the manner described in chapter 3. For 1718, 1719, 1720, repayment rates are given in table A3.1.

rentes were repayable at the discretion of the borrowers, few were repaid early in the inflation, because the borrowers were waiting for the inflation to devalue their debts.

We have computed the outstanding debt for each type of contract (rentes and obligations) by adding new loans and removing contracts that are repaid. Rather than focusing on the value of the contracts in calculating repayments, we have concentrated instead on the number of contracts in a two-step approach. The first step was to rely on our counts and our samples to estimate the number of quittances by quarter for each type of loan contract. The second step was to estimate the relationship between the quittances (recall that they are simply reimbursements where a notarized contract was drawn up) and total repayments, which would include both reimbursements with a notarized contract and reimbursements without such a contract.

For the first step, the number of quittances for each type of contract came from the detailed samples we drew for the Revolutionary period. Between 1790 and 1795, 22 percent of the quittances were rente quittances and 9 percent were obligation quittances. The samples allowed us to establish the relative importance of rente and obligation quittances for each quarter year.

The second step involved estimating the number of rentes and obligations whose repayment gave rise to a quittance. We began by establishing a benchmark using 1787 as a basis. The standard procedure we used to compute outstanding debts gave us total number of repayments by type of contract in 1787. We then compared those figures with the total number of quittances for each type of contract, which we estimated from a sample of quittance contracts drawn up in 1787. In that year, we calculated that some 2,563 rentes and 4,798 obligations were paid off. There were also 4,592 quittances, of which 12 percent were rentes and 10.5 percent obligations. Therefore, only one in four rente repayments led to a quittance and only one in eight obligation repayments led to a quittance.

Had this relationship between quittances and repayments remained stable, we could have simply multiplied the number of rente quittances by four and obligation quittances by eight to arrive at repayments during the Revolution. In that case, our estimate of rente repayments R_r in a given quarter would be $R_r = Q^*p_r/p_{qr}$ where Q is the total number of quittances observed in the quarter, p_r is the proportion of the quittances that are rente quittances, and p_{qr} is the proportion of rente repayments where quittances are drawn up.

It appears, however, that there was a dramatic shift in the propensity to draw up quittances during the Revolution. We in fact estimate that some 102,500 quittances were drawn up during the Revolution, of which 22,500 were for perpetual annuities and 9,225 were for obligations. Further, if we take into account the fact that many debt contracts were repaid without drawing up quittances, we can estimate that during the Revolution there were 105,000 repayments of rentes perpétuelles and 90,900 repayments of obligations. But if we take the number of rentes outstanding in January 1790 and add the number of rentes contracted during the Revolution, it only amounts to 48,000 contracts, and the corresponding figure for obligations is only 55,000. Clearly, the ratio of quittances to repayments rose at some point, and although we would like to have accurate estimates of how it changed for each type of loan contract, the necessary data do not exist.

The evidence does show that little debt contracted prior to the Revolution was outstanding after 1797. For the rentes, we therefore assumed that the propensity to draw up quittances doubled so that half of the rente repayments gave rise to quittances.[4] Our assumption is consistent with the view that during the inflation relations between debtors and creditors worsened, making formal contracts necessary when debtors

---

4. That figure is the largest possible one; making it any bigger would make indebtedness negative between 1789 and 1796. We did not let this figure vary because we wanted to limit the influence of this conjecture on the time path of repayments.

TABLE A3.3   DEBT REPAYMENT BY TYPE OF CONTRACT DURING THE REVOLUTION

Year and Half Year	Total Quittances in Paris Derived from Taxes	Numbers of Quittances from Detailed Sample		
		Total	Rentes	Obligations
1790.1	2,016	39	14	6
1790.2	1,776	0	19	6
1791.1	8,490	246	46	21
1791.2	10,404	52	12	7
1792.1	11,270	261	50	29
1792.2	6,640	175	23	10
1793.1	8,860	271	65	25
1793.2	7,950	370	101	36
1794.1	6,842	164	30	12
1794.2	7,374	192	29	7
1795.1	14,235	626	249	75
1795.2	13,091	621	108	51
TOTAL	95,162	3093	746	265

Source: A 12 percent sample of loan contracts and quittances from the études IX, XXI, XXVII, XLIII, LXII, LXX, LXXVIII, CXI, CXV, CXVII.

forced creditors to accept repayment in depreciated currency. For obligations, by contrast, the request for a prompt reimbursement did not necessarily lead to drawing up of quittance contracts. We therefore let the propensity to have a quittance drawn up for an obligation repayment increase slowly from one repayment in eight to one in four. Our assumption reflected the fact that obligations became the dominant debt contract after 1789. We also adjusted this propensity in 1795 to prevent the stocks of obligation from turning negative. In all cases, we sought to minimize the impact that our conjectures about the ratio of repayments to quittances would have on the time path of repayments.

Appendix 4:
Distribution of Loan Durations for Nineteenth-Century Obligations

The outstanding debt series after 1797 requires an estimate of the realized duration of obligations. By realized duration, we mean the actual duration of the obligations, which takes into account the possibility that they might be renewed by renegotiation of the loan or by the prorogation contract described in chapter 9. Because we do not have these realized durations for each year's worth of obligations, we cannot compute outstanding debt directly. Worse yet, the duration of obligations varied considerably in the nineteenth century, and that meant we could not simply use periodic samples to get durations, as we had in the eighteenth century. Finally, because debt as a whole had a much shorter maturity after 1797, renegotiation and prorogation could have a much bigger effect on outstanding debt estimates than was the case in the eighteenth century.

What we chose to do was first to estimate the initial durations of obligations and then to account for the rate of prorogation and renegotiation, which would have prolonged the obligations. (Here initial duration means the duration when the loan contract was first drawn up.) We began with initial durations that we extracted from prorogation and loan transfer contracts. For many of these contracts, entries in the chronological indexes revealed how long the original debt had been outstanding. On the basis of information we had about initial durations, we assumed that loans outstanding more than ten years had in fact already been prolonged via a prorogation. We therefore eliminated such loans from our calculation of initial durations. We then took the remaining loans and calculated three-year moving averages of their initial durations in order to reduce the volatility inherent in small samples. The resulting distribution of initial durations is given in the table A4.1.

TABLE A4.1   INITIAL DURATIONS FOR OBLIGATIONS BY YEAR, 1800–60

Initial Duration (Years)	Percent of Obligations Drafted in				
	1800	1815	1830	1845	1860
1	0.35	0.10	0.01	0.02	0.02
2	0.12	0.21	0.15	0.04	0.07
3	0.24	0.21	0.19	0.17	0.14
4	0.06	0.14	0.20	0.12	0.14
5	0.06	0.14	0.10	0.18	0.18
6	0.06	0.09	0.13	0.09	0.08
7	0.06	0.04	0.06	0.07	0.05
8	0.00	0.03	0.07	0.09	0.11
9	0.06	0.01	0.05	0.08	0.10
10	0.00	0.02	0.05	0.12	0.11

Source: Notaries' indexes for études IX, XXI, XXVII, XLIII, LXII, LXX, LXXVIII, CXI, CXV, and CXVII.
Note: The distribution of durations is estimated using a three-year average centered on the year of interest. The distribution for 1800, for instance, includes the durations observed for 1799 and 1801.

We then had to account for effects of renegotiating loan durations. Renegotiation became so common in the nineteenth century that it became the subject of a special contract, the prorogation. After 1815, there were in fact about one third as many prorogations as new debt contracts. Usually, a prorogation extended credit contracts by three years.[1]

To correct for the effect of the prorogation, we estimated the distribution of initial durations for each year. These initial duration profiles allowed us to determine what debts came due in what year and how long they had been outstanding. To do the estimates, we first deducted the number of prorogations in a year from the number of loan contracts that would have been repaid in that year had it not been for the prorogations. The difference gave us net repayments.[2] We then estimated new due dates for the contracts that were renegotiated via prorogations, under the assumption that prorogation repeated the original duration. We continued the process, allowing contracts to be extended several times. For instance, in the first three months of 1830, some 1,137 obligation contracts came due. These obligations had initially been signed between 1809 and 1829. There were 306 prorogations in the same period,

1. Using a sample of 144 contracts that gave us both the time a debt had been outstanding and its new duration, we found that the renegotiated durations rose with the length of time a debt had been outstanding. For simplicity, though, we decided that loans were extended by the average initial duration for debts of the same vintage.

2. In any given year, loans of different vintages come due, and we assume that the fraction of each that is renewed in that year is the same for all vintages.

which implied that 27 percent (306/1137) of existing contracts would be renewed in this period, while 73 percent would be repaid. Among the contracts renewed was one initially issued in 1810, which was extended in 1830 for the last time. Similarly, some 47 contracts initially signed in 1827 were extended, with the last one repaid in the early 1850s.[3]

3. The procedure is a matter of estimation, and the illustration in the text should not be taken literally. We do not know whether or not a given contract issued in 1810 was still outstanding in 1830, but our calculations suggest that such a thing was likely. The value of our procedure is that it leads to realized durations for obligations which are close to what the quittances suggest.

Archival Sources

Chronological Counts

We followed ten études from 1660 to 1869, and two more for intervening periods. These were the études for which we counted numbers of loans and repayments and estimated loan sizes and durations. The records presented gaps and other problems which we describe here étude by étude:

Etude IX. Dates: 1660–July 1864. Government quittances: 1698–21, 1760–96. Size of contracts: 1826–64.

Etude XXI. Dates: 1662–Nov 1705, June 1722–1869. Government quittances: 1669–79, 1698–1705, 1760–96. Size of contracts: 1826–60.

Etude XXVII. Dates: Aug 1695–August 1867. Government quittances: 1698–1721, 1760–96. Size of contracts: 1809–10, 1820–21, 1826–67.

Etude XLIII. Dates: 1664, Sept 1685–Dec 1819, Oct 1824–1869. Government quittances: 1698–1721, 1760–96. Size of contracts: 1826–69.

Etude XLIX. Dates: 1660–Mar 1679, Sept 1685–Feb 1694. Government quittances: None. Size of contracts: None.

Etude LXII. Dates: 1660–April 1670, Sept 1670–Oct 1686, Jan 1687–Sept 1864, July 1868–1869. Government quittances: 1698–1721, 1760–96. Size of contracts: 1826–69.

Etude LXX. Dates: 1660–Feb 1662, June 1683–1690, Feb 1692–Mar 1794, Sept 1794–1869. Government quittances: 1698–1721, 1760–96. Size of contracts: 1826–69.

Etude LXXII. Dates: 1660–87 government Quittances: None. Size of contracts: None.

Etude LXXVIII. Dates: 1660–61, 1667–1869. Government quittances: 1698–1721, 1760–96. Size of contracts: 1816–24, 1826–69.

Etude CXI. Dates: 1661–May 1685, Aug 1694–Mar 1794, Oct 1794–1869. Government quittances: 1698–1731, 1748–96. Size of contracts: 1799–1869.

Etude CXV. Dates: 1660–1869. Government quittances: 1698–1721, 1760–96. Size of contracts: 1822, 1824, 1826–69. Second Notary: 1746–67.

Etude CXVII. Dates: 1660–Sept 1666, Jan 1670–Aug 1677, June 1678–1869. Government quittances: 1698–1721, 1760–96. Size of contracts: 1822, 1824, 1826–69. Second Notary: 1660–Feb 1744.

In the above list, "Dates" refer to the periods for which we counted loans and repayments in the étude's répertoire. In the early stages of our research, we did not distinguish government debt quittances from private quittances. The "Government Quittances" therefore indicate the years for which we made this distinction; in the other years, private and government quittances were lumped together.

The "Size of Contracts" give the years when we gathered evidence about loan sizes not from samples of notarial records but from the étude indexes. We did not collect this sort of evidence systematically before 1826, even though some of the indexes listed loan sizes as early as 1800. Finally, if there is a "Second Notary," it tells when there were two notaries associated with the étude. That would happen when one notary owned the business and the other the office associated with the étude.

Detailed Samples

The detailed samples of loans described in chapter 3 began with a reading of loans from the minutes of études IX, XXI, XLIII, LXII, LXX, LXXVIII, and CXV. Our initial plan was to read all the surviving loans in the minutes of each étude roughly every forty years, beginning in 1700 and ending in about 1840. As our work progressed, we deviated a bit from this plan. First of all, the time involved and the unavailability of certain minutes forced us to eliminate some years or parts of years for certain études. We also realized that we had to make time for further detailed sampling beyond the forty year cross sections. We had to push the detailed samples back to include loans from 1690 and 1662, and we also wanted to add small detailed samples at roughly ten year intervals and during selected years in the 1750s and 1760s. Finally, because the delivery of bundles of notarial minutes *(liasses)* was slow, we made it a policy to read all the loan documents in a liasse once it was ordered. That policy gave us some additional years beyond those we had selected, because a given liasse might spill over into the preceding or following year, or the liasse we wanted might be tied together with a subsequent liasse from the same étude.

For the earliest year of our detailed samples (1662), a few liasses were unavailable, but we read all those which could be consulted: Etude IX, 427 (January through September); XXI, 181 and 182 (January through November); XLIII, 103 through 106 (entire year); LXII, 186 and 187 (entire year); LXX, 172 (January and February); LXXVIII, 292 and 293 (January through September); CXV, 156 through 159 and 199 (entire year).

For the detailed samples for the years from 1690 on, our data files do not indicate the liasse's entire call number *(cote)*, but they do give the number of the étude plus the months and years for which we collected data on loans. That is enough to allow other researchers to get the loan documents we used and replicate our samples. For each étude, we therefore list below the months and years for which we gathered detailed data on loans. In some instances, we actually read the minutes for additional months but found no loan contracts. If, on the following list, a year is given without any months, it means we read the entire year's worth of minutes for that étude:

Etude IX: 1690 (January); 1700 (all months but February); 1710 (January and February); 1730 (January through May); 1740; 1750 (January through March); 1760 (all but April and September); 1761; 1770; 1780 (all but June and November); 1799 (November and December); 1800 (January); 1809 (December); 1810 (January); 1820 (January); 1830 (February); 1840 (all but November and March).

Etude XXI: 1690; 1700 (all but February, June, and August); 1730 (February, March, April, and June); 1740 (all but November); 1750 (January through March); 1760 (all but January, February, and October); 1761 (all but February, March, and June); 1766 (all but July); 1770; 1780 (all but March through June); 1781 (March through August); 1799 (December); 1800 (January); 1807 (all but October); 1810 (January through March); 1820 (January); 1830 (January through March); 1840 (all but January, August, and October).

Etude XLIII: 1700 (January through August); 1740 (all but April); 1780; 1807; 1840.

Etude LXII: 1690; 1700 (all but February); 1740; 1780 (all but May); 1800 (January through March); 1807 (all but October and December); 1810 (January through April); 1820 (January through March); 1830 (January and February); 1840 (all but February, August, and December).

Etude LXX: 1690 (January and February); 1700 (April through December); 1710 (January through April, June); 1720 (January and February); 1730; 1740 (all but August); 1750 (January through June); 1751; 1752; 1753; 1754; 1755; 1756; 1757; 1758; 1759; 1760 (all but December); 1761 (all but February and April); 1770 (January and February); 1780 (January through August, October); 1788 (January through June); 1799 (October through December); 1810 (January); 1820 (January); 1830 (January); 1840 (all but January).

Etude LXXVIII: 1690 (January); 1700 (January through September); 1730 (January through March); 1740 ; 1750 (January); 1760 (January); 1761 (all but June); 1762 (January through August, October); 1766 (all but September and December); 1770; 1780 (all but November); 1790 (January); 1800 (January); 1807 (all but December); 1810 (January and February); 1820 (January through March); 1830 (January through March); 1840 (all but March, May, and November).

Etude CXV: 1700 (all but October and December); 1710 (January through March); 1720 (January); 1730 (January through March); 1740 (January through August); 1751; 1752 (September–December liasse is missing); 1753; 1754; 1755; 1756; 1757; 1758; 1759; 1760; 1761; 1770 (January and February); 1780 (January and February); 1788 (January and February); 1799 (September through November); 1807 (all but September); 1809 (November and December); 1810 (January through March); 1820

(January and February); 1830 (January through April); 1840 (February through June, August through October).

The detailed sample of minutes had two major gaps: the Law affair and the Revolution. For that reason, we undertook additional detailed sampling for the years 1718–20 and 1790–96. For 1718–20, we sampled every fifth liasse from eight of our ten études: IX 608, 614; XXI 112, 117, 122, 127, 131; XLIII 309, 314; LXII 312, 317, 322; LXX 258, 263; LXXVIII 585, 590, 295, 600, 605; CXI 90, 95, 100, 105, 110, 115, 120, 125; CXV 375, 380, 386, 390.

For 1790–96, we collected additional detailed data from études: IX 844; XXI 571, 573, 574, 583, 584, 589, 590, 592, 593, 594, 595, 606, 607, 610, 612; XXVII 502, 503, 505, 506, 507, 518, 527, 529, 531, 534, 535, 536, 537, 541, 542, 543; XLIII 578, 579, 582, 587, 588; LXII 656, 658, 659, 660, 661, 691, 694, 695, 696, 697, 699, 703, 704, 717, 718, 719, 720, 723, 724; LXVIII 636; LXX 588, 589, 590, 591, 592, 599, 600, 603, 604, 605, 611, 612, 613, 614, 615, 616; LXXVIII, 952, 953, 958, 962, 963, 972, 975, 976, 977, 982, 983, 985, 989, 998, 999, 1001, 1002, 1003; CXI 387, 388, 389, 390, 391, 397, 400, 402, 407, 408, 409, 410; CXV 959, 965, 966, 967, 968, 969, 970, 996, 997, 1000, 1003, 1005 1006, 1008, 1014, 1015, 1018, 1019, 1021, 1022, 1023; CXVII 946, 947, 949, 950, 951, 952, 953, 958, 959, 961, 963, 964, 965, 967, 970, 971, 975, 973, 976, 977.

Finally we also sampled loans sizes and durations in the following years and études:

In 1665–1666, from études IX, XXI, LXII, LXXVIII.

In 1670, from IX 440, 44; XXVII; LXII 203; LXXVIII 281, 314; CXVII 75, 76, 77, 78.

In 1682, from IX 471, 472, 473, 474; LXII 225, 226, 227; LXVIII 372, 373, 374, 375, 376, 377; CXVII 119.

In 1690, IX, XXI, LXII, LXX, LXXVIII.

In 1715, IX, XXI, LXII, LXX, LXXVIII, CXV.

In 1725, IX 626, 627; XLIII 351, 352; XI 301; CXVII 341.

In 1788, XLIII (March); LXII (January through April); LXXVIII (January through April).

Other Archival Sources

The list of archival sources here is not complete. It omits manuscript records that were read but never cited or used in our samples:

Archives de la Compagnie des Notaires de Paris
    Boxes 41, 46
    Délibérations: 1579–99, 1703–19, 1719–34, 1734–66, 1766–88, 1789–91, 1839–42.

Dossiers Individuels (Entry/exit dossiers for notaries, 1810–70).
Archives Départementales
  Côte d'Or C 4565.
We also relied on the various departmental archives to evaluate lending in
the provinces. Our sources there varied depending on the availability of
documents from the controle des actes and enregistrement. When these
were lacking, we utilized notarial documents themselves. The archival
sources we used concerned the following communities; in each case the
corresponding departmental archive and the relevant cotes are listed after
the name of the city:
  Apt: AD Vaucluse, 2C 62–64, 19Q 37–38, 86–88.
  Avignon: AD Vaucluse, 19Q 852–53, 1840 946–48.
  Bar-sur-Seine: AD Aube, IIC 434–38, 4Q 3769–70, 3790–94, 3828–
    31, 3873–76.
  Château-Thierry: AD Aisne, C1813–15, 68Q 56–58.
  Dijon: AD Côte d'Or, C* 8780–83 and 9Q2 45–50, 163–70.
  L'Isle-sur-la-Sorgue: AD Vaucluse, 3E37 583, 554, 568, 654, 667 688,
    632; 3E 38 1838, 1902, 1997; 19Q 37–38, 86–88, 852, 946–48,
    7985–90, 7915–58, 19Q 29–30.
  Lasalle and Saint-Jean-du-Gard: AD Gard, 6M728 and IIE51 437, 438,
    603 722, 16Q1, 28Q1.
  Nuits-Saint-Georges: AD Côte d'Or, C* 9879–81.
  Montbard: AD Côte d'Or, C* 9373–74, 19Q 111–12.
  Maubeuge: AD Nord, J942 115–17, 138; J1132 1, 6, 10, 24–25; J1133
    15, 23, 35–36; J1134 12, 21, 32, 68–72.
  Privas: AD Ardèche, 2C 2393–94; 3Q 1608–9, 1618–19, 1644–45; 3Q
    2073–74, 2088.
  Orange: AD Vaucluse, 2C 11–13, 19Q 7915–8, 7985–90.
  Rouen: AD Seine-Maritime, 2C 1840–46 and 3Q38 212–16.
  Rugles: AD Eure, IIC 2428; 499Q 12, 17–18, 25–26, 42–44.
  Salon: AD Bouches-du-Rhône, 2C 2012–14 and XII Q25/2 52–53.
  Tréguier: AD Cotes-d'Armor, 2C 7527–29 and 3Q 5710–11.
Archives du Ministère des Finances
  B 38930, B 31141, 38916–19, 38921, 38923
Archives Nationales
  BB[10] 100, 553, 709, 824, 846, 1064, 1065, 1206B, 1230B, 1244, 1260B,
    1326B, 1370, 1444, 1578, 1625, 1634, 1636, 1637, 1645, 1652 1661,
    1675, 1678, 1680, P 5934, 5936, 5937, 5939, 5947, 5970, 5973, 5975,
    6055, 6056, 6057, 6115, 6120.
  Y 9529, 17609, Y 18581 (registre 4).
  Computerized enumerations of all surviving notarial acts from 1751, 1761,
    and 1851.
Bibliothèque Nationale
  F 23717 ("Sentence rendue en la chambre criminelle du Châtelet de
    Paris, qui condamne André-Guillaume Deshayes [24 February 1764]").

Z 51471 *Journal encyclopédique* (March 1764).
Fonds français 6680, Journal of bookseller S. Hardy ("Notices d'événe-
   ments remarqables et tels qu'ils proviennent à ma connaissance").
Joly de Fleury Papers 385, 2148, 2150, 2425, 2538.

Finally, we also consulted ARTFL textual database of the French Language,
which is maintained by Centre National de la Recherche Scientifique and the
University of Chicago.

Bibliography

Periodicals and Serials

Almanach National, Paris. 1800–1869.

Almanach du commerce de Paris, des départements de la France et des principales villes du monde by Jean de la Tynna. 1805–15.

Almanach du commerce de Paris, des départements de la France et des principales villes du monde by Jean de la Tynna and S. Bottin. 1820–50.

Annuaire général du commerce, de l'industrie, de la magistrature et de l'administration ou Almanach des 500000 adresses, Paris. 1855.

Annuaire-Almanach du commerce et de l'industrie ou Almanach des 500000 adresses. 1862. Paris.

Annuaire statistique de la France. 1926, 1966. Paris.

Archives parlementaires de 1787 à 1860: recueil complet des débats législatifs et politiques des chambres françaises. Compiled by Jérôme Mavidal and E. Laurent. 1862–1994. Paris.

Bulletin des Lois de la République Française. 1792–. Paris.

Bulletin des lois du royaume de France. Paris.

Procès verbaux de la Convention Nationale. Paris.

Rapport au Roi [à l'empereur] sur les caisses d'épargne. (Annual volumes 1835–69 at the Bibliothèque Nationale.)

Moniteur Universel. 1800–1969.

Books and Articles

Anonymous. 1766. *Statuts et règlements des notaires parisiens.* Paris.

Anonymous. 1762. *Nouveau stile du Chatelet de Paris et de toutes les jurisdictions ordinaires du royaume tant en matière civile, criminelle, que de police.* Paris.

Anonymous. 1905–6. *Preussische Statistik,* v. 191, pts. 1, 2, 3. Berlin.

Abreu, D., D. A. Pearce, and E. Staccheti. 1986. "Optimal Cartel Equilibria with Imperfect Monitoring." *Journal of Economic Theory* 39:251–69.

Aftalion, Florin. 1987. *L'Economie de la Révolution Française.* Paris.

Aguesseau, Henri-François, d'. 1759–89. *Oeuvres.* 16 vols. Paris.

Akabane, Hiroshi. 1967. "La crise de 1724–1725 et la politique de déflation du

Contrôleur Général Dodun." *Revue d'histoire moderne et contemporaine* 14:266–83.

Akerloff, George. 1970. "The Market for 'Lemons': Quality Uncertainty and the Market Mechanism." *The Quarterly Journal of Economics* 84:488–500.

Alesina, Alberto, and Allan Drazen. 1991. "Why Are Some Stabilizations Delayed?" *American Economic Review* 81 (5): 1170–88.

Allinne, Jean-Pierre. 1983. *Banquiers et bâtisseurs, un siècle de Crédit Foncier.* Paris.

———. 1978. "Le Crédit Foncier de France 1852–1920." Doctoral dissertation, University of Paris II.

Amiand, Albert, and Pierre Voland. 1901. "Traité général théorique et pratique des honoraires des notaires: Commentaire du tarif légal et Etude sur les questions relatives à la rémunération notariale." *Journal des Notaires et des Avocats,* special issue.

Anderson, B. L. 1969a. "Provincial Aspects of the Financial Revolution of the Eighteenth Century." *Business History* 11:11–22.

———. 1969b. "The Attorney and the Early Capital Market in Lancashire." In R. R. Harris, ed., *Liverpool and Merseyside: Essays in the Economic and Social History of the Port and its Hinterland,* 50–77. London.

———. 1970. "Money and the Structure of Credit in the Eighteenth Century." *Business History* 1:85–101.

Antoine, Michel. 1970. *Le conseil du roi sous le règne de Louis XV.* Paris.

Antonetti, G. 1985. "Colbert et le crédit public." In Roland Mousnier, ed., *Un nouveau Colbert,* 189–99. Paris.

Arbellot, Guy. 1973. "La grande mutation des routes de France au millieu du XVIIIe siècle." *Annales: Economies, Sociétés, Civilisations* 28 (3): 765–91.

Arbellot, Guy, and Bernard Lepetit. 1987. *Atlas de la Révolution Française: Routes et communications.* Paris.

Archives Nationales. 1980. *Etat général des fonds,* vol. 4: *Fonds divers.* Paris.

Armstrong, Leroy, and J. O. Denny. 1916. *Financial California: An Historical Review of the Beginnings and Progress of Banking in the State.* San Francisco.

Arrunada, Benito. 1996. "The Economics of Notaries." *European Journal of Law and Economics* 3 (1): 5–37.

Asselain, Jean-Charles. 1989. "Continuités, traumatismes, mutations." *Revue Economique* 40 (6): 1137–88.

Bachaumont, Louis Petit de. 1784–89. *Mémoires secrets pour servir à l'histoire de la république des lettres en France depuis MDCCLXII jusqu'à nos jours.* London.

———. 1866. *Mémoires secrets pour servir à l'histoire de la république des lettres en France depuis MDCCLXII jusqu'à nos jours: Table alphabétique des auteurs et personnages cités dans les Mémoires secrets pour servir à l'histoire de la république des lettres en France.* Brussels.

Baehrel, René. 1988. *Une croissance: La basse Provence rurale de la fin du 16e siècle à 1789.* 2d ed. Paris.

Baker, Keith. 1990. *Inventing the French Revolution.* Cambridge.

Balzac, Honoré. 1898a. *The Rise and Fall of César Birotteau.* Philadelphia.

———. 1898b. *The Poor Parents, Part II: Cousin Pons.* Philadelphia.

———. 1962. *Le Cousin Pons.* Paris.

Barbier, Edmond-Jean-François. 1885. *Chroniques de la Régence et du règne de Louis XV.* 8 vols. Paris.

Barker, Nancy Nichols. 1989. *Brother to the Sun King: Philippe, Duke of Orleans.* Baltimore.

Baulant, Micheline. 1968. "Le prix des grains à Paris de 1431 à 1788." *Annales: Economies, Sociétés, Civilizations* 23 (3): 520–40.

Béaur, Gérard. 1984. *Le marché foncier à la veille de la Révolution.* Paris.

Bellanger, Claude. 1969. *Histoire générale de la presse française.* Paris.

Bercé, Françoise, Lizzie Boubli, and Franck Folliot. 1988. *Le Palais Royal.* Catalogue of an exposition at the Musée Carnavalet, 9 May–4 September 1988. Paris.

Benedict, Philip. 1990. "Was the Eighteenth Century an Era of Urbanization in France?" *Journal of Interdisciplinary History* 21:179–215.

Bergasse, Nicolas. 1790. *Lettre à ses commettans au sujet de sa protestation contre les assignats-monnoie, accompagnée d'un tableau comparatif du système de la Caisse d'escompte et des assignats monnoie, et suivie de quelques réflexions sur un article du Patriote francois.* [Paris.]

Bergeron, Louis. 1978. *Banquiers, négociants et manufacturiers parisiens du Directoire à l'Empire.* Paris.

Bergeron, Louis, and Guy Chaussinand-Nogaret. 1979. *Les "masses de granit": cent mille notables du Premier Empire.* Paris.

Bien, David. 1988. "Les offices, les corps et le crédit d'état: L'utilisation des privilèges sous l'ancien régime." *Annales: Economies, Sociétés, Civilisations* 43:379–404.

Bigo, Robert 1947. *Les banques en France au XIXe siècle.* Paris.

Bloch, Camille. 1912. *La monnaie et le papier monnaie: Instructions, recueil de textes et notes.* Commission de Recherche et de Publication des Documents relatifs à la vie économique de la Révolution. Paris.

———. 1912–13. *Procès-verbaux du Comité des Finances de l'Assemblée Constituante.* Collection des documents inédits de l'histoire économique de la Révolution Française. 2 vols. Rennes.

Bloch, Marc. 1954. *Esquisse d'une histoire monétaire de l'Europe.* Cahiers des Annales no. 9. Paris.

———. 1934. "Les mutations monétaires et les dettes." *Annales d'histoire économique et sociale* 6:383–87.

———. 1953. "Les mutations monétaires dans l'ancienne France." *Annales: Economies, Sociétés, Civilisations* 8:145–58, 433–56.

Block, Maurice. 1851. *Des charges de l'agriculture dans les divers pays de l'Europe.* Paris.

Bonney, Richard. 1981. *The King's Debts: Finance and Politics in France, 1589–1661.* Oxford and New York.

Bordo, Michael, and Eugene White. 1991. "A Tale of Two Currencies: British and French Finance During the Napoleonic Wars." *Journal of Economic History* 51:303–16.

Bosher, John. 1970. *French Finance 1770–1795: From Business to Bureaucracy.* Cambridge.

———. 1972. "The French Crisis of 1770." *History* 57:17–30.

Boucher d'Argis. 1786. *Edit de Louis XV, Roi de France et de Navarre, donné à Versailles du mois de Juin 1771*. Paris.

Bourquin, Marie Hélène. 1969. "L'approvisionnement de Paris en bois de la Régence à la Révolution." Doctoral dissertation, University of Paris.

Bouvier, Jean. 1970. "Vers le capitalisme bancaire." In Fernand Braudel and Ernest Labrousse, eds., *Histoire économique et sociale de la France*, 2:301–24.

Boyer-Xambeu, M. T., G. Deleplace, and L. Gillard. 1986. *Monnaie privée et pouvoir des princes: l'économie des relations monétaires à la Renaissance*. Paris.

———. 1995. *Bimétalisme, taux de change et prix de l'or et de l'argent: 1717–1873*. Cahier de l'Institut de sciences mathématiques et économiques appliquées. Serie A.F. 19–20. Paris.

Braesch, Frédéric. 1934. *Finance et monnaie révolutionnaires*. Nancy.

Braudel, Fernand. 1966. *La Méditerranée et le monde méditerranéen à l'époque de Philippe II*. Paris.

Braudel, Fernand, and Ernest Labrousse, eds. 1970–82. *Histoire économique et sociale de la France*. 4 vols. Paris.

Bresson, Jacques. 1825. *Des fonds publics français et étrangers et des opérations de la Bourse de Paris*. 5th ed. Paris.

Brissot de Warville, Jacques-Pierre. 1787. *Point de banqueroute ou lettres d'un créancier de d'état*. London.

Bruguière, Michel. 1987. "L'administration des finances de Louis XVI à Bonaparte: Ruptures et continuité." In François Bloch-Lainé and Gilbert Etienne. eds., *Servir l'Etat*, 161–85. Paris.

———. 1989. "Révolution et finances: Réflexions sur un impossible bilan." *Revue Economique* 40 (6): 985–1000.

———. 1990. "Préface" to Pierre-François Pinaud, *Les receveurs généraux des Finances, 1790–1865*. Geneva.

Bulst, Neithard, René Descimon, and A. Guerreau. 1996. *L'Etat ou le roi: les fondations de la modernité monarchique en France (XIVe–XVIe siècles)*. Paris.

Calmon, Marc Antoine. 1868–70. *Histoire parlementaire des finances de la Restauration*. 2 vols. Paris.

Calomiris, Charles. 1995. "The Cost of Rejecting Universal Banking: American Finance in the German Mirror, 1870–1914." In Naomi Lamoureaux and Daniel Raff, eds., *Coordination and Information: Historical Perspectives on the Organization of Enterprises*, 257–321. Chicago and London.

Cambon. 1793. *Rapports de la Commission des finances, la lois sur la dette publique, sur sa consolidation, sur l'emprunt volontaire, et sur l'emprunt forcé; suivis de l'instruction sur l'emprunt forcé*. Paris.

Cameron, Rondo. 1967. *Banking in the Early Stages of Industrialization*. New York.

Cannadine, David. 1977. "Aristocratic Indebtedness in the Nineteenth Century: The Case Reopened." *Economic History Review*, 2d ser., 30:624–50.

Caron, Pierre. 1909. *Tableaux de dépréciation du papier-monnaie*. Paris.

Carré, Henri. 1891. *La France sous Louis XV (1723–1774)*. Paris.

Carruthers, Bruce G. 1996. *City of Capital: Politics and Markets in the English Financial Revolution*. Princeton.

Chagniot, Jean. 1988. *Nouvelle histoire de Paris: Paris au XVIIIe siècle.* Paris.

Charlot, E., and J. Dupâquier. 1967. "Le mouvement annuel de la population de la ville de Paris de 1670 à 1821." *Annales de démographie historique,* 511–19.

Chartier, Roger. 1991. *The Cultural Origins of the French Revolution.* Translated by Lydia G. Cochrane. Durham, North Carolina.

Chevalier, Louis. 1950. *La formation de la population parisienne au XIXe siècle.* Paris.

Chevet, Jean-Michel. 1983. "Le Marquisat d'Ormesson, 1700–1840: Essai d'analyse économique." 2 vols. Doctoral thesis, Ecole des Hautes Etudes en Sciences Sociales. Paris.

Clark, Gregory. 1988. "The Cost of Capital and Medieval Agricultural Technique." *Explorations in Economic History* 25:265–94.

———. 1996. "The Political Foundations of Modern Economic Growth: England, 1540–1800." *Journal of Interdisciplinary History* 26:563–88.

Clavero, Bartolome. 1991. *Antidora: Antropologia catolica de la economia moderna.* Milan. Translated into French under the title *La grâce du don: Anthropologie catholique de l'économie moderne* (Paris, 1996).

Clay, Christopher. 1974. "The Price of Freehold Land in the Later Seventeenth and Eighteenth Centuries." *Economic History Review,* 2d ser., 27:173–89.

Clément, Pierre, ed. 1861–82. *Lettres, instructions et mémoires de Colbert.* 10 vols. Paris.

Collins, Michael. 1992. "The Bank of England as Lender of Last Resort, 1857–1878." *Economic History Review,* 2d ser., 45:145–53.

Conseil d'Etat. 1850. *Enquête sur le Crédit Foncier.* Paris.

Coquereau, Jean-Baptiste Louis. 1776. *Mémoires de l'abbé Terrai contrôleur général des finances.* London.

Courdurié, Marcel. 1974. *La dette des collectivités publiques de Marseille au XVIIIe siècle: du débat sur le prêt à intérêt au financement par l'emprunt.* Marseille.

Courtois, Alphonse. 1873. *Tableaux des cours des principales valeurs négociées et cotées aux bourses des effets publics de Paris, Lyon et Marseille.* Paris.

Cross, Ira. 1927. *Financing an Empire: History of Banking in California.* San Francisco.

Crouzet, François. 1993. *La grande inflation: La monnaie en France de Louis XVI à Napoléon.* Paris.

Cukierman, Alex, Sebastian Edwards, and Guido Tabellini. 1992. "Seignorage and Political Instability." *American Economic Review* 82 (3): 537–55.

Danieri, Cheryl Lynne. 1987. "Credit Where Credit Is Due: The Mont-de-Piété of Paris, 1777–1851." Ph.D. diss., University of California, Irvine.

Darnton, Robert. 1995. *The Forbidden Best-Sellers of Pre-Revolutionary France.* New York.

Daumard, Adeline. 1973. *Les fortunes françaises au XIXe siècle.* Paris.

Daumard, Adeline, and François Furet. 1961. *Structures et relations sociales à Paris au milieu du XVIIIe siècle.* Cahiers des Annales, no. 19. Paris.

David, Paul. 1985. "Clio and the Economics of QWERTY." *American Economic Review* 75:332–37.

Davis, Lance, and Douglass North. 1971. *Institutional Change and American Economic Growth.* Cambridge.

Davis, Lance, and Robert Gallman. 1978. "Capital Formation in the United States During the Nineteenth Century." In P. Mathias and M. M. Postan, eds., *The Cambridge Economic History of Europe*, vol 7., pt. 2:1–69, 496–503, 557–61. Cambrige.

Davis, Lance, and Robert Cull. 1994. *International Capital Markets and American Economic Growth.* Cambridge and New York.

Delarue, Amable Toussaint. 1786. *Registre des offices et pratiques des conseillers du roy notaires, gardes-notes et gardes-scel de sa majesté au Châtelet de Paris.* Paris.

Denisart, Jean Baptiste. 1775. *Collection de décisions nouvelles et de notions relatives à la jurisprudence actuelle.* 9th ed. Paris.

Deschodt, Eric. 1993. *Histoire du Mont-de-Piété.* Paris.

Descimon, Robert. 1983. *Qui étaient les Seize? Mythes et réalités de la Ligue parisienne, 1585–1594.* Paris.

Descimon, Robert, Jean-Frédéric Schaub, and Bernard Vincent. 1997. *Les figures de l'administrateur: Institutions, réseaux, pouvoirs en Espagne, en France et au Portugal, 16ᵉ–19ᵉ siècles.* Paris.

Dessert, Daniel. 1984. *Argent, pouvoir et société au grand siècle.* Paris.

DeVries, Jan. 1976. *The Economy of Europe in an Age of Crises, 1600–1750.* Cambridge.

———. 1984. *European Urbanization, 1500–1800.* Cambridge, Mass.

Dewald, Jonathan. 1980. *The Formation of a Provincial Nobility: The Magistrates of the Parlement of Rouen, 1499–1610.* Princeton.

———. 1987. *Pont-St-Pierre, 1398–1789: Lordship, Community, and Capitalism in Early Modern France.* Berkeley.

Deyon, Pierre. 1967. *Contributions à l'étude des revenus fonciers en Picardie, les fermages de l'Hôtel-Dieu d'Amiens et leurs variations de 1515 à 1789.* Lille.

Dickson, P. G. M. 1967. *The Financial Revolution in England.* London.

Diderot and d'Alembert. 1751–76. *Encyclopédie ou dictionnaire raisonné des sciences, des arts et des métiers.* 30 vols. Paris.

Donvez, Jacques. 1949. *De quoi vivait Voltaire?* Paris.

Doyle, William. 1996. *Venality: The Sale of Offices in Eighteenth-Century France.* Oxford and New York.

Ducloz-Dufresnoy, Charles Nicolas. 1789. *Origine de la Caisse d'Escompte, ses progrès, ses révolutions.* Paris.

Dumas, Auguste. 1935–65. "Intérêt et Usure." In R. Naz, ed., *Dictionnaire du droit canonique,* 5:1475–1518. 7 vols. Paris.

Dupâquier, Jacques, N. Felkay, J. Guérout, J. Jacquard, M. Lachiver, R. Lemée, C. Rollet, and A. Souriac. 1974. *Paroisses et communes de France: Région parisienne.* Paris.

Dupin, Charles. 1844. *Constitution, histoire et avenir des caisses d'épargne de France.* Paris.

Du Pont de Nemours, Pierre Samuel. 1790. *Effet des assignats sur le prix du pain, par un ami du peuple.* Paris.

Dupont-Ferrier, Pierre. 1925. *Le marché financier de Paris sous le Second Empire.* Paris.

Dutot, Charles. 1935 (1738). *Réflexions politiques sur les finances et le commerce.* Edited by P. Harsin. 2 vols. Paris.

Eaton, Jonathon, Mark Gersonvitz, and Joseph E. Stiglitz. 1986. "The Pure Theory of Country Risk." *European Economic Review* 30:481–513.

Edwards, Sebastian. 1996. "Exchange-Rate Anchors, Credibility, and Inertia: A Tale of Two Crises, Chile and Mexico" *American Economic Review* 86 (2): 176–80.

Egret, Jean. 1962. *La Prérévolution Française (1787–1788)*. Paris.

Ehrenberg, Richard. 1922. *Das Zeitalter der Fugger: Geldkapital und Creditverkehr im 16. Jahrhundert*. 3d ed. Jena.

Eichengreen, Barry. 1984. "Mortgage Interest Rates in the Populist Era." *American Economic Review* 74:995–1015.

El Annabi, Hassan. 1994. "Etre notaire à Paris au temps de Louis XIV: Henri Boutet, ses activités et sa clientèle (1693–1714)." Doctoral thesis, Université de Haute Bretagne, Rennes 2.

Emigh, Rebecca. 1996. "Landlords and Livestock: Comparing Landlords' and Tenants' Declarations from the Catasto of 1427." *Journal of European Economic History* 25:705–23.

———. 1997. "The Spread of Sharecropping in Tuscany: The Political Economy of Transactions Costs." *American Sociological Review* 62:423-42.

Engerman, Stanley, and Kenneth Sokoloff. 1997. "Factor Endowments, Institutions, and Differential Growth Paths Among New World Economies: A View from Economic Historians of the United States." In Stephen Haber, ed. *How Latin America Fell Behind: Essays on the Economic Histories of Brazil and Mexico, 1800-1914*, 260–304. Stanford.

Ensminger, Jean. 1997. "Changing Property Rights: Reconciling Formal and Informal Rights to Land in Africa." In John Droback and John Nye, eds. *The Frontiers of Institutional Economics*, 165–96. San Diego.

Farrell, J., and N. Gallini. 1988. "Second Sourcing as a Commitment: Monopoly Incentive to Attract Competition." *Quarterly Journal of Economics* 103:673–94.

Fauchois, Yann. 1989. *Chronologie politique de la révolution*. Brussels.

Faure, Edgar. 1977. *La Banqueroute de Law*. Paris.

Faure-Jarrosson, B. 1988. "Le contrat de vente de l'office de notaire: la pratique Lyonnaise sous l'Ancien Régime." *Le Gnomon* 60:4–11.

Felix, Joël. 1999. *Finances et politique au siècle des lumières: Le ministère L'Averdy, 1763–68*. Paris.

Felloni, Giuseppe. 1971. *Gli investimenti finanziari genovesi in Europa tra il seicento e la Restaurazione*. Milan.

Flammermont, Jules, ed. 1888–98. *Remontrances du Parlement de Paris au XVIIIe siècle*. 3 vols. Collection des documents inédits sur l'histoire de France. Paris.

Flandreau, Marc. 1995. *L'or du monde: la France et la stabilité du système monétaire international, 1848–1873*. Paris.

Flaubert, Gustave. 1926–1954. *Correspondance*. Paris.

Flour de Saint-Genis, V. B. 1889. *Le crédit territorial en France et la réforme hypothécaire*. Paris.

Foiret, F. 1912. *Une corporation parisienne pendant la Révolution (les notaires)*. Paris.

Fontaine, Laurence. 1994. "Espaces, usages et dynamique de la dette dans les hautes valles dauphinoises (XVII-XVIIIe siècles)." *Annales: Histoire, Sciences Sociales* 6:1375–91.

Forster, Robert. 1971. *The House of Saulx-Tavanes: Versailles and Burgundy, 1700–1830*. Baltimore.

———. 1980. *Merchants, Landlords, Magistrates: The Depont Family in Eighteenth-century France*. Baltimore.

———. 1960. *The Nobility of Toulouse in the Eighteenth Century*. Baltimore.

Frêche, Georges. 1974. *Toulouse et la Région Midi-Pyrennées au siècle des Lumières (vers 1670–1789)*. Paris.

Furet, François. 1981. *Interpreting the French Revolution*. Translated by Elborg Forster. Cambridge.

Gaston, Jean. 1991. *La communauté des notaires de Bordeaux (1520–1791)*. Toulouse.

Gerschenkron, Alexander. 1962. *Economic Backwardness in Historical Perspective: A Book of Essays*. Cambridge.

Gille, Bertrand. 1947. *Les origines de la grande industrie métallurgique en France*. Paris.

———. 1959. *La banque et le crédit en France de 1815 à 1848*. Paris.

———. 1965. *Histoire de la maison Rothschild*. 2 vols. Geneva.

———. 1968. *La sidérurgie Française au XIXe siècle, recherches historiques*. Geneva.

Glassman, Debra, and Angela Redish. 1985. "New Estimates of the Money Stock in France, 1493-1680." *Journal of Economic History* 45:31–46.

———. 1988. "Currency Depreciation in Early Modern England and France." *Explorations in Economic History* 25:75–97.

Goubert, Pierre. 1960. *Beauvais et le Beauvaisis de 1600 à 1730*. Paris.

———. 1970 "Le 'tragique' XVIIe siècle." In *Histoire économique et sociale de la France*, vol. 2: *Des derniers temps de l'âge seigneurial aux préludes de l'âge industriel (1660–1789)*, edited by Fernand Braudel and Ernest Labrousse, 329–66. Paris.

Grantham, George. 1995. "Time's Arrow and Time's Cycle in the Medieval Economy." McGill University, Montreal. Photocopy.

———. 1996. "Contra Ricardo: The Macro-economics of Pre-industrial Agrarian Economies." McGill University, Montreal. Photocopy.

———. 1997. "The French Cliometrics Revolution: A Survey of Contributions to French Economic History." *European Review of Economic History* 1:353–405.

Green, Edward, and Roger Porter. 1984. "Non-cooperative Collusion under Imperfect Price Information." *Econometrica* 52:87–100.

Greif, Avner. 1989. "Reputation and Coalitions in Medieval Trade: Evidence on the Maghribi Traders." *Journal of Economic History* 49:857–82.

———. 1993. "Contract Enforceability and Economic Institutions in Early Trade: The Maghribi Traders' Coalition." *American Economic Review* 83:525–48.

———. 1994. "Cultural Beliefs and the Organization of Society: A Historical and Theoretical Reflection on Collectivist and Individualist Societies." *Journal of Political Economy* 102 (5): 912–50.

———. 1996. "The Study of Organizations and Evolving Organizational Forms through History: Reflections from the Late Medieval Family Firm." *Industrial and Corporate Change* 5 (2): 473–501.

Grenier, Jean. 1822. *Traité des hypothèques*. Clermont-Ferrand.

Grosskreuz, Helmut. 1977. *Privatkapital und Kanalbau in Frankreich 1814–1848: Eine Fallstudie zur Rolle der Banken in der französischen Industrialisierung.* Berlin.

Guéry, Alain 1978. "Les finances de la monarchie française sous l'Ancien Régime." *Annales: Economies, Sociétés, Civilisations* 33:216–39.

———. 1991. "Les comptes de la mort vague après la guerre: Pertes de guerre et conjoncture du phénomène guerre." *Histoire et Mesure* 6 (3/4): 289–312.

Guinnane, Timothy. 1994. "A Failed Institutional Transplant: Raiffesen's Credit Cooperative in Ireland, 1894–1914." *Explorations in Economic History* 31:38–61.

———. 1997. "Cooperatives as Information Machines: The Lending Practices of German Agricultural Credit Cooperatives, 1883–1914." Yale University, Department of Economics. Photocopy.

Guyot, Pierre-Jean. 1784–85. *Répertoire universel et raisonné de jurisprudence civile, criminelle, canonique et bénéficiale.* 17 vols. Paris.

Habakkuk, Sir John. 1994. *Marriage, Debt, and the Estates System: English Ownership, 1650–1950.* Oxford.

———. 1952. "The Long-term Rate of Interest and the Price of Land in the Seventeenth Century." *Economic History Review,* 2d ser., 5:24–65.

———. 1968. "Economic Functions of English Landowners in the Seventeenth and Eighteenth Centuries." Reprint in *Essays in Agrarian History,* edited by W. E. Minchinton, 1:189–201. New York.

Hamilton, Earl. 1938. "Prices and Wages at Paris under John Law's System." *Quarterly Journal of Economics* 51:42–70.

Harris, Seymour. 1930. *The Assignats.* Cambridge.

Harsin, Paul. 1933. *Crédit public et banque d'Etat en France, du XVIe au XVIIIe siècle.* Louvain and Paris.

Hart, Oliver D. 1995. *Firms, Contracts, and Financial Structure.* Oxford and New York.

Hatin, Louis Eugène. 1866. *Bibliographie historique et critique de la presse périodique française.* Paris.

Hauser, Henri. 1936. *Recherches et documents sur l'histoire des prix en France de 1500 à 1800.* Paris.

Hautchamp, Barthelemi du. 1739. *Histoire du système des finances.* La Haye.

Hautcoeur, Pierre-Cyrille. 1994. "Le marché boursier et le financement des entreprises françaises (1890–1939)." Doctoral diss., University of Paris I.

Herbin, R., and A. Pébereau. 1953. *Le cadastre français.* Paris.

Henry, Louis, and Yves Blayo. 1975. "La population de la France de 1740 à 1860." *Population* 30 (special number, November): 101–2.

Heymann, Daniel, and Axel Leijonhufvud. 1995. *High Inflation.* New York, Oxford.

Hirsch, Jean Pierre. 1991. *Les deux rêves du commerce: Entreprise et institution dans la région lilloise, 1780–1860.* Paris.

Hoffman, Elizabeth, and Gary Libecap. 1994. "Political Bargaining and Cartelization in the New Deal: Orange Marketing Orders." In *The Regulated Economy: A Historical Approach to Political Economy,* edited by Claudia Goldin and Gary Libecap, 189–221. Chicago.

Bibliography

Hoffman, Philip T. 1986. "Taxes and Agrarian Life in Early Modern France: Land Sales, 1550–1730." *Journal of Economic History* 46:37–55.

———. 1991. "Land Rents and Agricultural Productivity: The Paris Basin, 1450–1789." *Journal of Economic History* 51:771–805.

———. 1994. "Early Modern France." In *Fiscal Crises, Liberty, and Representative Government, 1450-1789,* edited by Philip T. Hoffman and Kathryn Norberg, 226–52. Stanford.

———. 1996. *Growth in Traditional Society: The French Countryside, 1450–1815.* Princeton.

Hoffman, Philip, and Kathryn Norberg. 1994. "Conclusion." In *Fiscal Crises, Liberty, and Representative Government, 1450–1789,* edited by Philip T. Hoffman and Kathryn Norberg, 299–310. Stanford.

Hoffman, Philip, Gilles Postel-Vinay, and Jean-Laurent Rosenthal. 1992. "Private Credit Markets in Paris 1690–1840." *Journal of Economic History* 52:293–306.

———. 1994a. "Economie et politique: Les marchés du crédit à Paris, 1750–1840." *Annales: Histoire, Sciences Sociales* 1 (1): 65–98.

———. 1994b. "The Search for Stability: Credit Markets in Nineteenth-Century Paris." Caltech. Photocopy.

———. 1995. "Redistribution and Long-Term Private Debt in Paris, 1660–1726." *Journal of Economic History* 55:256–84.

———. 1998. "What do Notaries do? Overcoming Asymmetric Information in Financial Markets: The Case of Paris, 1751." *Journal of Institutional and Theoretical Economics* 154 (3): 499–530.

———. 1999. "Information and Economic History: How the Credit Market in Old Regime Paris Forces Us to Rethink the Transition to Capitalism." *American Historical Review* 104 (1): 69–94.

———. 2000. "No Exit: Notarial Bankruptcies and the Evolution of Financial Intermediation in Paris." Caltech. Photocopy.

Hoffman, Philip, and Jean-Laurent Rosenthal. 1997. "The Political Economy of Warfare and Taxation in Early Modern Europe: Historical Lessons for Economic Development." In *The Frontiers of the New Institutional Economics,* edited by John N. Drobak and John V. C. Nye, 31–55. San Diego.

Hufton, Olwen. 1996. *The Prospect Before Her: A History of Women in Western Europe.* New York.

Isambert, François-André et al. 1822–33. *Recueil général des anciennes lois françaises depuis l'an 420 jusqu'à la Révolution de 1789.* Paris.

Jardin, André. 1983. *Restoration and Reaction, 1815–1848.* Translated by Elborg Forster. Cambridge, New York, Paris.

Jardin, André and André-Jean Tudesq. 1973. *La France des notables: la vie de la nation 1815–1848.* 2 vols. Paris.

Jones, Eric Lionel. 1981. *The European Miracle: Environments, Economies, and Geopolitics in the History of Europe and Asia.* Cambridge and New York.

Jurgens, M. 1980. "En suivant les minutiers parisiens." *Le Gnomon* 18:39–64.

Kaiser, Thomas E. 1991. "Money, Despotism, and Public Opinion in Early Eighteenth-Century France: John Law and the Debate on Royal Credit." *Journal of Modern History* 63:691–722.

———. 1994. "Property, Sovereignty, the Declaration of the Rights of Man, and the Tradition of French Jurisprudence." In *The French Idea of Freedom: The Old Regime and the Declaration of Rights of 1789*, edited by Dale Van Kley, 300–339. Stanford.

Kindleberger, Charles P. 1993. *A Financial History of Western Europe*. New York and Oxford.

Kozminski, Léon. 1929. *Voltaire financier*. Paris.

Kreps, David M. 1990a. *A Course in Microeconomic Theory*. Princeton, 1990.

———. 1990b. "Corporate Culture and Economic Theory." In *Perspectives on Positive Political Economy*, edited by James E. Alt and Kenneth A Shepsle, 91–143. Cambridge.

Labrousse, Ernest. 1933. *Esquisse du mouvement des prix et des revenus en France au XVIIIe siècle*. Paris. Reprinted, 1984.

Laffont, Jean-Jacques, and Jean Tirole. 1993. *A Theory of Incentives in Procurement and Regulation*. Cambridge and London.

Laffon-Ladebat, André Daniel. 1807. *Compte rendu des opérations de la Caisse d'Escompte depuis son origine jusqu'à sa liquidation*. Paris.

Lamoreaux, Naomi. 1994. *Insider Lending: Banks, Personal Connections, and Economic Development in Industrial New England*. Cambridge.

Lamoreaux, Naomi, and Daniel Raff, eds. 1995. *Coordination and Information: Historical Perspectives on the Organization of Enterprises*. Chicago and London.

Lavisse, Ernest, ed. 1911. *Histoire de France depuis les origines jusqu'à la révolution*, vol. 8, pt. 1: *La fin du règne (1685–1715)*, by A. de Saint-Léger, A. Rebelliau, P. Sagnac, and E. Lavisse. Paris.

Lavoisier, Antoine-Laurent. 1864–93. "Résultats extraits d'un ouvrage intitulé 'De la richesse territoriale du royaume de France.'" In *Oeuvres de Lavoisier* 6: 403–513 (Paris, 1988).

Lee, Ronald. 1974. "Estimating Series of Vital Rates and Age Structure from Baptisms and Burials: A New Technique, with Applications to Pre-Industrial England." *Population Studies* 28:495–512.

Le Goff, T. G. E. 1996. "How to Finance an Eighteenth-Century War." York University. Photocopy.

———. 1997. "Les caisses d'amortissement en France (1749–1783)." In Comité pour l'histoire économique et financière de la France, *L'administration des finances sous l'Ancien Régime: Colloque tenu à Bercy les 22 et 23 février 1996*, 179–93. Paris.

Legros, Patrick, and Andrew Newman. 1996. "Wealth Effects, Distribution, and Theory of Organization." *Journal of Economic Theory* 70 (2): 312–41.

Lepetit, Bernard. 1988. *Les villes dans la France Moderne (1740–1840)*. Paris.

Lepetit, Bernard, and J. Hoock, éds. 1987. *La ville et l'innovation en Europe, XIV–XIXe siècles*. Paris.

Le Roy Ladurie, Emmanuel. 1966. *Les paysans de Languedoc*. Paris.

Le Roy Ladurie, Emmanuel, and Pierre Couperie. 1970. "Le mouvement des loyers parisiens de la fin du Moyen Age au XVIIIe siècle." *Annales: Economies, Sociétés, Civilizations* 25:1002–23.

Le Roy Ladurie, Emmanuel, and Micheline Baulant. 1980. "Grape Harvests from the Fifteenth through the Nineteenth Centuries." *Journal of Interdisciplinary History* 10:839–49.

Lescure, Michel. 1980. *Les sociétés immobilières en France au XIXe siècle.* Paris.

Levenstein, Margaret. 1991. "The Use of Cost Measures: The Dow Chemical Company, 1890–1914." In *Inside the Business Enterprise: Historical Perspectives on the Use of Information,* edited by Peter Temin, 71–112. Chicago.

Levine, Ross. 1997. "Financial Development and Economic Growth: Views and Agenda." *Journal of Economic Literature* 35 (2): 688–726.

Lévy-Leboyer, Maurice. 1964. *Les Banques européennes et l'industrialisation internationale dans la première moitié du XIXe siècle.* Paris.

Lévy-Leboyer, Maurice, and François Bourguignon. 1985. *L'Economie française au XIXe siècle: Analyse macro-économique.* Paris.

Liebowitz, S. J., and Stephen E. Margolis. 1990. "The Fable of the Keys." *Journal of Law and Economics* 33 (1): 1–25.

Limon, Marie-France. 1992. *Les notaires au Châtelet sous le règne de Louis XIV.* Toulouse.

Lin, Justin Yifu, and Jeffrey B. Nugent. 1995 "Institutions and Economic Development." In *Handbook of Development Economics,* volume 3A, edited by Jere Behrman and T. N. Srinivasan, 2301–70. Amsterdam, New York, and Oxford.

Loutchitch, Leonidas. 1930. *Allure et mécanisme des variations du taux de l'intérêt en France de 1800 à nos jours.* Paris.

Loyseau, Charles. 1606. *Traicté de la garantie des rentes.* 3d ed. Paris.

Luckett, T. 1992. "Credit and Commercial Society in France, 1740–1789." Ph.D. diss., Princeton University.

Lüthy, Herbert. 1959–61. *La banque protestante en France de la révocation de l'Edit de Nantes à la Révolution.* Paris.

Madero-Suarez, David. 1997. "Essays on Mexican Institutions for Monetary Stability." Ph.D. diss., UCLA.

Mallet, J. R. 1789. *Comptes rendus de l'administration des finances du royaume de France.* London and Paris.

Manski, C., and S. Lehrman. 1977. "The Estimation of Choice Probabilities from Choice-Based Samples." *Econometrica* 45:1977–88.

Marchand, Olivier, and Claude Thélot. 1991. *Deux siècles de travail en France.* Paris.

Marion, Marcel. 1927–31. *Histoire financière de la France.* 6 vols. Paris.

Martin, Marie-Joseph-Desiré. 1789. *Etrennes financières ou Recueil des matières les plus importantes en finance, banque, commerce.* N.p.

Martin, Germain and Marcel Bezançon. 1913. *L'histoire du crédit en France sous le règne de Louis XIV.* Paris.

Martin du Nord, N. M. F. L. J. 1844. *Documents relatifs au régime hypothécaire et aux réformes qui ont été proposées.* Paris.

Massaloux, Jean-Paul. 1989. *La régie de l'enregistrement et des domaines aux XVIIe et XIXe siècles.* Geneva.

Massé, A. J. 1827. *Le parfait notaire ou la science des notaires.* 6th ed. Paris.

McCloskey, Donald. 1975. "The Persistence of English Common Fields." In *European Peasants and Their Markets,* edited by W. Parker and E. Jones, 73–114. Princeton.

———. 1976. "English Open Fields as Behavior Towards Risk." *Research in Economic History* 1:124–70.

McCusker, John J. 1978. *Money and Exchange in Europe and America.* Chapel Hill.

Melon, Jean François. 1734. *Essai politique sur le commerce.* N.p.

Mercier, Louis-Sebastien. [1783–88.] *Tableau de Paris,* new ed., 12 vols. Amsterdam. Republished as *Le Tableau de Paris,* edited by Jean-Claude Bonnet (Paris, 1994).

Michaud, Claude. 1991. *L'Eglise et l'argent.* Paris.

Miles, M. 1981. "The Money Market in the Early Industrial Revolution: The Evidence from West Riding Attorneys." *Business History* 23:127–46.

Milgrom, Paul, and John Roberts. 1990. "Bargaining Costs, Influence Costs, and the Organization of Economic Activity." In *Perspectives on Positive Political Economy,* edited by James Alt and Kenneth Shepsle, 57–89. Cambridge.

Mitchell, Brian. 1988. *British Historical Statistics.* Cambridge.

Mitchell, Brian, and Phyllis Deane. 1962. *Abstract of British Historical Statistics.* Cambridge.

Michie, Ranald. 1988. "Different in Name Only? The London Stock Exchange and Foreign Bourses, c. 1850–1914." *Business History* 30:46–68.

Mokyr, Joel. 1990. *The Lever of the Riches: Technological Creativity and Economic Progress.* New York.

Moriceau, Jean-Marc. 1985. "Un système de protection sociale efficace: Exemple des vieux fermiers de l'Ile-de-France (XVIIe–début XIXe siècle)." *Annales de Démographie Historique* 127–44.

———. 1994. *Les fermiers de l'Ile-de-France XVe–XVIIIe siècle.* Paris.

Moriceau, Jean-Marc, and Gilles Postel-Vinay. 1992. *Ferme, entreprise, famille.* Paris.

Montaigne, Michel Eyquem, seigneur de. 1946. *The Essays of Montaigne.* Translated by George B. Ives. New York.

Mousnier, Roland. 1979–84. *The Institutions of France under the Absolute Monarchy, 1598–1789: Society and the State.* Translated by Brian Pearce. Chicago.

Muller, Daniel. 1920. *Les rentes viagères de Voltaire.* Paris.

Murphy, Antoin. 1986. *Richard Cantillon, Entrepreneur and Economist.* New York.

———. 1997. *John Law: Economic Theorist and Policy Maker.* Oxford.

Neal, Larry. 1990. *The Rise of Financial Capitalism: International Capital Markets in the Age of Reason.* Cambridge.

———. 1994. "'For God's Sake, Remitt Me': The Adventures of George Middleton, John Law's London Goldsmith-Banker, 1712–1729." *Business and Economic History* 23 (2): 27–60.

———. 1994. "The Finance of Business During the Industrial Revolution." In *The Economic History of Britain since 1700,* edited by Roderick Floud and D. McCloskey, 2d ed., 151–81. Cambridge.

———. 1997. "The Historical Development of Stock Markets." In *The Emergence and Evolution of Markets,* edited by Horst Brezinski and Michael Fritsch, 59–80. Cheltenham, England.

Nicolardot, Louis. 1887. *Ménage et finance de Voltaire.* 2 vols. Paris.

Noonan, John Thomas. 1957. *The Scholastic Analysis of Usury.* Cambridge.

Norberg, Kathryn. 1994. "The French Fiscal Crises of 1788 and the Financial

Origins of the Revolution of 1789." In *Fiscal Crises, Liberty, and Representative Government, 1450–1789*. edited by Philip T. Hoffman and Kathryn Norberg. Stanford.

North, Douglass. 1981. *Structure and Change in Economic History*. New York.

———. 1990. *Institutions, Institutional Change, and Economic Performance*. Cambridge.

North, Douglass, and Robert Thomas. 1973. *The Rise of the Western World: A New Economic History*. Cambridge.

North, Douglass, and Barry Weingast. 1989. "Constitutions and Commitment: Evolution of the Institutions Governing Public Choice in Seventeenth-Century England." *Journal of Economic History* 49:803–32.

Palerm, Angel Viqueira. 1990. "Price Formation and Relative Price Variability in an Inflationary Environment: Mexico, 1940–1984." Ph.D. diss., UCLA.

Perrot, Jean-Claude. 1992. *Une histoire intellectuelle de l'économie politique*. Paris.

Picard, Roger. 1912. "Les mutations monétaires et la doctrine économique en France du XVIe siècle à la Révolution." *Revue d'Histoire des Doctrines économiques et sociales* 5:343–67.

Pinaud, Pierre François. 1990, *Les receveurs généraux des Finances, 1790–1865*. Geneva.

Plessis, Alain. 1982. *La Banque de France et ses deux cents actionnaires sous le Second Empire*. Geneva.

———. 1987. "Le 'retard français': la faute à la banque? Banques locales, succursales de la Banque de France et financement de l'économie sous le Second Empire." In *Le capitalisme français, 19e–20e siècle: Blocages et dynamismes d'une croissance*, edited by P. Fridenson and A. Strauss, 199–209. Paris.

Poisson, Jean-Paul. 1985-90. *Notaires et société: Travaux d'histoire et de sociologie notariales*. Paris.

———. 1996. *Etudes notariales*. Paris.

Poitrineau, Abel. 1965. *La vie rurale en Basse Auvergne au XVIIIe siècle, 1726–1789*. Marseille.

Polanyi, Karl. 1944. *The Great Transformation*. New York.

Postan, M. M. 1935. "Recent Trends in the Accumulation of Capital." *Economic History Review*, ser. 1, 6 (October): 1–12.

———. 1942. "Some Social Consequences of the Hundred Years War." *Economic History Review*, ser. 1, 12 (1): 1–12.

———. 1972. *The Medieval Economy and Society: An Economic History of Britain, 1100–1500*. Berkeley.

Postel-Vinay, Gilles. 1998. *La terre et l'argent*. Paris.

Potter, Mark, and Jean-Laurent Rosenthal. 1997a. "Politics and Public Finance in France: The Estates of Burgundy, 1660–1790." *Journal of Interdisciplinary History* 27 (4): 577–612.

———. 1997b. "The Burgundian Estates' Bond Market: Clienteles and Intermediaries." In *Des personnes aux institutions: Réseaux et culture du crédit du XVIe au XXe siècle en Europe*, edited by L. Fontaine, G. Postel-Vinay, J.-L. Rosenthal, and P. Servais, 173–95. Louvain.

Priouret, Roger. 1966. *La Caisse des Dépôts*. Paris.

Quinn, Stephen. 1994. "The Economy of London's Goldsmith-Bankers, 1660–96: England's Free Banking Era Prior to the Bank of England." Ph.D. diss., University of Illinois.

———. 1997. "Goldsmith-Banking: Mutual Acceptance and Interbanker Clearing in Restoration London." *Explorations in Economic History* 34 (1997): 411–32.

———. 1994. "Tallies or Reserves? Sir Francis Child's Balance Between Capital Reserves and Extending Credit to the Crown." *Business and Economic History* 23:1–13.

Renaudot, Théophraste. 1654. *Inventaire des adresses (Recueil général des questions traittées ès Conférences du Bureau d'Addresse ès années 1633, 34, 35, iusques à présent, sur toutes sortes de matières, par les beaux esprits de ce temps)*. Paris.

Reinhard, Wolfgang, ed. 1996. *Les élites du pouvoir et la construction de l'Etat en Europe*. Paris.

Riley, James C. 1973. "Dutch Investment in France, 1781–87." *Journal of Economic History* 33:733–57.

———. 1986. *The Seven Years War and the Old Regime in France*. Princeton.

Roche, Daniel. 1981. *Le peuple de Paris*. Paris.

Rogister, John. *Louis XV and the Parliament of Paris*. Cambridge.

Rohrbasser, Jean-Marc. 1997. "Un pasteur actuaire? Ordre de la mortalité, durée de la vie et rentes viagères dans l'*Ordre divin* de Johann Peter Süssmilch." *Revue de synthèse*, series 4, 118:385–417.

Rosenthal, Jean-Laurent. 1993. "Credit Markets and Economic Change in Southeastern France, 1630–1788." *Explorations in Economic History* 30:129–57.

———. 1994. "Rural Credit Markets and Aggregate Shocks: The Experience of Nuits St. Georges, 1756–1776." *Journal of Economic History* 54 (2): 288–306.

Sagnac P. 1898. *La législation civile au temps de la Révolution française*. Paris.

Sahlins, Marshall. 1972. *Stone Age Economics*. Chicago.

Saint-Jacob, Pierre de. 1960. *Les paysans de Bourgogne du Nord au dernier siècle de l'Ancien Régime*. Paris.

Saint Marc, Michele. 1983. *Histoire monétaire de la France*. Paris.

San Francisco City Directory. 1861. *San Francisco City Directory*. Edited by R. L. Polk. San Francisco.

Sargent, Thomas. 1986. *Rational Expectations and Inflation*. New York: Harper and Row.

Sargent, Thomas, and François Velde. 1995. "Macroeconomic Features of the French Revolution." *Journal of Political Economy* 103:474–518.

Sargentson, Carolyn. 1996. *Merchants and Luxury Markets: The Marchands Merciers of Eighteenth-Century Paris*. London.

Sarrazin, Jean-Yves. 1991. "La situation sociale et l'activité professionnelle des notaires de Chalons-en-Champagne au XVIIIe siècle." Master's thesis, Université de Reims.

Schnapper, Bernard. 1957. "La fixation du denier des rentes et l'opinion parlementaire au XVIe siècle." *Revue d'histoire moderne et contemporaine* 2:161–70.

———. 1957. *Les rentes au XVIe siècle: Histoire d'un instrument de crédit*. Paris.

Schwartz, Anna J. 1986. "Real and Pseudo-Financial Crises." In *Financial Crises and the World Banking System,* edited by Forest Capie and Geoffrey E. Woods, 34–62. London.

Servais, Paul. 1982. *La rente constituée dans le Ban de Herve au XVIIIe siècle.* Brussels.

Shakespeare, Howard J. 1986. *France, the Royal Loans: Les emprunts royaux, 1689–1789.* Shrewsbury.

Shennan, J. H. 1979. *Philippe, Duke of Orleans.* London.

Sicard, Roland. 1987. *Parroisses et communes de France: Vaucluse.* Paris.

Snowden, Kenneth. 1987. "Mortgage Rates and American Capital Market Development in the Late Nineteenth Century." *Journal of Economic History* 47 (3): 771–91.

———. 1988. "Mortgage Lending and American Urbanization, 1880–1890." *Journal of Economic History* 48 (2): 273–85.

———. 1995. "The Evolution of Interregional Mortgage Lending Channels, 1870–1940: The Life Insurance-Mortgage Company Connection." In *Coordination and Information: Historical Perspectives on the Organization of Enterprises,* edited by Naomi Lamoreaux and Daniel Raff, 209–47. Chicago.

Stiglitz, Joseph E., and Andrew Weiss. 1981. "Credit Rationing in Markets with Imperfect Information." *American Economic Review* 71:393–410.

Sutherland, D. M. G. 1985. *Revolution and Counterrevolution, France 1789–1815.* Oxford and New York.

Sylla, Richard. 1969. "Federal Policy, Banking Market Structure, and Capital Mobilization in the US, 1863–1913." *Journal of Economic History* 29 (4): 657–86.

Szramkiewicz, Romuald. 1974. *Les Régents et Censeurs de la Banque de France nommés sous le Consulat et l'Empire.* Geneva.

Taylor, George. 1967. "Noncapitalist Wealth and the Origins of the French Revolution." *American Historical Review* 72:469–96.

———. 1962. "The Paris Bourse on the Eve of the Revolution." *American Historical Review* 67:951–77.

Théret, Bruno. 1991. "Le système fiscal français libéral du XIXe siècle: Bureaucratie ou capitalisme." In *Comité pour l'histoire économique et financière: Etudes et documents,* 3:137–224. Paris.

Thivaud, Emmanuel, and Eugene White. 1993. "The Paris Bourse before 1815." Rutgers University. Photocopy.

Thompson, F. M. L. 1963. *English Landed Society in the Nineteenth Century.* London.

Tommasi, Mariano. 1993. "Inflation and Relative Prices: Evidence from Argentina." In *Optimal Pricing, Inflation, and the Cost of Price Adjustment,* edited by Eytan Sheshinski and Yoram Barzel, 485–511. Cambridge and London.

———. 1994. "The Consequences of Price Instability on Search Markets: Toward Understanding the Effects of Inflation." *American Economic Review* 84: 1385–96.

———. 1996. "Inflation and the Informativeness of Prices: Microeconomic Evidence from High Inflation." *Revista de Econometria* 16 (2): 37–75.

Touzery, Mireille. 1994. *L'invention de l'impôt sur le revenu: la taille tarifée, 1715–1789.* Paris.

Tudesq, André-Jean. 1964. *Les grands notables en France (1840–1849): Etude historique d'une psychologie sociale.* Paris.

Tracy, James D. 1985. *A Financial Revolution in the Habsburg Netherlands.* Berkeley.

Velde, François, and David Weir. 1991. "Government Debt Policy in France, 1733–93. Unpublished manuscript.

———. 1992. "The Financial Market and Government Debt Policy in France, 1746–1793." *Journal of Economic History* 52:1–40.

Véron de Forbonnais, François. 1758a. *Recherches et considérations sur les finances de la France depuis l'année 1595 jusqu'à l'année 1721.* 2 vols. Basel.

———. 1758b. *Recherches et considérations sur les finances de la France depuis l'année 1595 jusqu'à l'année 1721.* 6 vols. Liége.

Vilar-Berrogain, Gabrielle. 1958. *Guide des recherches dans les fonds d'Enregistrement sous l'Ancien régime.* Paris.

Voltaire. 1953–77. *Voltaire's Correspondence.* Edited by Theodore Besterman. Geneva.

Voyer de Paulmy, René-Louis, Marquis d'Argenson. 1859–67. *Journal et mémoires du Marquis d'Argenson publiés pour la première fois d'après les manuscrits autographes de la bibliothèque du Louvre.* Edited by E. J. B. Rathery. 9 vols. Paris.

Vourric, [?] de. 1687. *De l'usure et des vrais moyens de l'éviter par l'usage de divers contrats licites et approuvés par le droit civil et canonique et par le droit de France.* Avignon.

Vührer, A. 1886. *Histoire de la dette publique en France.* 2 vols. Paris.

Wailly, Nathalis de. 1857. *Mémoire sur les variations de la livre Tournois depuis le règne de Saint-Louis jusqu' à l'établissement de la monnaie décimale.* Paris.

Wateville, Adolphe de. 1850. *Statistiques des établissements de bienfaisance: Rapport à M. le Ministre de l'Intérieur sur l'administration des monts-de-piété.* Paris.

Weber, Max. 1989. *Gesamtausgabe.* Edited by Horst Baier et al. Series 1, vol. 19, *Die Wirtschaftsethik der Weltreligionen,* edited by Helwig Schmidt-Glintzer and Petra Kolonko. Tübingen.

Weir, David. 1989. "Tontines, Public Finance, and Revolution in France and England, 1688–1789." *Journal of Economic History* 49:95–124.

White, Andrew Dickson. [1896] 1933. *Fiat Money Inflation in France.* New York.

White, Eugene. 1989. "Was There a Solution to the Ancien Regime's Financial Dilemma?" *Journal of Economic History* 49:545–68.

———. 1995. "The French Revolution and the Politics of Government Finance, 1770–1815." *Journal of Economic History* 55:227–55.

Williamson, Oliver. 1975. *Markets and Hierarchies, Analysis and Antitrust Implications: A Study in the Economics of Internal Organization.* New York.

———. 1985. *The Economic Institutions of Capitalism: Firms, Markets, Relational Contracting.* London and New York.

Woloch, Isser. 1994. *The New Regime; Transformation of the French Civic Order, 1789–1820s.* New York.

Wolowski, Louis. 1848. *De l'organisation du Crédit Foncier.* Paris.

Wrigley, E. A., and Roger Schofield 1981. *The Population History of England, 1541–1871.* Cambridge.

Index